TERRITORY, SOIL AND SOCIETY IN SOUTH ASIA

Territory, Soil and Society in South Asia

Edited by

DANIELA BERTI
GILLES TARABOUT

MANOHAR
2009

First published 2009

ISBN 978-81-7304-782-4

Published by
Ajay Kumar Jain *for*
Manohar Publishers & Distributors
4753/23 Ansari Road, Daryaganj
New Delhi 110 002

Typeset by
FineCurve Computers
Meerut City 250 002

Printed at
Salasar Imaging Systems
Delhi 110 035

Contents

Contributors

MICHEL ANGOT, Sanskritist and Philologist, is a member of the Centre of Indian and South Asian Studies, Paris, and teaches at the Ecole des Hautes Etudes en Sciences Sociales (EHESS). He has recently published (Edition, French Translation and Notes) the *Taittirīya-Upanishad* with the commentary of Shamkara (2007), and the *Yoga-Sūtra* of Patanjali with the commentary of Vyāsa (2008).

DANIELA BERTI is a social anthropologist, Research Fellow at the National Centre for Scientific Research (CNRS, Paris). She is attached to the research centre 'Cultures, Environment and Societies in the Himalayas' and has carried out fieldwork in Himachal Pradesh on different topics, e.g. spirit and divine possession, village gods and electoral politics, or the Hindutva programmes for collecting local history. Her recent project concerns the anthropology of District Courts and the study of judicial interactions.

CHRISTIANE BROSIUS is Assistant Professor at the Department of Social Anthropology, South Asia Institute of the University of Heidelberg (Germany). In *Empowering Visions* (2005) she analysed the iconography, rhetoric and production context of video propaganda of the Hindu Right. Her other research interests are urban anthropology, diaspora studies, and the anthropology of medias. She is currently writing a book about cosmopolitan 'Indianness' in the context of new-liberal India, where she explores the emerging middle classes through case studies about urban planning, religious leisure parks, heritage tourism, themed weddings, lifestyle specialists and magazines. She is co-founder of Tasveer Ghar/House of Pictures: A Digital Network of South Asian Popular Visual Culture (www.tasveerghar.net).

GÉRARD COLAS, Philologist and Sanskritist, is Senior Fellow at the National Centre for Scientific Research (CNRS). His publications are mainly concerned with Sanskrit architectural, religious and philosophical works, as well as with Indian palaeography.

PHYLLIS GRANOFF, Indologist, is the Lex Hixon Professor of World Religions, Yale University. She has worked on debates surrounding image worship in early and medieval India and is currently working on medieval Jainism, its philosophy, literature and art. She is the editor of the *Journal of Indian Philosophy*.

CATERINA GUENZI is Research Fellow at the French Institute of Pondicherry. She has academic training both in Social Anthropology and Sanskrit and has worked intensively on astrological knowledge and practices in Banaras. She is about to publish *Destiny and Divination: The Work of Astrologers in Banaras.*

CAROLINE OSELLA is Reader in Anthropology of South Asia as SOAS; FILIPPO OSELLA is Reader in Anthropology at Sussex. They have worked in Kerala since 1989 and their publications cover issues of caste, class mobility, modernity, religion, migration, consumption and gender. Major publications include: *Social Mobility in Kerala* (2000), *Men and Masculinities in South India* (2007), *Islamic Reformism in South Asia* (editors of *Journal of Modern Asian Studies* special issue, 2008), *Food: Memory, Pleasure, Politics* (editors of *South Asia* special issue, 2008).

SUNITA SINGH has been working for several years as a research assistant in Banaras. She holds a Masters in population and reproductive health research and is presently working as a programme officer in a Delhi based organization on health policy and reproductive health.

GILLES TARABOUT, Anthropologist, Senior fellow (CNRS), has specialized in the study of Kerala's society and popular religious practices. Apart from his own publications in the field, he has also co-edited various volumes in French on rituals, on the conceptions of the body, on Islam and Christianity in India, and in English *Violence/Non-Violence: Some Hindu Perspectives* (2003).

GÉRARD TOFFIN, Anthropologist, Senior fellow (CNRS), has extensively published on Nepal. His current studies concern the Vaishnavite sects in South Asia and the construction of democracy in Nepal. He is the author of *Newar Society: City, Village and Periphery* (2007).

Introduction

DANIELA BERTI AND GILLES TARABOUT

This volume has been prepared with a view to confront a widespread stereotype in academic studies about India. According to this stereotype, pre-colonial India consisted of territorial units with ill-defined, fuzzy boundaries. This is taken to be a specifically Indian characteristic as the very notion of territory in Indian civilization is said to be of secondary importance for cultural reasons (this notion may be part of a more general, and widespread way of opposing a reified West to an equally reified India). The arguments put forward may vary. However, they all converge to create the idea that, generally speaking, territory in India had, and still has, little value as a cognitive category. This book aims at radically reconsidering this perspective.

SOCIAL ANTHROPOLOGY AND THE STUDY OF TERRITORY

For long the social sciences have largely ignored the question of territory. It is only from the 1980s onwards that geographers, whom one would think to have been concerned with this topic long ago, have really begun to interest themselves in territories, not only in their political but also in their symbolic dimension, as objects of discourse and representation.[1] Paradoxically, debates among them seem to have been initiated by a perception of the 'end of territory' as a consequence of globalization. According to some, the category had thus become obsolete at the very moment it came into focus. The trend concerns now all the social sciences, so much that the French Ministry of Education and Research recently (2003) advertised an offer to substantially fund projects that would study 'Space and Territory: Society, Economy, Culture, Language, Representations', stating that 'social sciences and humanities have mostly elaborated their knowledge by ignoring the spatial dimension of human actions', but that processes at work in the contemporary world (i.e. globalization) involve a great number of academic disciplines in the *geographical turn* 'spreading in the social sciences, not only—as would be obvious—in geography, but also in economy . . . , in urban sociology, in political sciences . . . , in anthropology, in history, in linguistics, in the genetics of populations, and in cognitive sciences'.

As far as anthropology is concerned, a similar diagnostic has been made in numerous recent publications. As one of them put it, 'the exploration of how notions of belonging, localities and identities are constructed seems particularly relevant in current political contexts of "globalization" ' (Lovell 1998b: 1). One of the first and most influential publications on this theme was a collection of papers edited in 1988 by Arjun Appadurai for a special number of *Cultural Anthropology* on 'Place and Voice in Anthropological Theory', where the focus was more specifically on the problem of 'culturally defined locations to which ethnographies refer' (Appadurai 1988: 16). The discussion was further elaborated in various later works. Gupta and Ferguson (1997), for instance, emphasize that we should be raising questions about 'anthropology's implicit mapping of the world as a series of discrete, territorialized cultures', and that at a time when

> 'cultural difference is increasingly becoming deterritorialized because of mass migrations and transnational culture flows of a late capitalist, postcolonial world . . . , there is obviously a special interest in understanding the way that questions of identity and cultural difference are spatialized in new ways. The circumstances of an accelerating "global cultural ecumene" . . . make the project of exploring the intertwined processes of place making and people making in the complex cultural politics of the nation-state an especially vital part of the contemporary anthropological agenda'. (Gupta and Ferguson 1997: 3-4)

In this general context of rethinking the anthropologist's location as well as the way identities may relate to space in a globalized world, there have been essays reflecting on the very notions of space and place as something that may be a 'problem' in contemporary anthropological theory, which 'arises, paradoxically, because the meaning of place too often seems to go without saying' (Rodman

1992: 640).[2] However, as the author argues, places are socially constructed with multiple meanings, and 'anthropologists would do well to follow geographers' renewed interest [...] in reunifying *location* (i.e., the spatial distribution of socioeconomic activity such as trade networks), *sense of place* (or attachment to place), and *locale* (the setting in which a particular social activity occurs, such as a church) to yield a more rounded understanding of places as culturally and socially constructed in practice' (Rodman 1992: 643).[3]

In a short but influential seminal paper[4] on 'heterotopias', Michel Foucault stressed that 'the present epoch will perhaps be above all the epoch of space' (Foucault 1986: 22). 'In any case', he wrote, 'I believe that the anxiety of our era has to do fundamentally with space, no doubt a great deal more than with time.' But this was not to be the same space as was known earlier. According to him, 'today the site has been substituted for extension which itself had replaced emplacement. . . . Our epoch is one in which space takes for us the form of relations among sites' (ibid.: 23). How much this intuition had foreseen later developments in the social sciences (and especially in anthropology) is evident in the fact that all the works previously mentioned deal mostly, if not exclusively, with the question of sites, of identities in relation to space. In other words, the 'geographical turn' in social science studies appears also to be overwhelmingly a culturalist turn.[5] For instance, geographer Bonnemaison argues that 'human territoriality may be defined by the cultural relationship that a group or a society maintains with . . . the web of places and the system of itineraries that frame its space. References to biological-like concepts of "closure" such as appropriation or frontiers is not always a prime necessity: territory in fact refers more to the notion of identity than to security' (Bonnemaison 1995: 71, our translation).

This was indeed what S. Feld and K.H. Basso observed in their 1996 review of the then existing literature on the subject, when they wrote that 'the recent topicalization of place by cultural anthropologists has mostly been concerned with theorizing social identities' (Feld and Basso 1996b: 4). According to them, recent research in anthropology theorized place 'largely from the standpoint of its contestation', a development that 'surely reflects the now acute world conditions of exile, displacement, disaporas, and inflamed borders, to say nothing of the increasingly tumultuous struggles by indigenous peoples and cultural minorities for ancestral homelands, land rights and retention of sacred places'. As a consequence, anthropologists have come to worry 'about places as sites of power struggles or about displacement as histories of annexation, absorption, and resistance' (ibid.: 4-5).

This statement certainly accounts for the perspective taken in the two volumes edited by Appadurai (1988) and Gupta and Ferguson (1997). However, as Feld and Basso noticed, ethnographic accounts centred on the social construction of particular localities 'were few and far between' (ibid.: 6). Their own collection of contributions (as well as Rodman 1992, Hirsch and O'Hanlon 1995 and Lovell 1998a) therefore endeavoured to explore the 'complex ways in which places anchor lives in social formations ranging widely in geographical location, in economic and political scale, and in accompanying realms of gender, race, class, and ethnicity' (Feld and Basso 1996b: 7).

To sum up, the spate of anthropological writing on space since the late 1980s appears to follow two main trends. One is concerned with the location of the anthropologists and the people they study in a globalized world said to be characterized by deterritorialized culture. The other deals with perceptions and experience of lived-in places. Despite their differences, the two approaches partake of common preoccupations. Both are mostly, if not exclusively, focused on the question of the definition of identities. And both scarcely—if at all—mention such a word as 'territory', except in its derivative form 'deterritorialization'. Instead, there is a full array of seemingly connected notions such as 'space', 'place', 'location', 'site', and 'landscape'. Suggestive as they may be in their own right, these concepts are quite distinct from the notion of territory, which seems to have altogether disappeared from the profession's interests.[6] In thirty-one years of the *Annual Review of Anthropology*, significantly, there is not one bibliographical review that mentions in its title 'territory', or concerns itself with the topic. How can we account for such a disinterest?

The main cause could well be the exclusive stress put on culture and identities that has led most anthropologists in recent times to distrust the very notion of territory by assimilating it—we suppose—with the notion of cultural or ethnic boundaries. There is now a widely shared 'discomfort with the idea of bounded cultural units', to use Appadurai's words (Appadurai 1988: 20). Indeed, we too feel such a discomfort. But it is our contention that it has little to do with the question of territory, and that conflating the two notions, 'territory' and 'bounded cultural unit' (if it were to happen) would be groundless. They just are not co-terminous, as territory does not primarily refer to culture or identity, but to rights.

Ordinary definitions of the term in standard dictionaries give, for instance, 'land, especially land under one ruler or government' or 'the land and waters under a jurisdiction'; 'a political subdivision of a country'; 'an area for which a person is responsible as a representative or agent: a salesperson's territory', etc. Clearly, the notion of territory refers to notions of jurisdiction, of power, of rights,[7] but does not necessarily relate to cultural units or to group identities. People within a salesperson's territory may not be aware of the existence and the limits of this territory, and certainly need not develop a common perception of identity. While rights of a like nature define mutually exclusive territories, rights of different nature define different kinds of territories that may overlap and combine over a single stretch of land. A territory may be discontinuous geographically, its limits may be fluid, fuzzy, contested. But only in some specific cases does it intersect with the question of cultural identities.

A major example of such an intersection is, of course, the modern nation-state, where a territory, a political regime, a people and a culture are claimed to be ideally one and the same. This late development can by no means be taken as the model for reflecting on territory—such a standpoint, we feel, acted as a deterrent for fully recognizing the existence of territories in India, as we shall be showing later. Rather, one should consider its specificity against the many other forms of territorial organization that were, and still are, prevalent in the world.

While the present contributions participate in a wider movement currently taking place in the social sciences, which tends to give full importance to conceptions of space, they also try to explore a category—territory—that has elicited remarkably little interest among anthropologists in recent years. We feel, however, that there is much to gain in such a study, the more so because nation-state centred interpretations have tended to obscure the understanding of the complex interplay of territories in social life.

At the same time, the essays in this volume try to relate to a more specific tradition of Indian studies, and to contest some of its own peculiar stereotypes. The paradox is that for this region of the world, the notion of territory was far from being simply ignored. On the contrary it has been the object of diverse speculations, many of them concluding that it was of secondary importance and quite dispensable. Our discussion will first review the various arguments that were put forward to justify such a stand, before evoking the few attempts made to stress anew the importance of territory in India.

TERRITORY IN INDIA

The most enduring stereotype that characterizes so many studies of India is that in this society there were neither territories properly speaking nor boundaries, at least in pre-colonial times—an interpretation that has led scholars to assert for instance that 'territory cannot be seen as a primary constituent of the Indian state' (Wink 1986: 161), or that 'the Indian political tradition . . . ascribed but an ambiguous and subordinated place to territory' (Jaffrelot 1996: 75, our translation).

On the contrary, as has been said, the present collection of essays aims at showing through some well-defined cases the crucial import of territory in India since ancient times, not only in the definition and the regulation of effective social, political, and religious relationships, but also as a category that has explicit cognitive value, as an object of symbolic activity, representations, and debates. The scope is therefore wider than a study of political territories alone, as the very nature of the objections raised by various authors against valuing their importance could not but lead to take into account a diversity of domains related to the conceptualizations of territory in India. A brief review of these positions may not be out of place.

In their manifesto launched in 1957 at the occasion of the first number of *Contributions to Indian Sociology,* with the intention to contest the importance that was given at the time to the notion of the village as a sociological unit,[8] L. Dumont and D.L. Pocock wrote that the 'territorial factor, the relation to the soil is not, in India as a whole, one of the primary factors in social organisation. It is a secondary factor in relation to the two fundamental factors of kinship and caste' (Dumont and Pocock 1957: 18). Dumont himself had elaborated on this notion in his monograph study on the Kallars of Tamil Nadu, where he made a detailed study of local territorial units. In this work he concluded that 'kinship remains the fundamental principle of organization, and it becomes a factor in political organization once it is qualified or mediated so to speak, by the territorial principle' (Dumont 1986 [1957]: 184). With nuances, this was more or less the position held by many other authors. For example, A.C. Mayer, writing at the same period, underlined the importance of locality in breeding 'village patriotism' (overriding, often, caste divisions), but concluded also that kinship is essential in defining territorial units: 'this makes the region a fluid and rather unsatisfactory structural concept. . . . The "territory" of Ramkheri subcaste group is a variable kinship-territory' (Mayer 1960: 271-2). Similarly, Richard G. Fox found that in northern India 'the territorial state does not prove preeminent over local kin-defined political and economic bodies' (Fox 1971: 168).[9] In the present volume, Chapter 6 by Gérard Toffin is a critical contribution to this specific discussion and illustrates, among other things, that kinship and territory need not be set up as exclusive alternatives, but help mutually define each other.[10]

As an important variant in the arguments conducive to a devaluation of territory in relation to caste, Dumont later developed an alternative theory, in which kinship lost its role in favour of what he called the caste system's 'ideology'. According to his well-known formula, 'the ideology ignores territory as such' (Dumont 1966: 196). There, 'ideology' relates to the basic opposition between purity and impurity, the fundamental logic behind the 'caste system' in Dumont's theory. Such an assertion, in his view, was not meant to deny the empirical evidence of territorial facts, on which he himself had worked in detail. However, his quest for an overarching structural principle giving coherence to 'Indian civilization' (a preoccupation that went back to the first issue of *Contributions to Indian Sociology* in 1957) led him to an a priori subordination of what he called the empirical level to the ideological. In his words, the ideological level in India 'does not account for the territorial factor, ignores it and encompasses it' (ibid.: 67). Many essays in the present volume address and contest this perspective, for instance the contributions by Michel Angot and Gérard Colas (Chapters 1 and 2) that historicize the sharp contrast existing at the 'ideological level' between a Vedic ritualistic discourse, devaluing fixation in permanent places, and later Brahmanical developments, valuing the local entrenchment of gods.

Dumont's theory has been widely criticized from different perspectives,[11] but his specific point about territory was in fact little, if at all discussed. While most of his critics did not address the issue, some did so, but often considered territory as a mere part of the politico-economic sphere, a reductionism that could not really confront Dumont's perspective.[12] Thus, in a way, it is somewhat paradoxical that Dumont has been one of the few anthropologists to have discussed at length the notion of territory as such, under various aspects—village community, village gods, territorial segmentation of castes, concepts of property, and royal power[13]—in order to demonstrate that it was of secondary importance in relation to caste and 'ideology'.

Another line of argument that has tended to devaluate the importance of territory in India pertains to a denial of the links between people—or some of them—with the place they live in. For instance Sanskritist Charles Malamoud suggested once that there is nowadays a 'weak "territoriality" of the Indian village', to be paralleled with the fact that 'ancestors in India have no earthly abode' (Malamoud 1996 [1976]: 75 n. 7). A similar reasoning has been made by anthropologist Yasushi Uchiyamada (1995) when he argued that depressed castes in Kerala, who bury their dead, develop more attachment to the land than upper castes who practise cremation. On the basis of factual observation, the argument is altogether unconvincing, since in this region members of high castes, too, define their identity through strong references to an ancestral land (Tarabout 1991). However, coming from a social anthropologist who certainly would not see himself as an 'Orientalist', such a repetition of the argument suggests how widespread can be the scholarly prejudices against the importance of territory in India.

It has to be acknowledged that the so-called 'ethnosociology' approach theorized by McKim Marriott has fostered a much more nuanced approach towards the relationship between people and the soil. Inspired by transactionalism, 'ethnosociology' interprets many characteristics of Indian society, particularly castes, in terms of a circulation of substances, especially bodily substances (Marriott and Inden 1974; Marriott 1990). The qualities of various beings are determined by the nature of 'coded substances' that are exchanged between all of them. Interactions are thus able to constantly modify beings. In order to regulate these fluxes and these influences, rules of avoidance or acceptance are established, which are at the core of caste society. This theoretical frame leaves no room for the notion of territory, strictly speaking. It may have encouraged some forms of 'locationism', so to say, but no interest in delimited jurisdictions.[14] Yet it has definitely opened up a new line of analysis conferring a crucial importance to the soil, in the sense of a geographical milieu linked to identities, or more precisely as an ecological environment with which people are in a constant exchange of 'substances'.

Marriott did not himself elaborate much on the topic, but some of his ideas have been fruitfully developed by other scholars, most notably by E.V. Daniel (1984). Writing about the Tamil village he studied, Daniel begins by stressing the importance of the notion of soil: 'one of the most important relationships to a Tamil is that which exists between a person and the soil of his ur [village]' (Daniel 1984: 63).[15] He then proceeds to discuss the notion of *ūr*, which is not always restricted to 'village' but may take different meanings according to situations. For example, it is an external space 'defined person-centrically in terms of its relevance to a given ego rather than in terms of a purely semantic category that refers to a bounded territory common to all Tamils at all times and in all places' (ibid.: 68). When *ūr* specifically refers to the village, the corresponding territory can be conceived according to two contrasting modes: either as an administrative unit with fixed and continuous limits; or as a lived space with the 'focus on the center of the village and with a vulnerable "frontier" or a periphery' (ibid.: 77) marked by 'shrines of sentinel deities, entering points of roads and streams, haunted tamarind trees that dot the edge of the village' (ibid.: 74).

Daniel's book has become a reference for any discussion on the symbolic dimension of the relationships that people have with land in India. Indeed, he achieved a *tour de force* by conciliating the idea of humoral transactions in constant flux, at the core of ethnosociological theory, and its criticism by Moffatt: 'Why are physical, spatial boundaries so important in south Indian villages if flow is so valued?' (Moffatt 1990: 225). In stressing the crucial cognitive importance in India of the various bonds that link people to the land, Daniel has been able to hold together the notion of a flux of exchanges between people and the soil, and the notion of village territory, though he remained somewhat ambiguous in his formulations about the latter's limits.

In preparing this volume, therefore, we were faced with two disparate sets of arguments concerning a possible relationship between soil and territory. One argued that a supposed lack of territoriality was linked to a supposed lack of attachment to ancestors. The other one stressed the existence of constant flows of exchange between soil and people, but nevertheless entertained also little concern for territory proper, in the sense we have defined above (with the exception of Daniel's work). It was then necessary that the present book bring its own perspective on the question, and three chapters deal with the subject: Chapter 3 by Phyllis Granoff, Chapter 4 by Caterina Guenzi and Sunita Singh, and Chapter 5 by Caroline and Filippo Osella. It should be clear, however, that while these chapters amply demonstrate the elaborateness of conceptions that stress the mutual determination of places and people, they do not claim to establish that it equates soil with territory. As has been underlined before, the notions are just not of the same nature, though obviously they may intersect. But it was felt to be important, in this volume, to show that there exist in India explicit discourses establishing the identities of people with reference to their native or living well-circumscribed places.[16]

A third and last group of arguments may be described as the acknowledgement that territory did play a role in political relationships in ancient times (pre-colonial, or pre-Mughal, depending on the authors), but that it was no 'real' territory, so to say. Some would hold for instance that Hindu kingdoms, prior to the colonial period, were not so much defined by their limits than by the network of personal relationships that developed between the king and those who recognized his power. In this sense, the notion of territory is irrelevant, even 'fallacious' (Wink 1986: 47). Instead, 'we find a people-cum-territory or *janapada,* shot through with vested rights' (ibid.: 161). This notion was already pinpointed by Dumont when he argued that according to the (Brahmanical) model of Hindu kingship, territory was undifferentiated from its population (Dumont 1966: 372).[17] This standpoint, however, has been contradicted by other scholars using the same Sanskrit references as Dumont, and underlining the importance of territory in the exercise of royal power that these texts make clear. The historian of law R. Lingat (1967), for instance, showed that in the *Dharmaśāstra* and the *Manusmṛti*, royal power is closely associated with the notion of *kṣatra*, 'a power which is territorial in character, not only because it is applied within a territory and ends at the frontiers of the kingdom, but because it is conceived . . . as a regal right on territory, akin to a proprietary right that gives a direct power on land and soil' (Lingat 1967: 237, our translation). Lingat's conclusion, however, was seldom heard.

One argument that has been put forward was to affirm that, since every Hindu sovereign considered himself to be virtually a Universal Ruler, there was no room for the notion of territory, which thus had little pertinence for defining kingdoms. Based on texts and rituals that predate our era, this conception of kingship has been widely circulated and may be found in Buddhism as well as in the claims of any local Hindu chieftain of the recent past. We should however not confuse the image of power that these chieftains may have wanted to project, and the nature of this power. Some authors have been cautious enough in this respect and have considered that the symbolic order that was thus proclaimed, probably had only but 'a distant relationship with reality' and that, eventually, 'if there is an idea to remember, it is that kings ruled over a limited territory in the constant expectative of a war' (Biardeau 1982: 31 ff., our translation). Others have been less cautious. There has been for instance the suggestion that 'in the Hindu classical conceptions, the territorial extent was less important than its religious signification' (Jaffrelot 1996: 75, our translation; also Galey 1989).

Moreover, even authors who have recognized the past importance of the notion of territory in the relationships between kingdoms, have often dismissed the existence of their precise delimitation. Thus, according to some, 'the country was divided into political entities whose borders were defined by their centre rather than the peripheries, the opposite of the concept of *limes,* limits between states. That system continued till the reign of the Mughals' (Dupont and Landy 2005: 48). And even if the past existence of frontiers 'in the sense of zonal regions', with their fortified outposts and toll-bars, is readily acknowledged, 'this is no evidence that linear boundaries were known' (Embree 1977: 260).

Obviously, such conclusions rely on a comparison with an ideal-type of territory that closely corresponds to the specific form it has assumed in the modern nation state (Anderson 1983; Goswami 1998). In our view, as already pointed out, such a stand is detrimental for developing any fruitful analysis of the relationships that may exist between societies and space: such a definition of 'territory' necessarily ends up in an a priori negation of any territorial logic in societies prior to the appearance of the modern nation state; and even within today's nation states, the analysis would be applicable only at one level, that of the nation, and not at various scales of observation within it. In the wake we would lose any ability to shed light on the historical processes by which this specific form of territorial construction has emerged, or on the rather recent manifestations it has entailed in terms of 'ethnicity'. We stand by our definition of territory as primarily a notion about jurisdiction, and we argue that, yes, territories in India have been for centuries inseparable from the exercise of political power, and, yes, these territories were often known in very precise terms through well-defined limits. The last part of the volume is thus dedicated to this discussion. Two chapters (Chapter 7 by Gilles Tarabout and Chapter 8 by Daniela

Berti) are case studies of territorial entanglements between religious and political jurisdictions. A third and ultimate chapter by Christiane Brosius illustrates some aspects of the current 'ethnicization' of politics in contemporary India, as a recent development of territorial conceptions within the nation state.

Before concluding this review, it has to be stated that besides the general trends that have been presented, there has been also many works that have provided descriptions and analyses conclusively showing the importance of soil and territory in India, in observed individual and social practices as well as in explicit discourses.[18] Historian Nicholas Dirks has for instance criticised Dumont for his devaluation of the importance of territory (said to be secondary in relation to kinship) in the latter's monograph on Kallars: 'My ethnographic construction of the Kallars in Pudukottai leads me to challenge Dumont's theory on a number of important points. Territory, for example, plays a major role at every level of social definition. It is so embedded within social and political forms that we cannot say that it merely mediates the political and social domains as Dumont suggests' (Dirks 1993: 258). Other authors have underlined the importance and relevance of territory for a great variety of social contexts, such as the regional configuration of caste relationships (Miller 1954), the elaboration of a mythical past by inhabitants of urban neighbourhoods (Parkhill 1993), the power that is still today exercised by local deities within their specific jurisdiction (Sax 1991, Berti 2001, Tarabout 1999), the prevalence of localized codes of conduct for Brahmans (Chakrabarti 2000),[19] the bonds that migrant workers keep with their village of origin (Racine 1994), the territorial self-representation of commercial networks found in some merchant castes (Mines 1984), or the enduring links that married women maintain with their natal family (Sax 2000) or village (Lambert 1996). In the latter case, Lambert has shown that the birth-place is a significant dimension of one's identity, and that the stress put either on caste or on kinship, or on place in order to define one's identity, may be of a strategic nature. The author does not limit her critique to the question of the supposed subordination of territory to caste, but extends it also to its alleged exclusion from the system of conscious ideas and values: 'local identity is an indigenous value and thereby constitutes an aspect of conscious ideology different from that of caste' (Lambert 1996: 116).

Thus, territorial facts in India have imposed themselves on the attention of numerous observers, and could be negated or said to be of secondary importance only when there exists interpretative prejudice. At the same time, they still open a wide array of questions for discussion and interpretation. The present volume aims at addressing some of them. Without trying to be exhaustive in any way, given the immensity and the complexity of the Indian subcontinent, it is based on a diversified set of studies, varied both in historical and regional scope. The book therefore combines a great diversity of sources (ethnography, archives, texts and inscriptions), used by authors who have specialized in different disciplines (Indology, history of religion, social anthropology). Such diverse approaches and methodologies have been organized together in order to provide contrasting pictures of the plural conceptions and symbolic manipulations of territory in the Indian world. Three contributions by Sanskritists, each a specialist of a different period and of different texts, will precede papers of anthropological perspective. They introduce a necessary historicity, as some objections to the importance of territory in India relied on interpretations of Brahmanical texts, taken to express some kind of timeless cultural disinterest for attachment to place, for territory, and for boundaries.

SUMMARY

Without strictly following a chronological order, the succession of contributions is arranged so as to begin with the ancient period and end with today's developments. However, the main objective in organizing the book has been to deal step by step with the arguments that have just been presented. The volume is thus divided into three main parts. The first, 'Emergence of Divine Territories in Brahmanical Texts', is a preliminary discussion of some 'ideological' aspects of territory in ancient India. The second, 'Land, Soil, and Sense of Belonging', deals not so much with territory *per se* than with the allegation that cultural or theological reasons prevent some people in India from developing attachment with their native or living place. The third and most developed part, 'Religious and Political Territories', is a discussion of various kinds of territorial jurisdictions—with a last development about today's Hindutva claims for an 'ethnicized' national territory (Jaffrelot 1996).

EMERGENCE OF DIVINE TERRITORIES IN BRAHMANICAL TEXTS

We begin with a preliminary question: to what extent are there ideas in Brahmanical thinking that actually point to a devaluation of the notion of territory (and to what extent do they relate to practice)?

The first chapter by Michel Angot shows that Vedic texts definitely expressed a strong devaluation of the notion of localized, bounded *place*, and conversely put an extreme positive value on open *space* —at least as far as the Gods were concerned. While the hierarchy of values is unambiguous in these texts, understanding the way it did inform practice may prove more conjectural. Certainly, this was well in line with the way public sacrifices, the *srauta* rituals, could not be reiterated in the same spot, and with the full symbolism of such rituals. But, as pointed out by the author himself, these texts bear on ritual practice and on conceptions about the divine realm, and should not be taken as directly applying to the social world. As a matter of fact, even if these values are plainly congruent with the standard hypothesis of a nomadic origin of the first Vedic people, the development of Vedic rituals as elaborated in the ritual literature corresponds to a period when they applied for centuries within a well settled agricultural society. Today itself, Vedic *srauta* rituals may occasionally be re-enacted (with their valuation on open space) in the contemporary, well-territorialized Indian society. Clearly, values inform social life, but not necessarily in a mechanical way. In terms of a general theory, this should lead one to be very cautious about ideas about the 'spirit', the 'ethos' of a society or an economic system (Max Weber), or the 'ideology' of Indian civilization (Louis Dumont). In the specific perspective of the present volume, the positive value given to open space and the correlated devaluation of bounded places did apply well to the Vedic vision of the divine, but it may well have been circumscribed to this particular context in the developments of religion and society in India, and does not mean that Vedic society was devoid of territories, or that the ideology presented here was the only existing model. Contemporary ritual contexts that are proper to the Brahmans are still associated with Vedic deities that are 'delocalized', but often coexist at the same time with other models in which gods and goddesses are grounded in a specific territory, owned by them.[20]

Chapter 2 by Gérard Colas suggests some aspects of the historical shift in Brahmanical traditions from Vedic speculations towards later, very different conceptions. Epigraphic and textual sources of the fourth and fifth centuries CE refer to sedentary deities installed in temples in villages and towns. This sedentary character goes hand in hand with the existence of physical images of the divine (absent from Vedic references). Gods now have a physical body, more or less anthropomorphic, and are actors within a local society. The texts and inscriptions bear witness to the sometimes heated debates about the development of temple rituals and the possible implication of Brahmans in them. They testify also to the growing body of lands donated for the maintenance of cults. But if the link between divine image and temple ground is assumed quite early in the texts, there is a reluctance to admit that gods themselves may become landowners, and it takes many centuries for the literate society to accept it through various phraseologies. It is in this context that explicit discourses on divine territory appear—discourses that are plural and sometimes contradictory.

Taken together, these two chapters concur in their analysis of the decisive evolution in Brahmanical theories and ritual practices that lead from an uncompromised positive valuation of open space in the Vedic period, at least for the gods, to the latter's radical inscription in lands and territories. Clearly, when speaking about territory, the Brahmanical 'ideology'—to use Dumont's expression—is much more complex than a mere reference to Vedic speculation would suggest, not only in matters of land and society, but also in theological elaboration. The process has been a tense one, spanning centuries, but there is clearly no ground today to define Brahmanical conceptions of territory, even in the religious sphere, by referring merely to the early Vedic period. On the contrary, the process itself suggests the strength of territorial realities in Indian society for at least two thousand years, so much so that these forced themselves into the divine world.

LAND, SOIL, AND SENSE OF BELONGING

The following set of three chapters investigates a concept related to territory, but distinct from it, as already underlined: the concept of soil, and more generally the relationships between lands and identities. There are two points that are sought to be made.

At the general level of anthropological theory, the first illustrates that the interrelations between places and people do not necessarily entail the existence of a territory in the sense of a jurisdiction, as previously discussed. Nevertheless, it suggests also that 'space' does not exist as such (a point elaborately discussed in Casey 1996), and that land, in the sense of places or soil, cannot be dissociated from society in all its heterogeneities and particularities.

At the level of this volume's specific argument, the second point is to underline the importance of these perceptions for understanding how people in India come to identify themselves, or be identified by others, with the land—that is, how they claim, or are said to 'belong' to it.

This sense of belonging is addressed here in three ways. Chapter 3, by Phyllis Granoff, is a study of identifications made in medieval Buddhist, Jain, and Hindu texts between regions and the people living there or originating from them. These are strongly worded stereotypes in which the people's characteristics, qualities, and behaviour are said to be determined by the very place where they live or where they come from. Such kinds of prejudice, Granoff argues, may well have been of immediate import for the delimitation of so-called sectarian divisions of the time, where religious sectarian identities may have papered over deep social divisions grounded on regional differentiation. In her words, 'ritual was merely put in the service of a more fundamental marker of difference to give what was not originally a religious difference a definitely religious tone'.

The other two chapters in this part are based on micro-level field studies. Through a study of present-day Varanasi astrologers, Caterina Guenzi and Sunita Singh (Chapter 4) are able to show that Brahmanical elaborations and practices of geomancy are based on a typology of soils and on their supposed respective interactions with different classes of society. Land enables astrologers to divine good or bad prospects for its inhabitants, as they share its effects on them according to their own respective qualities, and as in turn they affect land's characteristics. One aspect of Brahmanical 'ideology', therefore, provides for a luminous illustration of the extent to which land, person, and society may be mutually determined.

Caroline and Filippo Osella's study of the interactions between land and people as they are conceived in Central Kerala (Chapter 5) amply corroborates this statement. By examining the rules that preside over the construction of a new house in order to establish harmonious relationships between a site and those who will live there, and by analysing the funeral practices of some of the castes of the region, they shed light on an intricate life-and-death cycle binding together people with their place and with the surrounding lands that provide them their sustenance. These findings accord well with previous anthropological works which stress the importance of humoral transactions in defining social identities in India (McKim Marriott, Daniel). They suggest, in addition, a possible specificity of Kerala in this matter, where it seems that a particular stress is given on the extremely intimate bonds that such transactions create between places and the life and identity of the people born or living there. Expressed in the specific language of transactionalist theory, this question is akin to the already much debated one about the relations between kinship and territory, to which many authors have answered by suggesting the primacy of kinship. This discussion is taken up again in the first chapter of Part 3, along a different theoretical line of analysis.

The second part, then, provides three examples of how places and people are said to determine each others in India, be it in the case of ancient regional stereotypes, or of the learned theories and practices of geomancy among contemporary urban Brahmans, or of the vital exchanges that are said to occur between specific places and their inhabitants in today's Kerala. Soil, identities and events are intimately intertwined. There is a perception of an 'inequality' of places (so to say) linked to personal or social inequalities, and eventually a strong sense of rooting in the land, a 'sense of belonging' (Lovell) to well-defined places.

RELIGIOUS AND POLITICAL TERRITORIES

While such a 'sense of belonging' points to a personal or social identity expressed in terms of place, it does not necessarily entail identification with a territory, as already underlined; conversely, one may belong to a territory without developing any specific 'sense of belonging' to it, as is often the case with administrative circumscriptions, for instance. However, and without any necessary connection with the model of the modern nation state, complex and multiple interplays between places and territories, between identities and jurisdictions, do often happen and they structure social groupings in depth. The last set of four chapters investigates such varying social and political dimensions of territories, understood as spatial divisions determined by the exercise of rights and power.

Gérard Toffin (Chapter 6) analyses the conception of territory among the Newars in the Kathmandu Valley of Nepal. Territory, there, is defined through various divine jurisdictions at the level of the whole village or of sections of it, through ritual marks at the boundary of villages, and through funerary associations whose membership relies on both lineage and residence, and whose elders are the effective chiefs of the village. Territory and kinship are particularly tightly bound together, so much so that the author speaks of 'territorial parentages', in which territory relegates to a secondary level the importance of blood relationships in the constitution of social groupings. Symbolic territories, imbued with a deep sense of belonging and local identities, are thus also in this case effective, well delimited judicial and political territories, in which the full control of the social life of the inhabitants is exercised.

The next two chapters are case studies of religious territories, with a very precise delimitation of their boundaries and an effective political import in the control of land and people. Such territories, which answer the strictest definition of the term, do not depend on the model of the nation state, and appear to have been widely prevalent in India. Historically, they did—and sometimes continue to—interact with the political organization of the former kingdoms, of the colonial power, or of the contemporary Indian nation state.

Gilles Tarabout (Chapter 7) develops a case study of a long-lasting dispute which involved the former kingdoms of Cochin and of Travancore over the territory of a temple. The case exemplifies the multiple forms of territory that once structured power relationships in Kerala, and the changes in their conception that occurred between the end of the seventeenth and the end of the nineteenth century. From a multiplicity of fragmented, embedded territories of different natures and importance, there is a progressive change to the notion of a unified territory that is characteristic of the modern nation state. Thus, far from a lack of territory in pre-colonial India, it could be said that there was an excess of them. But these territories were multiple, sometimes discontinuous, and overlapping, as very different rights applied to a same tract of land. At a broader level of observation this might give the impression of 'fuzzy' boundaries, while they were in fact very precise and well delimited at the micro level. The specific autonomy that was granted to some temple jurisdictions led in some cases to legal battles between growing state powers, which provide an exceptional opportunity for reconstructing what ultimately led to the establishment of modern bureaucratic states in the region. This evolution corresponds to a simplification, standardization, and political centralization of previous territories, but definitely not to the invention of the notion.

Daniela Berti's study of divine jurisdictions in Himachal Pradesh (Chapter 8) analyses the territorial aspects of the cults of village deities. These deities have specific and well-delimited jurisdictions, and the corresponding territories are examined in relation to the different political systems that have successively controlled the region—Hindu kingdoms, British colonial administration, and the democratic system of contemporary India. The author uses various sources, oral stories, manuscripts of former British administrators, and contemporary observation in order to demonstrate the extent to which local deities were, and still are, at the core of local perceptions of territory. Not only do they still function as ritual units, and as instances of arbitrage for ordinary litigation, but they have been the source for defining the limits of colonial and post-colonial administrative divisions, tax assessment units, and electoral circumscriptions. In this case, religious territories centred on village deities appear to have been the mould for economic administration and political dynamics, while retaining their relevance in the current religious life of the people.

The history of how India as a nation state has come into being has been told at length in numerous scholarly publications, and is not repeated here. The social and historical processes leading to the conception of India as a bounded whole has, for instance, been brought to light by Goswami (1998; 2004). The present volume concludes with a study by Christiane Brosius about the ways in which religious nationalism has developed in recent years (Chapter 9). Brosius explores particularly the relationships between the religious construction of territories and electoral politics at the time of the pan-Indian processions organized by the Hindu right at the end of the 1980s and the beginning of the 1990s.[21] The analysis focuses on some videos that were made about these so-called patriotic pilgrimages, which relied on an explicitly religious imagination and rhetoric so as to develop a 'mysticism of the territory', to use Jaffrelot's expression (Jaffrelot 1996: 92). For Jaffrelot, the ideology propagated by the RSS leads to a devaluation of administrative frontiers in favour of cultural ones. To the territorial nationalism it opposes an 'ethnic conception of the nation that structures the "Indian land" by exclusive reference to elements that are relevant in terms of cultural roots. Points of reference in the landscape are especially given a national value through a reinterpretation of the signification they may possess in the Hindu tradition' (Jaffrelot 1999: 93, our translation). Such a traditional sacred geography was particularly studied by D. Eck (1981, 1998), who has shown how ritual processions and pilgrimages are instrumental in the elaboration of Hindu visions of 'an "imagined landscape" in which networks of pilgrimage places have generated a powerful sense of land and location' (Eck 1998: 166). The author goes on to suggest that 'in a range of Hindu traditions, map-making has been the domain of both the cosmologists and mythmakers, and it is arguable that the imagined landscape they have created is far more culturally powerful than that displayed on the Bartholomew's map' (ibid.: 169).

As Christiane Brosius demonstrates in her contribution, this imagined landscape has been the support on which the Hindu right has tried to politically mobilize the electorate. The videos that are analysed here reveal the constant use of evocations of an impending menace collectively threatening a united Hindu people. This is expressed at the mythical level (the loss of a Hindu Golden Age), at the level of (a revised) history, and at the level of biological metaphors (the nation as a kindred family), all concurring in producing an imagined and diversified landscape for a claimed 'Hindu territory'. In this, we find a process of trying to redefine a political frame in terms of a religious and ethnicized territory. Militants identify the whole of India with a national soil (sometimes blurring the limits of international borders), towards which a sense of belonging is exclusively equated with Hinduness.

Soil and identities, divine and administrative jurisdictions, landmarks and territorial boundaries, all these ways in which relations to the land concur in the formation of social groupings are present and intertwined in this last case, as they were in the different other chapters of this volume. But they appear in a radically new configuration and organize the State at an unprecedented level in a typically nationalistic, nativistic way. 'Nation' in this understanding —and not the existence of territories—is the recent product of 'modernity'. It is thus a comparison with other societies that these studies eventually invite, but a comparison based on the recognition of the historicity and plurality of territorial organizations that are at the core of human relationships.

Acknowledgements: The essays in this volume are part of a collection originally published in Italian in 2003, as a special number of *Etnosistemi. Processi e dinamiche culturali* (no. 10, 'Terra, territorio e società nel mondo indiano'). We thank the publisher, CISU, Roma, for kindly authorizing their publication in English. The contributions have been revised, and the introduction entirely rewritten for the present edition—we are grateful to the anonymous reader for her/his insightful and stimulating comments.

NOTES

1. For instance in France, Lévy 1991; *Géographie et Cultures* no. 20; Di Méo 2000.
2. Also Geertz (1996).
3. At least three major volumes that reflect such preoccupations were published in the following years: Hirsch and O'Hanlon (1995); Feld and Basso (1996a); Lovell (1998a).
4. Published in English in 1986 but pronounced as a communication as early as 1967.
5. For a discussion see Bonnemaison and Cambrezy 1996.
6. Among the few exceptions (in French anthropology) may be mentioned Godelier (1978), and Vincent, Dory and Verdier (1995).
7. This was underlined by R.D. Sack in his sophisticated theorization of territoriality, defined as 'the attempt to affect, influence or control actions and interactions (of people, things, and relationships) by asserting and attempting to enforce control over a geographic area' (Sack 1983: 55). We thank Frédéric Landy for communicating us this reference.
8. See for instance Srinivas (1960), as well as Bailey (1959).
9. See also the critical reviews of this work by Galey (1973) and Stern (1973). More recently, see Jamous (2003 [1991]).
10. A perspective that had many exponents for other societies in the world (for instance, recently, Liberski-Bagnoud 2002), but was seldom applied to South Asia.
11. Contrary to arguments forwarded by many of Dumont's critics, his position should not be understood as merely resulting from an 'orientalistic' approach, in the sense popularized by E. Said. Dumont was a meticulous and scrupulous observer, whose monograph provides an impressive amount of precise empirical data. His choice of interpretation has to be referred to his overall intellectual project, which may be very roughly characterized as inherited from both Marcel Mauss (of whom he had been a student) and Max Weber (his notion of 'ideology' may not be very different from what Weber meant by 'ethics' [of a religion] or 'spirit' [of an economic system]). Besides, his programme of research was explicitly framed by a structuralistic perspective. Such a project, well in tune with the practice of social anthropology at the time, could not but lead to a form of essentialism.

12. See for instance the critique by F.G. Bailey of Dumont and Pocock's text: Bailey tackles indirectly with the question of 'territory' exclusively through a discussion of the 'sociological reality of the village' (he significantly substitutes 'village' for 'territory', the term used by Dumont and Pocock in the text he is discussing—Bailey 1959: 95). According to him, Dumont and Pocock deny such a reality because they discard the economic and political dimensions of the village.
13. The same preoccupations inform later studies of some of his former students, who have particularly worked out the ritual and symbolic dimensions of temple-centred territories (Galey 1985, 1986; Reiniche 1979, 1989, 1990).
14. See for instance Sax (1990: 493): 'Americans tend to think of their places of residence—houses, towns, states, or nations—as geographically bounded entities with definite borders. Residence is understood in the external terms of geographical location and/or legal definition, and places and persons are rarely considered parts of each other. Many South Asians, by contrast, think of their places of residence as biophysical entities'. There, 'biophysical entities' are opposed not only to Americans' supposed disregard for interactions between places and persons, but also, at least implicitly, to their notion of bounded entities with definite borders.
15. The importance of the interaction between ecology and human (or other species) physiology has been well brought to light in Zimmermann's study of Ayurvedic texts (Zimmermann 1982).
16. For a different line of enquiry on this question, making use of an explicitly culturalist definition of territory and concerning itself with territorial segregation in terms of religious/caste/race identities, see the comparative volume edited by Gervais-Lambony, Landy and Oldfield (2005).
17. This intellectual construction seemed to fit with observations made about some classical texts. For instance, C. Malamoud (1990, 1996 [1976]) showed that territory in Vedic times seemed to be less determining than human bonds: 'the term *grāma,* generally translated as "village", more often designates a concentration of people or a network of institutions than it does a set territory . . . the stability of the *grāma* depends more upon the cohesion of its constitutive group than it does upon the space that it occupies' (Malamoud 1996 [1976]: 75).
18. Moreover, territory has been a widely studied topic in anthropological studies on nearby Nepal (sometimes said to present a sharp contrast with India on this question!). See Toffin (1984, 1987, 1993), Lecomte-

Tilouine (1993), Krauskopff (1989), Höfer (1971). See also the studies by P. Dollfus, A. de Sales, G. Krauskopff in Formoso (1996).

19. This should lead to a considerable revision of the idea forwarded by C. Bouglé, according to whom, in India, there existed no *lex loci*. For a critique, see Derrett (1968), Conrad (1995).
20. Moreover, it is necessary to distinguish between territorial gods, installed in shrines but often said to have come from 'outside', and the deities and various invisible powers of more or less dangerous character who inhabit places in the landscape—trees, waters, mountains. This opposition has sometimes been arbitrarily interpreted in terms of a contrast between 'Aryan gods' and so-called autochthonous 'Dravidian gods' (Shulman 1980: 134).
21. See also her recent book on the question, Brosius (2005).

REFERENCES

Anderson, Benedict, 1983. *Imagined Communities*, London: Verso.

Appadurai, Arjun, 1988. 'Introduction: Place and Voice in Anthropological Theory', *Cultural Anthropology*, 3, 1: 16-20.

Bailey, F.G., 1959. 'For a Sociology of India?', *Contributions to Indian Sociology*, 3: 88-101.

Berti, Daniela, 2001. *La parole des dieux. Rituels de possession dans l'Himalaya indien*, Paris: CNRS Editions.

Biardeau, Madeleine, 1982. 'Dharma et frontières politiques en Inde', in J.P. Charnay et al., *Le bonheur par l'empire ou le rêve d'Alexandre*, Paris: Ed. Anthropos, pp. 29-35.

Bonnemaison, J. and L. Cambrezy, 1995. 'Le lien territorial, entre frontières et identités', *Géographie et Cultures*, 20: 7-18.

Bonnemaison, J., 1995. 'Les mots de la terre sacrée. L'exemple océanien', in *La construction religieuse du territoire*, ed. J.F. Vincent, D. Dory and R.Verdier, Paris: L'Harmattan, pp. 66-73.

Brosius, Christiane, 2005. *Empowering Visions: The Politics of Representation in Hindu Nationalism*, London: Anthem Press.

Casey, Edward S., 1996. 'How to Get from Space to Place in a Fairly Short Stretch of Time. Phenomenological Prolegomena', in *Senses of Place*, ed. S. Feld and K.H. Basso, Santa Fe: School of American Research Press, pp. 13-52.

Chakrabarti, Kunal, 2000. 'Cult Region: The Puranas and the Making of the Cultural Territory of Bengal', *Studies in History*, n.s., 16, 1: 1-16.

Conrad, D., 1995. 'The Personal Law Question and Hindu Nationalism', in *Representing Hinduism: The Construction of Religious Traditions and National Identity,* ed. Vasudha Dhalmia and H. von Stietencron, Delhi: Sage, pp. 306-37.

Daniel, E. Valentine, 1984. *Fluid Signs: Being a Person the Tamil Way,* University of California Press.

Derrett, J.D.M., 1968. 'Custom and Law in Ancient India', in *Religion, Law and the State in India,* Delhi: Oxford University Press, pp. 148-70.

Di Méo, Guy, 2000. *Géographie sociale et territoires,* Paris: Nathan.

Dirks, Nicholas B., 1993. *The Hollow Crown: Ethnohistory of an Indian Kingdom,* Ann Arbor: University of Michigan Press.

Dory, D., 1995. 'Religions et territoires. Eléments de théorie et propositions de recherche', in *La construction religieuse du territoire,* ed. J.F. Vincent, D. Dory and R.Verdier, Paris: L'Harmattan, pp. 367-75.

Dumont, Louis, 1966. *Homo Hierarchicus. Le système des castes et ses implications,* Paris: Gallimard.

———, 1986 [1957]. *A South Indian Subcaste: Social Organization and Religion of the Pramalai Kallar,* Delhi: Oxford University Press.

Dumont, Louis, and Pocock, David, 1957. 'For a Sociology of India', *Contributions to Indian Sociology,* 1: 7-22.

Dupont, Véronique and Frédéric Landy, 2005. 'Segregation and Territory: What do We Mean? A Discussion in the Indian and South African Contexts', in *Reconfiguring Identities and Building Territories in India and South Africa,* ed. P. Gervais-Lambony, F. Landy and S. Oldfield, Delhi: Manohar/CSH, pp. 43-72.

Eck, Diana, 1981. 'India's Tirthas: "Crossings" in Sacred Geography', *History of Religions,* 20, 4: 323-44.

———, 1998. 'The Imagined Landscape: Patterns in the Construction of Hindu Sacred Geography', *Contributions to Indian Sociology,* n.s., 32, 2: 165-88.

Embree, Ainslie T., 1977. 'Frontiers into Boundaries: From the Traditional to the Modern State', in *Realm and Region in Traditional India,* ed. R.G. Fox, Delhi: Vikas, pp. 255-80.

Feld, S., and K.H. Basso, eds., 1996a. *Senses of Place,* Santa Fe: School of American Research Press.

———, 1996b. 'Introduction', in *Senses of Place,* ed. S. Feld and K.H. Basso, Santa Fe: School of American Research Press, pp. 3-11.

Formoso, Bernard, ed., 1996. 'Dieux du sol en Asie', *Etudes Rurales,* 143-4.

Foucault, Michel, 1986. 'Of Other Spaces'[transl. Jay Miskowiec], *Diacritics,* 16-1: 22-7.

Fox, Richard G., 1971. *Kin, Raja, and Rule: State-Hinterland Relations in Preindustrial India,* Berkeley: University of California Press.

Galey, Jean-Claude, ed., 1985. *L'Espace du temple–I. Espaces, itinéraires, médiations,* Paris: EHESS.

———, ed., 1986. *L'Espace du temple–II. Les sanctuaires dans le royaume,* Paris: EHESS.

———, 1973. 'L'Etat et le lignage. Questions à propos d'un livre', *L'Homme,* XIII, 1-2: 71-82.

———, 1989. 'Reconsidering Kingship in India: An Ethnological Perspective', *History and Anthropology,* 4: 123-87.

Geertz, Clifford, 1996. 'Afterword', in *Senses of Place,* ed. S. Feld and K.H. Basso, Santa Fe: School of American Research Press, pp. 259-62.

Géographie et Cultures, no. 20, 1996 [special number on the seminar 'Territoire, lien ou frontière: identités, conflits ethniques, enjeux et recompositions territoriales', Paris 1995].

Gervais-Lambony, Philippe, Frédéric Landy and Sophie Oldfield, 2005. *Reconfiguring Identities and Building Territories in India and South Africa,* Delhi: Manohar/CSH.

Godelier, Maurice, 1978. 'L'Appropriation de la nature. Territoire et propriété dans quelques formes de sociétés précapitalistes', *La Pensée,* 198: 7-50.

Goswami, Manu, 1998. 'From *Swadeshi* to *Swaraj:* Nation, Economy, Territory in Colonial South Asia, 1870 to 1907', *Comparative Studies in Society and History,* 40-4: 609-36.

———, 2004. *Producing India: From Colonial Economy to National Space,* Chicago: Chicago University Press.

Guillaud, D., 1996. 'Les formes du territoire. Trois modèles d'organisation territoriale: Aribinda (Burkina-Faso), Jambi (Indonésie) et Koumac (Nouvelle-Calédonie)', *Géographie et Cultures,* 20: 19-30.

Gupta, Akhil and James Ferguson, 1997. 'Culture, Power, Place: Ethnography at the End of an Era', in *Culture, Power, Place: Explorations in Critical Anthropology,* ed. A. Gupta and J. Ferguson, Duke University Press, pp. 1-29.

Hirsch, Eric and Michael O'Hanlon, eds., 1995. *The Anthropology of Landscape: Perspectives on Place and Space,* Oxford: Clarendon Press.

Höfer, A., 1971. 'Notes sur le culte du terroir chez les Tamang du Népal', in *Langues et techniques, nature et société. T.2: Approche ethnologique, approche naturaliste,* ed. J.M.C. Thomas and L. Bernod, Paris: Klincksieck, pp. 147-56.

Jaffrelot, Christophe, 1996. 'La question du territoire en Inde: de l'universalisme aux particularismes ?', *Cultures et Conflits,* 21-2: 75-102.

Jamous, Raymond, 2003 [1991]. *Kinship and Rituals Among the Meo of Northern India: Locating Sibling Relationship* (tr. by Nora Scott), Delhi: Oxford University Press.

Krauskopff, Gisèle, 1989. *Maîtres et possédés. Les rites et l'ordre social chez les Tharu (Népal),* Paris: CNRS.

Lambert, Helen, 1996. 'Caste, Gender and Locality in Rural Rajasthan', in *Caste Today,* ed. C.J. Fuller, Delhi: Oxford University Press, pp. 93-123.

Lecomte-Tilouine, Marie, 1993. *Les dieux du pouvoir. Les Magar et l'hindouisme au Népal central,* Paris: CNRS.

Lévy, J., 1991. 'A-t-on encore (vraiment) besoin du territoire?', *Espaces-Temps,* 51-2: 102-42.

Libersky-Bagnoud, Danouta, 2002. *Les dieux du territoire. Penser autrement la généalogie,* Paris, CNRS Editions/FMSH.

Lingat, Robert, 1967. Les sources du droit dans le système traditionnel de l'Inde, Paris: Mouton/EHESS.

Lovell, N., ed., 1998a. *Locality and Belonging,* London/New York: Routledge.

———, 1998b. 'Introduction', in *Locality and Belonging,* ed. N. Lovell, London/New York: Routledge, pp. 1-24.

Malamoud, Charles, 1990. 'Sans lieu ni date. Note sur l'absence de fondation dans l'Inde védique', in *Tracés de fondation,* ed. M. Détienne, Paris/Louvain: Peeters, pp. 183-91.

———1996 [1976]. 'Village and Forest in the Ideology of Brahmanic India', in *Cooking the World: Ritual and Thought in Ancient India* (tr. by David White), Delhi: Oxford University Press, pp. 74-91.

Marriott, McKim and Ronald Inden, 1974. 'Caste Systems', *Encyclopaedia Britannica,* 3: 982-91.

Marriott, McKim, ed., 1990. *India through Hindu Categories,* Delhi: Sage.

Mayer, Adrian C., 1960. *Caste and Kinship in Central India: A Village and its Region,* London: Routledge & Kegan Paul.

Miller, Eric J., 1954. 'Caste and Territory in Malabar', *American Anthropologist,* LVI, 3: 410-20.

Mines, Mattison, 1984. *The Warriors Merchants: Textiles, Trade, and Territory in South India,* Cambridge: Cambridge University Press.

Moffatt, Michael, 1990. 'Deconstructing McKim Marriott's Ethnosociology: an Outcaste's Critique', *Contributions to Indian Sociology,* n.s., 24, 2: 215-36.

Parkhill, T., 1993. 'What's Taking Place: Neighbourhood *Ramlilas* in Banaras', in *Living Banaras: Hindu Religion in Cultural Context,* eds. B.R. Hertel and C.A. Humes, Delhi: Manohar, pp. 103-26.

Racine, Jean-Luc, ed., 1994. *Les attaches de l'homme. Enracinement paysan et logiques migratoires en Inde du Sud,* Paris: FMSH.

Reiniche, Marie-Louise, 1979. *Les dieux et les hommes. Etude des cultes d'un village du Tirunelveli, Inde du Sud,* Paris/La Haye: Mouton/EHESS.

———, 1989. *Tiruvannamalai. Un lieu saint sivaïte du sud de l'Inde–4: la configuration sociologique du temple hindou,* Paris: EFEO.

———, 1990. 'Redécouvrir un dieu—fonder un "royaume" (sud de l'Inde)', in *Tracés de fondation,* ed. M. Détienne, Paris/Louvain: Peeters, pp. 193-207.

Rodman, Margaret C., 1992. 'Empowering Place: Multilocality and Multivocality', *American Anthropologist,* n.s., 94, 3: 640-56.

Sack, Robert D., 1983. 'Human Territoriality: A Theory', *Annals of the Association of American Geographers,* 73, 1: 55-74.

Sax, William, 1990. 'Village Daughter, Village Goddess: Residence, Gender, and Politics in a Himalayan Pilgrimage', *American Ethnologist,* 17, 3: 491-512.

———, 1991. *Mountain Goddess: Gender and Politics in a Himalayan Pilgrimage,* New York: Oxford University Press.

———, 2000. 'Residence and Ritual in the Garhwal Himalayas', in *Himalaya: Past and Present,* vol. IV, ed. M.P. Joshi, A.C. Fanger and C.W. Brown, Almora: Shree Almora Book Depot, pp. 79-114.

Shulman, David, 1980. *Tamil Temple Myths: Sacrifice and Divine Marriage in the South Indian Saiva Tradition,* Princeton: Princeton University Press.

Srinivas, M.N., ed., 1960. *India's Villages,* Bombay: Media Promoters (2nd rev edn.)

Stern, Henri, 1973. 'Le pouvoir dans l'Inde traditionnelle. Territoire, caste et parenté. Approche théorique et étude régionale (Rajasthan)', *L'Homme,* XIII, 1-2: 50-70.

Tarabout, Gilles, 1991. 'Au "royaume" des brahmanes, les guerriers sont rois: souveraineté, pouvoir et statut au Kérala', in *De la royauté à l'Etat. Anthropologie et histoire du politique dans le monde indien,* ed. J. Pouchepadass and H. Stern, Paris: EHESS, pp. 75-122.

———1999. 'Corps possédés et signatures territoriales au Kérala', in *La possession en Asie du Sud. Parole, corps, territoire,* ed. J. Assayag and G. Tarabout, Paris: EHESS, pp. 313-55.

Thapar, Romila, 1989. 'Epic and History: Tradition, Dissent and Politics in India', *Past and Present,* 125: 3-26.

Toffin, Gérard, 1984. *Société et religion chez les Néwar du Népal*, Paris: CNRS.

———, ed., 1987. 'Paysages et divinités en Himalaya', *Etudes Rurales*, 107-8.

———, 1993. *Le Palais et le Temple. La fonction royale dans la vallée du Népal*, Paris: CNRS.

Uchiyamada, Yasuchi, 1995. 'Sacred Grove (kāvu): Ancestral Land of "Landless Agricultural Labourers" in Kerala, India', London: LSE (unpublished PhD dissertation).

Vincent, J.-F., D. Dory and R. Verdier, eds., 1995. *La construction religieuse du territoire*, Paris: L'Harmattan.

Wink, André, 1986. *Land and Sovereignty in India: Agrarian Society and Politics under the Eighteenth-Century Maratha Svarajya*, Cambridge: Cambridge University Press.

Zimmermann, Francis, 1982. *La Jungle et le Fumet des viandes. Un thème écologique dans la médecine hindoue*, Paris: Gallimard.

PART I

EMERGENCE OF DIVINE TERRITORIES IN BRAHMANICAL TEXTS

1

Land and Location: Errant Gods, Erring Asuras and the Land of Men: Place and Space in Vedic Literature

MICHEL ANGOT

> Being nowhere is being everywhere
>
> MONTAIGNE (Essays 1.8)

In this paper I refer to two groups of texts that are quite different from each other in their structure, significance, and literary flavour. First there is Vedic poetry, hymns that offer eulogies in a series of frenzied formulae. Composed in an archaic language, the hymns venerate, pray to, and above all celebrate the Devas, the 'gods'. Then there are the Brāhmaṇa texts which are analyses of sacrificial rites composed in a dry, even an astringent, prose. They deal mainly with the rituals of men, but men's rituals are based on rituals that the gods originally learnt to perform, and their description is enriched with myths, which are for the most part etiological. Here, as in the hymns, we meet the gods, their enemies the Asuras, and other secondary beings. The great lyrical poetry of the hymns contrasts sharply with the dry prose of the Brāhmaṇas. As for men, we meet them mainly in the *Atharva Veda* where we hear about their aspirations, their passions, and their fears; they are clearly men of flesh and bone who seek worldly happiness as their priority. This appetite for worldly success is in contrast with the Vedic Upaniṣads, short treaties that deal to some extent with concepts beyond ritual. It must be apparent that these texts can only be considered together if one is not too strict about the spirit of each category. There is more than a simple question of literary style between the Devas of the hymns and those of the Brāhmaṇas. The two bodies of texts have different concerns and different goals. The poets are addressing the gods while the technicians are charged with managing a poetic language and making use of it in community rituals. Despite this, our endeavour is probably legitimate since Indian tradition and subsequently the tradition of Indian scholarship in general[1] consider that these texts share the same inspiration. They are all seen as belonging to Veda, 'Knowledge',[2] which is also known as *śruti* or 'what has been heard'. Both words mean revelation.

We do not intend to give a purely historical interpretation of this rich body of literature when dealing with the question of territory and terrain.[3] We shall try to establish how the texts themselves consider this question and how they tackle it. If we end this essay with a few conclusions, the intention is only to say how the authors of these texts consider these questions and leave it to others to relate all this to history. The texts can be quite readily divided into 'texts of the gods' and 'texts of men', and we follow this pattern in the way we deal with them. This is to some extent simplistic because the division is rather arbitrary. The hymns of the Saṃhitās are, undoubtedly, 'texts of the gods' and the Upaniṣads deal only with men; but texts that deal with real sacrifices constantly have as their basis mythical sacrifices performed by mythical men.

Let us start by looking at the context. The Devas, whose names indicate that they either live in heaven or are destined to live there, are battling with the Asuras, a kind of demonic being, who deny the Devas their pre-eminence and their access to heaven. This perpetual war is the background to the myths of the Brāhmaṇas. Although Devas and Asuras are both born of Prajāpati, and so are brothers, they are enemies. The outcome of the war is uncertain. Even if the Devas are almost always the winners in the battles, that are related to us, the war starts again endlessly because neither side wants to accept a *status quo*. It seems that one side cannot really defeat the other: battles and wars are not events or even a series of events, but the normal way of life for these beings. 'The Devas and the Asuras were battling for these worlds.'[4] The Devas win heaven with difficulty and want to live there on their own but the Asuras who used to live there and have been chased away do not accept their lower status or their repeated defeats. The Devas and the Asuras battle each other for supremacy and the Devas win because they are precise in their performance of rituals. This allows them to regularly defeat the Asuras who are usually in too much of a hurry or simply have less knowledge of rituals. By being precise in their performance, the gods pay their respect mechanically to the procedures and sounds of the rituals. This has nothing to do with morality, but is enough to ensure that victory goes to the Devas and not to their opponents, the Asuras. Precision means being expert in action and speech, and this has nothing to do with any knowledge of the essence of things. Although the Asuras are 'more vigorous and stronger' (*AitB* IV.6), they fail when they compete with the Devas in rituals because they represent what is false which is only what is inexact.[5] Men who appear in the myths of the Brāhmaṇas are of little importance. The human condition seems to be the least desirable and the texts refer rarely to men. When they do, it is to note that men are subservient to the Devas. They owe their knowledge, which is strictly a knowledge of ritual—the only kind that exists in these texts—to specific beings, the *ṛṣis*, or to the intervention to one of the deities of sacrifice such as Iḷā. In any case, men cannot compete with the Devas or Asuras. Men debase the noble truths of the Vedic texts when they copy the Devas and perform their earthly rites, but they can only perform them in their own way. When men adapt the rites to a human scale, they introduce slight changes here and there and this only serves to emphasize their human status.[6]

These stories are short, often incomplete, and are generally etiological. The battles of the Devas and Asuras are not narrated for their own sake; their purpose is to explain and justify the mythical origin and practice of one part of a rite. The stories reveal how the rituals originated at a time when the Devas and the Asuras were learning to perform rites by trial and error, and how they finally gained their status. The lengthy apprenticeship of the Devas (the word comes from *dyu*, heaven) allowed them to leave earth and gain heaven.

When the texts refer to territory, the Devas, 'gods', attack and fight against all settled places and assign them to the Asuras who are presented as devilish creatures. The following account[7] is taken from the *Śatapatha Brāhmaṇa*, perhaps the most important text that deals with the speculations of the ancient scholars on their liturgy.

The Devas and the Asuras[8], both born of Prajāpati, were rivals. The Devas were driving the (chariots') wheels and the Asuras stayed within the walls. While the Devas were driving the wheels, they saw this rite; yes, they saw this rite while they were driving the wheels. That is why these formulae are addressed to a chariot when (the ritual is performed) with sacrificial cakes and that is why the formulae are addressed to a chariot when an altar is built for sacrifice.[9]

As usual, this account explains in an *ad hoc* manner why a ritual is performed in a particular way now[10] and why certain formulae are addressed to inanimate objects such as chariots.[11] The hymns and their explanation in terms of myth and ritual tell us what must be done and what must not be done, but not what must be known (although Veda means 'knowledge'). Praising a chariot is part of a eulogy for movement itself and this is widespread in the Veda: the gods move around and are not restricted to any specific place. The Vedic hymns raise chariots to the rank of a divinity (cf. *ṚS* VI.47, 26-8) and they retain this status in the different Indices (the *Anukramaṇī* which were composed at the end of the Vedic period). We do not know where the gods journey to nor is the space in which they move specified—it is an unlimited, indefinite setting for their actions. However, the Devas give less an impression of movement through space than of creating space as they travel and, to some extent, their activity seems to create space itself. It is almost an abstract space. The texts do not have a specific word for the space in which the Devas operate that would be the spatial equivalent of time.[12] What is of primary importance is the movements of the gods and their comings and goings. The Vedic words that are translated as space are for the most part the names of stations, points in space or more frequently divisions of space where the gods come for a specific purpose. Space is simply an undefined territory in which the gods act. There is of course *rajas*, but this is a complex word with different uses. *Rajas* is a word which often has dark associations. It is a general spatial framework that cannot be divided into specific locations. In the hymn *ṚS* I.35.2, *rajas* dies (ā-*√ṚT*—literally 'rolls towards us'): 'Rolling towards us with dark space, bringing men and Gods to rest, the God Savitar on his golden chariot comes seeing all creatures.' As we can see, this is a cosmic space and it arrives with the god who gives it a focus. Is this space the god's sovereign realm? If this is the case, it remains vague and poorly defined. The same hymn notes that demons, sorcerers, and other beings inhabit this same space. The god 'pushes them right away' but these beings are clearly present in the same non-territorial space. *Rajas* cannot be compared to *kāla* which is first a moment, or a point in time, and then a succession of moments or, in other words, time itself. A succession of moments creates time but it would appear that *rajas* cannot be divided and cannot create the units of space that could form a location. The notions of space and time are dealt with quite differently in the Veda.

On the one hand we have vast horizons, an unrestricted and open spatial freedom that leads to a positive outcome: the discovery of part of a ritual. If the gods have received the revelation, it is because they were moving about and were not stationary. On the other hand, everything that is stationary and solid represents failure, a lack of movement, an enclosed space that can at some point be given a name. The structure of divine space is not defined and so it is infinite and this contrasts with the finite structure of the places where the Asuras are found. Of course, the Devas win the battle, as they move through space with energy while their opponents remain enclosed in their forts. On the one hand, there is space without a name; on the other, places without space. The Devas wander about and are free whereas the Asuras seek out places where they can settle down and enclose themselves. They even come to represent these places.

The 'walls' in which the Asuras enclose themselves are often the fortresses to which they are attached. 'In that time, the Devas and the Asuras, both born of Prajāpati, were enemies. So the Asuras in the (three) worlds built themselves (three) citadels: of air for this world, of silver for the ethereal world and of gold for heaven.'[13] The Devas besiege these citadels and win the battle. The purpose of the myth is to legitimize the name of the *upasad*, a word that means the rites that take place at the end of the consecration (*dīkṣā*) in the *soma* rite. Strictly speaking, *upasad* means 'assize' or 'siege'. There is a pun here that gives a slant to the meaning of the word and justifies its name: the Devas by their 'siege' have conquered the fortresses (*púr*) of the Asuras. But nothing in the *Taittirīya Saṃhitā* version indicates that the Asuras and the Devas are at war.[14] It is just that the Devas cannot bear enclosed spaces—their immediate reaction is to conquer them, not in order to occupy but to destroy them, to remake space without locations. The story goes on to say, 'The gods broke down the fortresses of the Asuras and conquered these worlds and the sacrificer (that is to say, the man for whom the rite is performed) did the same here.' We are led to believe that the Asuras transformed each *loka* or world into a *púr* or fortress and that for the gods the battle consisted in changing back a fortress into open space. But however you read it, the outcome is the same: space is restored to its original status, the gods are its masters, and they can roam about at will. Like the Asuras, the Dasyus, the Dānavas, the Dāsas and other enemies of the Devas, are all associated with *púr*[15] and *Indra puro'bhinad ārhan dasyuhātye*, 'destroyed the fortresses in mortal combat with the Dasyus as he had to'. This verse is interesting because it shows in passing that Indra's usual work is to attack fortified places. These are destroyed and broken up but they are never occupied. *Pubhíd*, destroyer of fortresses, is even an attribute of Indra: 'Indra, destroyer of fortresses, destroyed the fort of the Dasyu with songs.' (*ṚS* III.34.1).

The high value that is accorded to space to the detriment of enclosed places can be found in the Vedic hymns that deal with the origin of the universe, although this theme is often dealt with in just a few stanzas. The story of Indra killing the dragon Vṛtra is found in many hymns of the *Ṛk Saṃhitā*, contrasts a luminous space, where movement is unrestricted, with an unmoving darkness: *idám súar idám id āsa vāmám ayám prakāśá urú antárikṣam / hánāva vṛtrám*: 'Here is the light, here is what was always the treasure, the luminous sign, the vast (space) between (heaven and earth); let us two kill Vṛtra.' This vast and luminous space is called *urúm lokám*[16] or often *uloká*, vast space, and the etymology of this word links space and light (*loka* is linked to lux in Latin, meaning light). The space of the gods is vast and luminous. The Devas dread what is narrow, as do men who repeatedly address the gods with prayers for protection from *áṃhas*:[17] 'O you of the two worlds, give us space. Masters of place, strengthen us with your speech! I praise heaven and earth; I who need help invoke them. May they save us from what is narrow.'[18] This fear of confinement does not come from the aerial nature of the divine. It is even found in the pressing of *soma*, the divine juice, and a liturgical god who is not associated with space: 'As we clarify you, pour for us the vital force, the vast pasture, the powerful refuge that stretches far; may constraint never reign over us' (*ṚS* IX.85.8). A location is always narrow and constraining; it generates worry. Unlike the Devas, in the Brāhmaṇas, the Asuras, who are enemies of the Devas,[19] are found in dark and enclosed places: 'The body of the (dragon) stayed there in the middle of currents that do not stop and do not rest: the waters flowed over Vṛtra's hiding place and he, the enemy of Indra, stays forever lifeless in deep darkness.'[20] The themes of darkness and immobility are constantly invoked, along with rest and sleep, to describe Vṛtra.[21] Indra murders Vṛtra because Vṛtra does not move and remains in a confined place; Vṛtra holds back the waters that carry life. Just as the Asuras are enclosed within their walls, so Vṛtra is confined in his dark cave. He is *gúhā hitáṃ gúhyaṃ gūḷhám*, 'he has put himself in his little hiding place; he is hiding, hidden'. Sometimes he hides inside a secret. Water or mountains can also be resting places for him as water is said to 'cross the secret (place) of Vṛtra'.[22] The enclosed places where he stays even come to mean the demon himself. *Vala* is a closed place or a cave where Vṛtra can be found and it is also one of Vṛtra's names. *Phaligá* is used less often but it always has a meaning as an object (a stable) and a personal meaning (*phaligá* = Vṛtra). The opposition between space/light and place/darkness even governs the value system in the *Ṛk Saṃhitā* that might be called morality.[23] 'Vṛtra is clothed in fog.' (*ṚS* II.30.3) and Indra 'dispersed the dark fog'.

We find the same contrast in the myth of the Paṇi which is less important than the myth of Vṛtra, although it follows the same structure. The Paṇi keep cows emprisoned in a *vrajá*, a stable or enclosed place, and Indra frees them. These words (*valá*, *phaligá*, *vrajá*) have an everyday use and only take on negative connotations because demons take up their residence there. What these words have in common is that they mean an enclosed place, sometimes dark, without light, and dedicated to whatever is stationary and held in check. The gods do not inhabit specific places and have no clear links with any single location.[24] There can be no question of a pilgrimage in the Vedas. To go on a pilgrimage you must have somewhere to go! Pilgrimages which are so important today only developed at a later date.[25] In any case such places are rare. You can read many Vedic hymns without coming across any locations and you must search through all of Vedic literature to unearth just a few. A territory implies boundaries, the segmentation of space, and this does not suit the Devas at all. On the contrary, they battle with all those who would divide up the world into territories.

The few rare hymns that are dedicated to the earth (*ṚS* V.84, *AS* XII.1, especially[26]), are not eulogies for land and soil, where peasants, protected by walls and warriors, await an uncertain harvest. There is no local, regional or national patriotism nor even a name:[27] 'The earth that carries in different ways many sorts of men speaking different languages with different customs, each according to his home—your numerous paths are used for men's journeys, your roads are used for travelling by car and chariot for both kinds of men, the good and the bad; may we conquer a path where there is neither enemy nor thief.'[28] The earth is seen as a vast, dynamic space that is open for men to travel on. It is fertile but dangerous.[29] The poets again appeal to the technology of the chariot in order to praise it: 'Your centre and your hub, O Earth, and all the strengths that come from your body' (*AS* XII.1.12). Space is immense and abundant, an earth without limits, a suitable setting for the actions of humans and gods. It is a land for travelling over and there is a prayer that its districts 'might be hospitable to me as I make my way' (*AS* XII.1.31). This is true for individuals and for communities: 'May we always walk the length of it' (XII.1.31). The hymn *AS* XII.1 might have been composed on Indian soil, but it depicts a land universal in its grandeur and diversity: snowy mountains, deserts, wandering rivers, forest and plains. It is 'the vast home' (XII.1.18) inhabited by 'peoples with different languages in many places' (45). The hymn is a celebration of a vast space that transcends, abolishes and refutes all specific locations.

All the vocabulary of Vedic Sanskrit reflects the high value accorded to movement and travel by the gods, represented as very positive beings. This means that locations are not given much value, partly because they are just unnamed stopovers, but mainly because they are ignored. Vedic vocabulary always refers to paths and not to the places where the paths might lead. There are plenty of paths in the Veda but they have no destination. The gods are beings who know the paths, they don't know where they arrive at. They can guide men, but only to take them on to a path, not to bring them to a destination. Consider this passage in a hymn that is quite banal and, for this reason, representative: 'Far from the paths, was Pūṣan born, / far off the way of Heaven, / far off the way of the Earth, / towards the two homes that are dear to him, / he comes, then he goes, knowing the paths. / Pūṣan knows and follows all the celestial regions that are here / so may he guide us very safely; / ensuring our well-being, keeping our men safe from all harm, / may he who knows walk before us with vigilance.'[30] True, Pūṣan is a god of prosperity and a guardian of roads and paths, but this is also true of other divinities. As the *Ṛgveda* consists mainly of formulaic eulogies, the same expressions are repeated again and again to glorify divine nature and the space where it can be found. This is true for the deities who inhabit the skies such as Sūrya 'Sun', Vāyu 'Wind', Uṣas 'Dawn', Rātri 'Night', but it is also true for the great gods of Vedic liturgy such as Agni 'Fire' and Soma 'Ambrosia', for warrior gods such as Indra, the Maruts, and Rudra, and for the sovereign gods Mitra and Varuṇa. What could be less relevant to the question of space than the preparation of Soma juice pressed from the stems of the plant of the same name? It is a simple operation that resembles an act of everyday cooking. Nonetheless the Vedic poets use a spatial metaphor to describe it: 'Make it flow through the pressing, spread the Soma wide, as a horse crossing the waters, crossing space, making a noise in the woods, swimming in the water' (*ṚS* IX. 108.7). The world to which the gods aspire is referred to in terms of a journey: 'The celestial world is a thousand (days') ride from (down) here.'[31] This is all the more odd as it is a question of gaining access in a very concrete manner to somewhere that is never described, although it is the goal of all the activities of the Devas. In the same way, when setting out a unit of measure, according to the *ṚS* I.92.3, a *yojana* is the distance that a team of horses yoked to a chariot can travel without having to be changed; it is not a fixed measure of distance. Elsewhere a *yojana* is a race of the Devas to determine the order in which they can drink the soma (*AiB* II.25). The same text tells of another race organized by the gods, in which each has his own mount, with various consequences.[32] Movement and speed in a race are a sufficient means for reaching decisions. It is not by remaining tranquil or by gathering their forces within themselves[33] that the Devas assert themselves and take decisions, but by clamouring noisily in competition and movement. Vedic order is dynamic. It is *ṛta*, the 'organized (good)', a word and an idea that is always contrasted with classical *dharma* whose root is linked with static values. Dharma is a cousin of the Latin *firmus*, firm, while *ṛta* can be linked to *art* in our languages.

The Devas have to move because they want to master sacrifice, but sacrifice does not agree to this, and flees. When a sacrifice is performed, it is described in terms of an animal that has escaped from the Devas. It can be a bird, a horse, a black antelope, or another fleet-footed animal: 'If we are walking silently, it is because sacrifice is like a quarry.' In order to calm sacrifice, 'so that it does not run away through fear (we go forward in this way)', says the *Pañcaviṃśa Brāhmaṇa* (VI.7.10). The quest for *yajña* involves prayers and eulogies, and these are all used to entreat the *yajña* to come back to those who seek it. In another piece in the same vein, the *Śatapatha Brāhmaṇa* tells how the Devas travel in search of sacrifice, followed by *ṛṣi* and men who, since they follow the Devas, have to imitate them. Once they have come to the *vāstu*, the place of sacrifice where the Devas first succeeded in performing a sacrifice, the *ṛṣi* and the men who want to know about sacrifice roam around (*pari-CAR*) the spot and the surrounding area looking for clues. This *vāstu* is just a place that has been abandoned. But through an odd evolution of language at a much later date, *vāstu* came to mean the location where the houses of gods and men are built. And *vāstuvidyā*, the knowledge of sites, is one of the words that mean architecture. Here *vāstu* is not the place on which a building is set,[34] but a place from which the Devas have departed, a departure that they consider final. The gods have left behind them the remains of a sacrifice that entitled them to gain access to heaven. *Vāstu*, thus, is just a place you leave behind.

All this is in striking contrast with late Vedic notions and *a fortiori* those of that Brahmanism which embraced renunciation, that is to say, yoga in all its forms. With yoga, being stationary is always seen in a positive light and given primary importance, while activity is negative and of secondary importance. The opposition between the two styles of thought can perhaps best be seen in the name that the *Yoga-Bhāṣya* (fifth-seventh centuries AD?) gives to activity. The text starts by saying that the nature of non-doing is the nature of *puruṣa*, 'the spiritual monad' (*YS* 1.3). This non-doing occurs when the mind is so completely at rest that it is absolutely devoid of any cognitive function. '(The master says that) in this state, the power of consciousness is fully established in its own nature, as in the isolation (of *puruṣa* from the mind).' But what happens if the mind is active? The text goes on: 'But when the mind is active, while it remains established in its own nature, it (i.e. *puruṣa*, the *citiśakti*) does not appear thus.'[35] According to Pāṇini, the origin of *vyutthāna*, translated here as activity, is interesting because it explains why the author of the *sūtra* chose this word. *Vy-ut-STHĀ-ana* is the negative of *utthāna*. This is derived from the root *STHĀ*—which means *gatinivṛtti*, absence of movement; accordingly *utthāna* means the action of being immobile while standing (the grammarians discuss about the nature of such an 'action'). *Vy-utthāna* is thus the cessation of being immobile. In other words, non-doing is in the primary state, and activity follows as an end to this base state. When the negative meaning of *vi* is added to its usual pejorative connotation (*vi* indicates a distortion cf. *prakṛti/vikṛti*, *samādhi/vyādhi*, etc.), *vyutthāna* is a bad end to an original state of non-moving. We can see how activity was regarded by Patañjali who had at his disposal other roots with positive connotations to indicate action (*CAR-*, *VṚT- KṚ-*, etc.). But these are the roots that are used to characterize the Vedic gods: they go, they roam about and they act.

In the Veda there is a rich vocabulary expressing the constant activity of the gods as they ceaselessly haunt the earth. But if they are endlessly active in their comings and goings, they only pass through space without ever turning any part of it into a location. When they visit men, they stay with a human community, not in a specific place: 'O Indra, may you be with the Yadu, with the Turvaśa.'[36] In fact, there are almost no names of places in the Veda and this rarity of place names is in contrast with much of the later literature.[37] The places where the gods, *ṛṣis* and men come and go, where they perform their deeds, have no clear names: 'He killed the dragon that was holding on to the mountain' (*ṚS* 1.32.2a). We have the impression that it is because Vṛtra was becoming associated too closely with one place, and even had a tendency to become a place, that Indra acts against him. In all of the extensive Vedic literature you never come across a sentence like: 'He went to X' where X would be the name of the place they are going to. Moreover, once the gods have arrived somewhere, the fact that one or another of them has been there does not *a posteriori* give the place an identity. A location does not have a name before the gods arrive it remains without a name after they leave. A high value is placed on proper nouns, and people's names abound (the *Bṛhad-Āraṇyaka Upaniṣad* ends with a long litany of those who composed it). Names are also created with divine epithets. This abundance of personal names is in marked contrast with an almost total absence of place names in the Veda. In sum, gods and men visit places that have no name and their visits are no excuse for naming them.

There are countless stories about battles between the Asuras and the Devas that could give rise to place names. These places often relate to a specific event, often a unique event, and they are important since they are worthy of being quoted in the stories about the gods. Despite this, the place where the Devas defeated the Asuras, where they saw part of a ritual, the place where they took off for heaven, or where Indra killed Vṛtra are all left without names.[38] The activities of the gods do not take place at such and such a location. Nevertheless there are a few examples of place names but they are not always clear. It is possible that Vinaśana, Disappearance, referred to in the *Pañcaviṃśa Brāhmaṇa* (XXV.10.16), and especially in the *Śrauta-Sūtra*,[39] is a place name but it could also be a geographic term since many rivers in central Asia do not reach the sea. So could not every river that disappears into the sands be known as Sarasvatī, following what the Brāhmaṇa say? It is possible that Sarvacaru (*AiB* VI.1.1 and *KauBB* XXIX.1) is also a place name, but it could also be an epithet or the name of a person. Some place names, however, are certain. While recounting a story, the *Aitareya Brāhmaṇa* (VII.1.1-3) explains that 'We still call this place Parisāraka, because the (river) Sarasvatī surrounded (*pari-SṚ-*) the *ṛṣi* on all sides.' It is so unusual to refer to a place name, that sometimes a myth is needed to justify it.[40] Alternatively the etymology of a place name can give rise to the kind of pun that the creators of these texts enjoy so much. In any case, we can see that these names refer more to localities than to permanent human settlements.

It is thus a mistake to identify in India or elsewhere such and such a place that is mentioned in the Veda. The desire to locate the hymns and words of the Veda in India leads to many errors. For instance, because the *Tāṇḍya Brāhmaṇa* says that the way to heaven passes by the Sarasvatī, and that the journey takes forty-four days on horseback, S. Shrava[41] states that the authors of this Brāhmaṇa 'lived in the north of Narmadā where the Himālayas are forty-four days' ride away on horseback'. The work shares in the belief and in the long-standing desire to situate the Veda in India, which is the only country that the gods visit. Simultaneously, it reflects the religious views of its author for whom 'the hymns do not refer to history or historical events. They, being eternal, had to have been revealed prior to any historical event' (p. XIV).

If among the names of the rivers we consider only the Sarasvatī, which has an important role in the Veda, we can see there is more than one Sarasvatī. The *Atharvaveda* talks about three Sarasvatīs (*tisráḥ sárasvatīr aduḥ sácittā viṣadūṣanam* 'the three Sarasvatīs provided an antidote with the same thought', *AS* VI.100.1cd) and a reference to three Sarasvatīs or a triple Sarasvatī can also be found in the *ṚS*.[42] In the same collection, the hymn VI.61 speaks of the river Sarasvatī and the goddess Sarasvatī. This example shows a tendency in the Veda to use the same word to refer to different things. A name cannot be limited to either a river in this world or a unique location. A sentence might start off by referring to this world and end on the celestial plane and you cannot be sure where the metaphor starts. We find rivers in this world sharing their name with celestial rivers, and celestial rivers turn out to be the source for the rivers that flow in this world. Sarasvatī 'endowed with many lakes' is the name of one or more rivers. It is also the name of a 'goddess who governs the fertility of women' and no doubt it is one of the names in the *Ṛk Saṃhitā* of the Milky Way which is the supreme celestial river. Sarasvatī is sometimes called Sindhu and this celestial Sindhu turns out to be the mother of the earthly Sarasvatī.[43] It is not always easy to make a clear distinction between the two and this technique is so widespread that it must be part of a desire to turn earthly locations into replicas of celestial space. In the same spirit, Brāhmanism and Hinduism claim that all rivers could be the Gaṅgā and that the Gaṅgā in this world is linked to a celestial Gaṅgā.[44]

One sometimes has the impression that a location has only a generic name. Where is the Kurukṣetra that the *Aitareya Brāhmaṇa* (VII.3.3) speaks about: 'Still today, at Kurukṣetra, they are called *nyubja*'? Kurukṣetra, the field of the Kuru, is first the name of the gods' sacrificial ground, the *devayajana*.[45] But is it also the place where Purūravas loved the nymph Urvaśī, where the armies of the *Mahābhārata* clashed, a place of which the *Gītā* (I.1) says is a *dharmakṣetra*? Is it not rather the case that the same name is used for different places and is therefore a generic name for several locations?

Moreover, if there are many questions in the Brāhmaṇa about when it is right and good, that is, effective, to perform certain acts,[46] there is absolutely no mention of where an act should take place. A location is defined by giving it dimensions that are not inherent to it. You choose a place and by doing so you give it an existence but it has no existence without this. A *vedi* is a site on which an oblation is made. It is measured with a measuring rod that is roughly the height of the sacrificer: 'You take the measure by using a man with his arms raised because the man is the sacrifice and here all things are measured with reference to a man.'[47] In fact, a sacrificial site is given a size, rather than being measured normally, because before the sacrifice the site did not exist and had no name, and at the end of the ritual it ceases to exist. When a site is being drawn up, the purpose is to mark out its orientation (*diś*), and this principle is valid for all locations. Turning a location into a site for ritual purposes means ignoring and even removing anything that makes the site unique. The ritual creates its own space but this does not make the space unique. Despite a few exceptions, place-names in the Veda are rare. The reason for this is that in the Veda a name indicates that something has an individual existence. The killing of Vṛtra by Indra means that the place where the demon lived ceases to exist and returns to the dynamic and unnamed space from which it emerged.

The Vedic Upaniṣads give primacy to men, and the gods are largely absent. But even here the relationship between an individual and where he lives is not developed. When an Upaniṣad refers to someone, it generally does so without describing where the person is, and without ever naming a place even if it is the person's home. When in the *Praśna-Upaniṣad* six seekers of *brahman* come to the sage Pippalāda, their names are listed. They greet the sage in an appropriate manner and he invites them to stay 'there' for a year. All we know about the location where they all live is that it is 'there'. The clear distinction between the manner in which people's names and place-names are treated is also found in the work of the grammarian Pāṇini (*c.* fourth century BC). A whole section of his work (*Aṣṭādhyāyī* IV.1.92-172) is devoted to names derived from forefathers, but there is nothing at all about suffixes that deal with place-names. There are no guiding principles for the formation of place-names. In the oldest of the Vedic Upaniṣads, the *Bṛhad-Āraṇyaka*, a man is given roots by linking him to a line of masters: a man is the son of someone else but his identity is not linked to a location. When India was given a name in Hindi, the name of a person and a whole people (Bharata and Bhārata) was turned into the name of a place: Bhārat(a)varṣ(a).[48]

The way the 'locative case'[49] is used and conceived in the grammar of Vedic poetry and prose is relevant here. If we put aside the very many instances where a 'locative' is used with a temporal dimension,[50] we can see that this case denotes less a place than the process of settling in a place. But it is not really a question of putting down roots or creating a permanent home; more a question of being in a place on a more or less temporary basis. Something has merely come on to a place or on to a person. Indra and Agni are 'among the Yadus and the Turvaśa', but they do not stay because they do not have a home there. Indeed they have no permanent nor impermanent home; they are just where they happen to be. Another example is the Vedic dream; it is an entity that visits both men and animals such as the 'bad dream' (*duṣvápnya* *ṚS* VIII.47.14) that is 'on the cows and the one that is on us'. In the same way, an error of some kind (X.132.5), does not have a permanent residence in the cows or in us. One tries to get free of bad dreams and errors by moving them on, mainly by displacing them onto a third party; and if one can do it, it is precisely because they have no permanent basis. When Indra has committed an error, Trita Āptya acts as a kind of emissary god.[51] Even if it is 'onto Śakapūta that the sin (falls)' Śakapūta is always aware of the process, for 'he who knows thus' knows how to move an error on and make it fall on his inferiors. This is true of mistakes and more generally of anything that is negative.[52] Since no entity such as error can have its own location, it can be moved on somewhere else. Even if what befalls someone is positive and that person is *śármaṇi*, 'under protection' or 'in good grace',[53] both this expression and its context indicate that the protection is temporary. In general the relationship between what affects someone and the person who is affected is contingent, transient, not essential. No such relationship defines something for all time or even for a limited period so that whether something is affected in a positive or a negative way, the affectation is not inherent. It is in this meaning that the locative case indicates a place where something happens or a place that is referred to. Many of the hymns of the *Atharva Veda* are formal invitations to entities that men wish for, such as good fortune or prosperity, and more often still, the hymns entreat beings that are not wanted, illnesses especially, to go and visit the neighbours. 'I consign Fever to the very depths, but not before I have paid homage to him. May the lady champion that is diarrhoea return to the home of the Mahāvṛṣa', says the *AV* V.22.4. Evil is *durita*, literally unwelcome, and the aim of the hymns is to make it go elsewhere. This hymn was composed in a style that was much used in the *Atharva Veda* but one imagines that it was not sung by the Mahāvṛṣas who must have had a similar hymn aimed at their neighbours. Often an illness or an unpleasantness is not given a specific people to visit but is asked only to go away. The same hymn from the *Atharva Veda* says in its first stanza: 'May Agni chase Fever away from here (. . .) May hostile things go far away!'.[54] The hymn mentions the kinship between *takmán*, Fever, and other people and invites Fever to go to those who will welcome it more readily: 'These are the grounds that we show to Fever; these lands here do not belong to him.' The locative is used here in just the way that we referred to above: *anyakṣetré ná ramase* 'You are not happy on land that is not yours', i.e. on our lands. The hymn ends (*AV* V.22.14) with a typical stanza: 'To the people of Gandhāra and Mūjarat, to those of Aṅga and Magadha, we are sending (*pari-DĀ-*) Fever to you as an emissary, as a treasure.' Thus bad things are invited to stay by some and sent on their way by others, running here and there without ever being satisfied anywhere.

If locations have no name and the locative case does not refer to the essence of a place, words that denote geographic places are fairly numerous, e.g. *párvata* for mountain, *sáras* for current, river or lake, and *samudrá* for ocean. The hymn *AS* XII.1 I have quoted above uses such words extensively. Nonetheless it would be very difficult to find a description that allowed a reader to distinguish between two places referred to by the same word. Every large country could easily be described in such a vocabulary. Just as in the poetic conventions of a later period, there are evocations of places in geography, or they are merely mentioned, to such an extent that you need to know that the text is referring to a mountain, for example, to make any sense of the text. An ocean might be a celestial ocean (*samudrâya tvā vâtāya YS* XXXVIII.7a) and we know that rivers flow down a mountain (*parvata*; *giri*), but that is about all. In the *Kauṣītaki-Upaniṣad* (II.13) there is a reference to 'the two mountains, that of the south and that of the north'. If we reach the conclusion[55] that 'this passage seems to have been written in the Madhyadeśa' and that the mountain in the north is the Himālaya and the mountain in the south is the Vindhya range, this is only because we know the geography of India and we can find it described in the text. The word *parvata* can be used for a range of mountains or for a single mountain. In many places there is a mountain to the north and one to the south. Simple words used only with their standard attributes can mean very vaguely a plain, a river, a mountain, or the sky. *Parvata* does not refer so much to a specific mountain, for example, as to any mountain without defining its characteristics. The many battles that fill the lives of the Devas are never given names. The hymns celebrate battle and war in general terms (*yúdh*, *saṃgrāmá*, *samohá*[56]) but there are no records of any battle that needs a place or date to help remember it. It is not only place-names that are affected by this desire to avoid being localised. The Veda generally avoid giving specific information and favour whatever is generic and just as there are no specific locations, there are no precise events. The techniques of war are reduced to a bare minimum. The hymn in the *Ṛk Saṃhitā* VI.75 is dedicated to the bow and its different parts and it describes the bow 'that comes right up to your ear as if it was going to speak to you, and kiss its sweet lover'. It speaks of 'the arrows (that) fly together like boys with their hair undone'. This passage might be poetry, but the prose of the Brāhmaṇas and the *Śrauta-Sūtras* is no more realistic, even though the dry and astringent style is unique in all of Indian literature. These two texts use the fewest possible words to recount their myths and they always favour generic terms.

Let us take as an example a place that is truly unique—the centre of the world. It is referred to in the *gavām ayana*, the walk of the cows. This is a ritual where the officers of the sacrifice, following the example of the gods, move upwards. When their journey is over, they come to the Prakṣa tree that is the source of the Sarasvatī[57] and also 'the centre of the world' (*tat pṛthivyai madhyam*).[58] Is this the *axis mundi*, the centre of the Vedic world? Certainly it is, but only in an ideological sense, as the tree is 'where speech ends. Where speech ends, there the shinning world ends'.[59] In the final analysis we cannot be sure where this place is, although it is unique and the origin of all space. The centre of the world is in fact the centre of a world; it is the centre of the poet who is reciting the poem.

The Veda use the same approach with words that denote place. A *sthāna* is always just a location sharing its characteristics with other. *Deśa* is another word for a piece of land, but it is not defined by its boundaries. It is derived from a root that means to show. A *deśa* is primarily what one shows to others; it is somewhere where one is not. The *Aitareya Brāhmaṇa* gives a very good definition: 'The Devas and the Asuras were battling in these worlds (*loka*). They fought in the direction (*diś*) of the east and the Asuras won. Then they fought in the direction of the south and the Asuras were again victorious; as they were when they fought in the west and the north. Then they fought in the place (*deśa*) located between the east and the north and this time the Devas were victorious'.[60] A *deśa* is defined by its direction and has no intrinsic identity. It is 'between', but without being between two places. This use of the word is an excellent example of the Vedic approach. A location is 'here' between different directions. The activity of the gods outside of the *deśa* gives it a temporary identity. The context gives a meaning to the word but this meaning need not be permanent. A *deśa* is purely 'there' but it could be elsewhere. It is the nominal form of an adverb of place. And this is true of all locations. Whereas *diś* are directions and could be directions to somewhere, the Devas do not act in specific locations, but in the direction of somewhere. 'It is in the Orient that the Devas bought the king Soma'.[61] The space where the gods meet their opponents does not remain untouched by the encounter. The gods do not protect a well-defined space, as one might expect. They want to organize space,[62] not to turn it into a territory but into a place of sacrifice that suits their needs. Moreover, the gods are always on the move; they break down barriers and push at all boundaries, but they must nonetheless stop to carry out the supreme act of *yajña*. Indra is the hero who transforms chaos into an orderly space where the gods, *ṛṣis* and men can sacrifice. Another word-meaning part of a space is *kṣetra*. It is an interesting word because it denotes the territory of a guardian deity (*kṣetrādhidevatā*) and more widely god's territory. In the Vedas, the link between *devatā* and *kṣetra* is never developed. You generally do not see the gods having a special relationship with a space that is theirs, or a place that they have made their own. A *kṣetra*[63] is simply somewhere the gods pass through and especially where men perform their actions. It is a field, whether cultivated or not. In the *Atharva Veda*, the minor divinity *kṣetrasya pati*, master of the field, is the lord of each field and *vāstos pati*, master of the home, is the lord of homes.[64] The god is not specific to anyone place nor has he made himself lord of a place. The divine being remains vague and undifferentiated and his presence anywhere does not confer an identity on that location.

Because *kṣetrasya pati* is anonymous, so too are all locations. The word *kṣetra* is so lacking in positive connotations in the *Atharva Veda* (*AS* II.8) that *kṣetra* and the adjective *kṣetriya* refer to a chronic illness that can be fatal. It is the illness associated with a place as if a place were something that can make you ill.

Everyone must have their place, but oddly enough this is not always true: 'The Asuras had a place; the Devas did not have a place; these worlds were the Asuras' place; whenever they met, the Devas were beaten because they had no place.' This shows that space is really just an idea and the fact that some beings have no place of their own in all these worlds does not stop them having a place elsewhere. It is just that it is a space without spatial dimensions. The Brāhmaṇas are full of stories and instances when either the Devas or the Asuras have no place in these worlds because their enemies have occupied them entirely. Nonetheless they survive: 'the Asuras, chased away from these worlds, retreated into the seasons'.[65] Each time the Devas or the Asuras are victorious, they force their enemies into a 'space' that can be a territory (the earth) but this space can also be related to time (the seasons or months, etc.) or be purely abstract (a direction, a metre in poetry or Vedic speech), or material (the elements of a sacrifice, etc.). The text does not always say where the defeated are: 'The Asuras were in these worlds. The Devas chased them out from (. . .) this world, from (. . .) the middle world and from (. . .) heaven' (*PB* VIII.9.2). The fact that the Devas occupy all these worlds does not prevent the Asuras being somewhere: space is not limited to the three worlds and it is perfectly normal that, having been chased out of everywhere, a few lines further on in the same paragraph we find the Asuras again and the battle can start once more (*PB* VIII.9.15).

The Devas and the Asuras do not manage to occupy all of this diverse space, either permanently or by right, nor do they manage to make it their own to the extent that they could be its masters. But this is not through lack of trying. Because the relations between Devas and the Asuras are characterized by perpetual rivalry (expressed by the root *SPARDH-*) and conflict, this inherent animosity stops either side from embedding itself anywhere on a permanent basis. They fight over space and, even when it is enlarged to encompass non-spatial dimensions, space is just the background for their conflicts. No part of space makes up a territory and when the Devas and the Asuras attempt to divide up space in a friendly manner, the gods usually trick the Asuras and win a complete, albeit temporary, victory: 'and they excluded their rivals from the division'.[66]

Space can grow and extend from within itself and the Devas wish repeatedly that space should grow bigger: 'How can these worlds be made to grow, how can we have more space? They said three syllables: *vītaye*, 'for expansion', and these worlds went away and the gods had more space'.[67] So we see space disappearing into the distance as if it was external to the Devas whereas the Devas, who have more space, must be within space. In any case, this is characteristic of the Devas who never have enough space.

This all results from the fact that space is unstable and fluid. The *āyatana*, place or home, is temporary and unstable and never becomes a well-defined area where there can be undivided sovereignty. The word *pratiṣṭhā*, base, is even more explicit: this stability is what all beings seek but they look in vain; the dynamism that is inherent in the whole Vedic universe makes space in general and the elements of which it is composed inherently unstable. Even 'this unsteady earth' that the gods have temporarily conquered hesitated 'as does a lotus leaf, blown here and there by the wind: it went to the Asuras; it went to the Devas'. The gods, whose virtual power needs a space where it can be used, tried to hold on to it: 'They consolidated it in order to make a stable base.' The paradox is that in the Brāhmaṇas, the Devas and the Asuras, to speak only of the main protagonists, are powers who do not have a space by right in which they can use their powers. Even Varuṇa, who is the supreme sovereign god, has a problem in acquiring space in which to use his powers: 'And the earth for its part was afraid of Varuṇa when he was big and thought: "Now that he is an important person, now that he is consecrated king, I am afraid that it might cut me in two!".' The 'kingdom' is not alone in being fearful: 'And Varuṇa for his part was frightened of the earth and thought: "I am afraid that he might get rid of me!".'[68] The fact that Varuṇa is king does not automatically make him a king of anything, still less a king of any specific location. And we do not know the space of which he is sovereign: the earth is not a passive place to be fought over by rivals who are keen on power.

Before the earth was transformed into a vast sacrificial ground, it was only *nirṛti*, disorder.[69] The nature of *nirṛti* is complex; it can be found in every hole, crack, crevice and hollow on the surface of the earth: 'If you offer an oblation in a fire that has been lit in a hole or in an opening to a crevice, these parts of the earth are *nirṛti*'[70] and 'every bit of the earth that is *nirṛti* by nature can be propitiated by means of this offering'. We need only bear in mind that there exist points in space dedicated to disorder. Although *nirṛti* is not linked exclusively to death, there is nonetheless a clear link between *nirṛti*, death, and fixed locations.

The space where the gods come to stay for a while, where they establish a *vedi*, a sacrificial ground, is full even before it becomes a place of sacrifice. The beings that occupy it did not wait for the gods or men to settle there. This space is full in the sense that nowhere it can be assumed to be empty. A space is lived in, if not by men, at least by all sorts of beings. To come to a place means adding oneself to those who are already there. The violence that is inherent in sacrifice starts when a sacrificial site is established. A kind of sword, *sphya*, is used to trace the boundary between the two worlds. It is not enough to transform an undifferentiated space into what is outside the site and what is inside by setting out boundaries;[71] it is also necessary to empty the space of all who live there. But these beings are its legitimate owners and there is no alternative but to chase them away and ensure that they do not return to reclaim what is theirs and so disturb the performance of the sacrifice. The owners are death personified (Yama) and all the *pitṛ*, that is to say, dead ancestors. They occupy the places that have been set up: 'It's Yama who is the master of places where one settles because Yama, yes!, reigns over settling on earth.' Yama grants[72] men the right to chase away those who occupy these spaces: '(He sweeps them away saying) Go, run, crawl away from here', that is to say: 'Leave! Get out! And crawl away from here.' He says this to all those who crawl on their stomachs. 'You who have been here the day before yesterday and yesterday', that is to say: 'You who have always been here or since this day.'[73] The site of the sacrifice is thus temporarily brought into being by violence and theft, and it seems that, even if this initial violence might not be the basis of sacrifice,[74] it might be inherent in settlement. Yama, death, is the lord of settled places and this fact is altogether noteworthy. Space is not understood in terms of territory, nor according to an established law; the unspecified open space can only be transmuted into a place through violence and death. The place of sacrifice, because it requires a specific location, has to be a place of death. There are many ways of creating a sacrificial site. It is not, however, a question of choosing one means over others, but more a question of imposing the one approach that the logic of sacrifice demands, the only approach that is respected by the gods and therefore by men.

What we see is straightforward: the Devas like open space and they do not like locations. Even in battle, typically 'the gods fight in their chariots while the Asuras stay behind their walls'.[75] However, some questions need to be answered: what is it in these settled places that the gods battle over constantly, and what is it that calls for their constant and repeated intervention? Does a location belong to those who live there, or to those who could live there? What is the danger hidden there that makes the gods decide to turn them back into open space? Why are words and names glorified so much in the Veda while there is such a total absence of place-names? Does this reveal a simple indifference to the place-names or to the places themselves? Why should a place not have an identity, or can it be identified? Why are generic words used systematically? Why do the gods not like the places they pass through? Since all Vedic texts[76] deal with the doctrine or practice of sacrifice, we shall now examine sacrificial space for the answers. The sacrificial site is the only place that the Vedic texts are interested in, whether they are dealing with the sacrifices of gods or those performed by men.

Yet we cannot altogether escape from ideology. The Brāhmaṇas and the sacrificial texts analyse the rites and speculate about them at the same time, making use of myth to overcome any difficulty that arises in a ritual or anything odd in its practice. It is not possible to say first what is the gods' idea of space and then what is man's conception of space, since the texts treat both together. Straightforward descriptions of a sacrifice, the events that take place, and the sequence and meaning are usually incomplete in the texts. There are always gaps between what the texts say and how they can be applied to a ritual. These need to be filled, and the theologians applied themselves to this task. The *Kalpa-Sūtras* describe the rites in minute detail. The lacunae that are apparent in the Saṃhitās and the Brāhmaṇas and the difficulty of adjusting the words of the former to the gestures of the sacrificers, described in the latter, are the *raison d'être* of these *sūtras*. Thinking about rites is also the origin of the Mīmāṃsā. The same texts must have given rise to different practices and these differences were even considered part of the rite.[77] Echoes of doctrinal disputes can be found in the Brāhmaṇas themselves but, despite these differences, it remains true that the sacrificial site is the only place of interest to Vedic texts.

Each of the solemn rites of the Vedic cult had a different status and this meant that two kinds of site had to be prepared for sacrifice. One group is suitable for the *agnihotra*, the bi-monthly lunar celebrations, etc., and these are said to be *nitya*, permanent. They are inaugurated when a new householder starts his independent ritual life. When he is newly married, he acquires the status of an *āhitāgni*, 'one who has installed his fires', with the rite of installing of the fires (*agnyādheya*). When he is installed with his fires, he settles in a specific place. He is then duty bound to perform some rites every day and others every fortnight. He sanctions activity on the site and this activity, together with the site itself, indicates his status. A site is a typically human place—the gods have no equivalent. The other kind of ritual acts are called *kāmya*, acts of offering. These are much more complex than the first category, and call for a new sacrificial site to be set up each time a sacrifice is performed. According to the *Śrauta-Sūtras* and the Brāhmaṇas,[78] this site is located near a village and must accord with certain very broad criteria such as orientation, levelling, and whether or not there is water nearby. But in general there is nothing that should prevent the performance of a rite. The *nitya* nature of the first site is in complete contrast with the strictly transitory nature of the second where everything is done to ensure that nothing to do with the site is permanent. The ground, the buildings made of earth and wood and the objects of baked earth and wood (but rarely metal) are all burnt, broken, destroyed and returned to the earth from which they came. What survives in spite of men's efforts is left on the site and simply abandoned.[79] Nothing in the area must commemorate the rite, and there must be no record of it, no name for it. The area must not in any way be recognized as the site of any act that could have occurred before the sacrifice, nor must it be cherished or maintained by the community after the sacrifice. The officiants of a sacrifice did not want to leave behind any trace of their activities, just as the gods do not want to be tied to any location.

The choice of a sacrificial site confirms the impression that the place itself is of no importance. We have seen that the site must conform to certain broad criteria but these impose so few restrictions that when listing them the *Śatapatha Brāhmaṇa* (III.1.1.4) says: 'Sātyayajña then said: "In fact, this whole earth is divine; you can sacrifice anywhere on its surface. When a location has been picked out and consecrated with sacrificial formulae, it is transformed into sacred ground".' When you read these texts, this feeling is clearly to the fore; the whole earth is suitable for sacrifice provided the surface is flat and inclines to the east which represents the direction of progress. When the boundaries of a site are traced—it's just a line on the ground—the whole earth is being enclosed. A sacrificial site is not created in opposition to the world. It is not even a concentrated version of it—it is a representation of the world on a smaller scale. The qualifications that make a site eligible are altogether relative. Even when there must be water present, this is not an insurmountable requirement since a tree, a well or a large path can be acceptable alternatives.[80] That the texts are indifferent about matters relating to location can be seen in the same part of the *Śatapatha Brāhmaṇa* (III.1.1.5) which ends by saying: 'In fact, it is the officiants of the sacrifice who make up the sacrificial site: wherever wise and learned Brāhmins perform a sacrifice, there is no mistake.' It is men who embody the true sacrificial site and the fact that a sacrifice must occur somewhere does not mean that it has to have a definite location. The world is the space in which gods and the men who imitate them can act and each sacrificial site represents the whole world. It is hardly a restricted field of action.

Once a site has been chosen, one might think that this constitutes a sacred terrain, even if only temporarily, but this is not the case. However you define sacred, the notion is completely unknown in Vedic *yajña*. There is no word to express the idea of sacredness, nor is there a bundle of metaphors that can convey it as there is for example for sacrifice and the acts that constitute a sacrifice. Since the sacrificial site is a mirror of the world, it cannot be closed to the world nor separated too much from it. In the *Śatapatha Brāhmaṇa* (XIII.2.4.2),[81] it is said: 'If he had ended (the sacrifice) with (domestic) animals, the paths would have met, the edges of the villages would have met, and the forests would not have harboured *ṛkṣīka* (ogres?), men-tigers, murderers or robbers. And with wild (animals) the paths would not have met, the distances (*grāmānta*) between the villages would have grown, the forests would have harboured *ṛkṣīka*, men-tigers, murderers and robbers.' This remark is used to justify the sacrificial practice of the god Prajāpati who seized domestic and wild animals and thus made himself master of the world of the gods and the world of men, the two only two worlds there are. The paths referred to (*adhvan*) have the same name as the main official, the *adhvaryu*, 'is the one who walks the paths'.[82] *Adhvara* is also a name for sacrifice and it is understood as a space where the main activity is wandering. However one considers what is outside (i.e. wild animals) and what is inside (i.e. domestic animals), they are considered jointly. In other words, a boundary makes it possible to distinguish what is outside from what is inside but its purpose is to bring them together, not to set them in opposition to each other.[83] In the same way, the *grāma*[84] or communities should not be so far away from each other that they cannot be joined by paths nor should they be so close that their paths are entwined. There should be a proper distance between communities. This is very relevant to the practice of sacrifice which always places a strong emphasis on the relationship between things.

The lines on the ground do not divide a sacred area from a non-sacred, or profane area because the space given over to sacrifice is a miniature version of the larger whole: 'The earth is as big as the altar because they gained the whole (earth) by means of the altar'.[85] This text explains the etymology of the word *vedi*, altar, which is directly linked to the root *√VID-* meaning to find. Since they have gained the earth, the *vedi* shows even in its name that it is equal to the earth. The sacrificial site as seen from the outside is a sacred place, i.e. it is distinguished itself from other places by its attributes, but still it remains a place like any other place. Yet in terms of operation it is an epiphany of space as place.

The sacrificial site is a space one passes though, a kind of stopping place and, as often in the Veda, the vocabulary is meaningful. In a *yajña* there is a highly structured order in which acts are performed, often in a systematic manner, as D-C-B-A-B-C-D. A *yajña* is a living being with a head (D) and a tail (D), a beginning and an end. The opening and closing ceremonies are marked by characteristic procedures. A *yajña* ends with a *udavasanīya-iṣṭi*, 'an offering for going away', and starts with an *adhyavasanīya-iṣṭi*, 'an offering for a pause' or 'an offering made while stopping'.[86] There is no error in this choice of these words. The names of these two offerings are associated with the vocabulary of travel, more precisely haulage. An *avasāna*, a pause or a stop, means in technical terms the moment when horses are unyoked from a chariot. It is the moment when you let go of the harness and also the place where you undo the harness. The *udavasāna* is both the moment of harnessing and the act of harnessing, so it is the moment of departure when you restart your journey. The two words *udavasāna* and *adhyavasāna* are derived from a root *ava-SO-* which means to tie-up or bind. The hitching of horses, means that wandering and travel are about to start again. The gods are perpetual nomads, and we have seen that the Devas defeat the Asuras because they travel and because they are precise in their rituals. This is partly why real chariots, which are the chariots of the Devas at a human level, are worshipped: the gods travel in them. The *Aitareya Brāhmaṇa* (VII.7) even says: 'The sacrifice is a chariot for the Gods.' Men need to move about in the same way, especially when they bring the sacrificial fires and then take them away. Like the Devas, men need a time when they are settled in order to perform a *yajña* which is understood in terms of an interruption to the usual state of travel. The moment when a sacrifice starts is, therefore, a cessation of movement and the end of a sacrifice is marked by a harnessing that marks a new start to a journey, even if in reality it is only to go home, which might be a journey of a few kilometres at most. Ideologically a sacrifice is just a pause that lasts as long as the ceremony does: travel is the norm for the gods and, to a lesser extent, for men.

A sacrificial site is a space that embodies movement, since where one stops is not really a place where you rest fully or come to a complete stop. The site is a smaller version of the cosmos and it must be a space where men, following the example of the gods, are active and move about. The Devas know the right paths and Vedic hymns are full of praises accompanied by prayers where men ask such and such a god to guide them on the *supáthā*, 'the right path'.[87] The sequential unfolding of a sacrificial rite is seen as a forward movement. A sacrifice advances, that is to say in terms of space the ceremonies start in the west of the site and end in the east, the direction of progress.[88] Movement in time, before and after the ceremony, is less important than movement in space, especially going forward. To go forward is to go towards the east and this movement in the ritual is highly valued. Of course, it is essential to know how to move correctly: the correct procedures of the Devas are contrasted with those of the Asuras. The purpose of the latter is to make an initial mistake that emphasizes the importance of ritual precision, the *ṛta* or *satya*, that is characteristic of the Devas and means that they can avoid error at the start of the rite. We have seen that men imitate the gods and sometimes alter what is needed, adapting their gestures according to their status and capabilities. In the following example, the participants in a sacrifice seek the correct sequence of moves within the site in order to set up their fires, and this is the cause of the rivalry between the Asuras and the Devas.[89] If it is necessary to move, it should be according to this sequence. And this is exactly what the Asuras do not do; they are beings who move incorrectly and in the end are committed to wander in error. The text (cf. schema)[90] tells how the Asuras installed the three equally necessary fires of a solemn ritual and first placed the *āhavanīya*, then the *gārhapatya* and finally the *anvāharyapacana* (also *dakṣiṇa*) fire. The *āhavanīya* is the most important fire for the offerings are poured into it and sent up to heaven. The Asuras act first but what they do fails, for even if they go to heaven because of what they do, they pass right through. Then it is the turn of the Devas, who start by installing the *anvāharyapacana* then the *gārhapatya* fire, and finally the *āhavanīya*. In the end this sequence takes them to heaven, that is say to happiness, where they remain. This is an etiological myth. Its purpose is to justify the sequence in which the gestures in a ritual are carried out, and we can see in it two themes that are typically Vedic. On the one hand, there is an error at the start of the ritual, i.e. the mistake inherent in every beginning, and, on the other, we see that the space in which this movement occurs is highly valued. This latter notion interests us here. The Asuras start off, then start off badly, whereas the Devas who come after them know the right path that leads to the goal and allows them to stay there. Among the right itineraries, the way of the Devas goes from the west to the east starting off in the south. This sequence makes the goal of the sacrifice accessible and the sequence of moves is resolved in a way that is necessary because it is effective. It is necessary to arrive at the goal in stages. There is a correct sequence which includes stopping and it is not a question of rushing at the goal. This is what the Asuras do: they are in too much of a hurry and seem not to know how the stages are necessary; they start with the goal (in the east, going forward), turned back (the word west is meaningful; it means backwards) and end up in the south. That is to say that they gain happiness but do not remain there. In the Brāhmaṇas, Iḍā is the offering eaten in communion made divine. She sees and analyses how the Devas and the Asuras act. She sees the consequences of the movements of both, interprets them and decides to imitate the gods for the benefit of men, and so adapts the procedures of the gods for men who set out not from the south, a place marked by death, but from the west and pass through the south.

The sacrificial site is a space to travel through; it is a place where movement is well-organized, and significantly, this movement can alter the site itself. In solemn rituals such as the *agniṣṭoma* that include an offering of *soma*, a second altar is created to the east of the first altar that holds the three main fires. The second altar is called *mahāvedi*, great altar, because it is bigger than the first. The hearth that is in the east in the first site, the *āhavanīya*, is transformed into the *gārhapatya* fire in the second site while another *āhavanīya* is built. As soon as the *āhavanīya* hearth becomes the *gārhapatya*, the former must be destroyed and the latter built in its place. In a way the locations of the hearths are moved around as part of the more general movement on the site. The root *TAN-*, to stretch out or to lay out, is used to express sacrificial activity in the texts: *deva ha vai yajñam tanvanah*, 'While the Devas laid out the sacrifice' (*ŚB* I.1.2.3). This stretching emphasizes the extension of the sphere of activity towards the east, but here it is more than that since there is a movement of the site itself. The transfer is significant and it is not a question of making a site ready for sacrifice. Reassigning locations within a site is part of the ritual and shows that the link between location and activity is temporary. Even the highest form of activity does not give a place its own identity.

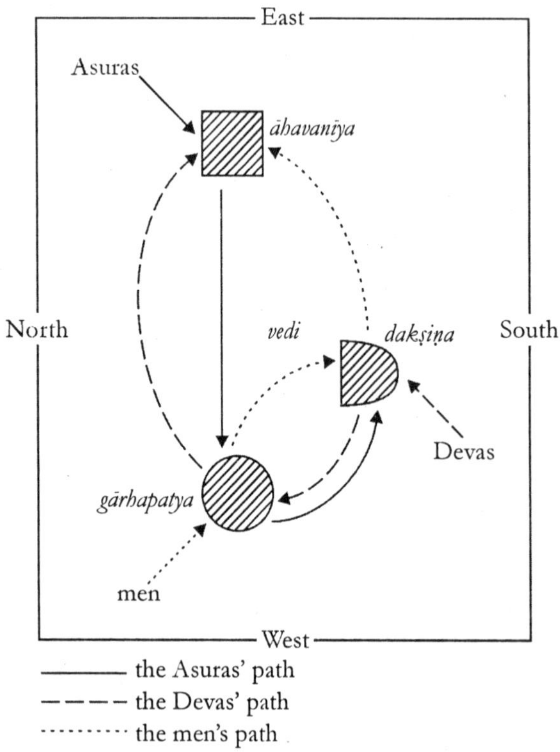

Fig. 1.1: The Disposition of sacrificial fires on the *vedi*, by Asuras, Devas and men.

It is worth noting that the words for sacrifice and ritual activity do not belong primarily to the family of *KṚ-* (to do). A rite is mainly a series of actions and, at a much later date, the two Mīmāṃsās placed great emphasis on its nature as *karman* or action. Yet, in the Brāhmaṇas, the root *KṚ-*, while not ignored totally, was not the main root denoting the activity of sacrificial ritual. A rite combines activity and movement and it brings different parts of a rite into relationship with each other. So the root *TAN-*, to lay out,[91] is more appropriate to mean sacrifice in its totality. It is even used to mean a simple action without any movement: *etásyām tāyámānāyām*, 'while he laid out (= made) this (offering)' (*ŚB* XIII.4.2.1).

However these movements were understood at a later date,[92] a site was far from being the centre of a space that surrounds it, nor was it defined mainly by the boundaries that could create a contrast with what was outside the site. The defining characteristic of a site is that it was a space through which one travelled.

We have seen that in order to uphold divine law men need to copy the actions of the gods. They do so by imitating the gods and by using metaphor. Men imitate the gods with a cult of chariots but these are chariots that come from nowhere and go nowhere. Yoking and unyoking are metaphors and these words are synonymous with beginning and ending. The separation of men from the gods is linked to their heaviness, and because of that, they are just not equal to the speed of the gods. But it is also due to the fact that in reality men have settled down in one place. The *grāma* is a human community in motion and it became the village of this community. For a society that had become sedentary, ritual was a positive and idealized memory of ancient times. When men settled in one place, the gods also ceased their wanderings and the places where they settled became sacred.

The journeys of the gods was an ideology; it allowed them to gather a fund of knowledge and to know the rituals, to defeat their enemies, and finally gain heaven where they made their home.[93] But this ideology could not be adopted by a human society that was slowly becoming sedentary and then finally became completely settled. If the hymns do not speak of villages and rural life, the texts on sacrifice that came later certainly do. In the *Aitareya Brāhmaṇa*, the story of Śunaḥśepa is interesting among those texts that celebrate wandering and travel, because it introduced a new way of dividing up space that was adopted later in the India of the Brāhmans. It clearly shows two kinds of space with opposing natures. There is the space in the village where *yajña* is celebrated and where the gods have their place. And there is the space in the forest where it seems the gods are not present. From this point on, the gods are constrained within a well-defined space. Without yet being fixed in one place, they have acquired a territory whose boundaries are defined by the limits of their activities.[94] They no longer wander at will, yet they sing in praise of wandering. *Cara*, wander, says Indra, who is stationed at the edge of the two worlds, to Rohita, the hero of the story. And Rohita wanders in space, protected from the power of both gods and kings, in spaces haunted by poor Brāhmans. We can see here a division of space between the village and the forest, especially as highlighted by C. Malamoud.[95] There is an astonishing contrast between the facts as told in the texts and what the protagonists in the texts actually say. The texts tell us that the king with his kingdom, his lands and his villages, is rich. He can afford an expensive sacrifice whereas the Brāhmans who wander in the forest outside of the villages are poor creatures. The same text praises both movement and wealth. The god Indra says that wealth comes to those who move, not to those who gather up their wealth and hoard it: 'He who stays sitting, his fortune also stays sitting; it does not move for him who does not move! He who stays lying down, his fortune also stays lying down. But it is lively for one who is lively.' (*AiB* VII.13) This divine speech proclaims values and ways of behaviour that are not in accord with the king with his wealth and his settled villages, or poor wandering Brāhmans who are prepared to sell their sons for a few cows. The texts say that those who are sedentary are rich and those who move are poor, but the protagonists say the opposite: wealth comes to nomads and wanderers. Men have stopped moving and have put down roots, but have turned their dreams and their memories into rituals. At the heart of their rituals, they continue to place a high value on movement and space, just as the gods do, whereas in truth their real space is now bound by the boundaries of their villages.

There is also a strong relationship between travel and knowledge. In the Veda travelling allows one to gain knowledge whereas remaining still is associated with ignorance. This is the opposite of Yoga where knowledge means staying still and closing one's eyes. The Devas move and so discover the way to heaven, and the same principle is valid for men. Naciketas, for example, goes on a journey in the afterlife to the land of Yama.[96] It is also a journey of knowledge as an episode in *Chāndogya-Upaniṣad* IV.4 explains: the child Satyakāma wants to know his origins, to find out whose child he is. It does not occur to him to ask his mother where he comes from, but he asks whose child he is.[97] His mother more or less tells him: she seems to have been a servant and not to have had a formal husband. But later when the young man has become a Brāhman[98] and wants to know *brahman*, his education takes place during several years when he is in charge of a herd of wandering cattle. Every night, 'at the place where those cows came together', Satyakāma kindled the fire there, and penned the cows. Then 'he sat down near them behind the fire, facing the east', and a being of some sort reveals to him a part of the nature of *brahman*. 'And the next day he set off again with his cows'. Throughout his journey of initiation, 'people other than men' teach him truth while during the day he herds his cattle.

The story comes to an end when he has nurtured the herd that was his charge and the child returns to the home of his master, which is the only settled point in this story about wandering. Here he finally gains access to the highest form of knowledge, in a place of learning that is not named. This story of men brings together the themes of the late Vedic period. Just like the gods, a young man gains knowledge by travelling. Also by travelling he nurtures the herd that has been given to him. In this Upaniṣad, it is clear that the earth is no longer an open space but it has become a space with a centre. But the focus of this story remains the teacher rather than his home. The young Brahmans comes back when he has finished wandering with his cattle and he returns not to a place but to a person.

Locations in this world are not highly valued, but space is. There is no connection between this and a divine space that could be the objective of the gods' searches. *Dhāman* is not a place but a function, a status, an institution and a state of being. *Nirukta's* commentary on this word and Sāyaṇa's is that it means *sthāna*, place, but this is a secondary meaning according to L. Renou.[99] If, as *AS* V.2 says, Agni and the Devas are *dhāsyus*, they are 'those who look for their *dhā(man)*'. They are searching for their own identities rather than looking for a place to settle. Moreover, *svarga* in this context is not a location but a superior, celestial space.

Vedic texts place a progressively greater importance on locations, and this can be seen in the story of Satyakāma. The vocabulary reflects this development: in the Brāhmaṇas, *antarvedí* means inside the sacrificial ground, but with time comes to mean *antarvedi*, the region of the Doāb.[100] When a myth as it appears in the Veda is compared with a later version, a tendency for people to settle and to put down roots is always apparent. This is true in the story of the human Purūravas and the nymph Urvaśī whose theme, the danger inherent in relationships between beings of differing status, is well known everywhere.[101] The two lovers are kept apart by their status but they remain united in their love. They live together on earth until the man commits an inappropriate act that makes him break a promise that separates them. The oldest reference to this story in Sanskrit texts can be found in *ṚS* X.95[102]. Although this *sūkta* belongs to the recent additions to the Saṃhitā, it contains characteristics of some of the oldest parts. There is no mention of a precise locality: The setting for the story is not clear and there is nothing that even suggests where it takes place. We can guess that the story takes place on earth and the text ends with the promise that, although the lovers are apart on earth, they will be reunited in heaven after Purūravas's death. In the meantime, Urvaśī 'fills the air, measures space'. This celestial nymph the Vedic Devas is characterized by her mobility and the speed with which she moves. The difference between celestial beings and humans is from the fact that humans are dull and this forces them to remain settled in one place, whereas the gods belong nowhere. The only names that are referred to in this *sūkta* are those of heroes and other nymphs. There are references to animals such as sheep, cattle, gazelles and horses, swans, foxes and jackals that shepherds could come across on the vast open spaces where their herds roam and where there were no forests to block out the horizon. The only fixed point in this story is 'the house opposite'.

The story of Purūravas and Urvaśī is next found in the *Śatapatha Brāhmaṇa* (XI.5.1), which clearly refers to the version in the *Ṛk Saṃhitā*[103] and quotes several stanzas. This later version fills in the gaps of the Vedic *sūkta* and produces a coherent narrative missing from the original. In the earlier version the story moves forward with a series of allusions rather than by clear descriptions of events and this makes it difficult, if not impossible, to follow what is happening.[104] The narrative framework gives importance to locations such as Kurukṣetra. The story is taken up again a thousand years later, most notably in a Purāṇa[105] where it is given a Hindu interpretation. The *Viṣṇu Purāṇa*, one of the oldest Purāṇas, provides a detailed version (VI.20-46) as a kind of fairy story in the context of a wider narrative, which was probably inherited from the *Śatapatha Brāhmaṇa.* Despite the fairy-tale nature of the story, there is a clearly defined spatial setting: the two lovers live at Alaka, the capital of Purūravas's kingdom; they go for walks in Caitaratha where they visit the groves and the shores of lotus lakes. They also visit other forests in a region that the text tells us is located next to Kurukṣetra. Even if the story itself has not changed, the setting clearly has. The open plain has become a forest broken up by villages and perhaps small towns. The animals that were clearly associated with pastoral activity have gone, except for two rams, which are Urvaśī's favourite animals. Other Purāṇas reinforce this tendency and place even greater importance on locality. The *Vāyu Purāṇa* (II.29.5-39) provides a list of eight places visited by Purūravas and Urvaśī during the sixty-four years that they lived together. The background to this development is the opposition between the village and the forest that is a major theme of Brahmanical ideology. By now values have changed: the forest has become a vast space but is dark, closed off, and hostile. In contrast, free space can be found in settled locations where men carry out their activities, and in the villages or towns where the king has his residence. And of course all these places have names. This is almost the opposite of what we find in the Veda.

All this can probably be placed in an historical context as far as we can determine one, but we must be careful not to confuse myth with history. An Indian myth is not necessarily a transposed or sublimated version of a historical fact. Nonetheless we are quite sure that India as we know it today and India in classical times with its villages and rural life, a settled India, were not always thus. At the time when Vedic sacrifices were held and when the Brāhmaṇa texts were composed, Vedic society was no longer nomadic. The people who regarded Indra as their warrior hero had gradually settled down. No doubt the culture, and the language(s), evolved, but the people themselves stopped moving, or moved only small distances. A. Minard remarks in a striking summary: 'By establishing themselves and proliferating in Mesopotamia (Doāb) that was known as Brahmarṣideśa, the Aryan tribes passed from a civilization that was still Indo-European, where the horse was dominant, people consumed meat and herded animals, to a civilization of a nilotic type, where cattle were valued, cereals grown and that had a vegetarian diet.'[106] This did not happen overnight and there are many variations between a truly nomadic life, whether complete or partial, with its memory of continual journeying, and an ideological view of travel that came once a people had settled down, even if they might not have considered their stops permanent. Even those Vedic hymns that are considered the most ancient praise the travels of gods and men but at the same time speak of fields and agriculture. This is how the Veda invites a rash gambler to get his feet back on the ground: 'Do not gamble with dice, cultivate your field, enjoy what you have, and value it highly! There are your oxen, O gambler, there is your wife' (*ṚS* X.34.13). This is undoubtedly a late hymn and it is unique in honouring mediocrity. But elsewhere the Veda does not hesitate to sing the praises of sowing seeds (*AS* VI.142) or to praise the stable where cattle live (*AS* VII.75.2). The Vedas refer to citadels, forts, and villages. Without doubt society at this time was settling down and adopting a mainly rural way of life. Perhaps they did not know that this settled way of life would last longer than they imagined but there was a real dissonance between an ideology where the gods are nomadic and where wandering (going 'forward') is a duty, and a society where men, who are obliged to copy the gods, are nonetheless fast putting down roots and becoming completely settled. An ideology based on movement, on the order to move on and on open spaces is clearly in conflict with a settled society where space has been more or less enclosed and divided into territories.[107] This ever-widening gap between the ideology of the ceremonies and how life was actually lived produced a language of metaphor. But the language of the liturgy did not change: it continued to speak of yoking and unyoking even when society had settled down.[108] In classical Sanskrit, *avasāna* is the site where a house is built:[109] the act of stopping became the place where you stop, but you no longer needed to travel to have to place to stop—the pause had become permanent.

Yet this is not how the texts describe this development. In terms of rituals and the values that are associated with them, in terms of understanding these rites, the point is that territory, place and name remain dangerous because they can close off an object from what surrounds it and isolate it from other objects. This is just what the gods fight against, as do those who formulated the doctrines and revered the gods. When translated into action, that is to say into rituals, the Veda as revelation is fearful of objects that are just present there, as separate from each other, since there is always a tendency for them to assert their individuality. The purpose of ritual is to limit the unique nature of objects and strengthen the relationship between words and objects, and between words and men. This is a fragile relationship, always threatened by the uniqueness of each object. The essence of these texts is that what is unique has no meaning. Vedic texts share a vision of life born of asserting the interrelationship of things and refuting their uniqueness. What is unique is only a means, albeit a necessary means, of gaining access to a world of fruitful plurality. Of course, only existing entities can be in relationship with each other but the purpose of all Vedic ritual, and of the speculation that goes with it, is to strengthen these relationships to the detriment of the entities themselves. What is unique strengthens substance but the Vedic universe is in its essence dynamic. It is a world of forces rather than things; it is a world of actions that link. The recurrent use of the root *TAN-*, meaning the act of sacrifice, can best be understood in this context. Weaving together sacrificial acts strengthens the links between beings and fills the void that always threatens to open up between them.[110] A sacrificial site should not become a place where an object can be located nor must the site become a place with too many boundaries. Rituals need to be located somewhere but these locations are seen primarily as places that link. This is how *ṛta* is understood. It is Vedic order, a space where inanimate objects as well as animate beings can be placed in relationship with each other. If beings must have a place, it should not be their own place because above all these beings have to move on, to be 'displaced'. In this sense disorder is seen as failed relationships, when objects are given too much importance. Uniqueness is a weight that inhibits free movement. This is exactly what the Asuras do: they do not like to create relationships between things and they direct their activity towards themselves and not to others. They enclose themselves in settled and fortified locations. Things by their own nature, because of their heaviness, seem committed to uniqueness and this is dangerous because it is a source of isolation. The gods in their battles and men in their rituals seek to break down this tendency to isolation. By asserting the primacy of relationship over what is related, rituals and the men who perform them create meaning. It is a dynamic meaning born of fruitful relationships established by ritual. Those who performed the rituals were fearful of the dominant effect of locations and large sterile objects that can be found there, so they cultivated paths to fruitful relationships.

Acknowledgements: I thank G. Tarabout and D. Berti for their comments on the first French draft of this paper. Translated from the French by Martin Creese.

ABBREVIATIONS

AiB	: *Aitareya Brāhmaṇa.*	*JB*	: *Jaiminīya Brāhmaṇa.*
ĀpŚS	: *Āpastamba Śrauta-Sūtra.*	*JS*	: *Jaiminīya-Sūtra and the Commentaries of Śabara.*
AS	: *Atharvaveda Saṃhitā.*		
BĀU	: *Bṛhad-Āraṇyaka Upaniṣad.*	*JUB*	: *Jaiminīya Upaniṣad Brāhmaṇa.*
BEI	: *Bulletin d'Études Indiennes.*	*KauB*	: *Kauṣītaki Brāhmaṇa.*
CS	: *Caraka Saṃhitā.*	*KS*	: *Kaṭha Saṃhitā.*
ÉVP	: *Études védiques et pāṇinéennes.*	*LŚS*	: *Lāṭyāyana Śrauta-Sūtra.*
JA	: *Journal Asiatique.*	*MS*	: *Maitrāyaṇī Saṃhitā.*

MDhŚ	: *Mānavadharmaśāstra alias Manusmṛti.*	*TB*	: *Taittirīya Brāhmaṇa.*
		TS	: *Taittirīya Saṃhitā.*
PB	: *Pañcaviṃśa Brāhmaṇa.*	*VS*	: *Vājasaneyī Saṃhitā.*
ṚS	: *Ṛk Saṃhitā.*	*YV*	: *Yajurveda.*
ŚB	: *Śatapatha Brāhmaṇa.*	*YS*	: *Yoga Sūtra.*

NOTES

1. In the Brahmanical tradition, one can get an idea of how Śaṃkara considered these elements by reading his commentary on *BĀU* V.I.I. In terms of Indian scholarship, L. Renou is particularly eminent; see the reeditions 1966 and 2003 of Lévi 1898. This work, which has never been superseded, might give a particularly dry and restricted idea of 'the Vedic religion', in contrast to the frenetic lyricism of the hymns and the highly introverted speculations of the Upaniṣad. Lévi placed great emphasis on mechanical efficiency in rites that were to be performed with precision and called it 'blind' efficiency. This interpretation was always criticized as too restrictive; see Colas 2006. Moreover the technicians and interpreters of the Brāhmaṇas must have visited those who composed or recited the hymns and also perhaps those who took refuge in solitude. But since we have no evidence of this, we are likely to remain ignorant of the Vedic religion and religious attitudes as they were lived and felt.
2. The word veda, 'knowledge', is not really suitable for this Revelation since, with the exception of the Upaniṣad, there is no exposition of doctrine. If it is a question of knowing, it is primarily a form of expertise. The treatise that provides an interpretation of the Vedas, the *Karmamīmāṃsā*, emphasizes the extent to which the Veda (which it often calls *śāstra*, 'instruction') imposes an obligation to act and not to know. At a later date, Śaṃkara makes the well-known division between *karmakāṇḍa*, 'section on action' and *jñānakāṇḍa*, 'section on knowledge'.
3. What is called *die textgeschichtlische Methode* consists in establishing a causal relationship between historical facts and texts, between what their authors did, where and when they did them, and what they said. A large part of contemporary science adopts this *Methode* with varying degrees of success.
4. *Devāsurā vā eṣu lokeṣu samayanta* (*AiB* I.14.5). The sentence is a *leit-motiv* in these works. Note the locative meaning 'concerning': the worlds are not so much the place of combat as their motive.

5. A particularly instructive passage in the *ŚB* shows that the Devas were initially identical with the Asuras and then separated out: whereas they both shared equally what was true and what was false, the Devas ended by seizing all that was true and the Asuras all that was false; henceforth, as usual, 'the Gods won and the Asuras lost everything' (*ŚB* IX.1.5.12-27); text and translation in S. Lévi 1898 (1966: 39-40).
6. Men move about on the sacrificial ground; their movement combine estimation and transformation: we see that men discover ritual after the Asuras and the Devas with the help of the goddess Iḷa who adapts divine procedures for them. This change indicates the status of men.
7. *ŚB* VI.8.1.1; cf. Eggeling 1894 : 289 and Minard 1949: 166, § 168a that refers to 'carting the fire around'.
8. In the *Aitareya Brāhmaṇa* and the *Śatapatha Brāhmaṇa*, the Asuras are the enemies of the Devas whereas in the *Ṛk Saṃhitā* the two words can be applied, with the exception of Indra, to the same entities: Soma and Varuṇa are Asuras and Devas at the same time.
9. Some rites that were not solemn mentioned in the *Gṛhya-Sūtra* need a *sthaṇḍila*, a 'site' in the shape of a chariot wheel (*Kāṭhaka-Gṛhyasūtra* 37, 2). Other references in Gonda 1980 : 231.
10. The 'now' refers to the time when the clerics composed the Brāhmaṇas. But it could also refer to our times since the rites can still be performed. This is true in this case since it is a question of an *agnicayana*, 'pilling up (of the altar) of fire', a ritual whose principle feature is building a fire altar that can have the shape of a falcon and where the altar is made by pilling up (*cayana*) five layers of bricks; an *agnicayana* of this kind was performed in Kerala in 1975 and was the subject of Agni (see Staal 1983).
11. The incongruity of addressing a prayer to an inanimate object, without awareness and without hearing, comes into the *mīmāṃsaka* discussion on the relationship between ritual gestures and the speech that accompanies them; it is one element of the thesis called *mantrāṇām ānarthakyam*, 'the non-significance of *mantra*', that is to say the thesis according to which the meaning of the *mantra* has to be ignored during the performance of a *yajña*. See *Acetane'rthabandhanāt* (*JS* I.2.35) and the commentary of Śabara: the *pūrvapakṣin* considers that the meaning of *mantra* in *yajña* is negligible because 'they are addressed to objects that are without consciousness'. Śabara gives as two examples prayers addressed to herbs (*TS* I.2.1.1.) and to stones (*TS* I.3.13.1). The *siddhāntin* answers (*JS* I.2.46) that it is figurative speech.

12. On *rájas*, see Renou 1958: 61-3.
13. *ŚB* III.4.4.3. Other versions of this myth can be found in *AiB* I.23 and *TS* VI.2.3. It is a theme that was taken up in Hinduism since it can be found in the *Mahābhārata* (VIII.33.17).
14. It is true that they are always hostile to each other since places are ceaselessly created in space.
15. For example *ṚS* I.51.5, X.99.7 for the Dasyu. Six of the seven *dasyuhátya*, 'slayings of Dásyu', are credited to Indra. For the Dāsa see *ṚS* I.103, IV.32.10. Hale 1986: 155 notes that in the battles between Indra and the Dasyu, we see a tendency to mention personal names (Śambara, Arbuda, etc.) and never the names of places. The fortresses are without names. It is not always possible to distinguish between Asuras, Dāsas, Dānavas and Dasyus.
16. For example in the hymn to the earth, *AS* XII.1.
17. This is a notion with many meanings (with its double *aṃhatí*) and it represents fairly well what the Devas and men of the Ṛk *Saṃhitā* are afraid of: narrowness, strangulation, oppression, anxiety (Sanskrit *aṃhas*, Greek αχοσ, German Angst, French angoisse have the same origin). For example: 'O Gods, we have reached a place (*kṣetra*) devoid of pastures for cows; the earth, although it is big, (*urvī*) has become narrow' (*agavyūtí kṣétram áganma devā urvī́ satī́ bhū́mir aṃhūraṇā́bhūt*, *ṚS* VI.47.20a): the association of *kṣétra/áṃhas* is particularly conclusive). See also *ṚS* X.25.8. Elsewhere the *ŚB* (I.5.1.22) refers to a *mantra* where the sacrificer calls on the six spaces to protect him from *áṃhas*. The Vedic hymns frequently call on the gods to deliver and protect men from *aṃhas* (for a list of constructions with *áṃhas* see *An Encyclopaedic Dictionary of Sanskrit on Historical Principles*, Poona, 1976 and Gonda 1957.
18. *MS* III.16.5: *urvī rodasī varivas kṛṇotaṃ kṣetrasya patnī adhi no bruvāthaḥ; staumi dyāvāpṛthivī nāthito johavīmi te no muñcatam aṃhasaḥ*. Quoted and translated by Rolland 1975: 118-19. The author translates *aṃhas* as 'anxiety' and I prefer 'narrowness'. The last sentence acts as a refrain (it is repeated twenty times!) in the hymn *AS* XI.6.
19. In the *Ṛk Saṃhitā*, that is to say the hymns of the *Ṛgveda*, except when referring to Indra, the Asuras and the Devas live in harmony and are even more or less merged together. It would be better to say that the word asura is an attribute of some Devas. Mitra and Varuṇa are the sovereigns of the Asuras and are themselves Asuras. It is only in the more recent Brāhmaṇas, that the Devas are hostile to their brothers,

the Asuras. This does not stop them cooperating in some instances but henceforth the old Deva-Asuras of the *Ṛk Saṃhitā* are completely integrated on the side of the Devas. Simultaneously, they lost their importance and are replaced by other deities such as Prajāpati. The transformation of Asuras into demons was further emphasized in the later texts and this happens in parallel with an evolution in the content of the myths. The immobility and the absence of movement that are characteristic of Vṛtra are not characteristic of Rāvaṇa of the Sanskrit *Rāmāyaṇa* and the demons of the Purāṇa.

20. *ṚS* I.32.10. This hymn is particularly interesting because it is one of the few hymns where the *vṛtrahátya*, 'the murder of Vṛtra', is told with a degree of precision.
21. Louis Renou studied the vocabulary of these themes in Benveniste and Renou 1934: 146. The verbal root of Vṛtra is *ŚĪ-* 'to lie'; *śáyana* 'a sojourn' is one of the preferred words for his cave. Also *DHĀ-* 'to pose' (*ṚS* I.32.10a-b).
22. The motif of 'secret sojourn' has a correspondence in the field of linguistics. The *pada*, 'sojourn' is also the gods' and became the technical term meaning words.
23. See in the remarkable work by Roesler 1997, especially pp. 242ff.
24. The fact that Varuṇa's palace (?) has a thousand doors is scarcely noted here and there (*sahásradvāraṃ jagamā gṛháṃ te* *ṚS* VII.88.5d).
25. See Vassilkov 2002: 133-58. The author notes especially (pp. 134-5) the *sārasvatasattra* 'session at the Sarasvatī', which is sometimes interpreted as a Vedic pilgrimage, and the expression *tīrthé síndhor* 'at the ford of a river' (*ṚS* VIII.72.7) which some scholars consider to be an ancient form of the cult of *tīrtha* 'the sacred places' of Hinduism. The fact that the cult of Soma is held preferably near a ford does not make the ford the location of a cult, still less the object of a cult.
26. There are only two hymns which are completely and exclusively dedicated to the earth; nonetheless the earth, either on its own or more often in association with the sky, is the subject of isolated stanzas. This hymn (*AS* XII.1) was studied by Renou 1956b: 59-69. It was composed at a time when the poets knew both rice and barley (as XII.1.42 shows). Barley (*yavá*) is the great cereal of the ancient texts, especially the *Ṛk Saṃhitā*, and its name is the subject of much speculation and, as Minard 1956: 49 (n. 118a) says, 'the growing importance of rice (unknown in the *ṚS*), which is noticeable in ritual, is linked to the progress of the tribes towards the East'.

27. It is interesting to compare this to the celebration of the earth of India of modern times in the *Vande Mātaram*. *AS* XII.1.12 says *mātá bhū́miḥ putró ahám pṛthivyā́ḥ* 'earth is mother, I am earth's son', but not obviously the earth of what is now 'India'.
28. *AS* XII.1.45 and 47.
29. One of the words that means the earth is the neuter *bhū́man* whereas the masculine *bhūmán* refers to abundance and multiplicity; they are both derived from the same root *BHŪ-* 'to be, to become', whereas the feminine *bhū́* is also one of the names of the earth.
30. *AS* VII.9.1-2 according to the translation by Henry 1892-6. See English translation in Whitney 1905 : 395.
31. *Sahasrāśvine vā itaḥ svargo lokaḥ* (*AiB* II.17.8). The unbounded value that is given to the number one thousand (*sahasra*) means that the sentence is not exact.
32. *AiB* IV.7-9. Since Agni races with a chariot drawn by mules, he burns their mould and 'that is why they do not conceive'. The theme of a chariot race can be found in different forms throughout the Vedas. In terms of poetry, we should point out the very strange hymn *ṚS* X.102 and in terms of ritual the *vājapeya* is worth noting; it mainly concerns a race whose outcome is fixed.
33. Once in a temple we expressed surprise to the officiating Brahman about the incredible din that accompanied the worship, he answered: 'Only thieves come without making a noise'.
34. See Malamoud 1990.
35. *Svarūpapratiṣṭhā tadānīṃ citiśaktir yathā kaivalye / vyutthānacitte tu sati tathāpi bhavantī na tathā* (*YBh* I.3)
36. *ṚS* I.108.8, transl. Renou 1965: 50. It is also possible, as noted by Dumezil 1971 : 263, that this ethnographic manner of speech refers to a spatial and geographic conception. In some cases, hymns list the points of the compass and associates them with different tribes. For example, *ṚS* VIII.10.5cd: *yád adyā́śvināv ápāg yát prā́k sthó vājinīvasū / yád druhyávy ánavi turváśe yádau huvé vāmátha mā́ gatam* 'O Aśvins, whether you are in the west or the east, O owners of the high good, whether you are with Druhyu, Anu, Turvaśa or Yadu, I call on you, come!'.
37. Macdonell and Keith 1912: 586, under the heading 'places', list twenty-two. But many of them are doubtful and after subjecting them to scrutiny only eight or nine remain. The emphasis on place-names seems to have grown with time and reaches a climax today with 'Indian' nationalism and its claims to make India 'the land of the Veda'. The

building of temples was an important point of this fixing of the Veda in an Indian context.

38. The contrast with the places where Kṛṣṇa or Rāma lived speaks volumes.
39. References in Macdonell and Keith 1912: 300 (but the reference to *Pañcaviṃśa Brāhmaṇa* should be corrected as above). We should remember that the Sarasvatī which is identified as a (sub-) tributary of the Indus could well originally have been the Helmand whose waters disappear in Seistan in Iran/Afghanistan. There is nothing unusual in this. The Seine, the Saône, the Sanne or the Rhin and the Rhône, which today are distinguished by differences in the way they are spelt and pronounced, originally had the same name. The Indo-European people who settled in 'India' arrived there with their hymns but also with names that they imposed on things. Many rivers that flow in regions of central Asia do not reach the sea: there certainly were more than one 'Sarasvatī' and indeed there still are. The *AS* VI.100.1 talks about three Sarasvatī. Witzel 1984, especially pp. 217-19, has shown that the Sarasvatī is also one of the names of the celestial river, the Milky Way. Imposing a name with which one is familiar on places that one discovers or on cities that one founds is a common practice. 'London' and 'Paris' are common names for towns in America. See Sergent 1997: 242.
40. Another case is the example that is always cited of *Munimaraṇa* 'Death of the Saints'. The explanation, which provides an opportunity to tell a myth about salvation, can be found in the *Pañcaviṃśa Brāhmaṇa* (XIV.4.7). Still more famous is the place called *Manor avasarpaṇam* 'Descent of Manu' where Manu disembarks from his ship at the time of the flood told in *ŚB* I.8.1.6. These three 'stories' from the Brāhmaṇas are translated and commented on by Lévi 1896: 146, 150-1 and 116. It should be noted that in the translation of the second passage the word 'place' is used several times by the translator but these are nothing other than adverbs of location (*atra*, *etarhi*).
41. For Shrava 1977: 270 'the hymns do not refer to history or historical events. They, being eternal, had to have been revealed prior to any historical event' (p. XIV). The work shares in the belief and in the longstanding desire to situate the Vedas in India, which is the only country that the gods visit.
42. *ṚS* X.75.1. It is the hymn to rivers, and the manner in which the earthly Sindhu and the celestial Sindhu are merged can be seen in its evocative

lyricism. The seven sacred rivers mentioned to remain seven in number at a later date but their names and locations change.

43. References in Lüders 1951: 153.
44. See Biardeau 1981. Hopkins 1912: 213ff. is full of information on this topic.
45. *ŚB* IV.1.5.13 and XIV.1.1.2. This place-name is not found in the *ṚS* or the *AV* but is seen in the liturgical *Saṃhitā* of the *YV* (*MS*, *KS* and *TS*). In the second passage of the *ŚB* quoted here, which is the most interesting, we can see that the Kurukṣetra of the gods and the Kurukṣetra of men is the same: 'That is why, when settling in the Kurukṣetra', we think: 'There is a place for divine sacrifice'. The best thinking on the Kurukṣetra in our opinion is to be found in Witzel 1984.
46. Discussions about when to offer the *agnihotra*, for example, are very frequent. The structure of time is a recurrent theme in the Brāhmaṇas, but thinking about space is much rarer and much less plentiful. In *caturviṃśe ha vai saṃvatsare'nuditahomī gāyatrīlokam āpnoti / dvādaśa uditahomī* 'he who sacrifices before the rising of the sun reaches the world of the *gāyatrī* during the twenty-fourth year; he who sacrifices after the rising of the sun, during the twelfth year' (*AiB* V.29.5), there is a clear contrast: information about time is questioned even when clear but information about places remains unspecified; what indeed is 'the world of the *gāyatrī*'? There are long discussions about the structure of time, as when it is said of the year that it is the *puruṣa* (*ŚB* XII.2.4). And in *ŚB* XII.2.2.13-23 the student provides a long answer to his master's question, 'My son, how many days does your father count in a year?' There is nothing along these lines about the structure of a place, or even the structure of space, even an abstract space. Prajāpati is never associated with a space.
47. *ŚB* X.2.2.6.
48. From a grammatical point of view, the word means 'the bharatide land'. The names *bharata* and *bhārata* 'Sons of Bharata' are ancient since people of this name appear in the *ṚS*: *áminthiṣṭāṃ bhāratā revád agním devāśravā devávātaḥ sudákṣam* (*ṚS* III.23.2a); references in the indices of the Veda and in Macdonell and Keith 1912.
49. Although this name is found in classical grammars, it is not a word translated from the Sanskrit nor is it an approximation of a technical term from the *vyākaraṇa*. This 'locative case ending' is known after its position in the declension, i.e. *saptamī* 'seventh'. Pāṇini sees a

relationship between this case ending and a *kāraka*, 'factor of an action' he calls *adhikaraṇa* 'support, reference', not a location. When he defines it (*ādhāro'dhikaraṇam* I.4.45), it is by means of the word *ādhāra*, from the root *DHṚ-*, whose link to location is not clear. 'In the final analysis it is making a noun of the preverb *adhi*, "concerning"', says Renou 1942: the *saptamī* expresses mainly a context, and to that extent it does denote location; the standard example is *gṛhe tiṣṭhati*, 'he stays at home'.

50. It is necessary to consider each case as it is found in the texts and not use the framework of a hypothetical 'Vedic literature'. I have particularly consulted Verpoorten 1977b, especially Chapter V, 'Place du locatif', pp. 89-102 which provides a survey of the use of the locative in the *Aitareya Brāhmaṇa*. The majority of the seventy-six examples of the 'locative' quoted by the author have a temporal value.

51. Example in *TB* III.7.12: *trité devā́ amṛjataitád énaḥ / tritá etán manuṣyèṣu mā mṛje / táto mā yádi kíṃcid ānaśé / agnír mā tásmād énasaḥ* 'The Devas wiped the mistake onto Trita, Trita wiped it onto men. If some bit of it reaches me, may Agni deliver me from this mistake'. It is in the *Atharvaveda* that this technique is most widely revealed.

52. An example of a transfer in *AS* XII.1.30b where it is a question of moving onto the enemy the *syédu* (or *sédu*) which seems to be the impure perspirations of the body taken as a whole: *yó naḥ sédur ápriye táṃ ní dadhmaḥ* 'what mucus (? *syédu*) is ours, that we deposit on him we love not (*ápriya*)' (tr. Whitney).

53. For example, *asya sumataú syāma* 'May we be in good grace' (*ṚS* VIII.48.12d).

54. *Agnís takmā́nam ápa bādhatām itáḥ (. . .) ápa dvéṣāṃsy amuyā́ bhavantu* (*AS* V.22.1a, d). In the same hymn (stanza 5), there is a reference to the *ókas*, 'house', of this terrible *takmán*. But here too, there is no notion that the illness has a house which is its home. The stanza must be understood as a kind of beseeching: 'Go, go and live with the Mūjavat; go on, go and live with the Mahāvṛṣa.' The last stanza is *Gandhā́ribhyo mū́javadbhhyó'ṅgebhyo magádhebhyaḥ / praiṣyán jánam iva śevadhíṃ takmā́naṃ pári dadmasi*. *Pari-DĀ-* is translated here by 'transfer' but is literally 'give around'. The idea of transfer from one place to another is expressed by a different vocabulary depending on the text. In the stanza *AS* XII.1.30 referred to *supra* n. 51, it is *ni-DHĀ-* 'to put down'. In *TB* III.7.12 the Devas and Trita wipe (*MṚJ-*) their fault on to their inferiors. In general in the *AS* the expression *A2 MṚJ- X7* means 'to shift A onto X': A, a word in the accusative, is a mistake, an illness, everything that is *durita*

'inappropriate' and X which is the locative case ending is the place (a people, somewhere that is not precise, etc.) on which it is wiped. The medical use of the Achyranthes Aspera is the result of the analysis of the Sanskrit name of this plant *apāmārgá in apā- MṚJ-* 'to throw off far' (cf. *AS* IV.17 and *CS*, *Sūtrasthāna* II).

55. Renou 1948: 44, n. 2 in the translation of this passage.
56. The hymn *ṚS* I.8, which is typical of the warrior hymns dedicated to Indra, celebrates the battles and massacres of the past and those that are to come: *muṣṭihatyá* (2), *yúdh* (3), *samohá* (6) are names of battles in general; neither dates nor places make any battle specific: in fact, battles never really end. Even the great victory of Indra over Vṛtra, to which many hymns refer, has no name; it took place *parvate* (*ṚS* I.32.2) 'on the mountain'. Reading the hymns dedicated to Indra, which are a long celebration of the god's victorious battles, is not in any way like reading an account of Alexander's campaigns. It is hardly possible to follow coherently the story of the *vṛtrahatyá* which remains full of gaps, multi-faceted, and sometimes contradictory.
57. Much has been written about the Vedic Sarasvatī and we note that it is described (exclusively) as a majestic river in the *ṚS* whereas the Brāhmaṇa mention its disappearance in the sands (*vinaśana*). There is much information in Khan 1978 (but the author pp. 12 *sqq.* should have take more note of the geomorphology before launching into his antediluvian flights of fancy).
58. *JUB* IV.6.12.
59. *Eṣa u ha vai vāco 'nto yat prakṣaḥ prāsravaṇaḥ / yatro ha vai vāco'ntam, tat svargo lokaḥ* (*JB* II.298).
60. *AiB* VIII.10. The text is one of those that glorifies the north-east. It is not certain that the translation 'battled over these worlds' is not better in this case as it can be seen in a similar expression.
61. *AiB* I.12.1. 'Orient' does not refer to the east of a place that thought as the centre of the world, but to a semi-abstract direction, a spatial, temporal and locational 'over there' of correct action. Translating *diś* by 'quarter' alludes too much to.
62. This organization is noted mainly by the roots Ṛ- (from which is derived *ṛta* which provides the principle name of the space for the rite), *DHĀ-* especially *vi-DHĀ-* 'to set off again', *MĀ-* 'to give one's measure' (from which is derived the word *māyā* 'the power of construction' of the gods, their creative magic). Space is organized for sacrifice: the universe is a vast sacrificial terrain for the Devas.

63. It should be noted how all this is diametrically opposed to the original yoga and to yoga as integrated into Hinduism where the knower is *kṣetrajña* 'knower of the field' (*YS* II.4; an attribute later adopted into Hinduism where *kṣetrajña* is, for example, applied to Viṣṇu in the *Sahasranāma*). Whereas the ultimate goal of Yoga (at least the *Yoga-Sūtra* and the *Yoga-Bhāṣya*) is *kaivalya* 'isolation', the ceaseless actions of the Devas have as their goal the establishment of relationships. For the *kṣetriyá* illness 'that belongs to the terrain', and its Vedic, Ayurvedic and grammatical references, see Filliozat 1975 : 93-6.
64. *AS* III.12 pour *vāstos patiḥ*. There is also a *kṣétrāṇāṃ pátiḥ* 'Master of the fields' (*VS* XVI. 18) to whom homage is paid with a formula (*kṣétrāṇāṃ pátaye námaḥ*) among the dozens of other similar formulae, a *kṣétraya pátnī* 'Mistress of the field' (*AS* II.12.1). Most often the *kṣétra* is a field (duly measured as in *ṚS* 1.110.5, X.33.6) but not necessarily cultivated (in the *ṚS* IV.57.1-3 it is associated more with animals). On the transition from the Vedic meaning to the classical meaning, see Renou 1939 : 351.
65. *AiB* IV.6.
66. *ĀB* II.1.1.10. *āyatana* becomes at a later date one of the names of the sanctuary (*devāyatana*). For *āyatana*, see Renou 1954. For *pratiṣṭhā*, almost a synonym of *āyatana*, see Geldner 1951; and Gonda 1967.
67. *ŚB* I.4.1.22-3.
68. *ŚB* V.4.3.21. This passage is taken from the long explanation of the coronation of an earthly king (*rājasūya*) and the myth is to do with salvation. On the *rājasūya*, see Heesterman 1957.
69. The notion is complex and difficult to translate by a single meaning. Nonetheless if one considers that *ṛta* is right order or the sacrificial order, *nir-ṛti* is its opposite etymologically, disorder. J. Varenne translated it by a word akin to void (but this *nirṛti*, far from being a void, is the presence of something); in the article which he dedicated to this notion, Renou 1955 says 'entropy', 'void', 'destruction', as well as 'disorder'. In order to avoid errors of interpretation, it is also necessary to emphasize that these disorders are necessary. Even though it is disorder, *nirṛti* has its place in the universal order and is not harmful. For this reason it is invited to the ritual and propitiated.
70. *ŚB* V.2.3.3
71. However these two spaces are not completely mutually exclusive; the boundaries are porous and, once the officiants have made boundaries, they bring back something of what was outside to the inside. The

sacrificial ground is not set in opposition to the world since it represents an organized version of the universal and is not a space from which impurity is absent.

72. *Yamó dadāty avasānam asmai*: 'Yama gives him a place of rest' *ṚS* X.14.9d. On Yama, master of places, see also *TS* V.2.3. On Yama, death and the dead, see Malamoud 1999.
73. *ŚB* VII.1.1.2-3. The gestures and the *mantra* that accompany them are recited as the domestic hearth *gārhapatya* is built. This cleaning is done by sweeping it with a branch of *palāśa* (*Butea fondosa* according to the translation of J. Eggeling). The term for 'point of fixing' is *avasāna*.
74. Malamoud 1989 has shown very well that the act of setting a foundation, however it is conceived, is absent from the Veda, although it is very widespread and important in some civilisations.
75. *ŚB* VI.8.1.1.
76. Except the Upaniṣad. But it is legitimate to ask if the definition of Veda, which is of a later date than the gathering together of the Saṃhitās and the Brāhmaṇas, is not a little generous.
77. Ritual is often described as repeatedly doing a series of actions in an identical manner; whether in a religious context or not, a ritual can be described as a series of actions that are known in advance, are of different kinds and from which certain results are anticipated. This is valid only to a certain extent for Vedic rites. Indeed, if the texts say what is standard in a sacrifice (*prakṛti*), they also state all the particular circumstances (which cannot be known in advance) so that what is standard in a sacrifice must of necessity be particular and unlike all other sacrifices, past or to come, which nonetheless have the same name.
78. For example, *Baudhāyana Śrauta-Sūtra* II.2, *Āpastamba Śrauta-Sūtra* X.20.1-11, *Lāṭyāyana Śrauta-Sūtra* I.1.14-19, *ŚB* III.1.1, etc. The qualities that are needed for sacred space are listed in Caland and Henry 1906-7 and the few lines quoted above are not simply a summary of the original texts: there really is nothing more. Let us quote as an example *LŚS* I.1.14-15: *prāgudakpravaṇaṃ devayajanaṃ lomaśam avṛkṣaṃ samam/purastāc cāsyāpaḥ syuḥ* '(The ground) where the offering is made to the gods should be inclined towards the north-east; it should be well covered with grass, without trees, and even. To the east of this (ground), there should be some water.' The name of the ground is *devayajana*, a word that means 'offering to the gods'. This recalls the original sacrifice of Kurukṣetra and is a metaphor for the ground.

79. F. Staal tells the story of how, at the time of the *atirātrāgnicayana* held in 1975, he asked about the ground of the previous ceremony held in 1956. The villagers pointed vaguely in one direction and he finally managed to find the bricks of the fire altar amidst the plants that were slowly undermining the construction and reclaiming it. See in Staal 1983 the commentary on the photo vol. I, pp. 189-90.
80. According to *LŚS*. I.1.1.16: *tadabhāve mahāvṛkṣa udāpāno mahāpatho vā.*
81. *ŚB* XIII.2.4.2.
82. Minard 1956: 146 n. 350b says that the best equivalent term to *adhvaryu* would therefore be 'acolyte' (αχολουθοσ 'companion on the road, follower, servant': χελευθοσ 'road, path'). But the word has unfortunate associations.
83. There are other procedures where a concern not to cut-off what is inside from what is outside can be seen. For example (*AiB* VI.3) the officiant *subrahmaṇya* proclaims the text (*subrahmaṇyā*) on the *utkara* 'the reject', inviting gods and brāhmins to come to the ground where the sacrifice will be held and to take their place there. The question needs to be asked how the work of the *subrahmaṇya* on the outside can have an effect on the inside.
84. The word means at least a community, a settled village at most. The following passage is often quoted *ápaśyaṃ grā́maṃ váhamānam ārā́t* (*ṚS* X.27.19a) 'Far off I see the *grāma* on the move'.
85. *ŚB* I.2.5.7.
86. *ĀpŚS* X.3.3.
87. For example *ágne náya supáthā rāyé asmā́n víśvāni deva vayúnāni vidvā́n* 'O Agni, lead us by the right path to riches, god who knows all the roads' (*ṚS* I.189.1ab). We can certainly understand that the roads and paths are metaphors but in this hymn and in others the theme of a journey is sufficiently strong for us to consider that, if the words are used metaphorically, this meaning has been added to the primary meaning.
88. The east is linked to Indra and it is the direction of sovereignty. When the Vedic Devas came to be only secondary gods in Hinduism, it is noteworthy that some of them (Indra, Varuṇa, Yama) remained primarily *lokapāla* 'guardians of the worlds'.
89. The Devas of the Veda are neither omnipotent nor omniscient: they must discover *yajña*. They either discover ritual or they learn its missing parts from a third party (the *ṛṣis*). The *yajña* has no other purpose

but to allow them to gain access to heaven and to ensure that they are pre-eminent there.

90. I use the version of the *Taittirīya-Brāhmaṇa* (I.1.4, 28), pp. 26-7 of the A.M. Sastri edition, Motilal Banarsidass, rpt. 1985.

91. The root *TAN-* also expresses the activity of weaving. The chariot and weaving are the two daily technical activities that the Veda refers to and they provide a large number of its metaphors. Following the important work by Silburn 1955, there is a tendency today to over-estimate the importance of this root *TAN-*. When you study the texts, you are lead to conclude that there is no single word that expresses the act of sacrificing in its totality and without using a metaphor. In the word of Haudry 1975: 344, sacrificial actions are a 'concluding'. The absence of a single word to express what is essential in the Brāhmaṇas means that language becomes highly inflated. Ritual activity is expressed primarily by roots that indicate one part of a rite and these words are very specialized: *HU-* is pouring the oblation; *YAJ-* is paying homage (to a god), etc. There is another option and that is using a metaphor. In addition to *TAN-* there are many other possibilities (*DHĀ-*, *BUDH-*, *VIDH-*, etc.). Moreover this lack of a single word shows that the Vedic ritual was not historically an activity of primary importance for the people who devised it. This is what Haudry, loc. cit., thought and it is a matter for further discussion.

92. The difference in the order in the text in which sacrificial hearths were laid out is used mainly to justify the immortal status of one group and the mortal status of another.

93. Where they find their *dhāman*.

94. The great gods of Hinduism who aspire to be universal visit places and live in places that become temples and also the capitals of a dharmic land. The same is true for regional deities. We know that Hindu gods have a tendency to adopt the practices of the community that venerates them. So the 'Sanskrit' gods of vegetarian communities are themselves likely to be vegetarian, etc. However, it is remarkable that the Vedic Devas did not become the great gods of Hinduism (with the exception of Viṣṇu) and it is possible that the mobility of the Vedic gods and the fact that they were not fixed in the locations and lands of 'Indian' society might have counted against them. On the other hand we know that some local deities are Asuras who have been converted.

95. See Malamoud 1989.

96. *TB* III.11.8 and in the *Kaṭha Upaniṣad* tells the legend.

97. Here again a comparison between Vedic texts and later texts shows a complete turn-around of the practices and values on which the former were founded. Thus in the *Mahābhārata*, one of the main texts on which Hinduism is founded, when Yayāti falls from Heaven and Aṣṭakas engages him in conversation, he asks (*MBh* V.119.15; 4078): *ko bhavān kasya vā bandhur deśasya nagarasya vā* 'Who are you? Of what race, from which country, from which town? Are you a Yakṣa, a Deva, a Gandharva, a Rākṣasa?' Henceforth you are defined by name, ancestry and place.

98. Although his father is unknown, the young boy is initiated as a Brāhman. We see that in this story you can acquire the status of a Brāhman by birth (and this seems to be the norm) and also by merit. This is not so great a problem that the text needs to insist on the point, but it seems already at this time to be sufficiently unusual that the text makes a note of it.

99. In any case it is a difficult word associated with *svadhā* and more generally with the root *DHĀ-* which is virtually an institution in the Veda. On *dhāman*, in addition to Gonda 1967, the following analyses can be consulted: Renou 1939 (reprinted Renou 1997, vol. I, pp. 199-200) and the article *dhāman* in Renou 1958, pp. 18-20. It is possible that the term *dhāsyu* which appears in only three hymns of the *AS* (II.1.4, IV.1.2 and V.1.2) can be analysed as a desiderative of *DHĀ-*, as L. Renou suggested to L. Silburn as recorded by the latter (n. 4, p. 45 of Silburn 1955). Even if *dhāsyu* is usually associated with *dhāsi* 'milk', the link between the two is easily made in the first stanzas of the hymn *AS* V.1 which can be seen as a variation on this root *DHĀ-*. On *dhāsi* see Janert 1956: 12 and Krick, *WZKSA*, XVI, p. 36.

100. References to *antarvedī* in the Brāhmaṇas can be found in the standard indices which provide what we hope is a complete list. Let us refer to *AiB* VI.3.2. The commentator Cakrapāṇidatta and *CS*, Indriya I.5, refer to the *antarvedī* as the name of a region as an example of *deśa*; the word is quoted in order to define *prakṛti* 'the standard' or 'original constitution'. Among his six elements, there is the *deśa*, 'the country' or 'region', says Caraka who lived before our era but the text was reworked after his death. Cakrapāṇidatta (XI c) gives standard examples in each category (brāhmans for *jāti*, etc.). With reference to the *antarvedīvāsin*, we see that they live in the purest of regions. This reminds us of course of the Manu's sociological geography of Manu (*MDhŚ*. II.17-22); but Āryāvarta has been replaced by the Doāb.

101. This can be compared with Lohengrin, Mélusine, etc. In the *ŚB* XI.5 version, Purūravas promises that he will not let Urvaśī see him naked. The Gandharva lay a trap so that Urvaśī will come back to them. While Purūravas gets up during the night to catch a ram that has been stolen by the Gandharvas, and of which he is very fond, the latter create lightning so that Urvaśī sees him naked, and she becomes invisible to Purūravas.
102. A translation can be found in Renou 1956b: 105-8.
103. He states that the poem of the *Ṛk Saṃhitā* of which he quotes five stanzas has fifteen stanzas. However the *sūkta* *ṚS* X.95 as we know it today has eighteen. Since the time of the *Śatapatha Brāhmaṇa*, it seems that a *apauruṣeya*, or non-human, work has grown by a few lines!
104. In the myths and legends of the Saṃhitā and to a lesser extent in the Brāhmaṇas we hear only one part of the myth. Thus in the story of Yama and Yamī (*ṚS* X.10), we hear Yama refuse to consummate an incestuous relationship with his sister Yamī. Nevertheless, elsewhere, Yama must have succumbed to her advances.
105. Generically by Purāṇa, 'ancients', we mean a collection of texts composed in the first millennium AD in a Sanskrit that is often lax. It contains mythological stories and the subject matter of the religion of the time. At times short, more technical, treatises are included (on grammar, lexicology, metre, etc.) which together comprise a work of reference for an 'honest brāhmin'. The major works include the *Vāyu*, *Matsya*, *Vāmana*, *Padma*, and the *Bhāgavata Purāṇas*. It is also referred to in the *Mahābhārata* and alluded to in the *Rāmāyaṇa* (III.48); references in V. Mani 1984. The *Vikramorvaśī*, Kālidāsa's play, should also be included.
106. Minard 1956: 327, § 888.
107. There is an impressive number of books dedicated to 'Vedic society' despite an almost total absence of evidence other than the Veda itself, and this continues to astonish me. In general contemporary Indian writers have a tendency to question the pastoral and nomadic aspects of Vedic society and emphasize quite rightly that in the *Ṛgveda* there is a vocabulary for fields and houses (an example is Nandi 2001: 32). They treat the Veda as indigenous to India and question its foreign origins. Authors who are not academics are more direct. One can read on this topic Kasyap 1998: 906-44, and especially the para. 941-3 'Date of the Rig-Veda': 'The motivation for the British administrators in India to include the invasion theory . . . is clear.

Indians who descended from the Aryans should not complain against the British rule since they themselves are immigrants and hence have no more right than the British to rule India.' 'The invasion is a myth propagated by historians'.

108. This phenomenon can be seen in our languages: in French it is still said 'dresser la table', but since the XVIII c. tables have remained erect and do not need to be 'dressées' or erected. For a long time we said 'remonter sa montre' as we used to raise (the weights of) a grandfather clock.

109. Thus in *avasānaṃ samaṃ samūlam*: 'The terrain (where the new house is to be built) is flat and provided with plants' (*Vārāhagṛhyapuruṣa*, section XIV, first sentence).

110. For more information on this question, we refer readers to the justly famous work by Silburn 1955.

REFERENCES

Angot, M., 2006. 'L'errance des dieux, l'erreur des Asura et la terre des hommes. Remarques sur l'opposition entre les lieux et l'espace dans la littérature védique', in *Studia Asiatica*, VII, no. 1, pp. 17-64.

Benveniste, É. and L. Renou, 1934. *Vṛtra et vṛthragna. Étude de mythologie indo-iranienne*, Paris: Cahiers de la Société Asiatique III.

Biardeau, M., 1981. 'Gaṅgā/Yamunā, la rivière du salut et celle des origines', in *Dictionnaire des mythologies*, Paris: Flammarion, pp. 442-4.

Colas, Gérard, 2006 : 'Jalons pour une histoire des conceptions indiennes de *yaja.*', in *Rites hindous, transferts et transformations*, ed. par G. Colas et G. Tarabout, collection Puruṣārtha no. 25, Paris: Éditions de l'école pratique des hautes études en sciences sociales, pp. 343-87.

Caland, W. and V. Henry, 1907. *L'agniṣṭoma, Description complète de la forme normale du sacrifice de soma dans le culte védique*, Paris: E. Leroux.

Dumezil, G., 1971. *Mythe et épopée* II, Paris: Gallimard.

Eggeling, J., 1882-1900. *The Śatapatha Brāhmaṇa According to the Text of the Mādhyandina School* (Sacred Books of the East), Oxford University Press.

Filliozat, J., 1975. *La doctrine classique de la médecine indienne*, Paris: École Française d'Extrême-Orient.

Fussman, G., 1986. 'Histoire du monde indien: La notion d'unité indienne dans l'antiquité. II. Les sources indiennes', in *Annuaire du Collège de France 1985-1986. Résumé des cours et des travaux*, Paris, Collège de France, pp. 637-46.

———, 1987. 'Histoire du monde indien: La notion d'unité indienne dans l'Antiquité. III. Les populations indiennes dans les textes bouddhiques et épiques. Āryas et Mlecchas', in *Annuaire du Collège de France 1986-1987. Résumé des cours et des travaux*, Paris, Collège de France, pp. 529-32.

Geldner, K.F., 1951: *Der Rig Veda aus dem Sanskrit ins Deutsche übersetz*, 3 vols., Cambridge (Mass.), HOS 33, 34, 35.

———, 2003: *Der Rig Veda aus dem Sanskrit ins Deutsche übersetzt mit einem laufenden Kommentar*. Cambridge (Mass.), HOS 63.

Gonda, J., 1957. 'The Vedic Concept of *Aṃhas*', *Indo-Iranian Journal*, I, pp. 33-60.

———, 1966. *Loka: World and Heaven in the Veda*, Amsterdam: New Holland.

———, 1967. *The Meaning of the Sanskrit Term Dhāman*, Amsterdam, Noord-Hollandsche Uitgevers Maatschappij (Verh. Kon. Ned. Wet. Letterkunde LXXIII, no. 2), 1967.

———, 1980, *Vedic Ritual: The Non-Solemn Rites* (Handbuch der Orientalistik. Zweite Abteilung. Indien. Vierter Band: Religionen. Erster Abschnitt. Vedic Ritual), Leiden-Köln: E. J. Brill.

Hale, W.E., 1986. *Asura in Early Vedic Religion*, Delhi: Motilal Banarsidass.

Haudry, J., 1975. *L'emploi des cas en védique L'emploi des cas en védique. Introduction à l'étude des cas en indo-européen*. Lyon: L'Hermès. (Collection Les Hommes et les Lettres).

Heesterman, J.C., 1957. *The Ancient Indian Royal Consecration: The Rājasūya Described According to the Yajus Texts and Annotated*, The Hague: Mouton.

Henry, V., 1892-6. *Les livres VII à XII de l'Atharva-Veda*, Paris.

Hopkins, E.W., 1912. 'The Sacred Rivers of India', in *Studies in the History of Religions Presented to C.H. Toy*. ed. D.G. Lyon and G.F. Moore, New York.

Janert, J.L., 1956. *Sinn und Bedeutung des Wortes dhāsi und seiner Belegstellen im Rigveda und Awesta*, Wiesbaden: Otto Harrassowitz (Göttinger Asiatische Forschungen 7).

Kasyap, R.L., 1998. 'Introductory Essay on Rig Veda', in *Rigveda Saṃhitā*, Bangalore, Sri Aurobindo Kapali Sastry Insitute of Vedic Culture.

Khan, M.I., 1978. *Sarasvatī in Sanskrit Literature*, Ghaziabad: Crescent Pub. House.

Krick, H., 1982. *Das Ritual der Feuergründung*, Wien: Österreichische Akademie der Wissenschaften.

Lévi, S., 1898 (2003). *La doctrine du sacrifice dans les Brahmanas*, with a preface of L. Renou (reprint of the 2nd edn., 1966), and with a postface of C. Malamoud. Turnhout: Brepols ('Bibliothèque de l'École des hautes études, Sciences religieuses' 118).

Lüders, H., 1951, 1959. *Varuṇa*, Göttingen: Vandenhoeck & Ruprecht. (I. *Varuṇa und die Wasser*, 1951; II. *Varuṇa und das Ṛta*, 1959).

Macdonell, A.A. and A.B. Keith, 1912. *Vedic Index of Names and Subjects*, Oxford (rpt. Motilal Banarsidass, 2 vols. 1982).

Malamoud, Ch., 1989. 'Village et forêt dans l'idéologie de l'Inde brāhmanique', in *Cuire le monde. Rite et pensée dans l'Inde ancienne*, Paris: Éditions La découverte, pp. 93-114.

———, 1990. 'Sans lieu ni date. Note sur l'absence de fondation dans l'Inde védique', in *Tracés de fondation*, sous la direction de M. Detienne, Louvain-Paris, pp. 184-91.

———, 1999. 'Les morts' in *Le fait d'analyse*, nouvelle série, no. 2.

Mani, V., 1984. *Purāṇic Encyclopaedia: A Comprehensive Dictionary with Special Reference to the Epic and Purāṇic Literature*, Delhi: Motilal Banarsidass.

Minard, A., I: 1949, II: 1956. *Trois Énigmes sur les Cent Chemins. Recherches sur le Śatapatha-Brāhmaṇa*. I Paris: Les Belles Lettres, II Paris: De Boccard II.

Nandi, R.N., 2001. *Aryans Revisited*, New Delhi: Munshiram Manoharlal.

Oldenberg, H., 1919. *Die Weltanschauung des Brāhmaṇa-texte*, Göttingen : Vandenhoecke und Ruprecht.

Ranade, H.G., 1998. *Lāṭyāyana Śrauta-Sūtra*, critically edited and translated, Delhi: Indira Gandhi National Centre for the Arts and Motilal Banarsidass.

Renou, L., 1939. 'Les éléments védiques dans le sanskrit classique', *JA* 231: 321-403.

———, 1942. *Terminologie grammaticale du sanskrit*. Paris: Champion, 3 vols. (Bibliothèque de l'École des Hautes Études, Sciences historiques et philologiques, fasc. 280, 281 and 282).

———, 1948. *Kauṣītaki Upaniṣad publiée et traduite*. Paris: Librairie d'Amérique et d'Orient Adrien-Maisonneuve (Coll. Les Upanishad VI).

———, 1954. *Vocabulaire du rituel védique*, Paris: C. Klincksieck.

———, 1955. 'Védique Nírṛti', in *S.K. Chatterjee Commemoration Volume*, Poona, pp. 11-15.

———, 1956a. *Études védiques et pāṇinéennes* II. Paris: Institut de Civilisation Indienne.

———, 1956b. *Hymnes spéculatifs du Veda*, Paris, Gallimard (Coll. 'Connaissance de l'Orient').

———, 1958. *Études sur le vocabulaire du Ṛg-Veda*. Première série, Pondichéry, Publications de l'IFI, no. 8.

———, 1965. *Études védiques et pāṇinéennes* XIV. Paris: Institut de Civilisation Indienne.

———, 1997. *Louis Renou. Choix d'études indiennes*, Paris: École Française d'Extrême-Orient.

Roesler, U., 1997. *Licht und Leuchten im Ṛgveda. Untersuchungen zum Wortfeld des Leuchtens und zur Bedeutung des Lichts*, Swisstal-Odendorf.

Rolland, P., 1975. *Compléments au rituel védique. La Vārāhagṛhyapuruṣa*, Éditions de l'Université de Provence.

Sergent, B., 1997. *Genèse de l'Inde*, Paris: Payot.

Shrava, S., 1977. *A Comprehensive History of Vedic Literature. Brāhmaṇa and Āraṇyaka Works*, Delhi: Pranava Prakashan.

Silburn, L., 1955. *Instant et Cause. Le discontinu dans la pensée philosophique de l'Inde*, Paris: Vrin.

Staal, F. et al., 1983. *Agni: The Vedic Ritual of the Fire Altar*, 2 vols., Berkeley: Asian Humanities Press.

Vassilkov, Y., 2002. 'Indian Practice of Pilgrimage and the Growth of the Mahābhārata', in *Stages and Transitions: Temporal and Historic Frameworks in Epic and Purāṇic Literature*, Croatian Academy of Science and Arts, ed. Mary Brockington, Zagreb.

Verpoorten, J.-M., 1977a. 'Unité et distinction dans les spéculations rituelles védiques', *Archiv für Begriffsgeschichte* XXI, I, pp. 59-85.

———, 1977b. *L'ordre des mots dans l'Aitareya-Brāhmaṇa*, Paris, Les Belles Lettres.

Whitney, D.W., 1905. *Atharva veda Saṃhitā*. Harvard: Harvard Oriental Series VII & VIII.

Witzel, M., 1984. 'Sur le chemin du ciel', BEI 2 (1984), 213-79.

———, 1987. 'On the Localisation of Vedic Texts and Schools (Materials on Vedic Śākhās, 7)', in G. Pollet (ed.), *Professor P.H.L. Eggermont Jubilee Volume: India and the Ancient World: History, Trade and Culture before A.D. 650*, Leuven (Orientalia Lovaniensia Analecteta, 25; Department Oriëntalistiek), pp. 173-213.

———, 1989. 'The Realm of the Kurus: Origins and Development of the First State in India", *Nihon Minami Ajia Gakkai Zenkoku Taikai, Hokoku Yoshi* (Actes du Congrès de l'Association japonaise des études sud-asiatiques), Kyoto.

2

Images and Territory of Gods: From Precepts to Epigraphs

GÉRARD COLAS

This paper will use Sanskrit documentation as the basis for exploring the relation between images of Hindu deities and the territory associated with them. At first sight, the textual approach, with regard to ancient India, seems ill equipped to explore the concrete aspects of this relation: it is scarce, ideologically limited, and often abstract. But the direct use of such documentation has the advantage of also directly introducing an ancient point of view, without the filter of an already established historiographical perspective. This inquiry will mainly be confined to two kinds of documents: several Sanskrit texts on rites and their exegesis, and a few selected inscriptions. I hope to illustrate how the joint use of these two kinds of sources can help diversify the approach to such topics as that of the present volume.

While these documents clearly point to a relation between deity and territory, they scarcely explain its nature in scholarly terms. This theological, or, more generally speaking, theoretical want of definition seems to stem, on the one hand, from the lack of an admittedly universal theological characterization of the divine person, and, on the other hand, from the difficulty in clarifying the relation between the deity, his/her material support (image or other), and the local environment. Indian classical theological and philosophical systems (which will not be dealt with here,[1] except for a brief exposition of Śabara's view) provide various definitions of the divine. They rarely examine the relation of the deity with its material substratum, and still less with its earthly abodes. Indian law dwelt on the question of the deity as an owner,[2] but did so from an almost purely juridical point of view, an aspect that will only be mentioned briefly here. The views of the temple priests will be examined at more length (through the example of the Vaikhānasas) since their manuals record a greater concern about the relation between the deity-image and his/her fields and the territory surrounding the temple. However, the way of reasoning of these manuals was situated on the border between devotion and ritual logic and remained non-systematized. Epigraphic documents, on the other hand, did not aim at elucidating the relationship between deities and territory. But a close examination of a few selected inscriptions will show that epigraphy can help in analysing how this relationship was built and regulated in the past practice of local or regional Indian societies.

The texts and inscriptions considered here speak either of images or of deities (or Buddha or Bodhisattvas) implicitly identified with images. Before going any further, we must solve the initial problem of deciding what generic name we should give to these images, since they are considered (in the limited context of the present study)[3] as incarnating or being intimately associated with a divine or Buddhist personality or presence. Such Indian terms as *arcāvatāra* and *svarūpa*[4] refer to specific doctrines and historical contexts, and therefore can hardly be used in a universally accepted sense. 'Idol' has pejorative connotations in Christian tradition. Its use would need numerous theoretical precautions. 'Icon' would inscribe the concrete image in the already fixed pattern of a relationship between representation and represented. In this paper, I shall therefore use the compound names 'deity-image' and 'Buddha-/Bodhisattva-image', the meaning of which we take to include non-anthropomorphic representation of deities or Buddha or Bodhisattvas (stones and rocks, for instance).[5] Since this paper only studies concrete 'deity-images', etc., it will not associate these terms with purely psychic representations.

Before considering the question in relation to concrete images properly speaking, we will briefly explore the Vedic context, where the material representation of gods is almost absent. There, gods are essentially mobile beings and their association with any specific earthly territory is difficult to determine. As we shall see, later classical Indian literature, by contrast, associated deities with specific geographical perceptions and with particular kingdoms. In the fourth-fifth century, Śabara, an author of Vedic ritual exegesis, minimized the literal interpretation of the deity as a landowner, perhaps partly in reaction to such ideas. At the same time, the epigraphy of his period (Buddhist as well as Hindu) displayed a contradictory tendency. Several centuries later, the temple-manuals (at least those of the Vaikhānasa priests), prescribed the gift of lands to temple-priests and obviously preferred it to the notion of landownership by deities. One of these texts, which may post-date the thirteenth century, records the epigraphic phraseology, thereby helping us to compare it with the priestly presentation.

THE ESSENTIAL MOBILITY OF GODS IN THE VEDIC TEXTS

The most ancient Sanskrit texts, which are Vedic, do not examine the question of the relation of a deity-image with a territory. One of the main reasons for this is that the Vedic god is not concretely represented. It is, however, essential to briefly examine this ancient point of view, because it durably conditioned later debates.

To propose any certain absolute chronology of the so-called 'Vedic' corpus remains impossible today.[6] The Vedic corpus, in the strictest sense, contains only the hymns of the four well-known collections, the *Ṛg-*, *Yajur-*, *Sāma-* and *Atharva-vedas*. The hymns of the oldest of these collections, the *Ṛgveda*, that is, the *Ṛk Saṃhitā*, could have been 'compiled between 1200 and 800 before our era'.[7] The definition of the Vedic corpus has often been extended to include other, later texts. Such a broadened definition generally includes the Brāhmaṇas, the Āraṇyakas, and the great classical Upaniṣads, these often being dated around 500 BC.[8]

The *Ṛk Saṃhitā* testifies to the nomadic existence that Indo-European tribes, who had come from the Eurasian steppes, led in the Indian subcontinent. The successive steps in building a hut, conjectured from the *Ṛk Saṃhitā*, are identical with those for building the yurt of Turks and Mongols: raising the structure, stowing it, trimming the cover on it, preparing an entry, fixing a ground sheet; each of these steps being identified in the *Ṛk Saṃhitā* with a cosmic phase (Christol 1987). Vedic texts in general (and not only the *Ṛk Saṃhitā*) perpetuate the ideals of a society 'constantly on the move as may be expected of cattle-loving warriors for whom the cow as well as the chariot are the epitome of wealth and prestige' (Heesterman 1993: 123). In such a society despising sedentary life, the values of the adventurers probably dominated over those of the stability seekers. The term *grāma* referred to 'a trekking warrior band' in older Vedic texts (although it came to signify 'village settlement' in the more recent ones). This ancient nomadic existence was probably more than mere errantry. It perhaps consisted in a continuous expansion with the installation of colonies and the local development of arable land (for more details, see Heesterman 1993: 123-4). Rites were organized to the rhythm of tribal movements and the establishment of new settlements. Several rites needed expeditions. The site of certain sacrifices was temporary (ibid.: 127-8). Vedic gods participated in this ideology of movement. They are by nature moving deities, travelling in their chariots while their foes, the 'demons' (*asura*), probably non-Vedic Indian deities, remain sedentary at home (ibid.: 123; Macdonell 1897: 18). Vedic texts do not appear to systematically mention the possession of stable and defined territory by the gods. However, this does not mean that Vedic society never conceived certain gods as privileged users or rulers of particular places or areas.

The ancient Vedic rites, at least those that the extant texts describe, neither address nor use divine images.[9] Nor do we know whether the above-mentioned 'demons', in their non-Vedic surrounding, were represented as images. Though the Vedic gods are probably imageless, they are not bodiless: Vedic hymns attribute multiple and separable bodies to them and occasionally mention their heads, faces, eyes, clothes, etc. Endowed with brightness and power, gods are intimately associated with natural phenomena. Several of them are said to possess the shape of the universe (*viśvarūpa*) (Macdonell 1897: 15-18; Malamoud 1989b: 129). In fact, the physical definition of Vedic gods most often remains allusive and their anthropomorphism uncertain. However, when Śabara, a specialist of Vedic exegesis in the fourth-fifth century, refutes the concept of the body of god in connection with his critique of landownership by deities, as we will see later, he probably does not conform faithfully to the ancient vision of the Vedic hymns.

SETTLED GODS AND TERRESTRIAL KINGDOMS

The Sanskrit texts that postdate the Upaniṣads (that is, the later texts of the Vedic corpus in a broad sense) mention the deity's territory as a kingdom. The kingdom of a god is often mentioned as being the universe, that is, a largely undefined and limitless space. But with the gradual recession of the Vedic conceptions, the god's kingdom is also made to conform to a terrestrial geography, which progressively gains both in steadiness and differentiation and whose final shapes were recorded in Purāṇas. We need to briefly outline this evolution. Instead of being so to say neutral, undifferentiated and open to conquest from any direction, space becomes stabilized and segmented, organizes itself and ranks its various quarters according to a cosmo-geography which progressively becomes prominent, the cosmo-geography of the Purāṇas. We cannot precisely date most of the Purāṇas, these collections of legends that were constantly being transformed and interpolated and that were intended for a wider public than the circle of the Brāhman specialists of the Veda. The Sanskrit language in which they are written is later than that of the Vedic corpus. Large portions of several ancient Purāṇas were probably completed before our era and Vārāṇasī could have been the site in which some of them were composed (L. Renou, J. Filliozat et al. 1985a: 416). Purāṇas often function as a sort of encyclopaedia. Their cosmo-geography includes islands of continental size, the island of mankind being divided into several regions and containing mountains. A description of this varied cosmo-geography would not be useful here.[10] Its geographical dimension represents a systematic attempt at mapping the earth, however different it may be from the modern scientific approach.

The mapping which early Purāṇas recorded cannot be precisely dated, but it could correspond to the growth of urbanization and, simultaneously, the strengthening of the road-network in the Indian subcontinent in the late first millennium BC (Ghosh 1973; Thapar 1974: 52, 150). During the third-second century, in the northern part of the subcontinent, for instance, Mathurā (situated to the south of the present Delhi) was a commercial and pilgrimage centre linked by roadways to Taxila in the north-west and to Kauśāmbī to its south-east; another road linked Kauśāmbī to Ujjayinī in the south (Meth Srinivasan 1997: 219). Around the beginning of our era, Vārāṇasī was another important religious centre, Vedic, Hindu and (in Sarnath) Buddhist.[11] Today, it is impossible to evaluate how far the development of these prestigious centres of pilgrimage and intellectual and commercial exchange contributed to the crystallization of the non-Vedic spatial conception recorded in Purāṇas, but the idea that the concrete strengthening of the road network stimulated the mapping could be an acceptable working hypothesis.

In the Sanskrit literature composed at that time, the ideals of village and town settlements replaced those of the nomadic group.[12] The spirit of conquest was concentrated in the figure of the king. In religion, such epithets as 'lord of the world'(*jagannātha*) for Viṣṇu, and 'master of the universe' (*sarveśvara*) for Śiva, for instance, reflect, at the divine level, the human ideal of political domination embedded in the title of Universal Monarch (*cakravartin*), that is to say, a monarch whose reign extends over the whole earth. Similar conceptions already existed in Vedic texts, but post-Vedic literature considerably reinforced and particularized the notion of universal sovereignty (Renou, Filliozat et al., 1985a: 375-6, 196). In Buddhism, the Universal Monarch is expected to act according to the Order (*dhamma*, *dharma*) and takes form like a 'lay double of Buddha' (my translation).[13] The king seeks to incarnate the condition of a *bodhisattva*, that is, a being about to reach the state of Buddha and, much later, from the ninth-tenth century, he is even contemporarily identified as a *bodhisattva* in Ceylon (Lingat 1989: 34, 136).

Various kinds of transactions between human monarchs and supra-human beings (gods or Buddha) are also conducted in relation to particular regional kingdoms. For instance, a king may institute a god as the owner of his kingdom. Such a conception is testified in AD 200-300 according to a passage in the *Nārāyaṇīyaparvan*[14] that describes the domestic rites and the behaviour of King Uparicara Vasu, he considers his kingdom and possessions as belonging to

Nārāyaṇa (Viṣṇu). Such abandonment of his kingdom by a monarch in favour of a god has Buddhist counterparts (unless the original idea itself comes from Buddhism). The *Mahāvaṃsa*, chronicles of the Ceylonese kingship, which may have been composed at the end of the fifth or the beginning of the sixth century (Lingat 1989: 69), relates events that occurred between the fifth century BC and the first half of the fourth century AD. It records how a statue of Buddha or his relics were given a kingdom or, again, how a king gave himself to Buddhist relics or even granted Buddha a royal status (Lingat 1989: 118-19). The gift of a kingdom to a Buddhist assembly and its subsequent repurchase by the monarch illustrate a more complex negotiation: monarchs ritually gave their kingdom to Buddhist monks, who in turn authorized them to buy it back 'at a fair estimation' (Derrett 1977: [87], n. 318). The *Aśokāvadāna* (perhaps written in the second century AD) relates a similar legend (the historical reality of which cannot be verified): the emperor Aśoka, who ruled in the third century BC and converted to Buddhism, is said to have given his own person, his wives, his ministers and his son to an assembly of Buddhist religious persons and then bought them back for the sum of 4,00,000 golden coins.[15] These facts can be interpreted in two ways, according to Lingat: either the king, owner of the land, is only its temporal ruler, or 'he renounces his sovereignty on the island [of Ceylon] in favour of Buddha . . . , the whole country is considered as being under the law of the *dhamma* [i.e. the Buddhist Order]. He is, as Aśoka probably thought, the trustee of the *dhamma* whence he gets his authority'.

The conception of a kingdom or empire entirely dedicated to a deity (or Buddha in the case of Buddhism), with the human monarch being no more than its administrator, thrived in Indian history until at least the eighteenth century (Sontheimer 1964: 75-6; see also Toffin 1986). Today, the idea is still perpetuated by rites in the Indian Himalaya (Berti 2001: 36-8). The origin of such notions is sometimes associated with an unfortunate event.[16] Deity-images sometimes symbolize the king's authority, or may even be local substitutes of that authority, as is the case, for instance, in remote areas of the Indian Himalaya.

UNSUBSTANTIAL GODS AS FICTIVE OWNERS: THE PRO-VEDIC REACTION OF MĪMĀṂSĀ

Along with the development of the concept of kingdom as a divine (or Buddhist) territory, the concept of deity-image or Buddha/Bodhisattva-image as owner and user of lands and villages progressively gained importance in Indian society. We have already mentioned the gift of a kingdom to a 'statue' of Buddha (in a fifth-sixth century record of earlier facts) and we will later examine two epigraphic testimonies to this conception, but we must underscore the fact that it met with strong resistance in specific milieus. This conception was probably current enough in the fourth-fifth century for Śabara, a follower of the pro-Vedic doctrinal and ritualistic system of Mīmāṃsā, to refuse the literal acceptance of the idea of usage of a land or a village by gods. Although he does not explicitly mention divine images in this context, he is probably referring to donations of land to deity-images.

The school of Mīmāṃsā, or 'Reflection', 'Investigation', focuses on explaining the Vedic ritual action as expressed in Vedic texts. Being an exegesis of Vedic ritual treatises, it became a full-fledged philosophical school, whose followers are the Mīmāṃsakas. Its founding text is the *Mīmāṃsāsūtras*, attributed to Jaimini. Its original composition is of uncertain date, perhaps 450 BC, and its final form (according to modern researchers) is of various dates.[17] The earliest available commentary on the *Mīmāṃsāsūtras* is that of Śabara, an author generally placed in the second half of the fourth century or in the fifth century. Śabara's position on the use of land or villages by gods is important because of its date and also because of its influence on traditional Hindu law (*dharmaśāstra*), although that law may have contributed to a certain distortion in Śabara's point of view.

Śabara's position is developed in Chapter 9 (1, 6-10) of his commentary on the *Mīmāṃsāsūtras*.[18] Śabara's main aim is to show the secondary character of the deity in Vedic sacrifice. To this end, he seeks to demonstrate that the deity, being bodiless, cannot receive offerings and cannot grant the fruits of the sacrifice, as indicated by the fact that it does not make use of the villages and lands attributed to it. In this passage, Śabara makes a fundamental distinction between Vedic sacrifice (*yajña*) and worship (*pūjā*). We know that Vedic sacrifice gives a large role to fire oblations and does not include any concrete representation of gods (in its ancient descriptions at least). By contrast, worship consists in offerings presented to one or several gods, during which a material image may be used (see, for instance, Heesterman 1993: 87). Śabara does not explicitly mention any image, but we can reasonably assume that he includes them in his reasoning. He disagrees with the thesis of his opponent that sacrifice consists in the act of nourishing a deity and would be the equivalent of 'worship' (*pūjā*). For Śabara, the Vedic sacrifice mainly aims at obtaining a fruit, and not satisfying a deity. The deity, like any substance used during the sacrifice, is only a secondary element as regards this aim and the fruit does not come from the deity, but from an abstract principle, the *apūrva*, the 'un-preceded one'.

Since gods are bodiless, they cannot consume food offered to them. By his denial of the possession of a body by gods, Śabara in fact goes beyond the ideology of the ancient Vedic corpus, which depicts gods as possessing features of the human body, however vaguely. Mīmāṃsā attributes mere linguistic existence to the gods.[19] To a certain extent, this conception echoes the ancient Vedic idea that 'Vedic utterances form what is the most substantial, concrete and individualized in the bodies of the gods' (Malamoud 1989b: 271, my translation). But Mīmāṃsā takes this conception to an extreme degree of abstraction.

Most importantly for our present investigation, Śabara considers the ownership of territories and villages by gods (which he implicitly associates with *pūjā*) as a kind of collective fiction resulting from human convention. He explains this in the following way. Having declared that the deity does not consume food, he adds that it does not own anything, and consequently cannot dispense any gift (and so cannot provide the fruits of sacrifice). The expressions 'village of the god' (*devagrāma*) and 'territory of the god' (*devakṣetra*) cannot be taken literally. One should consider them as the result of a custom (*upacāra*), that is, as conventional statements,[20] since things only belong to a person insofar as he or she can make use (*viniyuj*) of them at will. Obviously (for Śabara), a deity cannot make use of a village or territory at will. The so-called possessions of a deity are in fact in the hands of the 'servants of the deity' (*devatāparicāraka*), also named 'servants of the god' (*devaparicāraka*). For reasons which would be too long to go into here, the identification of these 'servants' with temple-priests is plausible.[21]

Śabara's argumentation links deities' ownership of villages or territories with their possession of a body and with a ritual genre, *pūjā*, that is distinct from the Vedic sacrifice, *yajña*. His reasoning does not explicitly imply causality between the gods' possession of a body and their ownership of land. However, both the concepts are carefully disconnected from Vedic sacrifice and associated with the worship of gods and with temple-rites. For Śabara, the worship of gods, like the bodies and territorial possessions attributed to them in connection with worship, have no other basis than conventional use (which we can interpret as socio-ideological use) and do not correspond to any theological or metaphysical reality.

Śabara's position illustrates a puristic reaction, a desire to preserve Vedic ritual and a fixed formulaic heritage, to the extent of partly distorting the ancient Vedic ideology. Śabara aims to define an idealized conception of the Vedic sacrifice and to preserve it from any 'contamination' by worship of the *pūjā* type, directly offered to deities. In Śabara's time, the Vedic corpus (even in its broader sense) was long since completed. This completion had been followed by the composition of ritual manuals (named *Kalpa-sūtra*), which sought to fix the domestic and solemn rites of Vedic ascendancy, trying to prevent their evolution.[22] While 'Vedic' rites survived or began their decline, non-Vedic domestic and public image worship progressively gained ground in Brahmanical milieus. The influence of this worship threatened the formal integrity of 'Vedic' aniconic rites. Although this historical and textual phenomenon still needs an encompassing study, one can observe that late ritual texts claiming to be based on the Vedic corpus integrate image-worship,[23] and that the public worship of divine images includes elements drawn from Vedic rituals.[24]

As regards spatial notions, the concept of deity-images (and Buddha/Bodhisattva-images) as landowners (which appears in fourth-fifth-century inscriptions, as we will see) is in sharp contrast with the Vedic ideology. The Vedic gods, who were previously so conceited in their conquering nomadic spirit, progressively settled in sanctuaries, like the stay-at-home 'demons' whom they had so proudly despised in the past. If one leaves Viṣṇu and, perhaps, Śiva-Rudra,[25] most of those who were 'at the centre of the Vedic ritual—Indra, Agni, Prajāpati, Varuṇa, the Maruts, the Aśvins, and others—lost their dominant positions in the later orthopraxis', that is, in *pūjā* rituals, and 'were relegated to secondary functions' (F.M. Smith 1987: 3).

Distinguishing the Vedic sacrifice (*yajña*) from worship (*pūjā*), Śabara criticized the conception of gods as possessors of bodies (consuming offerings and giving ritual fruits) and owners of lands and villages. By denying gods a body (in contradiction with Vedic hymns), he removed all metaphysical foundation for any anthropomorphic representation of the deities (hence for temple images, which, however, he does not openly mention).[26] By reducing the concept of the divine use of lands and villages to their use by 'servants of the god', he reduced divine ownership to a mere fiction. This, however, does not mean that Śabara vehemently opposed that fiction. He considers worship as a current practice of the 'world' (*loka*), and there is nothing to indicate that he condemns the set of conventions connected with that practice. Three or four centuries later, Kumārila (seventh-eighth century), another prestigious Mīmāṃsaka master, accepted deity worship even more obviously, though ranking it as inferior to Vedic sacrifice. He observed that 'well educated people' (*śiṣṭa*) who perform Vedic rites also practise deity worship (Colas 2004: 155). It may be surmised that he implicitly recognized (as Śabara also probably did) the principle of donation of lands to a deity, more precisely to a deity-image, as an acceptable current socio-religious convention. However, at a different metaphysical level of reasoning, these Mīmāṃsaka masters maintained the thesis of the quasi-non-existence of the gods. Other Indian scholastic systems (which recognize the authority of the Veda) also criticized (more or less openly) the notion of a divine presence in images (although they did not reject the possession of bodies by the gods),[27] while epigraphy currently expressed the concept of the deity-image as a landowner.

GODS AS DONEES OF LANDS: THE PHRASEOLOGY OF TWO INSCRIPTIONS

Śabara's questions addressed a circumstance that was already current in his time: donations, more precisely land donations, to temple-deities. Today, this circumstance is well documented,[28] but its history still needs more elucidation. At the time of Śabara, that is, during the Gupta dynasty, from the fourth to the sixth century, inscriptions immortalize the pious acts of Gupta kings, important persons, ordinary devotees and guilds of craftsmen (*śreṇi*). These acts included the construction of temples,[29] the raising of posts (*dhvaja*)[30] or pillars (*stambha*, *yaṣṭi*),[31] the donation of villages to Brāhmans,[32] the making and installation of images of gods, Buddha, Bodhisattvas and Jain fordmakers (*tīrthaṃkara*),[33] with the aim of increasing the glory or merits of the founder or his parents or simply out of devotion (*bhakti*). These inscriptions also eulogize the donations of money or villages for keeping charity houses, maintaining Buddhist monks or keeping lamps.[34]

The earliest known epigraphic mentions of Buddha-images considered as landowners apparently date from the fourth or fifth century.[35] Other inscriptions of the same period (though slightly later) mention donations of lands and villages to deity-images.[36] Only a limited number of epigraphic collections have been examined for this paper, and it is possible that several inscriptions older than those mentioned here also contain this sort of mention.[37] However, it may be said that the conception of Buddha-images and deity-images as landowners was well-established in epigraphy in Śabara's time. Let us analyse how the concept of deity-image as donee of villages or lands appears in two inscriptions of the Gupta period, and what phraseology these inscriptions use.

The first inscription, engraved on a stone pillar at Bhitarī (present Uttar Pradesh) dates from the second half of the fifth century. It records the donation of a village to a religious image, or to the deity which this image represents or in which this deity incarnated, depending on the interpretation of the reader. Verse 10 of this inscription mentions that Skandagupta, a king of the Gupta dynasty, made (that is, had made by a craftsman) an image (*pratimā*) of Śārṅgin (an aspect of Viṣṇu), installed it or had it installed (*pratiṣṭhāpya*),[38] then endowed (*vidadh[e]*) it (the image or Śārṅgin?) with that village (*grāma*) (which can be located in the present Bhitarī or in its neighbourhood) for the increase of the merits of his father (*pituḥ pu[ṇ]yābhivṛddhaye*).[39]

Since the sentence does not include a demonstrative pronoun in feminine gender (for *pratimā*, the image) or in masculine (for Śārṅgin himself), the grammatical formulation of the inscription leaves it open to doubt whether the donee is the image or the god. However, this present-day question might be judged rather artificial. Or it might be surmised that such a type of document gathered a faithful assembly or the local society around a fairly ill-defined ideological notion; it was simply not the role of an epigraph to clarify the theological relation between god and image. The factual succession was: an image, that is, a specific object, is made, then (ritually) installed and it is thereafter not simply an empty representation, but a donee, that is, a person. The representation has become a deity-image after the installation.

The inscription does not provide details on the installation itself, which is signified by *pratiṣṭhāpya*. In other places, the verb *pratiṣṭhā* and its derivatives are used to qualify Skandagupta's actions: this monarch re-established (*pratiṣṭhāpya bhūyaḥ*) his family (verse 7), the prosperity of his family (verse 6); his government is well established (*supratiṣṭhitaśāsanaḥ*, verse 11). The general meaning of the verb *pratiṣṭhā* in the causative form, as describing a religious practice, does not seem far from this: to install, fix, place firmly an important or worshipful object. This meaning is well known from ancient inscriptions, where derived forms of the verb or equivalent Prakrit forms designate the placing of tablets of homage,[40] of Buddhist relics,[41] etc. One may assume that the term also designates a rite at the time of the epigraph (second half of the fifth century): the *Bṛhatsaṃhitā*, a text of the sixth century, in other words slightly later, describes the *pratiṣṭhāpana* (a substantive whose equivalent is *pratiṣṭhā*), that is to say ritual installation, of Hindu, Buddhist, and Jaina images, in its Chapter 60.[42]

The second inscription, which belongs to the same period[43] and is engraved on a copper plate, needs longer examination. Its content is particularly instructive, since its very structure and phraseology clearly relate the process which ends with making the divine person a landowner: it describes this process, mentions the individual founder, explains its own function as an inscription, and instructs the administrators in charge of guaranteeing the donation to respect it with devotion. The inscription dates from the reign of Viṣṇugupta (sixth century) and comes from the village of Dāmodarpur (in Bengal). The inscription shows two phraseological levels, which find their respective expression in each part of the inscription and correspond to two separate phases of the process of donation.

Let us read the inscription closely. The seal of this copper chart is that of the 'Administrative Board of Koṭivarṣa' (*koṭivarṣādhi-ṣṭhānādhi[karaṇa]*).[44] The first part of the inscription gives an account of the concrete project and spiritual aim of the donation, as well as of the preparatory administrative and financial negotiations. The reigning monarch is described as 'king of the earth'. The composition of the administrative board of the Koṭivarṣa district, which belongs to the Puṇḍravardhana province, is described. Lines 6-10 quote *verbatim* the official request of the future founder, Amṛtadeva. This donor mentions that the current price of uncultivated and tax-free land amounts to 3 *dīnāras* per *kulyavāpa* (a unit of area) and he asks the administrative board, in the Koṭivarṣa district, to give (after receiving from him the equivalent in *dīnāra* currency), '[some] plots of ground' (*kṣetrastokān*), the revenue from which will allow for repairs to the temple (*devakula*) of the god named Śvetavarāhasvāmin, and insure certain offerings on a regular basis in that temple. Amṛtadeva wishes to increase the merits (*puṇya*) of his mother through this donation and he requests that this donation be 'registered on a copper plate according to the Law of inalienable donation' (*apradādharmmeṇa tāmrapaṭṭikṛtya*).[45] Lines 10-13 observe, among other details, that there is no practical obstacle to the process, especially in the eyes of the District Governor (*viṣayapati*) Svayambhūdeva, after verification of the validity of the request by the 'Chief Record-Keeper' (*prathamapustapāla*) Naranandin and two other persons, Gōpadatta and Bhaṭanandin, who may be administrative officers.

The second part of the inscription (lines 14-19) follows as a consequence of the first part: Amṛtadeva gives 15 *dīnāras* to the administrative board, corresponding to 5 *kulyavāpas* of land, situated in four different places; these 5 *kulyavāpas* are 'given to the glorious Śvetavarāhasvāmin according to the Law of inalienable donation' (*apradādharmmeṇa bhaga[va]te śvetavarāhasvāmine śaśvatkālabhogyā dattāḥ*) 'for the (spiritual) benefit (*anugraheṇa*) of his (that is, Amṛtadeva's) mother'. The inscription adds: 'From now on, the (official) administrators (*saṃvyavahārin*)[46] will have to respect these (*kulyavāpas* of land) out of devotion to the god (*devabhakti*).'[47] Verses which have the value of general maxims then follow: execration for land robbers, spiritual rewards for land donors (lines 20-1), etc.

This inscription clearly expresses the concept of a deity-image as a person to whom one gives a land donation. It incidentally seems to confirm that the donation of the slightly older Bhitarī inscription was addressed to an image considered as a person, and not to a god situated apart from that image. The process recorded in the Dāmodarpur inscription in fact ends with (and includes) the making of that copper-plate inscription: we are thus made the almost direct spectators of the transition from the administrative and legal conditions of the donation to its regulated religious understanding.

In its first part, the inscription records the administrative approach to the object of the donation. The god Śvetavarāhasvāmin, 'Lord White-Boar' (almost certainly Viṣṇu's incarnation as a boar), whose sanctuary was (and still is) in all probability situated in eastern Nepal,[48] is not mentioned as a person. This does not mean that he was not considered as such.[49] But this first phase concentrates on the terms of the negotiation with the local political authority, the administrative board, whose agreement is a preliminary condition to the realization of the project and its official registration on a copper plate. This first phase is not only legal in character, but also political. The rather complicated form of the donation (the official donor seems in fact to be the administrative board to whom Amṛtadeva gives the monetary equivalent of the land) would, however, require a separate comparative study.

The second part deals with the realization of Amṛtadeva's project. It opens another, specifically religious, perspective on the donee as a divine person. At the end of the whole process, the donation is, so to say, sealed by devotion that the administration is bound to authenticate and practise. The inscription itself, which registers the whole process, is the concrete sign of its social and political legitimacy.

The mere testimony of this epigraph would be an insufficient basis to build a theory. Only an extensive enquiry into the phraseology of inscriptions would make it possible to define and organize in a historical perspective the various political, social, and religious circumstances of the rise of the concept of deity-image in epigraphy. In spite of the limitations of our investigation, the Dāmodarpur inscription starkly illuminates Śabara's position at about the same time. It illustrates the institutional constraints of constituting the deity-image as a landowner and the political and administrative establishment of this conception in a devotional context. The inscription shows a clear dichotomy between the preparatory phase of the donation, which is administrative, commercial and political, and the phase of realization, which is strictly religious and devotional. This dichotomy does not entail incompatibility, but it testifies to two successive and complementary levels of understanding. After the completion of the second phase, a return to a purely legal perspective, abstracted from devotion, would be difficult: the first phase has been, so to say, absorbed in the devotion which the epigraphic document prescribes. Although the process included a legal dimension, the divine person of the image, or the rock (according to Bhandarkar),[50] is, at the end of the process, not only a legal person, but much more than that.

One may speculate on the definition of the divine person in this inscription. One of its final sentences, 'From now on, the (official) administrators will have to respect these (*kulyavāpa-s* of land) out of devotion to the god (*devabhakti*)', indicates the conventional and rather coercive aspect of the association of devotion with these lands. This presentation does not seem so distant from Śabara's, although its does not show any theoretical point of view. On the basis of this example, the epigraphic conception of the god as an owner of lands and villages seems to rest on a common social assent, sustained by a devotion which is itself voluntarily supported by the political power. Having no precise definition, this conception probably accommodated varied and more or less literate (according to the devotees' points of view) concepts. Like the fourth-fifth inscriptions that mention Buddha-images,[51] those which, around the same period (*c.* AD 400), mention deity-images owning lands and villages were necessarily composed by literate men knowing Sanskrit and were meant for literate readership. They did not exclude the agreement of its writer and readers with a specific religious sect, or an adherence to any particular philosophical doctrine, but they did not require them. The devotional concept of divine person that the Dāmodarpur inscription illustrates could convey and address the points of view of both the 'masses'[52] and the abstract theorists ('théoriciens abstraits').

While this epigraphic conception could well embrace the 'popular' idea that the image is a living person endowed with senses,[53] it cannot be reduced to this. According to Sontheimer, 'the deity as symbolized or personified by the idol is real and is not only the depository of the right, but also the beneficiary' from the perspective of the 'average donor' (p. 97). But the very existence of this popular 'average donor', a sort of common denominator to all those who donate to deity-images, seems improbable. A traditional Indian scholar could at the same time claim 'erudite', or even iconophobic positions, and worship a divine image according to his personal education and his family culture. Doctrinal activity concentrating on specific intellectual objects and philosophical or other discussions does not prevent adhesion to beliefs that are outside the scope of scholastic discussions. As we have seen, the Mīmāṃsaka Śabara (in approximately the time of the Bhitarī and Dāmodarpur inscriptions), though an unyielding defender of the aniconic Vedic rites, considered the concept of a god as owner as a custom connected with the 'mundane' practice of the worship of the gods and, as such, probably an acceptable custom. Mīmāṃsā, more generally, does not view temple rites in a purely negative way, but accepts them as belonging to Smṛti (Colas 2004: 154-5). Therefore the thesis of a conflict between ancient Mīmāṃsā (as represented by Jaimini and Śabara) and an image worship that would have been 'popular' (Sontheimer 1964: 49-50) needs to be seriously reconsidered.

In the parallel field of Buddhism, the most important epigraphic documentation of the fourth-fifth century mentioning the conception of a Buddha as a person residing in a monastery comes precisely from two sites which were also, during the same period, major sites of Buddhist scholasticism, as has been stressed by Schopen (1997: 277).

These inscriptions thus reflect a socially shared ideology of divine images and objects (rock or other) considered as persons. This indefinite notion could accommodate various types of devotion from believers whose individual ideas about images could contrast sharply, including followers of Mīmāṃsā who were highly sceptical about divine images at the philosophical level. In such circumstances, inscriptions fulfilled an essential function: they gave official expression to the political management of the devotion for divine representations that were donees of villages and lands. At the same time, the inscriptions literally inscribed devotion in a net of legal and political restrictions and legitimated this controlled devotion with the guarantee of the administration.

In contrast with the all-accommodating epigraphic concept of deity-image, the strictly legal perspective, that of traditional Hindu law, the Dharmaśāstra, provided only a reductive, non-devotional approach.[54] This approach was in no way appropriate for the definition of a divine personality, or, more precisely, a divine intelligence, in relation with ownership. No universally accepted legal doctrine arose from the debates of the nineteenth and twentieth-century courts of justice, whose judgements show various contrasting positions. Thus Rāmajaya Tarkālaṅkāra, a paṇḍit of the beginning of the nineteenth century, who had been influenced by the juridical and legal British environment, extended to deities the appraisal generally applied to minors and mentally deranged people: they possess a spark of intelligence, hence the capacity of being owners (Derrett 1977: [119]). On the contrary, according to Annoussamy, who writes on the basis of twentieth century judgements that have the value of case laws, 'although the idol acts through the intermediary of an agent, it is neither a perpetual minor nor an incapable person'.[55]

Traditional Hindu law often quotes Mīmāṃsā as its authority, especially on the subject of ownership by deity-images. It would be worth researching when this practice started and how it quotes the ancient Mīmāṃsā authorities, for, as we have observed above, neither Śabara nor Kumārila (seventh-eighth century) showed any fundamental hostility to the worship of the gods or to ownership by deities. Medhātithi, an author of traditional law of around the early ninth century,[56] does not reject the notion of ownership by deities. According to him, while this concept cannot be accepted literally, it can be accepted on a secondary level of meaning (Sontheimer 1964: 65). The deity-image or Buddha-image as owner of land and villages, as seen through epigraphy, could not be reduced to the legal personality of traditional Hindu law. This conception was not exclusively popular; it was also current among the literate and Sanskrit-reading milieus. Confirmed by the local political authority, it extended far beyond the legal sphere to establish itself in a devotion that was shared and agreed upon by the main actors in society. However, this general consensus was established at the cost of precision in the definition of the divine person: it corresponded to an ideology accepted by a large number of people rather than to a theoretical concept.

THE IMAGE AND ITS SANCTUARY IN THE PRIESTLY MANUALS

Śabara mentioned that the 'servants of the deity' were the real users of the properties given to that deity, these 'servants' probably being the temple priests. So we shall now turn towards priestly manuals to examine whether the concept of deity-image as donee of lands was defined more precisely in these texts than in inscriptions. We shall refer to the ancient temple-ritual corpus of the Vaiṣṇava Vaikhānasa tradition (written between the ninth and the thirteenth century for most of its texts). It postdates Śabara by at least four centuries, but has the advantage of showing a well-established and routine picture of the temple rites.

The Vaikhānasa manuals are written in an often simple and monotonous Sanskrit. For some of the assertions they contain, it is difficult to decide whether these should be considered as literary exaggerations, as part of an ideology or as the product of a real belief. This is especially the case when the relationship between the temple god and the priests is at stake, as we will see.[57] The idea of a specific relationship between a deity-image and a bounded territory appears only in a fragmentary and indirect manner. The Vaikhānasa manuals clarify the conditions that are favourable to the installation of a new image in a new temple. For this purpose, they provide elements of geomancy, instructions on city and village plans, and on the place in them of the sanctuaries of various gods: Viṣṇu (privileged by the Vaikhānasas) and deities around him. They also describe the spatial relationship between the plan of the future temple and the 'man of the site' (*vāstupuruṣa*) who is situated below the building. They sometimes mention the areas that are favourable to the installation of Viṣṇu temples.

According to these manuals, the destiny of the kingdom is closely associated with that of the image. Maintaining the concrete and ritual integrity of the temple and image and carrying out the material repairs or the ritual expiations are required to avoid calamities to the kingdom, king, ministers and various classes of the society (Colas 1986: 83). The monarch sometimes takes a small part in the image worship. Images are in a danger of being carried away by a king or robbers (ibid.: 83-4). The temple rites reinforce the stability of the kingdom. The 'counter-ritual' (*ābhicārika*) image is installed at the border of the kingdom and made to face the enemy to help vanquish him.[58] However, the Vaikhānasa corpus does not appear explicitly to mention territories situated outside the sanctuary over which the god would rule, except in terms of zones of influence, as we will see.[59] The notion of donation of lands to the god seems to be found only in a comparatively recent text of the corpus (see below).

Some words need be said about the very concept of image as a divine person in the Vaikhānasa corpus. It is not homogeneous. Its multiplicity is mainly perceptible in the rite of solemn installation or consecration of the image. On the other hand, it should be stressed that, apart from the Vaikhānasa corpus, the rite of installation of an image is variously interpreted in other religious traditions. There is nothing to show that the belief that a sentient being establishes itself in the image was at the root of this rite.[60] Several versions of the installation ritual tend to identify the image with a living body, others not. A comparative study of Hindu and Buddhist manuals would probably show important differences in the interpretations which the rites themselves suggested, and could provide significant results from a historical point of view.

The Vaikhānasa ritual corpus is markedly heterogeneous. It does not constantly consider the image as a divine person. Taken separately, its manuals do not uniformly maintain or reject the belief in life in the image. They consider the divine image from various perspectives of reasoning and understanding, some pertaining to ritual 'mechanism', others to belief. They develop and mix these various orientations within their prescriptions, not without apparent contradictions for the modern scholar.[61]

It cannot be denied that the anthropomorphic appearance of the divine image is omnipresent in the prescriptions of daily worship and festivals, where external homage (like feeding the image, bathing it, clothing it, etc.) forms the main part of the ritual actions and attracts the devotional attention. In this sense, the image is presented as a divine body.[62] The Vaikhānasa texts occasionally reinforce this corporeity by connecting several constituents of the image with physiological elements of the human body (Colas 2004: 167). However they do not connect the consecration of the image with the process of human birth.[63] In fact, their support of the anthropomorphic concept of the divine looks more like the admission of a diffused belief, anchored not so much in a ritual reasoning as in a properly devotional perspective.[64]

On the other hand, the image is sometimes presented as a mere abode, not a body. The permanence of the divine residence in that abode[65] is not unconditional. The god resides in the image only inasmuch as he is satisfied. Being a lover of plastic (and musical) beauty, he does not reside in a defective vase or in a damaged image (Colas 1996: 205). He is not pleased to stay on in a provisional temple after a sojourn of twelve years (Colas 1986: 189; 1996: 204-5). He remains independent from the material form where he has been installed. His departure from the image is never related to the notion of death or to a modification of his divine status. The vocabulary employed in these circumstances belongs to the range of human feelings (the god is satisfied or angry). The anthropomorphic dimension is not wholly absent, but confined to the psychological level. The stay of the god in the image depends on his will.

This divine presence in the image should probably be distinguished from the divine power, although the Vaikhānasa texts themselves do not clearly distinguish between the concepts, which seem to be complementary rather than fundamentally different. The concept of power (*śakti*) appears to be less devotional, more technical and closely linked with the ritual process. It is particularly important in the installation rite (*pratiṣṭhā*), of which one of the main aims in the Vaikhānasa manuals is the introduction of divine power into the image. This ritual consecration secures the legitimacy and efficiency of the daily worship and subsequent festivals. These few observations show the heterogeneity of the definition of the person of the deity-image in the Vaikhānasa temple ritual corpus.

Given this heterogeneity, let us examine how the notion of territory is associated with the deity-image. The only territory that the Vaikhānasa temple-ritual corpus seems consistently to consider as divine is the sanctuary. The temple is the abode of the god, but more than that, it is often considered as intimately linked with the main image.[66] The iconography of the main image largely determines the shape of the temple (Colas 1996: 301). The god and his sanctuary are in a symbiosis. Viṣṇu's temple is 'made of Viṣṇu' (Colas 1986: 81). The mutual permeability between the god and his abode is both intimate and complete. Furthermore, in several texts, the temple itself is to be consecrated in a way similar to the installation of an image, but adapted to its shape and dimensions. In the Vaikhānasa *Vimānārcākalpa* description of the rite, the eyes of the temple are opened like those of the image, and a sacrifice is offered to the 'limbs' of the temple, that is to say, to its structural and decorative elements, ritually hailed one after the other (ibid.: 80-1). The *Śrīpraśnasaṃhitā*, a text from the Pāñcarātra, another Vaiṣṇava tradition, devotes a full chapter to similar prescriptions.[67]

The god and his sanctuary are also conceptually merged as regards the evaluation of their power. To speak of the influence of a temple is also to speak of the influence of its image, and conversely. Three texts of the Vaikhānasa temple-ritual corpus show a progressive classification of Viṣṇu's sanctuaries according to the extent of their purifying and beneficial influence. The passages on the subject in fact deal with the power of the temple, although the corresponding Sanskrit term, *śakti*, is not used. Such a classification is not specific to the Vaikhānasa tradition, but the three Vaikhānasa texts are comparatively systematic. The five categories of temples are: 'human', 'antique', founded by 'seers' or '(spiritually) accomplished (persons)', founded by gods, and 'self-manifested'. The temple which is identified as 'human', that is, recently founded by a *yajamāna* (literally, patron of a sacrifice) according to a Vaikhānasa (or other) rite of consecration, purifies its close surroundings, according to one of the texts; it has an influence over a distance of 1 *yojana* (i.e. two marine miles in modern conversion), according to other texts. The 'antique' temple, founded by a human being, but of immemorial and legendary tradition, purifies the earth over a larger perimeter, namely 3 or 10 *yojanas*, according to the texts. The temple founded by a seer or a spiritually accomplished person has a beneficial influence over a perimeter of 5 or 50 *yojanas*. The influence of a temple dedicated to Viṣṇu and founded by another god extends to 10 or 100 *yojanas*. The 'self-manifested' temple, in other words the temple where the god manifested himself directly in the form of an image, purifies and protects all the created worlds (Colas 1996: 189-92 and 1997: 242-5). In all cases, the origin of the main image determines the category of the sanctuary and the nature of this origin defines the range of the temple's influence. So, for example, a temple is qualified as 'self-manifested' although it is in fact his divine image that is the 'self-manifestation' of the god.

The Vaikhānasa texts thus conceive the sanctuary and the divine image (sometimes identified as a habitation) as forming a whole impregnated with power. Therefore, a Vaikhānasa would probably hardly doubt that the god is the owner of the site. The legal Sanskrit literature perhaps applies the same implicit conviction when, like Raghunandana, it singles out the space within the sanctuary as a territory of an exceptional nature in comparison with the other lands and properties associated with the same sanctuary: while the deity is not in principle eligible for the right to property, according to Raghunandana and Gosvāmin, both legal authors, the space of the temple is an exception of which the deity is the donee in the proper sense of the term.[68] This space, which is in close relation or even symbiosis with the deity, forms a special territory; it is not an ordinary land property and, for several religious and legal authors at least, it is not subject to general rules.

PRIESTS AND LAND PROPERTIES OUTSIDE THE TEMPLE

Vaikhānasa manuals do not explicitly discuss the god's ownership of the sanctuary. They mention the lands dependent on the temple and situated outside it, but their ownership by the god is apparently mentioned, moreover incidentally, in one of the relatively recent texts of the Vaikhānasa temple-ritual corpus, as we will see. The question of the ownership of the temple lands arises for the 'human' temples of the above classification, which are the main object of the Vaikhānasa prescriptions.

One leitmotiv ceaselessly returns: at the time when a founder finances the building of a temple and the making and installation of images, he must also carefully provide assets for the families of the Vaikhānasa priests who live around the temple. He may give cows and gold, but the gift of lands is recommended above all else, for, it is said, lands are an indestructible and unmovable property. The gift of lands 'ensures the continuity of worship after the decease of the priest who was responsible for it', as well as the welfare of his descendants. The texts sometimes emphasize that these lands must be fertile and that their donation should be made at the very beginning of the consecration of the image, to ensure the permanent presence of the god on the site. According to the *Samūrtārcanādhikaraṇa*, one of the most ancient texts of the corpus, 'one institutes enjoyment of (certain) lands (*bhūmibhoga*)[69] to keep the worship uninterrupted' (4, 43). This passage does not mention the identity of the donee. It goes on to state that one must institute 'land enjoyment' for the priests, the assistant-priests, the singers, etc. It adds: 'all that is given with water into the hand of the master-priest is (in fact) given into the very hand of the god of the gods' (4, 49).[70] But there is nothing to show that these lands are really given to the deity or considered as being his/her property. The ancient texts of the corpus (around the tenth century) apparently recommend only the land donation to priests, assistant-priests, singers, dancers, and other employees, on the occasion of the foundation of the temple and various other rites, such as the yearly festival, the offering of cooked oblations, etc. They do not appear to discuss the legal ownership of these lands. The occasional praises of the gifts of lands as being gifts to the god himself, should not be understood literally, but considered as mere hyperbolic statements. This fact is in sharp contrast with the epigraphic documentation, which clearly shows land donations to deity-images as early as in the fifth century.

The Vaikhānasa prescriptions apparently mention land donations to image-deities only at a comparatively late period and they do so in connection with the charts that record these donations. A minimum of caution is required, since the ancient temple-ritual corpus of the Vaikhānasas has not yet been entirely published. But one can speak of a general tendency. In the present state of our knowledge, the *Prakīrṇādhikāra* is the only text of the corpus that mentions the ownership of lands by the god Viṣṇu, and then with some ambiguity, as we will see. The *Prakīrṇādhikāra* belongs to the latest stratum of the (*circa*) ninth to thirteenth-century temple-ritual Vaikhānasa corpus. One of its chapters takes into account epigraphy itself in regard with the donation of lands. The passage involved can be translated as follows:

Then, the wise man should arrange diligently, by means of land enjoyment (*bhūmibhoga*), the establishing (*sthiti*) of the priest for (him to continue) the worship and for his family. He presents[71] the priest a piece of land, which is very large, very fertile and exempted from taxes.

He then causes to be written[72] on a copper plate, etc. the fixing of the limits (*sīmāviniścaya*) (of the given land) and it is with the name of god (as a donee on this document) that he gives this land, which makes the livelihood of the priest. He should do that at the beginning (of the temple consecration ritual): the establishing (*sthiti*) of Hari (Viṣṇu) (in that place) depends on that (*tadadhīna*). For, the glorious (*bhagavant*) Hari is considered as a father and the priest as (his) son. According to the (normal) procedure (*kramāt*), one should not write the name of the son when there is a (living) father. The satisfied priest is but Hari himself. Or the wise man writes (the land donation) with the name of the priest[73] Then, after he has built a solid house with stones for the priest in the vicinity of the temple, (that house) is declared as (being) the house of the (priest).

Let him do (that) diligently so that the well-settled priest lives without suffering until the moon and sun last. For, when the priest suffers, the glorious Hari suffers. When the priest is well pleased, Janārdana (Hari) is well pleased. One speaks of two forms for Hari: the image and the priest himself. For, before his invitation (*āvāhana*) (to come) in the image, he (Hari) is always present in the priest. (12, 111cd-120)

This passage prescribes the donation to the priest of a land exempted from taxes. It then describes the typical epigraphic way of recording this donation. The conventional epigraphic phraseology which this Vaikhānasa text exceptionally mentions, and which encourages the donation of lands to the god, differs from the usual Vaikhānasa prescriptions on land donations, which recommend the donation of lands to the temple priests. The two discursive levels, as well as the two types of document that convey them, priestly manuals and epigraphs, in fact correspond to two different readerships.

The first discursive level is intended for the priestly readership. For the Vaikhānasa priest who composed this text, the temple servants are the obvious owners of the lands situated outside the temple; the reason for the gift of lands is to enable the priests to live comfortably with their families. The donation is made for the benefit of the priest as such and the property is indissolubly linked with the practice of priesthood, or, rather, conditioned by it. This is the current phraseology of the ancient nucleus of the Vaikhānasa corpus, where the exceptional interpretation of the donation made to the priest as a donation to the god is only hyperbolic. In this respect, the *Prakīrṇādhikāra* does not break with the ancient conception.

The second discursive level belongs to the epigraphic literature and not to the Vaikhānasa culture as such. The *Prakīrṇādhikāra* presents an inscriptional model. The epigraph, intended for the society at large (although we can hardly define its readership) includes a legal dimension, but is not confined to this dimension. The document on a copper plate or other support is expected to mention the limits of the gifted land and either the god or the priest as the donee. If the god is the donee, only his name is indicated, not that of the priest. The reason given is that the priest is the son of the god and one should not make a gift to the son in the presence of his living father. Is this a Dharmaśāstra rule or simply a custom of social priority of the father over the son? Should we consider this reason as a mere hyperbolic statement, similar to the identification of the priest as a form of the god, at the end of the passage? When ritual texts venture beyond their purely technical prescriptions, it is difficult to appreciate whether their statements are hyperbolic or denote a real belief. Whatever the answer, the gift of land directly to the priest is only mentioned as the second possibility, and without further comment: the *Prakīrṇādhikāra* appears to indicate that epigraphy favours the temple deity as donee.[74] The gift of a residence to the priest seems to be registered on the same document, whoever the main donee may be.

The Vaikhānasa author of the *Prakīrṇādhikāra* was probably conscious of the phraseological difference between epigraphs and contemporary statements of the Vaikhānasa manuals. This discursive difference echoes Śabara's observation, in the fourth-fifth century, that such expressions as 'village of God' and 'territory of God' pertained to conventional custom, the alleged possessions of the deity being in fact in the hands of the 'servants of the deity'. Epigraphy consolidated conventional custom. The mention of a god as a donee in preference to a priest may have helped to disengage land property from individual human ownership and give it a sacred, hence perennial character. In return for the perpetuity of the land gift, the families that in practice used these lands and derived revenues from them had to take on the duties of priesthood. This blurring of the identity of the human beneficiary should be connected with yet another fact: the responsibility of the surrounding society, village or city for the preservation of the temple buildings and rites. For, as we have seen, the establishment of an image and a sanctuary generated collective duties that reached beyond the historical individuals associated with its foundation. Apart from the provisions arranged by the founder, the community, which is believed to benefit from the divine presence, is also held responsible for the condition of the image and temple. Damages occurring to them have negative consequences on the whole community (Colas 1996: 193-5). On the other hand, the blurring of the human individuality of the temple land-user helped to change the temple from the status of a historical, datable foundation to that of a legendary or undatable site, 'antique', according to the classification of sanctuaries described above.

The presentation of the epigraphic model in the *Prakīrṇādhikāra* also confirms an aspect of the Dāmodarpur inscription. Such inscriptions implemented a kind of contract between the deity-image and society. This contract was in part legal, but involved the local society far beyond the juridical sphere. The society had a religious and devotional commitment to an image that was commonly and conventionally accepted as a divine person, and not only as a legal one. Hence, the *Prakīrṇādhikāra* does not consider its own phraseology and the epigraphic phraseology which it reports as being contradictory. The point of view it expresses confirms a specific dichotomy between the fact and its socio-religious interpretation; these two are not in a relation of opposition, but of superposition, as observed in Mīmāṃsā and the Dāmodarpur inscription.

CONCLUSION

Several centuries before our era, the question of the relation between gods and territory was not a main concern in the hymns of the Vedic society, which valued movement and not sedentariness. Vedic rites do not appear to have been closely and permanently linked with particular sites or areas. By contrast, Hindu and Buddhist texts from the early centuries of our era onwards testify to the interaction between gods (or Buddha, Bodhisattvas) and earthly kings with respect to universal sovereignty. Historical data illustrate this interaction up to the eighteenth century at least. Rituals sometimes gave another dimension to this relation by connecting it with Purāṇic geography and associating it with concrete images of gods in temples. This embodiment of gods in images differs from Vedic ideology, where the possession of a body by gods was ambiguous and mentioned in a fragmentary way, and where there was no image-worship as such.

Donations of lands and villages to Buddha- and Bodhisattva-images are recorded from around the fourth century, and to Hindu deity-images from at least the fifth century. The earliest inscriptions to record this tendency must be correlated with the contemporary view of Mīmāṃsā on donations to deities. For during the same period, Śabara rejected the idea of deity as landowner, although he did acknowledge it as a convention apparently acceptable to him (though he did not explicitly mention images themselves, but only deities considered as owners). Śạbara's position was connected with his denial of any metaphysical foundation to the worship (*pūjā*) of gods. The question of ownership by deity-images was probably important enough to the Brahmanical milieus to induce Śabara to pronounce on ownership by deities and to accept this conception as an established (and probably acceptable) custom, even while he considered it as a mere fiction from a doctrinal point of view. Later on, Kumārila (seventh-eighth century), another Mīmāṃsaka, stressed that the practitioners of Vedic rites, 'well-educated people', also worshipped the gods: he thus agreed with the practice of worship and thereby, perhaps, with the concept of land donation to deity-images.

The period when traditional legal literature started examining the relation between the deity-image and its ownership of land remains to be determined, as does the influence of British law on this issue in modern times. The Dharmaśāstric approach to the subject is often clear, but remains limited by its own concerns. Moreover, this legal discipline does not seem to have settled on any common position concerning the status of a deity-image as an owner. Its interpretation of the position of Mīmāṃsā in this regard has apparently evolved. The philosophical Sanskrit literature, which we have not examined here (except Mīmāṃsā, very briefly), does not deal systematically with the relation between deity-image and territory. After the twelfth century, the school of the 'non-dualism of the specified' (Viśiṣṭādvaita)[75] elaborated the notion of 'divine descent', that is to say incarnation, 'in the form of an image of worship' (*arcāvatāra*), but its theory about this remained metaphysical,[76] and largely ignored the link between deity-image and territory. Perhaps the Indian systems of philosophy saw no need to conceptualize such a subject, which was left to the area of daily practice.

The priestly manuals which we have examined implicitly distinguish three notions: the divine territory that is the whole sanctuary, the land ownership of the priests, and the field of influence of the temple. They do not provide a unique and homogeneous theory of the personality of the deity-image nor of its relation with a specific territory and with the lands of the temple or of the priests. Remarkably, the *Prakīrṇādhikāra*, a ritual text which could postdate the thirteenth century, while confirming the priestly view that temple lands should be given to priests (and not to deity-images), accepts and strengthens the role of epigraphy in instituting the deity-image as a donee of land. This apparent paradox could be explained by the fact that epigraphy expressed a common social ideology shared by communities of divergent interests or opinions, whether practical (about the ultimate beneficiary of temple land donations) or metaphysical (about deity as a donee, for instance). Epigraphy illustrates and reinforces the convention which Śabara had mentioned and apparently accepted.

The inscriptions, which we have examined here through two examples, addressed a literate public, but did not advocate a particular doctrine, erudite discipline, or even any specific point of view. They illustrate the ideological concept of a deity-image which can accommodate numerous opinions, from the belief in the presence of life in the deity-image to the idea that the deity-image as an owner is a mere social convention. This epigraphic indeterminacy about the personality of the deity-image was probably not considered problematic in the society of the time. On the contrary, it perhaps answered a common social desire to reach a consensus on the issue. This concept therefore transcends the purely legal point of view and the doctrinal differences and should not be overly contrasted with them.[77] Strikingly, very pragmatic legal, political, and commercial negotiations preceded the donation of lands to the deity-image, but this pragmatic aspect merged into the much broader dimension of devotion to the image as a new owner, a devotion that the inscriptions decreed. Institutional devotion seems to have been a means of including and going beyond the merely legal and political rules, whose formulations were under constant revision and debate. In such a context, the universal recognition of the deity-image as a person may well have contained or helped to resolve potential crises relating to the management of temples and the lands connected with them. Furthermore, it may have helped to crystallize a system of values approved by society at large in the absence of a universally recognized political and legal system.

Acknowledgements: I thank D. Berti, G. Tarabout and M. Lecomte-Tilouine for their observations on the first draft of this paper.

NOTES

1. See Colas 2004.
2. I use the terms 'property' and 'owner' in a broad, not in a strictly legal, sense. Derrett has shown how the complexity of the concept of 'property' in India (which involves several degrees of interpretation) is far-removed from the concepts of Western law (1977: [86]).
3. There are many other possible points of view; for the philosophical ones, see Colas 2004.
4. *Arcāvatāra* (Sanskrit) means '(divine) descent', i.e. incarnation 'in the form of an image of worship', a concept elaborated by the Viśiṣṭādvaita school, which first developed in south India. *Svarūpa* or literally 'one's own form', a concept elaborated among various Vaiṣṇava sects of northern India.
5. These notions can be extended to Buddhist relics, like the Tooth of the Buddha in Kandy (Sri Lanka): see Seveniratne 1992. On Buddhist relics in general, see Schopen 1997, Chapters 6-8. Among non-anthropomorphic representations, stones, for instance, are said to bleed, etc., in Nepal (Lecomte-Tilouine 2003: 175-83, especially 181-2); in northern India: 'Dhanā asked for an image to worship. The Brahman gave him a round stone and Dhanā fixed his mind on it. He fed the stone and organized *darśan* before it, but the deity would not eat anything and Dhanā was very upset' (Callewaert 2000: 115). Unfortunately, we could not take Jaina material into account here.
6. For the content and date of this corpus, see Renou, Filliozat et al., 1985a: 270-308, *passim.*
7. According to recent research: see Fussman 2002: 746. Fussman 2002: 743-8 contains a useful summary of the present state of knowledge about Āryas, the Indo-European tribes mentioned below.
8. Renou, Filliozat et al., 1985a: 288, 294; for the dates of the Upaniṣads,

they say (p. 299), without committing themselves, that 'the often proposed date of 500 BC is not unreasonable' ('n'est pas inadmissible', my translation).

9. Malamoud 1989b: 260 mentions simulacra of the patron of the sacrifice, not representations of gods.
10. See, for instance, L. Renou, J. Filliozat et al., 1985a: 547-9. For more details, see Kirfel 1920.
11. See Eck 1983: 45, 57, where details of historical nature are unfortunately often scattered.
12. On this evolution, see Stietencron 1977.
13. See Lingat 1989: 16, 146-50; Renou, Filliozat et al., 1985b: 533-4.
14. The *Nārāyaṇīyaparvan* is a part of the *Mahābhārata* (12, 321-39). For the date of the *Nārāyaṇīyaparvan* passage referred to here (12, 322, 17-25), see Schreiner 1997 and Oberlies 1997: 86.
15. Lingat 1989: 56; p. 50 for the date of the text.
16. Sometimes with a crime to be expiated: see Berti 2001: 36.
17. 250 BC or AD 300 ? See Verpoorten 1987: 5.
18. For more details, see Clooney 1988: 279-84; Colas 2004: 151-5.
19. For a summary of the position of Mīmāṃsā in this regard, see Malamoud 1989b: 272.
20. Therefore they can be understood only as metaphors. For the meaning 'metaphor' of *upacāra* (= *lakṣaṇā*), see Kunjunni Raja 1969: 231, 233 (reference to *Nyāyasūtra* 2.2.62 in note 1), 235 and 247. According to some Sanskrit authors, confirmation by common usage is a main requirement for the validity of a metaphor (Kunjunni Raja 1969: 231-2).
21. M. Biardeau (1964) proposes a more general interpretation: she sees these expressions as probably designating devotees of one or the other of the great gods ('de l'une ou de l'autre des grandes divinités') who had already acquired great importance in Śabara's time (ibid.: 87, n. 3).
22. Conjectural date: 400 to 200 BC for most of these texts, according to Renou, Filliozat et al., 1985a: 302.
23. See, for instance, the *Vaikhānasasmārtasūtra*, composed from the fourth century AD and, probably, before ninth century (Colas 1996: 49-50).
24. See, for instance, the installation rite of the image in Chapter 60 of the *Bṛhatsaṃhitā* (sixth century).
25. Insofar as he is considered an 'original' Vedic deity: see F.M. Smith 1987: 43-5.

26. Seven centuries before Śabara at least, Yāska, also a defender of Vedism, raised the question of the anthropomorphism of gods in his *Nirukta* (7, 6-7), but did not take a position on this issue. The answer to this question may have not been so crucial at that time. Yāska lived between the seventh and third century BC, according to Kahrs 1998. For generalities on the *Nirukta*, see Renou, Filliozat et al., 1985a: 306-7.
27. See Colas 2004. Buddhist scholasticism, which, of course, does not accept the authority of the Veda, is not taken into account here.
28. See, for instance, Sircar 1966, under *deva-dāna* (gift made to a god); Announssamy 1979, Bagchi 1933, Sontheimer 1964 (especially, pp. 69-71), Derrett 1977 ([61]). See Diserens 2001: 267-70, about this type of donation in Kullu Valley (in the present state of Himachal Pradesh).
29. See, for instance, *C.I.I. III* Bhandarkar, no. 2 (reign of Samudragupta) (pp. 222-4), no. 11 (reign of Candragupta II) (pp. 255-7), no. 20 (reign of Kumāragupta I) (pp. 278-9), no. 35 (AD 473-4, rebuilding of a temple financed by a guild of silk weavers) (pp. 324-32).
30. See, for instance, *C.I.I. III* Bhandarkar, no. 12 (Candragupta) (p. 259).
31. See, for instance, *C.I.I. III* Bhandarkar, no. 16 (AD 415-16, Kumāragupta I) (pp. 269-70), no. 32 (reign of Skandagupta), no. 37 (reign of Budhagupta) (pp. 334-5), no. 39 (reign of Budhagupta) (pp. 340-1).
32. See, for instance, *C.I.I. III* Bhandarkar, no. 3 (Samudragupta, a village given to Jayanta Bhaṭṭa) (pp. 227-8), no. 4 (AD 328-9, Samudragupta, a village given to a Brahman) (pp. 230-1).
33. See, for instance, *C.I.I. III* Bhandarkar, no. 5 (fourth century, reign of Rāmagupta) (pp. 233-4), no. 18 (reign of Kumāragupta I) (p. 273), no. 25 (reign of Kumāragupta I, an image of Buddha) (p. 293), no. 34 (AD 473-4, reign of Kumāragupta II, an image of Buddha) (pp. 321-2), no. 29 (AD 459-60, reign of Skandagupta, five Tīrthaṃkaras) (pp. 307-8), no. 36 (reign of Budhagupta) (pp. 333-4).
34. *C.I.I. III* Bhandarkar, no. 8 (pp. 246-7), no. 9 (pp. 250-2).
35. See Schopen 1997, Chapter 12, especially, pp. 260, 278.
36. Thus a donation of lands to the gods Kokāmukhasvāmin and Śvetavarāhasvāmin mentioned in another inscription on a copper plate from Dāmodarpur and dated from the reign of Budhagupta (second half of fifth century) (*C.I.I. III* Bhandarkar, no. 40, p. 344, lines 5-6 of the inscription; see also below, notes 48-9); donation of a village to the 'Divine One' (that is, to a Viṣṇu deity-image) in 496-7 (*C.I.I. III* Fleet,

no. 27, p. 122, lines 6-8 of the inscription: 'I give this village to the two feet of the Divine one . . . as a rent-free village (*agrāhāra* [= *agrahāra*]) of the god for increasing the merits of several persons of the same family, which will be thereafter tied down to maintain the temple and ensure regular offerings.' I interpret this passage differently from Fleet. I understand *sva* according to the context, as must be done most often, rather than by a mechanical application of grammar.

37. South Indian inscriptions mention from the end of the fifth century the 'enjoyment (of land) by the god' (*devabhoga*), that is, the ownership of land by the god: cf. Fleet 1876: 52 (Uruvupalli inscription on copper-plate dated from the 11th year of the reign of Siṃhavarman).
38. This verbal form can be interpreted in any way, but it is clear that, in practice, the monarch who orders the (probably ritualised) setting up of the image is symbolically its author.
39. *C.I.I. III* Bhandarkar, no. 31, p. 315. For the date of the inscription, see ibid., p. 81.
40. For instance, in a Prakrit inscription written in a pre-Kushan script (Lüders 1984: 203-4, who restores the term *pra[ti][ṭhāpito]* with certainty).
41. Numerous instances (some of them already before the Christian era): see *C.I.I. II, 1*, no. 1, p. 28 (year 6 BC), no. 73 (AD 52), etc. Inscriptions also use this verb for the building of *stūpas:* ibid., p. 87.
42. While it may be possible that the divine image was considered as a permanent resident of the place where it was installed, this shade of meaning does not seem to be contained as such in the verb *pratiṣṭhā* in causative form itself. The interpretation of this verb in Schopen 1997 (pp. 263-4) about similar Buddhist facts seems to me slightly forced.
43. *C.I.I. III* Bhandarkar, no. 47 ('Dāmodarpur Copper-plate inscription of Viṣṇugupta'), pp. 360-4. The exact date of this inscription is probably AD 542-3.
44. Sircar (1966: 8) defines the *ādhiṣṭhānādhikaraṇa* in the following way: 'administrative office or board at the headquarters of a territorial unit; office of the administrators of a city; the city office'. About Koṭivarṣa as the capital of the district (*viṣaya*) of the same name, see *C.I.I. III* Bhandarkar, pp. 284-5; according to the same source (p. 285), this Koṭivarṣa can be identified with Bāṇgarh or Bāṇnagar, situated 'in the West Dinajpur District of West Bengal'.
45. On the expression *apradādharma*, see *C.I.I. III* Bhandarkar, pp. 363 (n. 4),

290 (n. 8). According to Sircar 1966, p. 26: *apradā* = '[gift land] not to be alienated'; *apradā-dharma* = 'custom regarding inalienable gift land'. *Tāmra-paṭṭa*, a term that means 'copper-plate', is sometimes used to name the chart itself, which is inscribed on the copper plate: see Sircar 1965: 101.

46. The exact meaning of this term cannot be discussed here. For more details on official administrators, see *C.I.I. III* Bhandarkar: 106-7.
47. We more or less follow Bhandarkar's literal translation: 'these (*kulyavāpas*) should be respected by administrators in times to come, out of devotion to the god (*devabhaktyānumantavyāḥ*)'.
48. This is probably the same site as that mentioned in another Dāmodarpur inscription of the same period (*C.I.I. III* Bhandarkar, no. 40, p. 344), which Bhandarkar placed 'somewhere in Darjeeling and Sikkim' (ibid.: 343). According to the same author (ibid.: 343), 'it looks that the images of these gods [that is, Kokāmukhasvāmin and Śvetavarāhasvāmin] . . . were natural formations of the rock'. However, according to a personal communication of M. Lecomte-Tilouine, it is now agreed that this site corresponds to the Varāhakṣetra, a main pilgrimage site situated at the confluence of Sunkoshī and Kokākholā rivers in eastern Nepal, near Dharan. Here, one also finds a temple dedicated to Kokāmukhasvāmin. Moreover, the deity-images here appear to be sculptured images, not natural formations of the rock.
49. Compare with the phraseology used in another Dāmodarpur inscription of the same period (*C.I.I. III* Bhandarkar, no. 40, p. 344: see previous note), which records the donation of a piece of land for building temples to Śvetavarāhasvāmin and Kokāmukhasvāmin.
50. Cf. n. 48, above.
51. According to Schopen 1997, these inscriptions 'were obviously written by literate individuals familiar with Buddhist doctrines of the day' (p. 277), but they also show that the 'théories abstraites' (the 'abstract theories', an expression of L. de la Vallée Poussin) of Buddhism which were current at that time, like the doctrine of the Buddha's four bodies, for instance (ibid.: 259), 'had little, if any, direct detectable influence on a large segment of even the already limited number of literate members of the "Buddhist" society of their day—most of whom were probably monks' (ibid.: 277).
52. My point of view here probably slightly differs from that of Schopen (1997: 277).
53. Cf. Sontheimer 1964: 49; Clémentin-Ojha 1990: 115-16.

54. Sontheimer 1964: 99, concludes: 'to search for a legal personality merely in order to enable suits to be brought or defended in the interests of the endowment, is quite superfluous'.
55. Annoussamy 1979: 616 ('l'idole, bien qu'elle agisse par l'intermédiaire d'un agent, n'est pas un mineur perpétuel, ni un incapable').
56. Date taken up by Sontheimer 1964: 62, n. 42.
57. On such hyperbolic statements, see also Colas 2005: 39.
58. Colas 1996: 195, 207. *Abhicāra*, from which *ābhicārika* derives, is often translated as 'black magic', but 'counter-ritual' seems more precise.
59. The *Rauravāgama*, a Śaiva manual, mentions the 'Guardian of the field' (*kṣetrapāla*), a sort of 'agrarian spirit' of which it describes the worship (Dagens and Barazer-Billoret 2000: 50-1), but there are probably other Śaiva manuals which describe this spirit. *Kṣetrapāla* also designates one of Śiva-Bhairava's forms in one of the supplementary chapters of the same text (ibid.: 50, n. 2).
60. According to Sontheimer, the *prāṇa-pratiṣṭhā* ('installation of breath', that is, of life) 'can hardly be said to have only a symbolic character, but at the root of this ceremony there must have been the belief that a sentient deity begins to "reside" in the idol for the purpose of a personal relationship between the worshipper and the deity' (p. 49). On the other hand, it should be stressed that the name *prāṇa-pratiṣṭhā* itself is not universally used: more often, texts merely name this rite *pratiṣṭhā*.
61. See Colas 1989: 146-7, especially about the eye-opening of the image and its place in the succession of the ritual acts; Bentor 1996: 35-6.
62. Compare with Clémentin-Ojha 1990: 119-22, 127-8.
63. By contrast with, for instance, the Buddhist *Kriyāsaṃgrahapañjikā* which includes in the ritual ten ceremonies through whose names they symbolically correspond to the life-cycle of a Brāhmaṇa, from the preparation for conceiving a child, through the birth, up to marriage: see Tanemura 2001: 54-8. This text was 'written during the last phase of Buddhist tantrism in the Indian Subcontinent' (ibid.: 52).
64. See Colas 2004: 167. As has been underscored, ritualists would probably replace a damaged image with less reticence than devotees: for examples in the nineteenth-twentieth century, see Clémentin-Ojha 1990: 126-7.
65. See also Reiniche 1988: 380. Sontheimer's remark (1964: 49, n. 12) about the permanence of the divine presence in the image needs to be qualified.

66. See above; Annoussamy 1979: 614 ('the temple . . . is nothing but the abode of the idol', my translation).
67. H.D. Smith 1975: 453-4. See also D. Eck, *Darśan*, p. 59, quoted in Strickmann 1996: 452, n. 41.
68. The deity is then 'a primary recipient', while it is an owner only in a secondary sense in other cases: see Sontheimer 1964: 66-7.
69. Bhoga: 'enjoyment', that is, 'possession'. On this term, see especially Derrett 1977: [19] and n. 31 (especially the reference to Kane).
70. See Colas 1996: 130, n. 1, and, more generally, for this paragraph, pp. 129-32.
71. *Samarpayet*, a term that does not have any particular shade of meaning here, and is merely the equivalent of *dadyāt*.
72. *Lekhya*, for *likhya* (literally 'having written', hence 'having caused to write') or *ālekhya* ('having caused to write').
73. The Sanskrit sentence here shows *vā* ('or') twice, which suggests that the second *vā* is merely expletive.
74. The donation to a god residing in a temple is largely confirmed by epigraphy: see the instances in Sontheimer 1964: 70-1.
75. Its earliest well-known representatives are Nāthamuni (ninth century), Yāmunācārya (tenth century), Rāmānuja (eleventh century).
76. See, for instance, Śrīnivāsācārya (seventeenth century), *Yatīndramatadīpikā*, Avatāra 6, p. 55.; Avatāra 9, pp. 86ff.
77. Compare with Schopen 1997: 278.

REFERENCES

Sanskrit Texts

Prakīrṇ ādhikāra, ed. by the Śrīvaikhānasavidyānilaya, Ākulamannāḍu, 1929.

Rauravāgama, critical edn. N.R. Bhatt, vol. III (Kriyāpāda 47-65 and Anubandha), Pondichéry: Institut Français, 1988, Publications de l'Institut Français d'Indologie no. 18, 3.

Śabara. *Śābarabhāṣya on Jaimini's Mīmāṃsāsūtras*, ed. Maheśacandra Nyāyaratna, 2 vols., Calcutta: Bibliotheca Indica, 1863, 1887.

Śrīnivāsācārya. *Yatīndramatadīpikā*, ed. Aṇṇaṅgarācārya, Vṛndāvana, 1976.

Varāhamihira. *Bṛhatsaṃhitā*, ed. H. Kern, Calcutta: Bibliotheca Indica, 1865.

Yāska. *Nirukta* in L. Sarup, *The Nighaṇṭu and the Nirukta: The Oldest Indian Treatise on Etymology, Philology and Semantics*, Critically edited [. . .] and translated [. . .], Delhi: Motilal Banarsidass, 1984 (rpt.).

EPIGRAPHICAL RECORDS

C.I.I. II, 1 = *Corpus Inscriptionum Indicarum,* vol. II, Part I: *Kharoshṭī Inscriptions with the Exception of those of Aśoka*, by S. Konow, Calcutta: Government of India, 1929.

C.I.I. III Fleet = *Corpus Inscriptionum Indicarum,* vol. III: *Inscriptions of the Early Gupta Kings and their Successors*, by J.F. Fleet, Calcutta: Government of India, 1888.

C.I.I. III Bhandarkar = *Corpus Inscriptionum Indicarum,* vol. III: *Inscriptions of the Early Gupta Kings*, revised by D.R. Bhandarkar, ed. B. Chhabra and G.S. Gai, Delhi: Archeological Survey of India, 1981.

Epigraphia Indica, vol. XXIV: see Lüders 1984.

SECONDARY SOURCES

Announssamy, David, 1979. 'La personnalité juridique de l'idole hindoue', *Revue historique de droit français et étranger,* 57: 611-21.

Bagchi, S.C., 1933. *Juristic Personality of Hindu Deities [Asutosh Mookerjee Lectures, 1931]*, Calcutta: University of Calcutta.

Bentor, Y., 1996. *Consecration of Images and Stūpas in Indo-Tibetan Tantric Buddhism,* Leiden: Brill, Brill's Indological Library 11.

Berti, D., 2001. *La parole des dieux. Rituels de possession en Himalaya indien,* Paris: CNRS Editions.

Biardeau, M., 1964. *Théorie de la connaissance et philosophie de la parole dans le brahmanisme classique,* Paris-La Haye: Mouton.

Callewaert, W.M., 2000. *The Hagiographies of Anantadās: The Bhakti Poets of North India,* Richmond: Curzon Press.

Christol, A., 1987. 'Les huttes cosmiques. Pour une archéologie formulaire du Veda', *Bulletin d'Etudes Indiennes,* 5: 11-36.

Clooney, F. X., 1988. '*Devatādhikaraṇa*: A Theological Debate in the Mīmāṃsā-Vedānta Tradition', *Journal of Indian Philosophy,* 16: 277-98.

Clémentin-Ojha, C., 1990. 'Image animée, image vivante. L'image du culte hindou', in *L'image divine. Culte et méditation dans l'hindouisme*, ed. A. Padoux, Paris: CNRS, pp. 115-32.

Colas, G., 1986. *Le temple selon Marīci*, Pondichéry: Institut Français d'Indologie.

———1989. 'L'instauration de la puissance divine dans l'image du temple en Inde du Sud', *Revue de l'Histoire des Religions,* CCVI: 129-50.

———1990. 'Le dévot, le prêtre et l'image vishnouite en Inde méridionale', in *L'image divine. Culte et méditation dans l'hindouisme,* ed. A. Padoux, Paris: CNRS, pp. 99-114.

———1996. *Viṣṇu, ses images et ses feux. Les métamorphoses du dieu chez les vaikhānasa*, Paris: EFEO.

———1997. 'Etres supérieurs, temps et rite. Les sources du pouvoir du temple hindou', in *Religion et pratiques de puissance*, ed. A. de Surgy, Paris: L'Harmattan, pp. 239-52.

———2004. 'The Competing Hermeneutics of Image Worship in Hinduism (Fifth to Eleventh Century AD)', in *Images in Asian Religions: Texts and Contexts*, ed. P. Granoff and K. Shinohara, Vancouver: University of British Columbia Press, pp. 149-79.

———2005. 'Rites Among Vaikhānasas and Related Matters: Some Methodological Issues', in *Hindu and Buddhist Rituals in South Asia*, ed. J. Gengnagel, U. Hüsken and S. Raman, Wiesbaden: Harrassowitz, pp. 23-44.

Dagens, B. and M.-L. Barazer-Billoret, 2000. *Le Rauravāgama, Un traité de rituel et de doctrine śivaïtes*, Translation, 2 vols., Pondichéry: Institut Français de Pondichéry.

Derrett, J.D.M., 1977. 'The Development of the Concept of Property in India *c.* AD 800-1800', in *Essays in Classical and Modern Hindu Law*, vol. 2, Leiden: Brill, pp. [8]-[130].

Diserens, H., 2001. 'Castes, privilèges et divinité tutélaire. Pages d'histoire d'un village en Himalaya occidental au XIXe siècle', *Journal Asiatique*, 289: 237-84.

Eck, D., 1983. *Banāras: City of Light*, Delhi: Penguin.

Fleet, J.F., 1876. 'Sanskrit and Old Canarese Inscriptions No. XII', *The Indian Antiquary*, V: 50-3.

Fussman, G., 2002. 'Histoire du monde indien', *Annuaire du Collège de France 2000-2001:* 733-58.

Ghosh, A., 1973. *The City in Early Historical India*, Simla: Indian Institute of Advanced Study.

Heesterman, J.C., 1993. *The Broken World of Sacrifice: An Essay in Ancient Indian Ritual*, Chicago: University of Chicago.

Jha, G., 1936. *Śābarabhāṣya*, Translation, vol. III (*Adhyāyas* IX-XII), Baroda: Oriental Institute, Gaekwad's Oriental Series LXXIII.

Kahrs, E., 1998. *Indian Semantic Analysis: The Nirvacana Tradition*, Cambridge: Cambridge University Press.

Kane, P.V., 1941. *History of Dharmaśāstra*, vol. II, part II, Poona: Bhandarkar Oriental Research Institute.

Kirfel, W., 1920. *Die Kosmographie der Inder nach den Quellen dargestellt*, Bonn-Leipzig: Kurt Schroeder.

Kunjunni Raja, K., 1969. *Indian Theories of Meaning*, 2nd edn., Madras: Adyar Library and Research Centre.

Lecomte-Tilouine, M., 2003. 'Le paysage népalais, exégèse et appropriation du pays', in *Histoire et devenir des paysages en Himalaya*, ed. J. Smadja, Paris: CNRS Éditions, pp. 165-92.

Lingat, R., 1989. *Royautés bouddhiques: Aśoka et la fonction royale à Ceylan*, Paris: EHESS.

Lüders, H., 1984. 'Seven Brāhmī Inscriptions from Mathurā and its Vicinity', *Epigraphia Indica* XXIV, ed. N.P. Chakravarti, New Delhi: ASI (rpt. 1st edn.: 1942), pp. 194-210.

Macdonell, A.A., 1897. *Vedic Mythology*, Strassburg: Trübner.

Malamoud, Ch., 1989a. 'Village et forêt dans l'idéologie de l'Inde brahmanique', in *Cuire le monde. Rite et pensée dans l'Inde ancienne*, Paris: La Découverte, pp. 93-114.

———, 1989b. 'Briques et mots. Observation sur le corps des dieux dans l'Inde classique', in *Cuire le monde: Rite et pensée dans l'Inde ancienne*, Paris: La Découverte, pp. 253-73.

Meth Srinivasan, D., 1997. *Many Heads, Arms and Eyes: Origin, Meaning and Form of Multiplicity in Indian Art*, Leiden: Brill.

Oberlies, T., 1997. 'Die Textgeschichte der Śvetadvīpa-Episode des Nārāyaṇīya (Mbh 12, 321-326', in *Nārāyaṇīya-Studien*, ed. P. Schreiner, Wiesbaden: Harrassowitz, pp. 75-118.

Padoux, A. (ed.), 1990. *L'image divine. Culte et méditation dans l'hindouisme*, Paris: CNRS.

Reiniche, M.-L., 1988. 'Un nom, une forme, un lieu. L'invention hindoue de l'autre et du même', *Revue de l'Histoire des Religions*, CCV-1: 367-84.

Renou, L., J. Filliozat, et al., 1985a. *L'Inde classique: Manuel des études indiennes*, Tome I, rpt., Paris: Librairie d'Amérique et d'Orient Adrien Maisonneuve.

———, 1985b. *L'Inde classique: Manuel des études indiennes*, Tome II, rpt., Paris: EFEO.

Schopen, G., 1997. *Bones, Stones, and Buddhist Monks: Collected Papers on the Archaeology, Epigraphy, and Texts of Monastic Buddhism in India*, Honolulu: University of Hawai'i Press.

Schreiner, P., 1997. 'Introduction', in *Nārāyaṇīya-Studien*, ed. P. Schreiner, Wiesbaden: Harrassowitz, pp. 1-29.

Seneviratne, H.L., 1992. 'The Meaning of Space in the Temple of the Tooth in Kandy', in *Religion in India*, ed. T.N. Madan, Delhi: Oxford University Press, pp. 111-26.

Sircar, D.C., 1965. *Indian Epigraphy*, Delhi: Motilal Banarsidass.

———1966. *Indian Epigraphical Glossary*, Delhi: Motilal Banarsidass.

Sontheimer, G.-D., 1964. 'Religious Endowments in India: The Juristic Personality of Hindu Deities', *Zeischrift für vergleichende Rechts Wissenschaften*, 87: 44-100.

Smith, F.M., 1987. *The Vedic Sacrifice in Transition: A Translation and Study of the Trikāṇḍamaṇḍana of Bhāskaramiśra*, Poona: Bhandarkar Oriental Research Institute.

Smith, H.D., 1975. *A Descriptive Bibliography of the Printed Texts of the Pāñcarātrāgama*, vol. I, Baroda: Oriental Institute.

Stietencron, H. von., 1977. 'Orthodox Attitudes Towards Temple Service and Image Worship in Ancient India', *Central Asiatic Journal*, XXI: 126-38.

Strickmann, M., 1996. *Mantras et mandarins. Le bouddhisme tantrique en Chine*, Paris: Gallimard.

Tanemura, R., 2001. 'One Aspect of the Consecration Ceremony of Images in Buddhist Tantrism: "The Ten Rites" Prescribed in the *Kriyāsaṃgrapañjikā* and their Background', *Journal of the Japanese Association for South Asian Studies*, 13: 53-75.

Thapar, R., 1974. *A History of India*, rpt., Hardmondsworth: Penguin.

Toffin, G., 1986. 'Dieux souverains et rois dévots dans l'ancienne royauté de la vallée du Népal', *L'Homme*, XXVI: 71-95.

Verpoorten, J.-M., 1987. *Mīmāṃsā Literature*, Wiesbaden: Otto Harrassowitz (A History of Indian Literature, vol. VI, Fasc. 5).

PART II

LAND, SOIL, AND SENSE OF BELONGING

3

The Place of Ritual: Geographical Boundaries and Sectarian Identity in Medieval Indian Religions

PHYLLIS GRANOFF

This paper was originally the third of four studies on rituals in medieval India. In my first paper (Granoff 2000: 399-424) I argued that the ritual culture of medieval India in some cases and contexts could be regarded as 'eclectic'. By this I meant that groups self-consciously allowed the use of rituals or ritual elements that they acknowledged were not their own. I chose to illustrate this with a discussion of select verses from an early medieval Buddhist text, probably of the eighth century AD, entitled the *Mañjuśrimūlakalpa*.[1] I further presented some evidence from Jain texts that supports the notion that at least in some cases Jains could also see rituals transcending established boundaries. Although Jainism is slightly older than Buddhism, throughout their history the two religions have had much in common; both began in protest against the priestly cult of the sacrifice around the sixth century BC and they often adopted similar strategies in the face of Hindu ritual culture. While I did not discuss Hindu evidence in any detail in this first essay, I did propose that Hindu texts also were 'ritually eclectic' to some extent, although the boundaries they erected could be different from the starker Buddhist/Hindu or Jain/Hindu boundaries of some of the Buddhist and Jain texts discussed. In addition, I suggested that in an environment where rituals could cross boundaries, groups had to be constantly vigilant to preserve for themselves a distinctive ritual identity. They did this in many ways.

In my second paper (Granoff 2001: 109-31) I attempted to examine how and when rituals could serve as dividing lines between groups that wished to distinguish themselves from each other. I explored the use of ritual boundaries in two broad categories. In the first I dealt with ritual boundaries between groups who are otherwise very different in terms of doctrine and belief structures. The main example for this category was Jains and Buddhists as against Hindus. Among the categories of rituals I discussed was the broad one of rituals to conceive children, a class of rituals that both Jains and Buddhists rejected. They offered instead a scientific theory closely related to the theories of the medical texts of the conditions required for conception. In their self-descriptions, indeed both Jains and Buddhists could insist that their refusal to believe in rituals for procuring children was an important point that distinguished them from the non-Buddhists and non-Jains who did believe in their efficacy. The evidence indicates that over the course of time such ritual boundaries were not as successful in defining group identity as one might have thought.

As a second category of the use of ritual to distinguish religious groups I dealt with intra-group rivalry. Jainism split into two main sects, the Śvetāmbaras, whose monks wear white robes, and the Digambaras or 'sky-clad', whose monks go naked.[2] In addition, monks were organized into various lineages, which traced their descent to the founding figure of Jainism, the Jina Mahāvīra, who was probably an older contemporary of the Buddha, or to later charismatic monks. These lineages or *gacchas* were often rivals for local patronage in medieval times. In the cases of the competing lineages of Śvetāmbara Jainism, ritual was often the most obvious differentiating feature between the groups. In their general belief system and sacred writings, these groups had little to differentiate them from each other. My tentative conclusion was that ritual works better as a boundary marker precisely in cases like these Jain *gacchas*, where there is so little else by way of doctrine to distinguish one group form another. I return in this paper to the sectarian politics of the Jain *gacchas*.

Medieval Jain sectarianism offers an opportunity to study the religious rhetoric and the complex social and economic factors that underlay sectarian splits in medieval India. We have a number of small but lively polemical texts that give us access into the issues that fired sectarian disputes. From these sources we learn that Jain sects or *gacchas* most often berated each other for not following the proper ritual calendar or ritual sequence; nonetheless, I would like to explore here the possibility that their basic differences may have been more than simply differences in how they practised particular rites. I will suggest that competing religious groups in medieval India, like these Jain *gacchas*, may indeed have used ritual boundaries to mark themselves off from each other, but that in fact what differentiated the groups may well have been not religious at all. The Jain evidence shows that competing groups were often tied to specific geographical areas, and that it was such regional/linguistic affiliation that was, at least in some cases, the primary identity marker, the clearest point of differentiation that set these groups apart from other like-minded groups. In such cases, I would like further to suggest, ritual was merely put in the service of a more fundamental marker of difference to give what was not originally a religious difference a decidedly religious tone. Medieval India often classified people on the basis of regional and linguistic identity. I will argue here that such classifications also coloured the way in which religious groups saw themselves and others.

Little is known of the actual history of Śvetāmbara sectarianism. While lineages of monks are mentioned in one of the earlier Jain sacred scriptures, the *Kalpa-Sūtra,* which may date to the second century BC, and in Kuṣāṇa inscriptions of 200 BC to AD 200, the proliferation of monastic lineages known as *gacchas* seems to have occurred around the eleventh century AD.[3] Many of the medieval *gacchas* did not survive into modern times, but it is clear from their inscriptions that most of them, with two or three exceptions, were active in a small geographical area. Indeed, many of the *gacchas* known to us by name seem to have been comprised of local monks who exerted their authority over the village from which they came. This village also gave their *gaccha* its name. Thus we have the Māḍara Gaccha, named after the village of Māḍara in Sirohi state in Rajasthan. Most of the inscriptions of this *gaccha* in fact come from the area around Māḍara. The Nānavāla Gaccha took its name from another village in Sirohi, named Nānā. It too seems to have been active primarily in the area of its origin. The same may be said of the Jīrāvalī Gaccha, which seems to have been nothing more than a local branch of a larger monastic group, the Bṛhad Gaccha. Judging from the inscriptions, such local groups of monks seem to have formed independent units or *gacchas* that were then responsible for ritual services in their local area. Thus we learn that the Varmāṇa or Brāhamaṇa Gaccha controlled the Jain temple of Mahāvīra at Varmāṇa (Jain 1963: 63-4). In theory *gacchas* could extend their influence over larger areas, of course, and in practice, much of medieval Śvetāmbara Jain monastic politics may well have been the result of the rivalry between monks of different *gacchas* over areas of influence and patronage, particularly the patronage of local rulers.

Geographical ties were not the only ties that bound monks in their *gacchas*. It is possible to document cases in which the monks of a given *gaccha* were not just from the same village but from the same family (Granoff 2006). Monks in a *gaccha* thus formed a closely knit group with shared origins in the same village and in some cases with strong ties of kinship. In addition, there is evidence to indicate that the lay members of a monk's family would participate actively in making donations that supported his *gaccha*. For example, they would fund the ceremonies at which a monk was installed in a position or given a particular honorific title (Laughlin 1999). Some Jain sectarian groups, then, were often defined by ties to place and by strong kinship ties.

For most of the small local *gacchas* we do not know what, if any, ritual differences existed between them and other groups. The examples I gave in my discussion of ritual exclusivism were taken from the polemical writings of the sixteenth century AD Tapāgaccha monk, Dharmasāgara. While he vehemently attacks other *gacchas* and castigates them for their improper interpretation of Jain ritual practice, it is worth noting that he mentions only a few of the many *gacchas* that must have existed in his day. Some of the groups he mentions, it would appear, had more than local authority, but they were a minority. The majority of Jain *gacchas* were strictly local phenomena. The only written records that these *gacchas* have left us are inscriptions that commemorate the dedication of images and temples, in themselves rituals that were shared between groups, at least in their broad outlines. We know virtually nothing of the details of how these rituals might have been practised, and it is in those now vanished details that ritual differences may well have surfaced. But at least the Jain *gacchas* offer us an example of the divisions in a religious community that seem to have had roots in non-religious factors: birthplace and kinship ties. These geographical roots or kinship links may well have carried further significance in medieval India. I now discuss the kinds of associations with place that are made in a variety of medieval texts. Belonging to a certain place or a certain group was often seen as implying something about a person. Geography was not morally neutral in medieval India, and, as we shall see, a definite preoccupation with classifying peoples and places was coming into vogue just at about the time the Jain regional *gacchas* were proliferating. I examine now a number of examples of such classifications and speculate about what they might mean for medieval Indian religious groups and how they saw themselves as distinctive from other groups.

CLASSIFYING THE WORLD

While there has always been an awareness of local and regional differences in Indian literature, the interest in classifying and describing such differences seems to have increased at about the same time as the Jain *gacchas* were developing. Medieval texts show both a growing consciousness of these differences and an almost irrepressible desire to codify them in readily accessible lists. The Dharmaśāstras, texts that define for the Hindu community orthodox religious and social behaviour, had always made an effort to define the geographical sphere of *dharma* or proper conduct.[4] We see this concern persisting into medieval times in the compendia on *dharma*, where it leads to elaborate lists and descriptions of places that are propitious for ritual activity.

The twelfth-century *Dānasāgara* (1.35) of Ballālasena, for example, has a section on *puṇyadeśa* or 'auspicious places'. It begins with a quote from the *Viṣṇu Purāṇa* which defines the limits of Bhārata, the sacred land of India.[5] It then cites the law book of *Manu,* one of the earliest and most influential of the Dharmaśāstra texts.[6] Manu (2.23) had defined 'civilization', the area in which it is possible to practise the correct religion (the ancient sacrifice) as that territory in which the *kṛṣṇasāra* deer roams naturally. By Manu's definition, 'civilization' was confined to the area between the Himālayas and the Vindhyas. Another statement in the *Dānasāgara* says that the place where the strict regulation of the duties of the four castes is not observed is beyond the pale of *dharma.* Having thus defined the broad limits of a geographical area in which religious activities can take place, the text proceeds to specify particular places within those broader outlines that are uniquely suited for religious ritual. Passages from the *Liṅga* and *Matsya Purāṇa* are quoted, listing specific *tīrthas* or holy places that are considered most auspicious for ritual bathing and giving. These texts have expanded the range of sacred geography to include places in southern as well as northern India.

The concern for defining the limits of sacred terrain persisted in medieval times. Hemādri in his *Caturvargacintāmaṇi, vrata khaṇḍa,* probably written around 1260, likewise included a section on where rituals are to be performed. He begins with a quotation from the *Mārkaṇḍeya Purāṇa* and then proceeds with many of the passages cited by Ballālasena. It is clear that there is something very important in these texts about place and the practice of religion. Some places are simply unsuited for ritual activity and some places are ideally suited for it. We shall see that this extends to the people who come from these places as well.

From the beginning, the concern with identifying propitious places for religious ritual had as its corollary identifying or labelling places as totally unmeritorious. By medieval times both aspects of sacred geography are greatly expanded. Ethnic or regional stereotyping, sometimes without malicious intent, becomes a familiar exercise in texts from about the eleventh century AD. There is no question that ethnic slurs or stereotypes existed before this period; thus in the great Sanskrit epic, the *Mahābhārata,* portions of which may date as early as the fourth century BC, when the warrior Karṇa is furious with his charioteer Śalya who is trying to prevent him from going into battle against Kṛṣṇa and Arjuna, one of the worst terms of abuse he can think of is to call Śalya, 'Pāpadeśaja' or 'Kudeśaja', 'Born from a wicked or evil place'. He goes on to describe in some detail the perfidy of the place Śalya comes from, the land of the Madrakas, located in what today is the Panjab.[7]

Listen, Śalya, to what they say about the wicked Madrakas, to what everyone says, women and children, even old men as they chat together; even men who devote themselves to study say the same. Listen, Śalya, carefully, and then either accept what I say or be ready with your reply. The Madraka is always a false friend; if there is someone who goes against us, you can be sure he is from Madraka. One should have nothing to do with a person from Madraka, who is the lowest of the low, a born liar. The man from Madraka is always evil minded, false and dishonest. The Madraka is the epitome of all evil. (8.27.71-4)

The text continues with a litany of the Madraka's immorality; the women are licentious; men and women drink and eat beef; they are lustful and immoral in every way and there is no act so base that they will not do it. In Chapter 30 the slurs continue. People from Bāhlīka in the far north-west are not even human (v. 44); they are the offspring of two demons, Bahis and Hlīka. Karṇa then goes on to tell Śalya a story to back up his abusive comments about the Madrakas. A Brāhmin once came to the home of an artisan. He was pleased with the artisan's behaviour and said to him,

I once dwelt alone for a long time on a peak of the Himālaya. And I saw many different lands with all of their different customs. In none of them did the people ever go against what was right. They all followed the definition of what constituted proper behaviour that had been set down by those who know the Veda. But as I wandered through many lands, each with its different customs, I came finally to the land of the Bahlīkas. There I heard that a man who is a Brāhmin suddenly takes to behaving like a Kṣatriya; the Bāhlīka becomes a Vaiśya and then a Śūdra and then a barber. The barber then becomes a Brāhmin once again. And having been a twice-born, he becomes again a servant. In the same family one man might be a proper Brāhmin, well-behaved, while his brothers just do anything they desire. The Gāndhāras, Madrakas, and Bāhlīkas, are indeed stupid. This was what I heard; I heard that they do not maintain the proper conduct; this is what I heard as I wandered the entire earth, I heard that everything is topsy-turvy in the land of the Bahlīkas. (8.30.50-6).

The text continues in this vein, singling out certain lands for opprobrium and praising others as the abode of those with proper conduct. In his criticism of the Bāhlīkas, the Brāhman specifically notes that the distinction between the four castes, with the Brāhmin at the top and the Śūdra at the bottom, is not maintained. Eventually Śalya is allowed to reply. He protests against the very notion that certain places are inherently good or bad or that people in a given place can be uniformly characterized in one way or another. He even suggests that Karṇa's own kingdom, the territory of Aṅga in the north-east, has a mixture of good and bad. Here is what he says (83-7)

> O Karṇa, even in the territory of Aṅga, in the country over which you rule, there are men who sell their wives and children or those who abandon others in need. In every country there are good Brāhmins or Kṣatriyas, Vaiśyas or Śūdras, there are pious women of chaste conduct. Every man is an expert when it comes to the faults of others; but he does not see his own faults; even if he sees them, he does not know what to do.

The exchange between Karṇa and Śalya has many points of interest; it is an early example of 'moral geography', of stereotyping peoples or places and judging them on moral grounds, that becomes so familiar in the Purāṇas. The list of vices, from drunkenness to licentiousness and failure to observe caste restrictions in behaviour and occupation, will become a familiar list over the centuries as one group describes another. These are the vices of the *mlecchas,* of the Buddhists, of the Jains, or more generally of the wicked at the time of the last of the four declining world ages, the *kali yuga*. The accused and accuser may change but the accusations stay relatively constant. In fact, in a story in the Buddhist *Sūtrālaṃkāra* attributed to Aśvaghoṣa of the second century AD (Chapter 4), and preserved in Chinese, a Gandhāran Buddhist comes to Mathurā. He worships at a Buddhist *stūpa*, only to be accosted by some hostile Brāhmans who worship Śiva, a god who they say is capable of destroying one's enemies. There follows a debate between them, after which the Gandhāran Buddhist concludes that Mathurā and its people are indeed unwholesome. Gandhāra is the place of morality and pure religion!

Regional stereotypes in Indian texts often include the kind of harsh censure that we see in the exchange between Karṇa and Śalya. Kṣemendra, an eleventh-century author, in his *Kalāvilāsa* describes the first appearance of *dambha* or deceit in the world.[8] Brahmā sees that mortals in their honesty have no way to earn a living and so he creates *Dambha,* whom he orders to go to earth. It is in Gauḍa (Bengal) that *Dambha* is most victorious, but he lodges in the words of the Bāhlīkas and the religious observances of the easterners and southerners. He plants a firm foot in every aspect of the lives of the Gauḍas. Kṣemendra does not just paint certain peoples as deceitful; he also depicts certain castes and occupations as particularly deceitful, for example courtesans, doctors, and scribes.

But descriptions of peoples and places did not have to have this kind of negative edge that we see in Kṣemendra. Certain genres of medieval texts simply show a growing fondness for describing the complex variety of the world and its many lands. Such descriptions were not confined to texts like the Jain *Jambudvīpaprajñapti,* something we might consider a specialized text on cosmography. The idea of assigning different countries and people uniform traits became a part of mainstream literate Indian culture. The *Nāṭyaśāstra*, a text on dramaturgy, had shown some interest in different lands and their languages and customs, but not to the same degree as later medieval texts.[9] Thus in Chapter 21 of the *Nāṭyaśāstra* on costumes, as the discussion turns to how humans are to be portrayed, a distinction is made about how women from Avantī, for example, or Gauḍa, are to wear their hair.[10] It is repeatedly stressed that all characters should be costumed and coiffed according to local custom (21.70; 21.100). Even the skin colour of the actors must be authentic (21.101ff.). Compared to later texts or to the *Mahābhārata*, the *Nāṭyaśāstra* is somewhat temperate in its descriptions, saying that 'for the most part' the Pulindas, a tribal people, and southerners are dark, while 'for the most part' people in the north are fair (21.103). It also includes in its classifications castes and activities, and thus avoids the impression we get from other sources that place of birth or geographical origin is the sole or even the main determinant of the appearance and nature of a person. Chapter 17, in its discussion of the languages to be used in drama, further characterizes the languages of different regions, describing them as having a preponderance of one sound over another. The text is thus clearly aware of the need for accuracy in character portrayal and of the importance of being able to provide simple lists of what was typical about the customs and languages of different lands.

A similar motivation lies behind the later texts on poetics that include a separate section on different lands, insuring that the dramatist and the actor could know how to depict different peoples. Given the emphasis on verisimilitude, such descriptions served to aid both author and actor in their need to become familiar with the customs and appearance of the characters who would appear in a drama. The *Bhāvaprakāśa* of Śāradātanaya was written some time between 1150 and 1250. Its tenth chapter contains a description of Bhārata, which it defines as the land extending from the Himālaya in the north to the Setubandha, the bridge Rāma is said to have built to cross over Laṅkā, in the south, a notable expansion, as an early text like Manu excluded all of south India. In the *Bhāvaprakāśa* we are told that in the first of the four world ages, the golden age or *kṛta yuga,* the entire area was inhabited, but as the ages have progressed, people have begun to shun the cold and move further and further south. The text offers concise descriptions of different peoples, describing their physical features, their attire and their language. Thus we hear how one group lives in mountain caves; their language has a lot of the letter *śa* in it; they are ruddy complexioned and have black hair; they are corpulent and have buck teeth and wear clothing of coarse cotton (180). Another group lives in the forests and along river banks; their language has a lot of *ca* and *ṣa.* Like the wicked Madrakas, some of these groups are said to eat beef (thus the Caṇḍālas in verse 182), and many are fond of intoxicating drinks (vv 182, 186). One group is said to violate the norms of decent society and eat meat, drink wine and make offerings of meat (186). It is further recommended to the aspiring playwright that he include characters like these and other forest dwellers to amuse the audience. The descriptions, purporting to be objective accounts of the customs and languages of the groups described, are nonetheless somewhat pejorative. The implications of eating beef and drinking spirits would have been most evident to a contemporary reader.

Another text on poetics, the slightly earlier *Kāvyamīmāṃsā* of the tenth-century author Rājaśekhara, in Chapters 17 and 18 includes a description of different lands and the cycles of time. The text stresses why it is important for the poet to know about different peoples and what they are like: the poet who knows the cycles of time and geography will not lack for subjects. The information that this text gives includes the names and borders of countries, and a brief list of local fruits and trees or products that are unique to a place; it also has a description of the skin colour of different peoples. Rājaśekhara adds that a poet must be careful to get his information correct when he writes about a place or a people; to describe someone or some place wrongly is a flaw or *doṣa* in composition. He recommends that poets consult his *Bhuvanakośa* or *World Encyclopedia*, a text no longer extant.

The description of the world and its countries and peoples seems to have become so popular a topic that it crept into a variety of texts of different genres. The *Śaktisamāgamatantra*, a late medieval text on rituals devoted to Hindu goddesses (vol. III, chapter 7), includes a description of different places in India. The areas it outlines are no longer just political entities (like Madraka or Bāhlīka in the *Mahābhārata* or the lands of Rājaśekhara). The boundaries of the territories are mostly either natural objects (rivers, mountains, etc.), or sacred places (temples). Thus we read:

> O Śivā, the land of Aṅga extends from Vaidyanātha to Bhuvaneśvara. There is nothing wrong with making a pilgrimage there. (16)
>
> O Śivā, I have proclaimed that Vaṅgadeśa is the land from the ocean to the Brahmaputra; it yields every kind of accomplishment. (17)
>
> From Jagannātha in the East to the banks of the river Kṛṣṇā is the land of Kaliṅga; people there practice the left-handed Tantra. (18)

The text continues, occasionally describing the special products of a place. Maru, which corresponds to the desert area of Rajasthan, is the place that camels come from, for example, while Kāmboja, usually located in the far north-west, is famous for its horses. We may learn of the general characteristics of groups; Mālavaites, or people from Mālava in central north India, are devoted to making money and to agriculture, while those in Tiliṅga, which corresponds to Andhra Pradesh, to study and meditation; Khurāsana or Khorasan in Central Asia follows the way of the *mlecchas*. We are also told of the suitability of certain places for certain religious practices. Thus the land of Malaya (Kerala) is said to be especially propitious for the cultivation of mantras, and Gauḍa or Bengal for the cultivation of magic spells. Both Aṅga and Magadha in the north-east are suitable for pilgrimage. The geographical range of the *Śaktisamāgamatantra* is certainly wider than many of the other texts; it knows Khurāsana, Cīna (China), Nepāla and Bhoṭa (Tibet), for example. The *Śaktisamāgamatantra* is also interesting in that it includes both the kind of information the authors of treatises on poetics had emphasized (skin colour, local products) and the kind of information that had interested the authors of ritual texts like Ballālasena and Hemādri, namely what places were particularly propitious for the performance of specific religious rituals. Some places are praised as suited for pilgrimage, while others are noted as particularly good for cultivating magic powers, *vidyās* or *siddhis*. Some places are simply said to be excellent, while others are most wicked. Thus Sauvīra (Saurashtra) is described as the worst of all places while Simhala (Śrī Laṅkā) is the best. The *Śaktisamāgamatantra* seems to combine the 'objective' list of external characteristics that had interested the texts on poetics, and the 'moral geography' that we had seen in the *Mahābhārata*, the Dharmaśāstras and their descendants, the ritual texts.

The history and development of medieval Indian attitudes towards place in texts like these remain to be studied.[11] I have given here examples from a number of texts that belong to different genres to point out one general feature that they have in common. All of them assume, unlike Śalya, that each country or each people characterized can be described in uniform terms. Thus all people from place *x* have the same skin colour, dress the same, and follow the same goals (making money or pursuing Vedic study, as the case may be). They may also be equally good or equally wicked; a place may simply be the best or the worst. I would like to suggest that this willingness to see people as representatives of a place and as uniformly characterized by virtue of their place of origin also affected the ways in which religious disputes could be understood and described. In what follows I hope to illustrate that some disagreements, even those about ritual rules or doctrinal interpretation, could in fact be described in religious texts in terms of a similar geographical stereotyping. What divided religious groups in such descriptions was as much their place of origin as their views. I turn now to one such quarrel in Buddhist literature.

THE KAUŚĀMBĪ MONKS AND THE VAIŚĀLĪ MONKS: STICKING TOGETHER AGAINST OUTSIDERS

The rules for the behaviour of Buddhist monks are preserved in Pāli and in Sanskrit. The quarrelsome monks of Kauśāmbī figure in both the Pāli Vinaya, *Mahāvagga* 10.1 and the Sanskrit *Mūlasarvāstivādavinaya* (*Kośāmbīvastu*).[12] There is also a *sutta* in another Pāli text, the *Majjhimanikāya*, called the *Kosambiyasutta*, that speaks of the quarrelsome Kauśāmbī monks.[13] In fact, the two *vinaya* accounts of the squabbles of the Kauśāmbī monks differ considerably and in intriguing ways. In the Pāli *vinaya* account, as in the Pāli *sutta*, the fight seems to be an internal one; that is, the monks of Kauśāmbī are fighting among themselves. We are not told exactly why in either of the Pāli texts; in the *vinaya* we are told only that one of the monks has been accused of some offence; others have rallied to his defence, while still others have sided with the accusers. The situation threatened to get out of hand, and the Buddha eventually had to persuade the contending monks that their actions threatened the unity of the saṃgha which should be preserved at all cost. But here is how the *Mūlasarvāstivādavinaya* describes the problem:

> The Blessed Buddha was in Kauśāmbī in the Ghoṣilārāma. At that time there was a certain monk from Kauśāmbī who was troublesome and argumentative, practised in the sūtras, the vinaya and the abhidharma. He had many loyal monks as followers, who were similarly troublesome and argumentative, practised in the sūtras, the vinaya and the abhidharma. Now in Vaiśālī there was a certain monk who was native to that place, that is, a Vaiśālaka, who was troublesome and argumentative, practised in the sūtras, the vinaya and the abhidharma. And he had many loyal monks as followers, who were similarly troublesome and argumentative, practised in the sūtras, the vinaya and the abhidharma.

Now it so happened that one time the monk from Vaiśālī in his wanderings chanced to come to Kauśāmbī. Tired from his journey, he rested a while and then he went to see that Kauśāmbī monk. The two of them exchanged pleasantries and then they set about discussing in earnest the meaning of certain things in the sūtras, the vinaya and the abhidharma. One of them would say, 'This is the way the sūtra is to be read. This is the meaning of the sūtra.' The other would reply, 'Oh no. The sūtra must not be read like that. That is definitely not the meaning of the sūtra. You are wrong. I am right. You have made a mistake.' 'I have not made any mistake. It is you who are wrong.' And in this way they became enemies. The monk from Kauśāmbī was always on the alert for any slip committed by the monk from Vaiśālī.

Now the monks had agreed upon a certain arrangement. 'Whoever saw that the pot for water to be used at the toilet was empty, was void, had no water in it, was to fill it and put it back in its place. Or he was to tell the monk who occupied the position of *upādhivāraka*, saying, "The water pot used in the toilet is empty." If he does not fill the pot himself or tell the *upādhivāraka*, then he will be considered to have committed an act of carelessness. We will say that he has committed an offence requiring expiation.'

One day some householder invited the Buddha and the monks to eat in his house. Some of the monks had already gone and others were about to go. The monk from Vaiśālī had taken the pot of water and gone to the latrine. His attendant ran after him, calling out, 'Master! Some of the monks have already gone to the meal and others are about to go. Come on. Let's go!' And so he put the water pot down somewhere and set off. Now that Kauśāmbī monk suddenly arrived on the scene. And so the monk of Vaiśālī picked up the pot and was about to go into the monastery. His attendant said, 'Master, why are you going back in?' He replied, 'Son, that monk from Kauśāmbī is just waiting for me to do something wrong. I'm going to fill the water pot.' 'Is it completely empty?' 'No, it's not completely empty. But there's not enough water in it to be of use to anyone.' 'Master, as long as it's not completely empty. We'll all stick up for you. Come on. Let's go!' And so the monk from Vaiśālī left the water pot right there and went with his attendant. The monk from Kauśāmbī took a good look at the pot. Furious, with a grumble he filled it and used it and then set off. After the monks had eaten and when they were all back at the monastery, that monk began to stir them up, 'Noble brothers! The monk from Vaiśālī has broken the rules.' He discussed it with all of the monks there, in order of seniority, and then proceeded to where the monk from Vaiśālī was.

'Noble brother', he said, 'Allow me to speak'. 'You are allowed.' 'You have committed an offence. You must do what is right now.' 'I don't see anything wrong that I have done.'

'Noble brother! The monks had made an agreement. If anyone sees that the water pot used for the toilet is empty, void, has no water in it, he is to fill it himself and put it back in its place or tell the *upādhivāraka*, saying, "Noble Brother! The water pot used for the toilet is empty." If he does not fill it himself and he does not tell the *upādhivāraka,* then he will be considered to have committed an act of carelessness. We will say that he has committed an offence requiring expiation.' The monk from Vaiśālī said, 'It wasn't empty.' 'It doesn't matter if it wasn't empty. There wasn't enough water in it to be of use.' The Vaiśālī monk was silent.

The monk who was from Kauśāmbī had a large group of followers there. And so he was able to use his power to have the monk from Vaiśālī temporarily excluded. The monks of Vaiśālī got angry. And so a fight, a quarrel, an argument, arose between the monks of Vaiśālī and the monks of Kauśāmbī, the one group saying he was guilty and the other saying he was not guilty.

The story continues, and eventually the Buddha is disgusted with the monks of Kauśāmbī and their quarrels. He flies through the air and goes to Śrāvastī. In the meantime, the monks of Vaiśālī and the monks of Kauśāmbī spend their days, fighting with each other. 'They went out for alms in the morning, and then shut the doors of the monastery and fought for the rest of the day.' Things went on this way for twelve years when the Brāhmans and householders finally began to ask themselves and each other why the Buddha was avoiding them. They decided they would no longer speak to the Kauśāmbī monks or give them alms. The Kauśāmbī monks then went to Śrāvastī. At this point the Vaiśālī monks seem to disappear from the scene. The text resembles more closely the Pāli version, and it seems that the Kauśāmbī monks are divided amongst themselves on the question of whether a certain monk has committed an offence. The text concludes with the Buddha counselling the Kauśāmbī monks to patch up their differences.

When we examine this sometimes humorous account it seems clear that what fuels and sustains the hostility between the two groups of monks must be something more than the actual offence committed.

A friendly discussion on Buddhist sūtras, on the monastic rules or vinaya and the scholastic doctrinal discussions or abhidharma, as the text puts it, turns into a personal hostility that then becomes a matter of general concern with the lines firmly drawn by who comes from where. The Kauśāmbī monks are lined up against the monks from Vaiśālī. A reader is left with the impression that the real issue is not whether the accused, in his eagerness to attend the feast, did really violate the rule about the water pot; there is no substantive discussion of his case. The issue is the power of the Kauśāmbī group with their connections to force the expulsion of a monk who is an outsider. This is not about ritual or doing things differently. The Kauśāmbī monks are about to split the community on geographic lines. This is in fact what we see happening in medieval Śvetāmbara Jainism; splinter groups form in the monastic community along geographic lines. I might add that the *Mūlasarvāstivādavinaya* in its telling of the story seems to judge negatively not only such quarrels in general, but more specifically the monks of Kauśāmbī who started the fight. This is at least the impression we are given when the householders of Kauśāmbī blame the Kauśāmbī monks for the absence of the Buddha and the monks of Vaiśālī drop out altogether as the quarrelsome Kauśāmbī monks go to the Buddha in Śrāvastī and are told to patch up their differences.

The Vaiśālī monks, however, do not fare very well in another story in the *Mūlasarvāstivādavinaya*, this time from the *adhikaraṇavastu*.[14] There we hear of the monk Kāla Mṛgāraputra, who has come to Vaiśālī from Śrāvastī. He has become very popular with the local people, which angers the Vaiśālī monks. Here is how the text describes the conflict:

> At that time the venerable monk Kāla Mṛgāraputra was in Vaiśālī, staying in the *kūṭāgāra* on the bank of lake Markaṭa. The people of Vaiśālī, the Licchavis, all came to him and through their reverence of him they greatly honoured the Buddha, dharma and saṃgha. The monks of Vaiśālī reflected, 'This venerable Kāla Mṛgāra was born somewhere else; he was raised somewhere else. He was born in Śrāvastī. But the people of Vaiśālī, the Licchavis, seem to be quite taken with him. We must find some excuse that is the cause of expelling him from the community so that the people of Vaiśālī, the Licchavis, will no longer be so pleased with him.'

The Vaiśālī monks are all treated to a special bath by one of the householders, and they make sure that the unsuspecting Kāla Mṛgāra takes someone else's robes by mistake. They accuse him of theft and without due procedure they temporarily expel him from the community of monks. Eventually, they repent of their wrongdoing and take Kāla Mṛgāra back. This story is absolutely unambiguous in its depiction of the source of the Vaiśālī monks' hostility: they do not like Kāla Mṛgāra simply because he is not one of them; he is an outsider.

I would like to consider another story from the monastic rules which also exists in the Pāli Vinaya section known as the *Culla Vagga* and in the section of the *Mūlasarvāstivādavinaya* known as the *Saṃghabhedavastu*. It suggests that regional allegiances could result in more serious quarrels, less easily repaired. The story is about the efforts of the Buddha's cousin, Devadatta, to split the saṃgha or monastic community by proposing five strict rules for the monks: that they should live only in the forest; that they should subsist only on alms and never accept invitations to eat in homes; that they should only wear a robe of rags and never wear the clothes of a householder; that they should dwell only under trees and never in huts; and that they should never eat meat. The two versions again have telling differences. In the Pāli, Devadatta is able to convince 500 monks to follow him. Furthermore, we are clearly told that these are 500 monks from Vaiśālī. It is this detail that the *Mūlasarvāstivādavinaya* account omits; all we are told there is that some 500 monks joined Devadatta. The text again seems to be partial to the monks of Vaiśālī in its telling of these stories. This can only raise the intriguing question of the role of regional groups in the compilation of these vinaya texts and in dividing the community.

I turn now to another story from the *Mūlasarvāstivādavinaya* that again suggests a special connection between a place and its inhabitants and a religious position. In the account of the life of the Buddha, the *Mūlasarvāstivādavinaya* offers this description of the conversion of the Buddha's relatives, the Śākya clan (Gnoli 1978b: I-200):

King Śuddhodana saw the ascetics who had become followers of the Buddha, with their matted locks. He said to himself that because of their calm deportment their mental attitude brought pleasure to others; but skinny and scrawny from all their austerities, their bodies were certainly not any pleasure to look at. He looked at them again and thought once more, 'These ascetics with their matted locks display a calm deportment and so their mental attitude may well bring pleasure to others; but skinny and scrawny from all their austerities, their bodies are certainly not any pleasure to look at. What kind of followers would do the Buddha justice?' Thus he wondered and he came to the conclusion that the Śākyas would make handsome followers for the Buddha. And so he called all the Śākyas together and said to them, 'If the prince Sarvārthasiddha had not renounced the world, what would he have been?' 'The Emperor over the entire world.' 'And what would you have been?' 'His followers.' 'Well, now the prince Sarvārthasiddha is the King of the Dharma. Why do you not become his followers?' 'King, do you mean to say that we should become monks?' 'You should become monks.' 'All of us?' 'One in each family.' 'So we shall.' And King Śuddhodana had this proclamation made throughout the city Kapilavastu: 'Thus the king commands. Let every Śākya living in my territory become a monk, one from each family.'

In this brief account of the conversion of the Śākyas, it is clear that following the Buddha is not entirely an individual decision. The Śākyas as a whole are to become followers of the Buddha. Buddhism is the clan religion. There is no corresponding story in the Pāli texts; there we learn only that the Śākyas were initially reluctant to bow down to the Buddha but when they saw the king worship the Buddha they followed suit.

There are other stories in the *Mūlasarvāstivādavinaya* in which the practice of religion is described as a community decision and community affair. In one story, we meet again the Buddhist community of Vaiśālī. The Buddha has arrived with his monks and the householders have made an agreement that no one of them is to invite the Buddha and the monks to dinner. If any one of them were to invite the Buddha and monks, this would mean that everyone else in the community would be deprived of the opportunity to do so themselves. Thus they all agree that only the community as a whole, the *gaṇa,* will invite the Buddha and the monks to dinner.

The story centers around the particular events that unfold when one wealthy and meritorious householder, not having heard of the group agreement, proceeds to invite the Buddha on his own. Eventually, the conflict is resolved, and the Buddha goes as well to the community dinner (Bagchi 1967: 138).

In another story we see that belonging to a particular place influences religious preference in several different ways. This is the story of the Buddha's sojourn in the city of Bhadraṅkara, a place that is described as a bastion of heretics or *tīrthikas*. The Buddha has decided that the wealthy layman Meṇḍhaka is ready to receive the Buddhist teaching, and thus decides to go to Bhadraṅkara. The heretics make the inhabitants of the entire city agree that no one will go and see the Buddha; whoever does so must pay a fine of 60 *kārṣāpaṇas*. Only one person violates their common agreement, and she is an outsider. A young Brāhman girl from Kapilavastu has been married into a family in Bhadraṅkara. She is standing on the city wall and sees the Buddha in the darkness. In her heart she wishes there were a staircase so that she might descend from the wall and worship the Buddha. The Buddha knows her mind and makes a staircase for her. The Buddha accepts her worship and tells her to go to Meṇḍhaka and tell him to come to the Buddha; why should Meṇḍhaka, whose son has an inexhaustible purse, be afraid of a fine of 60 *kārṣāpaṇas?* Meṇḍhaka hears the Buddha preach and then wants everyone in Bhadraṅkara to do the same. He agrees to pay their fines. This is not necessary, however; for if the community as a whole (*gaṇa*) could agree to prohibit worship of the Buddha, it can also lift the prohibition! Now the entire city *en masse* rushes to see the Buddha; the throng is so great that the Buddha's guard, Vajrapāṇi, must break open the city gates so that the people can get out of the city and see the Buddha! (Bagchi 1967: 145-8)

In this story, religious belief is very much associated with group or civic identity. The pious Buddhist lady is from Kapilavastu, a city closely associated with the Buddha as his native place. The citizens of Bhadraṅkara are devotees of the heretics, probably Jain, and agree as a group not to worship the Buddha. When one of them becomes a Buddhist, his goal becomes conversion of the others. As the story concludes all the citizens of Bhadraṅkara pour through the city gates.

The heretics are elsewhere in the *Mūlasarvāstivādavinaya* depicted as keen to link place and religion. When Anāthapiṇḍaka, one of the most famous lay donors in Buddhism, decides to build his Jetavihāra for the Buddha, the heretics attempt to stop him. Here is what they say, 'We have divided up the cities; the ascetic Gautama has Rājagṛha; Śrāvastī belongs to us' (Gnoli 1978a: 20). The *Mūlasarvāstivādavinaya* seems in stories such as these to link place or place of birth with a particular religious affiliation. We shall see that as time progresses this link becomes firmer and lends to religious debates a unique complexion.

Thus far we have looked at the role that geography may have played in setting boundaries between religious groups. The Jain example of the medieval lineages or *gacchas* suggested that what differentiated groups may well have been something as fundamental as where they originated and operated. I then took us on a tour of something I called medieval moral geography, to show that place becomes increasingly important in the medieval Indian text and often serves as a marker of ethical traits as well as physical traits. Place can also determine what kinds of religious practices are capable of being cultivated and bearing fruit. I then looked at a few Buddhist stories in which quarrels may have occurred and dividing lines may well have been drawn with more consideration to place of origin of the participants in a dispute than to other factors. I would now like to draw some of this disparate material together by discussing a late medieval Vaiṣṇava group in which we see place play an important role. The Oriya Vaiṣṇava writers known as the Pañcasakhā sought to define themselves in a way that was distinctive. One of the major issues for them was place: they were intent on finding a unique identity for themselves that was different from that of the dominant group of Vaiṣṇavas in north India, the Bengali followers of Caitanya. Both groups relied on the same texts and both worshipped the same god in the same temple, Jagannātha at Purī in Orissa. The Oriya Vaiṣṇavas sought for themselves a distinctive religious identity in a number of ways, some of which include using ritual as markers. But their texts make clear that the issue was not so much ritual difference as place. How were they to maintain an identity different from that of the Bengali? I suggest in what follows that ritual was the means to the end; it was not the reason why the Oriyas had to be distinct from the Bengalis, but it was how they could describe their desired distinctiveness in more acceptably religious terms.

MEDIEVAL VAIṢṆAVA MOVEMENTS: COUNTERING THE INFLUENCE OF THE BENGALIS

Increasingly in the late medieval period disputes between religious groups come to be couched in terms of regional rivalries rather than debates about doctrine or ritual. Much of the evidence for how groups regarded themselves and others comes from biographical literature of important figures in the traditions, with their obvious biases. Nonetheless these texts reveal that it was one particular regional or ethnic group who exercised power at certain medieval sacred sites, and against whom others would struggle to maintain their authority and establish their legitimacy. This group was Bengali, the followers of Caitanya. It would seem that the Bengalis played an important priestly role at both major Vaiṣṇava pilgrimage sites in north India, Vṛndāvan and the temple of Jagannātha Purī in Orissa. This brought them into potential conflict with other Vaiṣṇava groups, the Puṣṭi Mārga followers of Vallabha whose cultic centre was later in Rajasthan, the Pañcasakhā poets of Orissa, and the Assamese followers of Śaṅkaradeva.[15] Elsewhere I discussed some of the techniques that the Assamese biographers employed to maintain the supremacy of Śaṅkaradeva over the temple priests of Jagannātha Purī. In the Assamese biographies, for example, Jagannātha comes at night to Śaṅkaradeva and eats his leftovers, taking the divine gift of food that is usually presented at a temple to the pilgrim this time from the pilgrim himself, who does not even need to go to the temple that is controlled by the priests. Eventually even the priests come to Śaṅkaradeva; if they are left to exercise their authority in the temple, they nonetheless must in some way acknowledge the superiority of Śaṅkaradeva (Granoff 2003).

Other medieval groups faced similar problems and many of them described the struggle as one between the Bengalis on the one hand and a group from another linguistic area on the other hand. Here is what the seventeenth-century *Śrīnāthajī kī Prākaṭhya Vārtā* of Harirāyajī has to say:

Śrīācārya (Vallabha) had two sons. To the first, Śrī Gopīnāthajī, he gave the Lord Jagannātha's image, and the second, Śrīguṃsāījī, that is Śrī Viṭṭhalanāṭhajī, he put in control. That was when he removed the Bengalis and in accordance with the Divine wishes appointed Gujarati Brahman priests to do the worship. He made Rāmadāsa the head and appointed all the Brahmans to do the worship.

Earlier in the text we had learned that the Bengali Mādhavendra Purī had been responsible for looking after the crown of the Lord and on festival days for seeing that his turban was put on; something he was doing did not please the lord. And so after a period of fourteen years during which the Bengalis had looked after the image, the Lord gave these curt instructions to the disciple Avadhūtadāsa: 'Tell Kṛṣṇadāsa that the Bengalis are stealing from me. Get rid of the Bengalis.' (p. 18)

It would be hard to find a clearer example of polarization of ethnic groups than this. It is the Bengalis against the Gujaratis, and what they are fighting over is control over the worship of the image of Kṛṣṇa known as Śrīnāthajī that has appeared at Mount Govardhana. Indeed, the entire story of the miraculous appearance of Śrīnāthajī on Govardhana is a story of competition between the followers of Vallabha and the Bengalis. The Bengalis claimed that the image from the start was destined for worship by one of them, Mādhavendra Purī, whom we have just met. In the *Caitanyacaritāmṛta* of Kṛṣṇadāsa, completed in AD 1615, we are told that Mādhavendra Purī had been granted a vision of Kṛṣṇa, who told him to set him up for worship at Mount Govardhana.[16] It is this claim that is disputed by the Vallabhaites, particularly in the *Śrīnāthjī kī Prākaṭhya Vārtā.* As the text opens, Mādhavendra Purī is indeed on the scene, but the partially manifested image refuses to accept his offerings and tells Mādhavendra Purī that he is waiting for Vallabha to come. Until that point, the image tells him, it will take only milk. The image further advises him that when Vallabha comes and a temple is built for the image, then Vallabha will appoint Mādhavendra Purī to look after the worship of Śrīnāthajī. Initially, Vallabha had wanted a Gujarati Brāhman, Sādu Pānde, to look after the worship. Sādu Pānde had been one of the first of the residents of Vṛndāvan to have seen Śrīnāthajī on Mount Govardhana; indeed Śrīnāthajī had asked Sādu Pānde to give him milk. But if Sādu Pānde felt comfortable making the simple offering of milk to Śrīnāthajī he does not feel that he knows enough about ritual to accept Vallabha's request to superintend the formal worship of the image. He tells him that there are some Brāhmans, followers of Śrī Kṛṣṇa Caitanya, at the Śrīkuṇḍapa. He advises Vallabha to appoint them to tend the Lord. Vallabha does so; he puts Mādhavendra Purī in charge of the worship. Some of his Gujarati devotees like Sādu Pānde and Kṛṣṇadāsa are then given lesser roles.

The text never makes entirely clear what it is that the Bengalis have done wrong; there is a brief mention that they have put an image of the Goddess Vṛndā next to Śrī Nāthajī and that Śrīnāthajī does not like it, and then the Lord accuses them simply of stealing from Him. What is clear, though, is that they are always known in the text as 'the Bengalis'. The dividing line is drawn between these Bengalis, who are in a position of dominance and are removed from that position, and the Gujaratis, who replace them. While there is no question that the Vallabhaites developed a complex form of ritual that was very different from Bengali rituals, that does not seem to be at issue in our miracle text about the appearance of Śrīnāthajī. Ritual difference here seems less of a boundary marker than regional origin.

The Vallabhaites met the Bengalis at Vṛndāvan, a place that belonged to neither of them originally, and yet we have seen that the contest between them for control over the worship of one particular image there was intense. The Oriya poets to whom I now turn met the Bengalis on Orissan ground, but the Bengalis were nonetheless already established in a position of religious authority in and around the temple of Jagannātha Purī. Orissan Vaiṣṇavism would develop its own distinctive philosophical literature, its own rituals and its own practices of meditation, but the problem of what their relationship to the towering figure of Caitanya would be was one with which they struggled in a number of ways. The five Vaiṣṇava poets, active in the sixteenth and seventeenth centuries, were Balarāma Dāsa, Jagannātha Dāsa, Acyutānanda Dāsa, Yaśovanta Dāsa, and Ananta Dāsa. Acyutānanda Dāsa was particularly prolific and has left us a number of accounts of his own life as well as of some of the others in the group. There are problems for the modern scholar in dealing with these texts and my own research has only just begun. One obvious problem is authenticity; not all texts attributed to Acyutānanda Dāsa are his work, and the same is no doubt true of the other poets. This is blatantly obvious when we look at one genre of text, the *Mālikās* or accounts of the future. Some of the *Mālikās* attributed to Acyutānanda Dāsa speak of nylon, of Russia and Gandhi. Rather than assume that Acyutānanda Dāsa did indeed have knowledge of the future I find it easier to assume that the texts in which such things occur are definitely later texts! Another serious problem is the state of the editions; many of the printed texts have changed readings to make them more comprehensible to a modern audience. Prabhat Kumar Mukherjee pointed out one stunning change in the *Śūnya Saṃhitā*, where the Vaiṣṇava saint meets someone called Buḍā mātā, 'the Old Mother'. In fact, Mukherjee notes, this reads 'Buddha Mātā' in the manuscripts, "Mother of the Buddha"' (Mukherjee 1981: 171). With these limitations in mind, the printed texts, cautiously used, still have much to tell us about the Oriya Vaiṣṇava poets and how they defined themselves. In what follows I focus on their relationship to the Bengali Vaiṣṇavas, particularly Caitanya.

Although the Bengali accounts of Caitanya do not mention the five Oriya poets, the Oriya poets in their own writings trace their lineage back to Caitanya. Acyutānanda Dāsa describes himself as a disciple of Caitanya; in his *Śūnya Saṃhitā*, Chapters 1 and 11, he mentions a prediction that Kṛṣṇa makes that in the Kali Yuga, Kṛṣṇa will be born as Caitanya and Sudāmā, his companion, will be born as Acyuta. In Chapter 2, Acyutānanda tells us how Caitanya then predicts that Acyutānanda will spread the devotion to Kṛṣṇa in Utkala, Orissa. In another text, the *Varṇa Ṭikā,* Acyutānanda again tells us that he was initiated by Caitanya. But in yet another text, the *Varaṇa Carita Gītā* (p. 296), Acyutānanda tells us both that he was initiated by Caitanya and that he did not accept Caitanya's doctrine.

When Caitanya became exceedingly popular, he says, he left Purī and retreated to the Devī Pīṭha at Jhaṅkaḍa. There is no question that goddess sites play an important role in the eschatology of the Oriya Vaiṣṇava poets. The destruction of the wicked at the end of the *kali yuga* is a major theme in their writings, and the final battle is said to be set for Yājapur, a famous goddess site in Orissa. It is also clear from their writings that the five Oriya poets consciously attempt to distinguish themselves from the Bengali Vaiṣṇavas from whom they claim their spiritual descent. This is clearest in their rejection of the Bengali *mantra*, *Hare Kṛṣṇa*, in favour of their own *Hare Rāma.* My own suspicion is that the *Varaṇa Carita Gītā* is being honest about the conflict or contest between the Oriya and Bengali Vaiṣṇavas.

This conflict is clearest in a seventeenth-century biography of Jagannātha Dāsa, 1487-1547. *Śrī Jagannātha Caritāmṛta* was written by his disciple Dibākara Dāsa in Sanskrit and Oriya. In this text the rivalry between the Bengalis and the Oriyas is a central theme. Like the rivalry between the Gujaratis and the Bengalis in the *Śrīnāthjī kī Prākaṭhya Vārtā,* the rivalry here centres on the control of a sacred object and sacred space, the temple of Jagannātha at Purī; Yājapur is an alternative sacred space to which the losers occasionally retreat. And the rank order of the Bengalis and Oriyas is reversed; here Caitanya is the disciple of the Oriya Jagannātha Dāsa.

As the text opens, we learn that Caitanya has been born from the smile of Kṛṣṇa and Jagannātha has been born from the smile of Kṛṣṇa's favourite consort, Rādhā, as Rādhā and Kṛṣṇa gazed lovingly on each other in heaven. Caitanya first meets Jagannātha Dāsa when Jagannātha is reciting the *Bhāgavata Purāṇa* in Oriya. The *Bhāgavata Purāṇa*, probably composed in south India in the tenth century, in its tenth book has a detailed account of the life of Kṛṣṇa. It became the single most important text for all medieval Vaiṣṇava groups devoted to the worship of Kṛṣṇa. Jagannātha Dāsa translated the Sanskrit text into Oriya. It is this text that he was reciting in our story. Caitanya is said to have been overwhelmed by its teachings of divine love; he goes to see Jagannātha every day. This does not please the Bengalis who are with Caitanya. They peremptorily tell Caitanya not to have anything to do with the 'Utkala Brāhmin', the Brāhman from Orissa. We are on familiar ground; a religious rivalry is explicitly described in terms of regional rivalries. The Bengalis further warn Caitanya that if he refuses and continues to associate with Jagannātha, he might well start to behave like him. Again, we see the familiar association between correct ritual practice and place. The assumption is that no one from Utkala, or Orissa, could know or do the proper things. Then follow two verses, one in Sanskrit and one in Oriya, castigating the Oriya Brāhman for not worshipping Kṛṣṇa exclusively:

> I think it is better to hug a snake or a tiger or a crocodile than to consort with sinners who worship many gods.
>
> Hug a snake or a tiger or a crocodile. The wise man would never consort with someone who worships other gods.

As the text continues, Jagannātha Dāsa says that he has been told by the Lord Jagannātha that he should be initiated by Caitanya. What is even more interesting is that the *mantra* or sacred formula that he gets from Caitanya is not the *mantra* of the Bengalis at all; it is not *Hare Kṛṣṇa* but *Hare Rāma*. Here Caitanya has been made over into the originator of the unique Oriya rituals and doctrine! The text acknowledges that there is something highly irregular in the transmission of this *mantra*; it has to be validated by a dream that Lord Jagannātha gives to both Jagannātha Dāsa and Caitanya.

There are further indications that all is not well between the Bengalis and the Oriyas. In Chapter 3 Caitanya bestows upon Jagannātha the honorific epithet, *atibaḍa*, 'the greatest'. The Bengali Brāhmans are angry that such an honour should be given not to one of their own, but to an Utkala Brāhman,

> Hearing the word 'greatest', the Vaiṣṇavas were sad. Why should he (Caitanya) be calling a Brāhmin from this place in that way?
>
> Now he uses the term 'greatest' for an Oriya Brāhman; all these years we have been faithful devotees and now we are put in a position of inferiority.

The Bengali Brāhmans seem to object not just to being superseded; their pride seems doubly wounded by the fact that the one who surpasses them is not a Bengali, but an Oriya! This comes out again and again and the language of the text is explicit: there is a sharp polarity between those who come from Bengal and those who come from Orissa.

Now you associate with this Brahman from Utkala and call him 'The greatest one'; we Vaiṣṇavas are something lesser; O lord, this is not the proper way to treat us.

The Bengali slurs against their Oriya rival are of no avail. Caitanya refuses to leave Purī and the company of the Utkala Brāhman. The Bengalis in their anger abandon Caitanya and Purī and go to Yājapurī, in a reversal of what happened to Acyutānanda Dāsa. Acyutānanda, remember, disgusted with Caitanya's fame at Purī and his doctrine, left Purī for a goddess centre. The Bengalis make repeated efforts to get Caitanya to come to them and to get Caitanya to leave Jagannātha Dāsa. Caitanya replies with praise of Jagannātha Purī and Jagannātha Dāsa. The Bengalis are adamant; their only concession is that they agree to go to Purī once a year to the chariot festival.

As the text continues, the rivalry between the Bengalis and the Oriyas seems to assume less importance; the case has been settled. The Bengalis have left Purī for all but one short period during the year. Caitanya dies and Jagannātha Dāsa continues to worship in the temple at Purī. His troubles are not over, however; in what is surely one of the strangest episodes in medieval hagiography, Jagannātha Dāsa is accused of being unchaste when someone reports to the king that two women always serve Jagannātha Dāsa. The king goes to see for himself and finds that, lo and behold, the accusation seems to be true. There he finds Jagannātha Dāsa and the two women. Jagannātha explains that it is only right for women to serve women; he says the women are heavenly damsels, and he strips to show the king that he, Jagannātha, has female genitals. He says that he is Rādhā/Kṛṣṇa; for 27 days of the month he is a man and for three days he is a woman and menstruates.

There is no question, I think, that the notion that the saint is Rādhā and Kṛṣṇa combined in one body is something that the Oriya poet has taken from Caitanya's followers. The biography of Jagannātha Dāsa is clearly struggling with the Bengalis, with the towering figure of Caitanya, with Caitanya's doctrine, and with

Bengali control over or influence at the temple at Purī. The text deals openly with the conflict between the Bengalis and Oriyas, allowing the Oriyas to emerge victorious in the figure of Jagannātha Dāsa. At the same time, it makes clear that what was defining religious groups could be such factors as geographical origin, whether one was Bengali or Oriya, and it makes every effort to combat such views. The Bengalis who believe that no Utkala Brāhman could possibly be an acceptable worshipper are virtually expelled from Purī and the Utkala Brāhman is revealed to be God.

CONCLUSION

I have tried to show that defining boundaries between medieval religious groups could be a complicated process. The Oriya and Bengali Vaiṣṇavas have numerous points of difference between them, most fundamentally in the sacred formula or *mantra* that they recite. But this is not entirely the issue between them in their texts; often it boils down to the simple fact of being a Bengali or being an Utkalīya. I attempted to show that this was not confined to the Bengalis and the Oriyas; indeed in texts of the Puṣṭi Mārga of Vallabha we hear the same language of polarized groups set apart from each other on the basis of regional origins. There we hear of the Bengalis and the Gujaratis. I have also tried to argue that in medieval India where one comes from became increasingly important; regions were classified and moral as well as physical traits assigned to different peoples. Finally, by going back to the Buddhist rules for monks, the *Vinaya* texts, I hoped to suggest that categorizing competing religious groups in terms of regional origin was not something new to medieval India. The Buddhist texts suggest that it may not only have been place of origin that provided group cohesiveness to religious groups; kinship ties may also have played a role. This is supported as well by evidence from Jain sectarian groups. All of these points and the texts in which they are found, I think, merit further study.

In terms of the issues I have tried to outline in my presentations on ritual and boundaries in medieval India, highlighting the role of regionalism I believe can alert us to the possibility that even when rituals seem to divide religious groups they may not necessarily be the primary reasons for the divisions observed. In medieval India the assumption could often be that coming from a certain place naturally made your rituals the right ones, or the wrong ones, as the case may be. Regional affiliation marks some groups as fundamentally different from each other; adopted ritual differences offer a means to describe such differences in religious terms. As these examples suggest, behind the heated arguments about ways of performing rituals may be other contested spaces.

Acknowledgements: This paper was originally presented as part of a series of lectures organized in Paris in 2000 by Gérard Colas and Gilles Tarabout. I thank those individuals present for their comments. I also thank Gregory Schopen and Heidi Pauwels for their comments on some passages in the translations.

NOTES

1. On the date of this text see Matsunaga 1985: 882-94 and Lalou 1936: 327-49.
2. On the history of this split, which probably began in the fifth century AD, see Dundas 1992: 40-52. Long after this paper was written, Paul Dundas's masterful study of Jain sectarianism (Dundas 2005) appeared. This book contains a wealth of information about the groups I discuss here, particularly the Tapāgaccha.
3. On the history of the *gacchas* see Jain 1963: 53-69. On the date of the *Kalpa-Sūtra* see Dundas 1992: 58.
4. On the dating and nature of this literature see Kane 1968.
5. The Purāṇas are notoriously difficult to date. They are compilations of diverse material, including myths, semi-historical accounts, cosmogonies, and ritual rules. The *Viṣṇu Purāṇa* is often dated to the fifth-sixth century AD. On Purāṇic literature in general see Rocher 1986.
6. On its date and importance see Kane 1968: 306-49. Kane suggests that the earliest portions of the text may be around the second century AD (Kane 1968: 330).
7. Scholars agree on this identification, although not all of the places named in early or medieval texts can be identified with certainty. I am relying for my identifications on Dey 1971.

8. I thank Judit Törzsök for reminding me of Kṣemendra's penchant for ethnic slurs.
9. When I presented this paper Charles Malamoud reminded me that the *Kāmasūtra* had its own way of describing regional differences, classifying women and their sexual habits according to the place they came from.
10. There has been considerable debate about the date of the *Nāṭyaśāstra,* which is the foundational text of the classical Indian theatre. Recently Bansat-Boudon (1998: 18 n. 2) suggested a date of the second century AD. For some of the discussion see Konow 1969: 3.
11. Benoytosh Bhattacharya, who edited the *Śaktisamāgamatantra,* noted a number of Sanskrit texts that include descriptions of places. The subject deserves a separate monograph. When I presented this paper, Sanjay Subrahmanyam suggested that the tendency to classify entire populations of peoples in uniform terms that we find in these texts may well relate to beliefs in the medical texts that eating fruits of the soil and drinking the water of a given place result in a particular physical and psychic state; this would explain why all Bengalis are the same as each other or all people from Magadha are the same as each other and yet why populations from different regions differ from those in other regions. Zimmermann 1987 discusses the role of the environment in determining human nature according to the medical texts. It seems to me that the medical texts, while arguing for the influence of environment on the body and psyche, also argue that these influences can be modified by a change in environment. But in the texts I am citing a Bengali or a Madraka is always false, no matter where he happens to find himself. Nonetheless, medical texts do show an interest in classifying the habits of different regions, particularly the food habits, and the physician who does not take such things into consideration is said to be unlikely to succeed in his medical treatment. See for example the *Caraka Saṃhitā, Cikitsāsthānam,* Chapter XXX, vr 316-20.
12. *Mahāvagga*, pp. 368-73: *Mūlasarvāstivādavinaya*, pp. 258-70.
13. *Majjhimanikāya*, vol. 1, no. 48.
14. *Mūlasarvāstivādavinaya, Adhikaraṇavastu*, p. 102.
15. Vallabha, Caitanya, and Śaṅkaradeva were all active in the early sixteenth century. Vallabha died in 1530, Caitanya in 1533, and Śaṅkaradeva in 1569.
16. I have discussed some of this material in Granoff 1983: 12-25.

REFERENCES

PRIMARY SOURCES

Bhāvaprakāśa of Śaradātanaya, ed. Madan Mohan Agrawal, Aligarh: Aligarh Muslim University, 1978.

Caraka Saṃhitā, ed. Vaidya Jādavajī Trikamji Âchārya, Bombay: Nirnaya Sagara Press, 1941.

Caturvargacintāmaṇi of Hemādri, ed. Paṇḍita Bharatacandra Śiromaṇi, Kashi Sanskrit Series, no. 235, Varanasi: Chaukhambha Sanskrit Sansthan, rpt. 1985.

Cullavagga, ed. Bhikkhu J. Kashyap, Nalanda Pali Text Series, Nalanda, Pali Publication Board, 1956.

Dānasāgara of Ballālasena, ed. Bhabatosh Bhattacharya, *Bibliotheca Indica*, vol. 274, Calcutta 1953.

Kalāvilāsa of Kṣemendra, in *Kṣemendralaghukāvyasaṃgraha*, ed. E.V.V. Rāghavāchārya and D.G. Padhye, Hyderabad: The Sanskrit Academy, Osmania University, Sanskrit Academy Series, no. 7, 1961.

Kāvyamīmāṃsā of Rājaśekhara, ed. C.D. Dalal and Pandit R.A. Sastry, Gaekwad's Oriental Series, 1934.

Mahāvagga, ed. Bhikkhu J. Kashyap, Nalanda Pali Texts Series, Nalanda: Pali Publication Board, 1956.

Majjhimanikāya, ed. Bhikkhu J. Kashyap, Nalanda Pali Texts Series, vol. 1, no. 48, Nalanda: Pali Publication Board, 1958.

Mūlasarvāstivādavinaya, ed. S. Bagchi, Buddhist Sanskrit Texts Series, no. 16, Darbhanga: Mithila Institute, 1967.

The Gilgit Manuscript of the Śayanāsanavastu *and the* Adhikaraṇavastu, *Being the 15th and 16th Sections of the Vinaya of the* Mūlasarvāstivāda, ed. Raniero Gnoli, Roma, Instituto Italiano per il Medio ed Estremo Oriente, 1978a.

The Gilgit Manuscript of the Sanghabhedavastu, ed. Raniero Gnoli, Roma, ISMEO, 1978b.

Nāṭyaśāstra, ed. Pandit Kedārnātha, Kāvyamālā no. 42, Bombay: Nirṇaya Sāgara Press, 1943.

Śaktisamāgamatantra, ed. Benoytosh Bhattacharya, Baroda: Baroda Oriental Institute, 1947.

Śrījagannātha Carita, Puri: Baḍa Oḍia Natha, 1963.

Śrīnāthjī kī Prākaṭhya Vārtā of Harirāyjī, Nathdvara: Vidyāvibhāga Mandira Maṇḍala, 1981.

Śūnya Saṃhitā of Acyutānanda Dāsa, ed. Mṛtyuñjaya Nayak, in *Santha Kavi Acyutānanda Dāsa o Śūnya Saṃhitā*, Katak: Friends Publishers, 1992.

Sūtrālaṃkāra, attributed to Aśvaghoṣa, Taisho 201, tr. into French by Edouard Huber, Paris: Ernest Laroux, 1908.

Varana Carita Gītā, in *Bhakta Kabi Acyutānanda*, compiled by Brajmohan Mohanty, Cuttack: Orissa Book Store, 1995.

Varṇaṭikā of Yaśovanta Dāsa, in *Yaśovanta Mālikā o Varṇa Ṭikā Avatāra Mālikā*, Katak: Dharma Grantha Stores, n.d.

SECONDARY SOURCES

Bansat-Boudon, Lyne (ed.), 1998. *Théâtres Indiens*, Paris, EHESS.

Dey, Nundo Lal, 1971 [1927]. *The Geographical Dictionary of Ancient and Medieval India*, New Delhi: Oriental Books Reprint Corporation (rpt.).

Dundas, Paul, 1992. *The Jains*, London: Routledge.

———2005. *History, Scripture and Controversy in a Medieval Jain Sect*, London: Routledge.

Granoff, Phyllis, 1983. 'God as Idol: The Role of Special Images in Sectarian Conflict in Medieval Vaiṣṇavism', *South Asian Religious Art Studies*, 3: 12-25.

———2000. 'Other People's Rituals: Ritual Eclecticism in Early Medieval Indian Religions', *Journal of Indian Philosophy*, 28, 4: 399-424.

———2001. 'My Ritual, My Gods: Ritual Exclusivism in Medieval India', *Journal of Indian Philosophy*, 29, 1-2: 109-31.

———2003. 'Pilgrimage as Revelation: Śaṅkaradeva's Journey to Jagannātha Purī', in *Pilgrims, Patrons and Place: Localizing Sanctity in Asian Religions*, ed. P. Granoff and K. Shinohara, Vancouver: University of British Columbia Press, pp. 181-203.

———2006. 'Fathers and Sons: Some Remarks on the Ordination of Children in the Medieval Śvetambara Community', *Asiatische Studien*, LX, 3: 607-33.

Jain, Kailash Chandra, 1963. *Jainism in Rajasthan*, Jivaraja Jaina Granthamala, no. 15, Sholapur.

Kane, Pandurang Vaman, 1968. *History of Dharmaśāstra*, vol. 1, Poona: Bhandarkar Oriental Research Institute.

Konow, Sten, 1969. *The Indian Drama*, tr. S.N. Ghosal, Calcutta: General Printers and Publishers.

Lalou, Marcelle, 1936. 'Mañjuśrīmūlakalpa et Tārāmūlakalpa', *Harvard Journal of Asiatic Studies*, 1: 327-49.

Laughlin, Jack, 1999. 'Ârādhakamūrti/adhiṣṭhāyakamūrti: Popular Piety, Politics and the Medieval Jain Temple Portrait', Ph.D. thesis, Department of Religious Studies, Hamilton, McMaster University.

Matsunaga, Yukei, 1985. 'On the Date of the Mañjuśrīmūlakalpa', in *Tantric and Taoist Studies in Honor of R.A. Stein*, ed. Michael Strickmann, Brussels: Mélanges Chinois et Bouddhiques, pp. 882-94.

Mukherjee, Prabhat Kumar, 1981. *The History of the Gajapati Kings of Orissa and their Successors*, Cuttack: Kitab Mahal.

Rocher, Ludo, 1986. *The Purāṇas, History of Indian Literature*, vol. 2, fas. 3, Wiesbaden: Otto Harrassowitz.

Zimmermann, Francis, 1987. *The Jungle and the Aroma of Meats: An Ecological Theme in Hindu Medicine*, Berkeley: University of California Press.

4

The Smell of Soil: Geomantic Practices among Banaras Astrologers

CATERINA GUENZI AND SUNITA SINGH

> On one occasion, while cowherd-boys headed by Balarāma were playing, they complained to the mother (Yaśodā) that Kṛṣṇa had eaten earth. Thereupon, Yaśodā, anxious about his well-being and health, caught Kṛṣṇa by his hand and rebuking him, . . . spoke: 'You naughty boy! Why did you eat earth secretly? These your playmates tell me and your elder brother also says the same.' 'No mother, I did not eat earth. All these are liars. If (you still think) they tell the truth, look into my mouth personally.' 'If that be the case, open your mouth.' Thus ordered, the glorious Lord Hari of unlimited supreme powers and who, out of sport, had assumed the form of a human child, opened his mouth. She (Yaśodā) beheld therein the universe consisting of mobiles and immobiles, the ethereal dome, the cardinal points, the sphere of the earth along with the mountains, continents and oceans, the wind, the fire, the moon, the stars, the planetary system. . . .
>
> *Bhāgavata Purāṇa* X.8, vv. 32-8[1]

In the city of Banaras, astrologers not only look at the heavens, planets and stars, but also at soil and land. In analysing their clients problems, astrologers examine horoscopes (*janam kuṇḍalī*), almanacs (*pañcāṅg*), and astral charts (*cakr*), as well as the soil (*miṭṭī*, *bhūmi*) and land (*zamīn*) where people live. According to them, soil, land, and house play a fundamental role in determining the destiny of living beings. In some cases, people's suffering, diseases, or conflicts are attributed to 'soil defects' (*bhūmidoṣ*) or 'site defects' (*vāstudoṣ*) rather than to 'planetary defects' (*grahadoṣ*).

In this article we examine the geomantic techniques used by Banaras astrologers when they inspect the qualities and properties of different kinds of soil and land. To do this, we consider the point of view of the astrologers and clients as well as theories codified in sacred texts that speak of the reciprocal relationship between living beings' destiny and 'the fate of the soil' (*miṭṭī kā bhāgya*) or 'the fate of the land' (*zamīn kā bhāgya*). As we shall see, not only does the land have an influence on the lives of its inhabitants, but conversely the actions taken by human beings are thought to affect the properties of that land.

The theoretical knowledge referred to by astrologers whenever they conduct a divinatory investigation on soil and land is termed *vāstuśāstra*, 'the science of sites and buildings', a corpus of sacred texts (*śāstra*) that defines the principles of architecture (*vāstuvidyā*).[2] Astrologers consider *vāstuśāstra* to be a part of *jyotiṣa*, astronomical and astrological knowledge, and use this science in order to detect defects (*doṣ*) present on a plot. Rules codified in *vāstuśāstra* establish how to examine the qualities and orientation of soil, the shape of plots, and the internal configuration of domestic space. Special consideration is given to spatial directions (*diśā*).[3]

Vāstuśāstra is not the only source of knowledge used by astrologers who divine soil and land. Geomantic specialists also resort to other divinatory techniques drawn from *saṃhitā*, the branch of astrology that specializes in the interpretation of omens, and from *horā* (or *phalita*), predictive astrology based on horoscope reading. Most astrologers rely on both theoretical competence codified in Brahmanical texts and divinatory skills obtained through initiation (*dīkṣā*) from a tantric guru. Tantric initiation is thought to endow the astrologer with supernatural powers (*siddhi*) that enable geomantic divination.

In Banaras, today, divination of soil and land is so much in demand that some astrologers have decided to specialize in this kind of work, and discontinue reading horoscopes and almanacs. Many Hindus consult astrologers at the moment of buying a plot of land or constructing a house. The investigation of the site is undertaken to make sure that the soil, land, and building will suit a person and his family. The geomantic inspection carried out by the astrologer before buying land or building a house is thought to be as important as the matching of a bride and groom's horoscopes prior to marriage. In both cases, a major change will affect the life of the family and the astrologer has to verify that the choice is *anukūl*, in accordance with the cosmic order as defined by temporal and spatial dimensions.

Another time astrologers are consulted is when difficulties and obstacles repeatedly afflict those who live in a certain house or on a certain piece of land. The astrologer will ascertain whether the soil or the building characteristics could be the cause of the problems. Examples of when an astrologer might be consulted might include a household where parents do not earn enough money, children have trouble in school, or family members are continuously disputing; a farm that is not productive or a factory plagued with problems; a building site where work is not progressing well. In each case, an astrologer would be asked to conduct a geomantic inquiry.

Clients seeking the astrologer's geomantic advice come from different social strata and walks of life. *Vāstuśāstra* is very popular among the urban middle and upper classes, who can afford to buy land and build their own houses, or who already own one or several pieces of real estate. The inspection of the ground is also often requested by people from lower classes, who rarely resort to 'classic' astrological counselling based on personal horoscopes. Aside from individuals, one finds owners of private companies requesting astrologers' geomantic surveys in order to guarantee the success of commercial activities, and officials from the Indian government seeking *vāstu* consultation before undertaking major building projects.

INVESTIGATION PROCEDURES

Astrologers follow two main geomantic procedures, 'soil inspection' (*miṭṭī śodhan*) and 'land investigation' (*zamīn kī parīkṣā*). According to the first procedure, the client brings to the astrologer a soil sample taken from his house and wrapped in paper or in a plastic bag. In the second case, the astrologer goes to the client's place in order to analyse not only soil qualities, but a whole range of land characteristics.

In traditional houses, still common in villages, the floor is made of mud and those consulting an astrologer can collect a soil sample from inside the house.[4] In the case of urban houses made out of cement or bricks, there are two ways soil samples may be collected. Either the sample is taken out from the ground surrounding the house, or a 'soil substitute' is found. Instead of the 'true soil' (*sahī miṭṭī*, *sahī bhūmi*), the client will submit to the astrologer a surrogate, *dhūl*, composed of dust and dirt collected while sweeping the house.

When collecting a soil sample around one's house or in the surrounding proximity, it is best to select a 'mixed' (*miśr*) sample of earth taken from the 'four corners' (*cār kon*). This expression refers to a sample consisting of earth selected from different areas that make up the plot where a house is situated. Earth is collected near the walls of the house, in the garden, near trees, near a water source, and up to the external borders of the plot.

When the soil sample is collected from inside the house—be it mud or dust— it should be selected from specific areas. In traditional mud houses, the most appropriate place for taking a sample is the *nābhi sthal*, the spot of the 'navel', situated in the middle of the courtyard (*āṅgan*). This place is considered to be the 'hearth' of the house and the place where its qualities are concentrated.

In those houses where there is no *nābhi sthal*, a soil sample is taken from the room corresponding to the kind of problem that afflicts the consultant. In the case of conflicts between husband and wife, for example, the sample will be collected from the bedroom. In the case of economic problems, soil will be taken from the storeroom, and so on. Sometimes, someone consulting an astrologer will collect several samples, each wrapped in a numbered packet corresponding to a certain room so that the astrologer can detect in which part of the house a *doṣ* is located.

When a person wants to buy a piece of land, or build a house, or major problems persistently afflict the members of a household, an astrologer will be called to personally visit the place, to conduct a detailed inspection of all the characteristics of the land, and detect possible omens (*lakṣaṇ*) present on the territory. Land investigation and soil sample inspection are not mutually exclusive procedures. They may constitute two phases of a same diagnostic process. If problems persist after an astrologer has analysed a soil sample, he may discern that a visit to the place is necessary. A soil sample appropriately collected, however, is often deemed sufficient. This is how astrologer Chandra Mauli Upadhyay describes the divinatory power of a soil sample:

Through the inspection of a soil sample you can find out everything about the land, about whatever is in the four corners of the land . . . for example, you may come to know that on a certain land there are four trees in one corner, a pond in another corner, a house in a third place and a channel in a fourth . . . all this you can find out through a soil sample. . . .

Astrologer Nilkanth Shastri, the most popular and renowned astrologer in Banaras, whose office is always crowded with clients, further describes the richness of information an astrologer can get from a soil sample:

When people bring me earth (*miṭṭī*) collected in the different areas of their land, near the house and near its external borders, or, which is even better, when they bring me a soil sample taken from the *nābhi sthal*, I am able to detect everything about the land where these people live. . . . I can grasp (*pakaṛnā*) all the details of their land: its shape, the house position, in which parts the land is pure (*śuddh*) or impure (*aśuddh*), in which parts it is alive (*jīvit*) or dead (*mṛt*), if any ghost (*bhūt-pret*) is there. . . . I can come to know the full history of the land, what happened in past generations, which kind of person is the actual owner, if he is an alcoholic, a criminal, I can even find out his son or his son-in-law's job. . . .

In sum, a soil sample is considered to contain, in condensed form, the totality of land characteristics. Most astrologers consider that both geomantic procedures—soil inspection and land investigation—are valid, and many practice hybrid versions of these separate models of divination. Nevertheless, it is important to clarify that these two procedures are expressions of two very different divinatory models. Their distinctiveness becomes more evident when we consider two other specialists who operate in Banaras and conduct geomantic inquiries: the *ojhā* and the *vāstuśāstrī*.

Ojhās are exorcists who generally hail from low castes and treat clients afflicted by ghosts. They divine through soil-sample inspection (or rice inspection, as we will see later on) and examine the earth by invoking one or more deities. *Ojhās* follow a divinatory procedure described as 'intuitional' (Paulme 1956), 'inspirational' or 'revelatory' (Zeitlyn 2001). *Vāstuśāstrī*—experts in *vāstuśāstra*—for their part personally visit the land of their clients and analyse soil, land, and building characteristics.[5] The geomantic inquiry conducted by the *vāstuśāstrī* is based on rules well established in *vāstuśāstra*, the Sanskrit literature on sites and building. This kind of specialist follows what has been called 'inductive divination' (Paulme 1956) or 'mechanical divination' (Zeitlyn 2001). While the *ojhā's* clients largely come from the lower classes and rural areas, the *vāstuśāstrī's* clients are generally urban families from middle or upper classes.[6] Both specialists, in spite of these differences, aim to identify the possible defects and faults (*doṣ*) or the ghosts (*bhūt-pret*) responsible for problems afflicting people living on a land or inside a house.

Banaras astrologers, whose geomantic practices join technical skills and textual knowledge, on the one hand, with spiritual power and tantric rituals, on the other, combine both divinatory models, 'inductive' and 'inspirational'. Their clientele is quite large and socially heterogeneous. Generally, soil sample inspection, which is very cheap (10 to 50 rupees) is requested by low-caste and rural clientele, whereas land investigation is more often demanded by better-off urban families, who can afford to spend hundreds or even thousands of rupees. These families will pay for the astrologer's travel expenses as well as for the sophisticated rituals he will perform for the well-being of their land and house.

Let us now examine the technical knowledge required for soil inspection. The scrutiny of soil properties and qualities is the first stage of any astrologer's geomantic inquiry, wherever it is conducted.

'TRUE SOIL' AND ITS SUBSTITUTES

As we have noted, the soil sample scrutinized by an astrologer must be selected according to precise instructions. A badly selected soil sample will invalidate the results. Astrologers and clients talk of obtaining 'true soil' (*sahī miṭṭī*) or 'authentic soil' (*aslī miṭṭī*). This kind of soil is rich in terms of information about the land in question. It is of that place and in contact with the people of that place.

Soil has peculiar qualities that other substances also utilized for divinatory purposes do not have. Although the practice of submitting dust and dirt (*dhūl*) sweepings from the floor is common, there are astrologers who do not recognize the divinatory value of *dhūl* and refuse to examine it. Consider the opinion of a Brāhman client from a village near Banaras, who had come to consult an astrologer:

To bring *dhūl* is a mistake. The dust and dirt that deposits inside the house is nothing but soil (*miṭṭī*) that comes from outside . . . it is the soil on which we trample when we are outside and that we bring inside the house, but it is not the soil on which our house is built. How could soil that comes from outside make you know the problems of your own place? At most, it can tell you problems that are outside your place!

While soil belongs in a permanent and constitutive way to the place where people live and where their house is built, dust is incidental. Soil is then considered a reliable source of information because of being an autochthonous substance.

Aside from earth and dust, some astrologers analyse rice in order to know about a household's problems. Rice taken from the storage container of the household is deemed a viable substitute of soil for divination. It is thought to contain a trace, a 'sign' (*sanket*, *lakṣaṇ*) of family difficulties.[7] Nevertheless, according to some informants, rice is a particular potent resource enabling the divination of physical afflictions (*śārīrik kaṣṭ*), especially if a person is a victim of sorcery (*ṭonā-ṭoṭkā*). Being absorbed inside the body, rice is believed to be one of the most common vehicles for transmitting charms. Astrologer Ramanand Pandey's assistant noted:

Both earth and rice make you knowing obstacles (*bādhā*) that are inside the house. But people bring earth when they can't see any progress (*barkat*), when, despite the fact that they work very hard, they don't have enough money, or when there are disputes and tension among family members. . . . Conversely, people bring rice when someone is ill, if he has stomach ache or headache, if he is victim of *jādū* (black magic) or *ṭonā* (sorcery).

In order to make rice more potent as a source for divination, an afflicted person may be asked to touch the rice or spend a night sleeping on a pillow filled with that rice. When rice is imbued with a person's sufferings in this way, it is termed the body's rice (*śarīr kā cāval*). A woman who had brought a soil sample from home and the rice touched by her cousin who was in hospital, explained the following to us:

> Through the soil sample you can find out the complete picture (*āvaran*), the full history (*pūrā itihās*) of the entire household (*pūre ghar kā*). On soil, we sleep everyday, we eat everyday, we walk everyday . . . soil is twenty-four hours a day under our feet . . . that is why it can tell the full history of the family. . . . 'Body's rice', on the contrary, will tell you just one person's history (*vyakti kā itihās*). If, for example, the person who touches the rice is you, then, we can know your own health problems, but not your full household problems. When you bring both soil and rice to the astrologer it is precisely because you want to know if the troubles concern one specific person or, conversely, the land (*zamīn*), the house (*ghar*), or the full family (*parivār*). This is why I came with both.

Soil and land are submitted to inspection whenever all the members of a household are going through difficult times. This is how the head of a building enterprise of Ramnagar, a village a few miles away from Banaras, describes a situation when a divinatory investigation of soil and land is required:

> If you start living on some land and after six months or a year someone in the family falls ill, or the cows are not giving milk, you start wondering what is happening. If, for example, a child or a calf dies in his first years, you'll be wondering what could be the cause. In these cases you'll consult an astrologer; for that he will inspect the soil. If children are sick and we are having lots of problems (*diqqat*), we'll ask the astrologer to examine our *miṭṭī* . . . we'll ask him to check if there is any defect in our land, if there is anything bad hidden inside our land. We'll ask him to tell us why we are not able to increase our income, or, if we are getting enough money, why our children have to suffer so badly . . . these are the cases when we show soil to the astrologer.

Soil divination as a means to discover the causes of household history and obstacles rests on the link between the inhabitants of land and the qualities of the land itself. To discover this link astrologer Shree Kanth Shastri insisted on visiting land personally in order to detect the original earth of a site that would reveal its true history:

It is necessary to go and visit the land personally, otherwise you'll never be able to identify the kind of earth that is original to the site. Soil is often levelled with earth taken from other land: how can you check it if you don't go there and examine the land? You should always inspect the earth that is six inches under ground level, so that you'll avoid the layer of dust and dirt that each year leaves on the ground. Six inches under the ground level you find the true soil, the 'pure soil' (*pavitr miṭṭī*). You'll never know, however, if someone, one or two hundreds year before, hasn't brought some earth from another land and put it there . . . but if you don't go on the land, you'll never be able to understand where the earth which comprises the soil comes from, you'll never know if grass that grows on that soil is original.

Tantric astrologer Harihar Pandey spoke of the difficulties of divining in urban areas, where people utilize earth and refuse taken from very different and faraway sites in order to level the land (*pāṭ denā*):

In villages to inspect soil is very simple: you just have to examine earth that is one hand span (*bittā*) under the ground level. But in cities, *pakkā* houses are built on soil that is leveled with earth or garbage taken from different places . . . that's why in cities there is always confusion and it is very difficult to find the pure soil (*śuddh miṭṭī*).

When conducting geomancy, autochthonous soil should be distinguished from the layers of 'new soil' (*nayī miṭṭī*) that are applied before building a house. This is why astrologers follow precise rules when seeking the original, authentic and pure soil, as opposed to the recently imported matter. One method is to analyse the earth that is found under ground level (the depth can vary, according to the type of land). The presence of big stones on the site is another criterion that signifies the authenticity of soil, for rocks are almost never transported from one land to another. Conversely, soil composed of small stones, often used for levelling, is considered suspicious, and rarely selected as a significant soil sample.

Another method followed in order to identify pure soil consists in comparing the different kinds of earth present on the site. This is how astrologer Shree Kanth Shastri explains this criterion:

If you bring a stone belonging to a land to another land, you'll notice that it has a different colour compared to all the other stones that you'll find in that land . . . it is exactly like you [*pointing at the Italian anthropologist*], even if you are here, you are different from all Indian woman, because you come from abroad, from faraway, you have a fair complexion, while Indian women have dark complexion . . . in the same way you can distinguish original soil from soil that comes from outside.

Soil that is homogeneous with the rest of the site is considered autochthonous. The more a kind of soil is common to a certain region, the more it will probably be original to the site.

Now that we have reviewed different methods that astrologers follow when selecting a soil sample, let us consider divinatory techniques used in order to scrutinize it.

THE *VARṆA* OF SOIL

A fundamental principle through which different kinds of soil are classified is *varṇa*, a category that in geomantic science is used in its triple meaning of colour, function and social class that composes the caste hierarchy.

Varāhamihira, a sixth-century astronomer and astrologer, writes the following in *Bṛhat Saṃhitā*, a renowned treatise on divination:

Soil (*bhūmi*) that is white, red, yellow and black is beneficial to Brāhmaṇa, Kṣatriya, Vaiśya and Śūdra respectively; Similarly, if soil smells like clarified butter, blood, food or liquor, it is good for the four classes in order; . . . likewise, a sweet, astringent, sour and pungent soil bestows prosperity on these classes in order.[8]

This same way of classifying soil according to the four *varṇas* is frequent in *vāstuśāstra*, ancient sacred texts on architectural principles, and it is still very much in use in contemporary Hindī literature on the subject.[9]

In the Banaras astrologers' inventory of soil typologies, however, the *varṇa* category is often used in a different way. Instead of indicating the caste that should live on the soil, the *varṇa* category is used to denote the colour and the function of a plot of land. Astrologer Kameshwar Upadhyay, who teaches in the department of Astrology of Banaras Hindu University, describes the way different soils vary according to *varṇa*, making them more suitable for different purposes:

> Brāhmaṇa soil is a bright, light-coloured, white or yellow soil. This kind of soil is appropriate for educational institutions. This is why schools, colleges and universities work very well on this type of soil. This kind of soil is also very much beneficial for temples and worship. Those people who have their house built on this kind of soil will be very peaceful. They will not desire too much money, they will not be ambitious, they will be very quiet and peaceful people. But this soil is not favourable for agriculture: harvest will not be abundant on this kind of soil. . . .
>
> Kṣatriya soil is red. People who live on this kind of soil never stop fighting and quarrelling, their behaviour is always oriented toward conflicts. This kind of soil is very much used for military defence operations. Police and army should always build their headquarters on kṣatriya soil. But if you build a school on this kind of soil, it will be a total disaster, and there will be lots of disputes.
>
> Wherever you find several types of soil mixed together, we call it vaiśya. It is a kind of soil that is quite beneficial for trade and commercial exchanges.
>
> A dark, humid and varied soil is śūdra soil. This is not auspicious soil for human beings. People living on this kind of soil always suffer from some disease, they waste money and their thoughts are impure. If you live on this kind of soil, your kids will probably not pass exams at school. Notwithstanding, from an agricultural point of view, śūdra soil is very fertile and gives very rich harvest. It is good for the meat and fish trade as well.

It is claimed that each type of soil, according to its *varṇa*, has an influence (*prabhāv*) on the behaviour and personality of those who live on it. A house built on a kṣatriya soil is said to bring disputes and disagreements between family members, brāhmaṇa soil makes people devoted to learning and worship, and so on. One astrologer told us that the influence of soil type is particularly evident in multi-storeyed buildings, where people of different castes live together. He referred to such a building in Banaras, which was built on śūdra soil:

> All the families living in that building were eating meat, you could smell meat everywhere . . . this is the influence of the place (*sthān*): on śūdra soil,

even Brahmans end up eating meat and fish . . . even if at the beginning they will try to resist, after some time they will surrender . . . this is the influence (*prabhāv*) of the place where we live.

The influence of soil is thought to be significant not only at the level of the building plot, but also at larger levels of urban or regional space. An astrologer explained to us, for example, that in the Ayodhya region of Uttar Pradesh, soil is 'white', brāhmaṇa, and is therefore poor from an agricultural point of view but very 'fertile' from a religious point of view.[10] In the Hazaribagh district of Bihar, rich in coalmines, soil is black, śūdra, and this would be the reason for frequent diseases and premature deaths affecting the inhabitants of that area. In the Banaras urban area the most widespread soil is a yellow kind, that is brāhmaṇa soil that favours knowledge (*vidyā*) and learning (*vidvattā*). This is how astrologer Nilkanth Shastri describes Banaras soil:

What characterizes Banaras region is that this is a site (*aḍḍā*) for learning (*vidvattā*) and scholars (*vidvān*). From the Varaṇā river up to the Asī river, 15 or 16 kilometres inside the Pañcakrośī (the pilgrimage route that surrounds Banaras), you find a *miṭṭī* that constitutes the base (*ādhār*) of knowledge (*vidyā*). On this type of soil, even a servant's daughter has a double M.A. I'll tell you a story. One day our servant was sick and we asked her to send here her daughter so that she would do the washing-up. When her daughter got here, my daughter realized that she was one of her classmates in College! Such a soil (*bhūmi*) is Banaras. . . .

Nilkanth Shastri, an astrologer with over 50 years of 'field experience' in different areas of Banaras, classifies the different city neighbourhoods as follows:[11]

If you go in the residential area in front of Besant College, you'll see that over there soil is reddish and most of the inhabitants are millionaire businessmen. Reddish soil (*lālpan miṭṭī*) is in fact beneficial for economic growth. . . . From Daśāsvamedh ghāṭ up to Hariścandra ghāṭ, you'll find a mixed soil (*miśr miṭṭī*), full of stones, which is quite appropriate for doing *tantr sādhanā* (practice of 'accomplishment'). This is why in this area you'll see many temples and excellent ascetics. If you go to the area behind the Railway Station, you'll find that over there soil is dry and mixed with lime, what in Sanskrit we call *kaṭhora mṛttikā*, or hard soil . . . if you keep a small amount of this soil with you, you'll see that very soon it becomes hard like a stone. On this kind of soil, the behaviour is theft-oriented, that's why you'll find plenty of thieves and robbers in that area. . . .

From the examples above, we see that different types of soil are thought to predispose different kind of human behaviour: behaviour oriented towards knowledge, business, non-vegetarianism, stealing and so on. Geomantic thought found in astrology suggests human behaviour is cultivated in the same sense as crops are cultivated. Human culture is like a cultivation, varying according to the type of soil where it is implanted.

THE SMELL OF THE SOIL

Another important characteristic of soil is smell (*gandh*). Through smell astrologers detect the history of a territory and in which way this history is affecting the actual life of the inhabitants. Astrologers say that by smelling a soil sample you may come to know whether any *adharmik* act (an act contrary to *dharma*) has been committed on that land, or whether any corpse has been buried there. Through smell astrologers can detect if any *garant*, an object over which a charm has been uttered with malefic ends, is hidden in the land.

After having sniffed a soil sample, an astrologer is able to say if a plot is pure (*śuddh*) or impure (*aśuddh*), auspicious (*śubh*) or inauspicious (*aśubh*), fruitful (*phalit*) or non-fruitful (*aphal*), alive (*jīvit*) or dead (*mṛt*). Such qualities are not intrinsic properties of soil, but the result of acts (*karm*) committed by human beings on the land. Soil absorbs and assimilates bad acts (*duṣkarm*) and transforms them into bad smell (*durgandh*) which becomes embedded.

Before analysing soil smell, an astrologer utters a formula (*mantra*) and blows on the soil that he holds in his hands. This procedure is meant to purify soil so that 'authentic smell' (*aslī gandh*) will come out.[12] Astrologers' olfactory inventory is quite varied, but fundamentally structured around the main opposition bad smell and perfume. In the 'perfume' category—*achhī khuśbū*, *sugandh*, *mahak*—come soils that smell of rose, jasmine, sandalwood, 'cleanliness' (*sāph*), *sondhi-sondhi* (the fresh scent that comes from the earth after rain), clarified butter, curd, rice, cow-dung or just earth. Among the 'bad smells' (*kharāb khuśbū, badbū*), astrologers discern the smell of urine, excrement, rotten substances, garbage, blood, and fish.

A perfumed soil is a pure, auspicious soil, where people can live in good health and peacefully without need of celebrating any propitiatory ritual act. A bad-smelling soil is one that contains some *doṣ*, a word that means 'fault, sin' and 'defect, or error'. In the geomantic context, this word is used to designate land that has a negative influence on its inhabitants. Thus, land on which people suffer from diseases, mental disturbances, economic troubles, family tensions or the death of cattle is suspected of having some *doṣ*. Usually, a land's *doṣ* (*bhūmidoṣ*) is investigated when several members in a house compound—animals included—are simultaneously afflicted with some suffering, while a planetary *doṣ* (*grahadoṣ*) affects people as individuals, each one at a specific and different time.

A client who had come to consult an astrologer with a soil sample told us that: 'just like doctors who take your pulse, do radiographies and then diagnose if you have cancer or tuberculosis, so astrologers do the same when they smell soil samples and tell you what kind of problem you have'. Geomancy specialists actually utilize expressions like *miṭṭī kī jāñc*, 'soil test', which is similar to that used for 'blood test' (*rakt-jāñc*) or 'urine test' (*mūtr-jāñc*). 'Soil tests' through smell enable the astrologer to detect what kind of *doṣ* land suffers. Land defaults are most often attributed to something that has been introduced by human beings inside the 'womb' (*garbh*) of the soil. For example, land may be negatively affected by the corpse of a person who died in violent circumstances (murder, suicide, accident), an animal's carcass, the placenta of a woman who had a miscarriage, or any object (metal pots, small statues of deities) buried after being imbued with a curse.

Soil in which corpses and carcasses have been buried becomes the abode of ghosts who molest human beings, obstruct progress, and cause suffering. Yet in most cases, astrologers do not deal with spirit possession and leave these cases to the exorcists. Astrologers deal with ghosts that do not enter a person's body, but roam around on land or in a house creating obstacles (*bādhā-vighn*) that put a family in trouble.[13]

The examination of soil colour (*varṇa*) and smell (*gandh*) is the first step of any geomantic enquiry and can be done both in the astrologer's or in the client's place. For a deeper enquiry, the astrologer will then go in the client's place to scrutinize the full range of characteristics and 'symptoms' (*lakṣaṇa*) of the land.

GEOMANTIC FIELDWORK

Whenever an astrologer visits a land site, he will take into consideration both objective characteristics of the land and subjective sensations he feels during the fieldwork.

The first characteristic examined is the overall shape (*ākār*) of the plot. In general, plots of square, rectangular, or circular form are worth taking (*grahaṇ yogya*), whereas those with a triangular, pentagonal, hexagonal, or any irregular form are worth leaving (*tyāgne yogya*), defective, and harmful. Let us see, for example, the way the *Kriyātmak Vāstu Śāstra* (1997), a contemporary Hindī handbook on *vāstuśāstra* principles, defines plots with a bad influence on human beings:

> Triangular plots (*tribhujākār bhūkhaṇḍ*) are inauspicious (*aśubh*) and whoever builds a house on this type of land will suffer economic and legal problems; he might be arrested and go to jail.
>
> Those who live on a plot having the shape of a *mṛdaṅg* (*mṛdaṅgākār bhūkhaṇḍ*) [i.e., hexagonal form] will become widowers and will be attracted to others' women; they will lose their wealth and destroy household happiness.
>
> People living in plough-shaped (*śakaṭākār bhūkhaṇḍ*) [i.e. having pentagonal form] plots will be afflicted with all sorts of obstacles (*bādhā*), ghosts, and economic loss.[14]

Trapezoidal plots constitute a special category and can be of two types: 'having a cow muzzle' (*gau mukhī*), when the entry to the land is smaller than the far end, or 'having a lion muzzle' (*siṃh mukhī*), when, conversely, the entry is into the longer side. Plots, lands or houses with 'cow muzzles' are considered auspicious (*śubh*), the others are not.

Inclination and orientation constitute another criterion according to which lands are classified. Lands which are 'turtle backed' (*kūrmapṛṣṭh*), rising in the middle, or 'elephant backed' (*gajapṛṣṭh*), with a depression in the centre, bring prosperity, longevity, and success. On the other hand, lands 'demon backed' (*daityapṛṣṭh*), higher in the eastern direction and lower in the western direction, or 'snake backed' (*nāgapṛṣṭh*), higher in the northern and southern directions, are harmful.

Another important factor that astrologers consider whenever they analyse parcels of land is how they are traversed by travellers and inhabitants, the 'situation' or *sthiti* of the land. Here they are classified as auspicious or inauspicious according to the following: the number of roads that pass near to the land, the side from which roads pass—east, south, west or north side—the position of the land according to the road (at the beginning, in the middle, at the end), the position of the surrounding houses, and so on.

Land auspiciousness is also checked through a method called the 'pit (*gaḍḍhā*) test'. This method, still currently used by astrologers, is described in the *Bṛhat Saṃhitā*, Varāhamihira's sixth-century treatise on divination:[15]

> After having dug in the middle of the land a one cubit pit and after having filled it back with the same earth, [it should be checked] if the pit is insufficiently filled, the land is harmful (*aniṣṭa*); if it is filled up to the ground level, it is average (*sama*); and if earth comes out from the pit, land is auspicious (*dhanya*).[16]

There is another version of the same test. Here, the pit is filled at evening time with some water and the next morning the water level is checked. If some water is left in the pit, the land is auspicious; if the earth is wet, the quality is average; if the pit is completely dry, the land is inauspicious.

B. Dagens (1977: 24-5) has remarked that these tests, though we could think of them as being 'divinatory', have in fact an empirical foundation. Through these tests, the compactness and the humidity of the soil can be evaluated. These are qualities that should be checked before building a house. If you fill a pit with its own earth, for example, and the earth is coming out from the pit, this means that the soil is extremely compact and therefore appropriate. Banaras astrologers would agree, but further use these tests for knowing if a piece of land is appropriate for a specific owner. According to their view, the pit depth and width should be measured according to the length of the arm of the person who is going to buy the land.

Another way of examining qualities and properties of land is the interpretation of 'omens' (*lakṣaṇ, śakun*).[17] Through the observation of vegetation, animals, bones, anthills, and other characteristics, the astrologer will try to understand whether the site is auspicious or whether a ghost could afflict people living on that land. So, for instance, thorny shrubs, which are called *kaṣṭ kārak*, 'suffering makers', and holy trees such as the pīpal, banian and nīm, are considered to be signs of ghosts roaming on the land, for ghosts are thought to choose this kind of vegetation for their abode. Generally, however, flourishing vegetation with fruit trees or flowering trees is considered to be auspicious, while scarce vegetation is looked upon as a bad sign.

Among omens, major importance is attributed to bones visible on the ground or hidden inside the earth's 'womb' (*garbh*).[18] Let us briefly list the effects (*pariṇām*) attributed to different types of bones, according to the *Kriyātmak Vāstu Śāstra* (p. 57):

Human bones: death, nightmares
Donkey bones: wealth and cattle destruction
Monkey carcass: death, danger
Horse bones: economic losses, fights
Child's bones: robbery, economic losses
Brahman's bones: death, poverty
Men's bones: family destruction

Bones, ashes, or pieces of burned wood are generally looked upon by astrologers as tangible proof of the presence of ghosts. Human bones are the most dreaded relics, and their effect is thought to vary according to the nature and qualities of the dead person. This is how one astrologer described the way human bones affect people living on a land:

> Problems caused by bones depend on the kind of person who died. If it is an evil person (*durjan*), his bones are going to bring many sufferings, but if it is a good person (*sajjan*), his bones are not going to create many. The effects of human bones depend on the dead person's intrinsic qualities (*svabhāvik*

guṇ). Children's bones, for example, create all sorts of obstacles concerning marriage and procreation; adult's bones generate health problems: someone will get ill, someone will fall from a roof. . . .

Besides observing vegetation and bones, an astrologer pays attention to anything that he perceives, not only while he is 'in the field', but also during his journey to a client's place. The sight of a snake on the way to the place, for example, is considered to be a sign that the land is protected by some 'snake-deity' and that some ancient wealth is hidden inside the land. The astrologer S.C. Chaturvedi, whose skills in *vāstuśāstra* and omen interpretation are well known in Banaras, told us that once he had to discourage his clients from buying a parcel of land because a snake had appeared several times:

> The first time I went to visit that parcel of land [in the state of Madhya Pradesh], I saw a snake very close to me, nobody else saw it. I was scared. Six or seven months later, while we were going back to that same place, we saw it again, it was crossing a footpath. . . . I was with the person who wanted to buy the land, and the snake went straight in the direction of his son, there were only ten steps between the snake and us, and the snake was whistling. . . . Then I screamed out. 'All of you get away! The snake is coming back because it doesn't want us to get to the land where the treasure is kept!' I explained that if a snake was appearing, this meant that there was an ancient treasure and it could be very dangerous to touch it . . . the *ātmā* (soul) of the treasure owner was living on that land and would bring all sorts of suffering and obstacles, it would keep frightening the family.

While visiting a plot of land, an astrologer has also to take into account his own physical and psychic reactions. A shiver, a brow quivering, nausea, unusual heart beating, bad thoughts, or nightmares may all be signs. An astrologer, after becoming impregnated with 'place influence' (*sthān kā prabhāv*) considers his own symptoms as significant. This has been explained by astrologer S.C. Chaturvedi in the following manner:

> Whenever you go to visit a place, you feel things with your own body . . . if it is a good place, then you'll have good thoughts, whereas if it is a bad place, you'll have bad thoughts. Once I went to Bihar to visit a place and I stayed over the day after. During the night I had nightmares but in the morning, when I woke up, I forgot them. I asked, however, if there hadn't

been a murder in that place . . . and actually there had been one! Someone had been killed in that place. If you are a pure, wise and honest person, omens come out by themselves.

An astrologer becomes the privileged mediator between land and human beings. Through a full array of procedures that range from objective and measurable tests to subjective perceptions, an astrologer deciphers signs of soil and land in order to make them clear to inhabitants.

LIVING LANDS, DEAD LANDS

Having described the way soil and land are classified and analysed, we may now direct our attention to the way astrologers and clients express the idea of reciprocal influence (*prabhāv*) between soil qualities and human behaviour.

First, the reciprocal influence between human beings and soil is not an immediate one. It becomes evident after a prolonged period of 'cohabitation'. Soil does not instantaneously absorb the influence of human acts (*karm*), and human beings do not usually perceive the influence of the land that they live upon immediately. A man who had come to the astrologer's place in order to have home soil divined explained to us why he had waited fifteen years before seeking advice from the geomantic specialist:

> If there is a problem with soil, you will not realize it soon . . . even if the *doṣ* (defect) has been there since the first day you started living on that land, at the beginning you will not perceive it. It would be like a battle. At first you are able to resist, you are able to fight, but then you become weaker and weaker . . . and at the end you succumb, and lose the battle. The same thing happens with soil and land . . . if there is a *doṣ*, people, without knowing it, keep fighting, try to resist as much as they can, but after some time they become so weak that they give up . . . at that point they realize that there is a problem with land.

Human beings assimilate and incorporate the influence of the land and soil gradually, over periods of several months or years. So too, soil is not immediately affected by human behaviour, as astrologer S.C. Chaturvedi explained:

If a bad act is accomplished just once on a particular piece of land, that land will make up for it by itself. But if evil acts are repeatedly perpetrated, then the fate of the land (*zamīn kā bhāgya*) will be diverted and 'will turn its face away'.

To say that the land's fate will be 'diverted' draws on the idea that, in the natural state, soil and land are seen as being 'alive' (*jīvit*). A land on which several inappropriate acts (*anucit karm*, *duṣkarm*, *burā karm*) have taken place becomes 'dead' (*mṛt*). As astrologer Nilkanth Shastri said,

> Because of bad human actions a piece of land that is alive becomes dead. The bad *karm* kills the land. Like someone who dies when killed, in the same way soil dies when killed. The soil might have been auspicious, but because of bad human behaviour it will die (*miṭṭī kī mṛtyu ho jātī hai*). When I visit a land and I realize that soil is dead—and some metres away it can be still alive—then I ask: 'What happened in this place? Something bad happened . . .'. And then I come to know that there is always something, a murder, a rape, or something else.

Another common way to express the opposition between 'live' and 'dead' lands is the distinction between 'awake' (*jāgṛt*) and 'asleep' (*supt*) lands. A land where *adharmik* (against the moral order) acts are committed, after some time 'will fall asleep' (*so jātī hai*). For example, a family lacking in religious devotion, who doesn't regularly make fire offerings (*havan*) or *pūjā* will make the land 'sleep'.[19]

A 'sleeping' plot, rather than being harmful and one that brings sufferings, disease or disputes, is a land that makes human efforts fruitless. A common saying is that 'whatever profit you make in one year on land that is awake (*jāgṛt*), you'll get in ten years on a sleepy (*supt*) land'. Similar binary oppositions between lands of different profitability are expressed by the distinction between *dhanī*—that which bring wealth (*dhan*), fruitful—and *ṛṇi*—that bring debts (*ṛṇ*), unfruitful—lands; and between bright, radiant (*ujlī*) and dark (*kālī*) lands. These latter categories, however, express intrinsic land qualities, whereas the dead or sleeping condition is created by human behaviour.

If human beings can kill lands or make them sleep, they also have the capability to revive, 'to awaken' (*jagānā*) lands. For instance, whenever a family living on a dead or sleepy land observes a *dharmik* (virtuous) behaviour, full of meritorious acts for a long time, the land will be gradually awaken up. However, this process is considered to be very slow because several years or even generations are required before the land is revived.

Astrologers know faster solutions that can arouse land in a short time. If the land to be revived is devoid of any building, an astrologer might suggest applying a layer of auspicious soil taken from a land that is alive to the unfortunate ground. After that, the celebration of ritual acts and uttering of sacred formulas is required in order to purify the land. Rituals for purification differ according to the land problem, as explains astrologer Ramanand Pandey:

> First we start with preliminary remedies (*prāthamik cikitsā*), . . . for example some flowers that come from the temple, that we have ground up and mixed with water, will be spread on the ground while lighting some incense. Otherwise I can give a *jantar* (amulet) containing some *mantra*. But this is just first aid, it is like putting band-aid on a wound. If I see that is not sufficient, that they are not getting rid of problems, that their economic situation is not improving, then I go myself with ritual technicians (*paṇḍit*) in order to celebrate *havan* (a fire sacrifice with vegetal oblations).[20]

Through the ritual, as well as through means like applying a layer of earth that is 'alive' in order to cover 'dead' soil, human beings are able to obliterate the embedded memory of evil acts inscribed in the territory.

STARS DOWN TO EARTH

Up to now we have considered astrologers' geomancy in the literal sense of earth (Greek: *geo*) divination (*manteia*), that is, divination through investigation of physical characteristics of the soil and land. Another way astrologers inspect the land consists in studying the astral configurations associated with a particular plot or territory. Astrological methods are mainly used to ascertain the degree of compatibility between land and its owner.[21]

There is more than one astrological method for investigating the degree of compatibility between a person and a plot of land. One consists of examining the fourth house (*bhāva*) of the consultant's natal chart. Through an analysis of this, the astrologer finds out what the person's situation is with regard to land property and real estate. According to the position of the planets, opportunities and difficulties of buying land or building a house will be deduced by the astrologer.

A second way calls upon the astrological branch of *praśna* (horary astrology). According to this method of divination, astral configurations that are in the sky at the moment one seeks a consultation with an astrologer and asks him a 'question' (*praśna*) indicate the answer. When a person goes to the astrologer in order to know if a particular land is worth of buying, the astrologer will examine the 'query-horoscope' (*praśna kuṇḍalī*). Planets in the first house—the *lagna* or ascendant house—are thought to hold the clue.

Other ways of evaluating whether a land will suit a particular person consist in comparing the person's and the land's zodiacal signs (*rāśi*). The person's zodiacal sign is calculated according to the position of the Moon at birth or, more commonly, on the basis of the first syllable of the person's name.[22] The land's zodiacal sign can be calculated in one of several ways. One method associates zodiacal signs with the *varṇa* of soil that composes the land. Land having brāhmaṇa soil is Cancer, Scorpio and Pisces; land having kṣatriya soil is Aries, Leo and Sagittarius; vaiśya soil land will be Taurus, Virgo and Capricorn and śūdra soil land will be Gemini, Libra and Aquarius. Another way of calculating the zodiacal sign of land is using the direction where the entry is situated: thus land with the entry on the eastern side (*pūrv diśā*) is Aries, Leo and Sagittarius; on the southern side (*dakṣiṇ diśā*) is Taurus, Virgo and Capricorn; on the western side (*paścim diśā*) is Gemini, Libra and Aquarius and on the northern side (*uttar diśā*) is Cancer, Scorpio and Pisces.[23]

According to these classifications, a Cancerian should look for a parcel of land whose *varṇa* is brāhmaṇa or whose entry is on the northern side; an Arian should live on an east oriented land or a land that has kṣatriya soil, and so on. When a purchase is contemplated, in order to have these astrological criteria respected, astrologers recommend that the plot of land should be in the name of that member of the family whose zodiacal sign is compatible with the zodiacal sign of the land. Thus, if a couple want to buy a plot of land having the entry on the western side and the husband's sign is Aries while the wife's is Libra, the astrologer will explain that, in order to have auspicious (*śubh*) and fruitful (*phāydemand*) land, the plot should be put in the wife's name. Otherwise problems and suffering will arise. Because of this, astrologers often recommend transfers of property among family members in order to make the land beneficial for those who live on it.

As we have noted, astrologers evaluate the compatibility between a plot of land and its owner by matching zodiacal signs. Yet, astrologers can also calculate a full horoscope for land and territories in the same way that they calculate horoscopes for human beings. According to the date the land has been bought or a territory created, astrologers study the fate (*bhāgya*) of that land or territory through time. For example, the horoscope of India has been calculated on the basis of the date of Independence (actually this date was chosen after consulting several astrologers). Having Taurus (*vṛṣa*) as ascendant (*lagna*) and Capricorn (*makara*) as the lunar sign (*rāśi*), India's astral chart enables astrologers to set forth diagnostics and predictions about the economic and political life of the nation. In the same way, astrologers calculate 'the horoscope of a piece of land' (*zamīn kā cakr*, *zamīn kī kuṇḍalī*) for their clients according to its date of purchase. Astrologers calculate the positions of planets in the different houses of the horoscope and analyse the defects and qualities of the land, what kind of profit it will give, what kind of activities will be profitable on that land, and so on.

CONCLUSION

The vast array of geomantic techniques that we have described—soil sample inspection, 'fieldwork' inquiry, omen interpretation, astrological correspondences—show the importance that astrologers attribute to the qualities of soil, land, and territory as determinants of well-being.

The geomantic procedures suggest how individuals and collectivities are affected by soil and territory. Through the matching of horoscopes, astrologers evaluate the compatibility between an individual and his land. Other geomantic techniques reveal the link between land and a collectivity. Astrologers divine how the members of a household share the qualities of the land where their house is built. Inhabitants of the same urban area are also thought of as sharing the characteristics of the soil that is spread in that area. The inhabitants of a city share the qualities of the soil on which the city is built. For example, the soil of Banaras is considered predisposed towards knowledge and spirituality. In the same way, all inhabitants of Indian territory are thought of as sharing the destiny written in the horoscope of the Indian nation. Geomantic procedures show that the common destiny shared by people living on the same soil is not only synchronic, as in the examples cited, but can also be diachronic. This is specially the case with dead lands, where astrologers diagnose the presence of ghosts: people living on a plot of land are bound to the destiny of those who have preceded them. A binding that ties people who live on the same land at different times.

Acknowledgements: The authors are grateful to Daniela Berti, Mark Nichter, Stefano Piano, Bo Sax, Gilles Tarabout and Rick Willet for their helpful comments and suggestions on earlier drafts. All errors of interpretation are ours.

NOTES

1. In G.V. Tagare (1978: 1302-3).
2. *Vāstuśāstra* is currently translated as 'Hindu geomancy'. This subject is becoming increasingly popular in urban India, and English and Hindī literature that reinterprets the principles of ancient Sanskrit texts is flourishing on the subject.
3. In this article we shall limit our analysis to soil and land conceptions, and we shall not deal with domestic-space related issues. While the first subject is very little explored, several authors have treated house-structure conceptions, with special concern for the harmonious relationship between domestic activities and spatial directions (*diśā*). See, for example, M.A. Moore (1990) and M.-L. Reiniche (1981); for directions and space classification, see M. Gaborieau (1992).
4. Indian houses are usually classified according to two categories: *kaccā* (raw or untreated) houses, that is mud houses, and *pakkā* (processed) houses, that is, of brick and cement.

5. Though original *vāstu* literature is in Sanskrit and most of the experts in this branch of knowledge are Brāhmans, there are also *vāstuśāstrī* who are not Brāhmans. Kunja Bihari, for example, a lawyer from the Agrawal business caste, after having studied astrology for several years, is now specialized in *vāstu* practitioner in Banaras.
6. The Bollywood film *Raaz* (Secret), one of the 2002 biggest successes, contains a meaningful characterization of a professional *vāstuśāstrī* in contemporary India. In this film by Vikram Bhatt, a newly married couple—rich, Westernized and very much stressed because of Mumbai's frenetic pace of life—decide to go back to the resort of Ooty, where they had been for a honeymoon. But, as soon as she enters the beautiful villa they have rented, the bride starts feeling restless. A friend who starts worrying about the bride's health tells the couple to take the advice of a *vāstuśāstrī*, Prof. Agni Svarup (from the Kāyastha caste). The *vāstuśāstrī* goes to examine the villa and its surroundings and makes an 'inductive' test: he leaves a lemon for a night in the attic and the day after goes to check its colour. As the lemon has become red, the *vāstuśāstrī* explains that this means that some blood has been split in the house and that the bride is afflicted by the soul (*ātmā*) of the person who has died in such a violent way. After a further inspection of the house, the *vāstuśāstrī* comes to know that a young woman who had been the groom's lover, had committed suicide inside the house after the couple's marriage, out of grief. In this movie, we see that *vāstuśāstrī's* professional behaviour seems to better satisfy urban and Westernized elite expectations than an *ojhā*-exorcist would do, even if both are dealing with spirit possession.
7. Rice is often examined by low-caste exorcists as well: besides rice, exorcists also inspect rupees or cloves that clients bring from home. Astrologers, however, do not frequently inspect these latter substances.
8. *Bṛhat Saṃhitā*, chap. 53, vv. 96 and 97b (M.R. Bhat's translation, 1982).
9. Classification of soil according to *varṇa* in *vāstu* literature is found in *Mayamata* (chap. II, vv. 10-15a) ; *Vāstusaukhyam* (chap. II, vv. 14-15) and *Kriyātmak Vāstu Śāstra* (chap. II, v. 8).
10. The city of Ayodhya, considered as god Rām's native place, is a major Hindu pilgrimage centre (*tīrtha*).
11. Astrologer Nilkanth Shastri has elaborated a soil classification system that is much more sophisticated than the classical fourfold *varṇa* classification: he has identified sixteen different types of soil according to the colour, texture, and substances contained (i.e. lime, coal, mica).

12. In fact, the literal meaning of the word *śodhan*, that we have translated as 'investigation', is 'purification'.
13. About the relationship between territory, ghosts, and spirit possession, see the Kerala-based works of G. Tarabout (1999) and Y. Uchiyamada (1999).
14. *Kriyātmak Vāstu Śāstra*, pp. 48-9.
15. The origin of this test seems to be even prior to the *Bṛhat Saṃhitā*. This land checking method is in fact described in the *Āśvalāyana-Gṛhya-sūtra* (II.8), a text that, according to P.V. Kane (1962: vol. 2, part II, pp. 833-6), can be attributed to a period between 800 and 400 BC.
16. *Bṛhat Saṃhitā*, chap. 53, v. 92.
17. Sanskrit literature about omen interpretation is vast: for a bibliography, see D. Pingree (1981: 67-80).
18. Astrologers use different divinatory techniques in order to find out bones that are under the surface. They draw a 9, 12 or 27 cases diagram on the ground and, according to the positions of planets or asterisms at the moment of the enquiry, the location of bones will be identified.
19. C. Malamoud (1996) notes that in Vedic literature, soil is considered the receptacle of human falsehood: 'soil is therefore filled with lies, pierced with the *anṛta* that human beings introduce on it day after day' (p. 77). *Anṛta* —whatever is 'badly articulated', 'false', 'confused'— fills earth holes and cracks (and it is there that lives the goddess Nirṛti, the mythological representation of *anṛta*).
20. Among the most frequently celebrated *havan* for purification and awakening of land, there is *kṣetrapāl bali* (sacrifice for field guardians) and *vāstuyajña* (fire sacrifice for site and building).
21. As we have seen, the 'pit test', where the owner's arm constitutes the unit of measure, is used as well as a means to certify the compatibility between a person and a land.
22. Names starting with 'cū', 'ce', 'lā', 'lī', 'lū', 'le', 'ā' designate Aries (*meṣa*) persons; names starting with 'ī', 'u', 'e', 'o', 'ba', 'bī', 'bū', 've', 'bo' designate Taurus (*vṛṣa*) persons, and so on (*Sulabh Jyautiṣ Jñāna*, 1997: 36-7).
23. Plots of land are not the only territorial sections where the astrological compatibility between an inhabitant and his territory is taken into consideration. Astrologers can in fact compare as well a person's zodiacal sign with a village or a town's zodiacal signs (these latter being calculated on the basis of the first syllable of the village's name).

Compatibility between persons' and villages' zodiacal signs, however, is not frequently taken into consideration by Banaras astrologers. For more about this in other Indian contexts, see V. Daniel (1984: 81-95) and G.G. Raheja (1988: 52-6).

REFERENCES

Hindī and Sanskrit Texts

Bhāratīya Vāstu Śāstra, T.N. Shastri, Calcutta: Bholanath Pustakalaya, 1996.

Bṛhat Saṃhitā of Varāhamihira, ed. and tr. M.R. Bhat, Delhi: Motilal Banarsidass, 1982

Kriyātmak Vāstu Śāstra, J. Gaharana and A. Kulashreshth, Agra: Dip Publications, 1997.

Mayamata. Traité sanskrit d'architecture, ed. and tr. B. Dagens, Pondichéry: Institut Français d'Indologie, 1970.

Sulabh Jyautiṣ Jñāna, V. S. Khankhoje, Varanasi: Chowkhamba, 1997.

Triskhandh Jyotiṣam, 16, 5th year, Varanasi, 1997.

Vāstusaukhyam, Ṭoḍaramalla, with Hindī commentary of K. Shukla, Varanasi: Sampurnanand Sanskrit University, 1999.

Secondary Sources

Dagens, Bruno, 1977. *Les enseignements architecturaux de l'Ajitāgama et du Rauravāgama*, Pondichéry: Institut Français d'Indologie.

Daniel, E. Valentine, 1984. *Being a Person the Tamil Way*, Berkeley: University of California Press.

Gaborieau, Marc, 1992. 'Des dieux dans toutes les directions. Conception indienne de l'espace et classification des dieux', in *Classer les dieux ? Des panthéons en Asie du Sud*, ed. V. Bouillier and G. Toffin, Paris: EHESS, pp. 23-42.

Kane, P.V., 1962. *History of Dharmaśāstra*, Poona: Bhandarkar Oriental Research Institute.

Malamoud, Charles, 1996. 'L'arbre aux racines de mensonge. Variations indiennes sur le vrai et le faux', *L'inactuel, "Mensonges, Vérités"*, n. 6: 69-80.

Moore, Melinda A., 1990. 'The Kerala House as a Hindu Cosmos', in *India Through Hindu Categories*, ed. McKim Marriott, Delhi: Sage, pp. 171-202.

Paulme, Denise, 1956. 'Oracles grecs et devins africains', *Revue de l'Histoire des Religions*, CXLIX: 145-56.

Pingree, David, 1981. *Jyotiṣśāstra: Astral and Mathematical Literature*, Wiesbaden: Otto Harrassowitz.

Raheja, Gloria G., 1988. *The Poison in the Gift: Ritual, Prestation and the Dominant Caste in a North Indian Village*, Chicago: University of Chicago Press.

Reiniche, Marie-Louise, 1981. 'La maison au Tirunelveli (Inde du Sud)', *Bulletin de l'École Française d'Extrême-Orient*, 70: 21-57.

Tagare, Ganesh Vasudeo, 1978. *The Bhāgavata Purāṇa*, Delhi: Motilal Banarsidass.

Tarabout, Gilles, 1999. 'Corps possédés et signatures territoriales au Kerala', in *La possession en Asie du Sud. Parole, corps, territoire*, ed. J. Assayag and G. Tarabout, Paris: EHESS, pp. 313-56.

Uchiyamada, Yasuchi, 1999. 'Soil, Self, Resistance: Late-Modernity and Locative Spirit Possession in Kerala', in *La possession en Asie du Sud. Parole, corps, territoire*, ed. J. Assayag and G. Tarabout, Paris: EHESS, pp. 289-312.

Zeitlyn, D., 2001. 'Finding Meaning in the Text: The Process of Interpretation in Text-based Divination', *Journal of the Royal Anthropological Institute*, 7, 2: 225-40.

5

Vital Exchanges: Land and Persons in Kerala

CAROLINE OSELLA AND FILIPPO OSELLA

INTRODUCTION

Valentine Daniel, in what is still one of the most useful analyses on land in South Asia, sets out some fundamental principles governing the ways in which a specific soil on a particular territory forms and shapes those who live on it. He writes that, 'The *ūr* [village] can have an effect on its inhabitants . . . for this . . . to be accomplished, there need be no ingestion of food or water.' (1984: 84). Further, 'The soil of an *ūr* changes the *putti* [mind] of its residents. The *putti* and *kuṇam* [disposition] of the residents, however, can also change the substance of the soil' (1984: 94). Daniel shows how people planning to migrate search carefully for territory which will be compatible with their own natures, and outlines some ways in which character and dispositions are held to be transmitted to people by the land on which they live. We have also alluded to this phenomenon in the context of Kerala, where we have found that by contiguity even the most apparently impermeable matter can be altered by the subtlest of influences (Osella and Osella 2002).

In this paper, drawn from several periods of fieldwork in Kerala, we explore Malayāḷi ideas about the interconnections between land, houses, and their residents (who may be human, or animals, or spirits). We will summarize knowledge—held more deeply and in better detail by artisan and service castes, more superficially among the general population—about the forces and influences present on the land, and ways in which they can be managed. In exploring the ways in which people try to maximize auspiciousness within their plots of garden land, house, and outbuildings, we find that they are searching to bring territory into harmony with the beings—both living and dead—resident on and around the land.[1] Kerala's rather unusual—from a pan-Indian perspective—funeral practices lead the way towards understanding how humans are able to settle successfully on a patch of land and make it 'theirs' by virtue of actually coming to participate in its substance. Thinking about the opposition made between garden land—as a place suitable for human habitation—and paddy-land—suitable for paddy but widely felt as dangerous and polluting to humans—also distinguishes the marginalized social position of those castes that live and labour to produce rice. While we will suggest that recent work stressing the partibility, permeability and mutability of the person is also useful in understanding data on land, we will take issue with the suggestion that all phenomena can be understood as examples or types of 'body metaphors' or 'body symbolisms'.

The various periods of fieldwork on which this paper is based took place from 1989 to 1999 in and closely around one panchayat we call Valiyagramam.[2] This consists of two named villages which have no clear boundary either between them or between their neighbouring panchayats, representing the type of dense flat land settlement for which Kerala, with its enormously high population density, is famous. Valiyagramam is a mixed *grāmam* (here: village, rural settlement) characterized by a rapidly expanding middle class, a small and declining elite, and a substantial and increasingly impoverished working-class sector. Villagers are also divided and stratified by *sammudayam* or *jāti*, community or caste. Hindu families of traditionally high caste status (such as Brāhmans and aristocratic Nāyars) live largely in the village interior near to temples; Christians and lower-caste Hindus live scattered around the village. Residential areas are divided between a few neighbourhoods inhabited by single communities, and several mixed areas. Members of Dalit castes—Pulayars and Paṟayars—continue to live in segregated areas (some of which are formally designated 'Harijan colonies') at the edges of the paddy-fields; they are still overwhelmingly employed as labourers, moving into areas such as house-construction or inland fishing as the agricultural economy continues to decline.

LIVING PLOTS

Kerala's land is divided by geographers and inhabitants alike into three natural longitudinal divisions: the 'shore-land' or low-lying coastal and backwater strip; the 'same-height-land' or central zone, 30-200 m, characterized by red laterite soil and scrub land; and the 'mountainland' which used to be thickly forested, now less so. Valiyagramam lies in the flat lands, bounded on the south and east by a river and on the west by an artificial irrigation canal separating its paddy fields from those of the neighbouring panchayat. The northern border, not demarcated by any boundary, is where the village runs into the next panchayat, a small Muslim and Christian trading town. Following state land registry boundaries, the panchayat of Valiyagramam (covering the two villages) spreads over 5,577 acres, divided into three types of land: to the west stands the *puñja*, 2,985 acres of one-crop paddy land, which gets flooded during the monsoon, being 2 m below sea level. This land forms the south-east corner of Kuttanad, Kerala's rice-growing region. To the east is the *viruppu*, 758 acres of land lying just 0.5 m below sea level, and which yields three harvests (two of paddy and one of sesame). Between the *puñja* and the *viruppu* lies the 1834 acre strip of *paṟampu*, or garden land, which is used for habitation and the cultivation of coconut, banana, jackfruit, areca, mango and cashew trees; root vegetables such as *kappa* (cassava/tapioca), *cēna* (*Arum campanulatum*, a type of yam), and *cēmpu* (*Caladium esculentum*, a large yam indigenous to Sri Lanka); and secondary cash crops such as pepper and, most lately, rubber. The distinction between habitable and non-flooding garden land (*paṟampu*) and the rest is the major feature differentiating village land. Land in the seasonally flooded *puñja*—thickly planted with paddy and home to the lowest castes and fiercest spirits—is viewed with ambivalence by those not living on it. The vast majority of people living on the western *puñja* are Pulayars, former agrestic slaves who even now are identified as an agricultural labouring caste. The eastern *viruppu* is home to a mixed settlement of Pulayars and poorer Īḻavars, again mostly working as agricultural labourers. These two areas, especially the *puñja*, are avoided by most villagers and held to be both the abodes of dangerous and ambivalent spirits, fierce and wild deities and demons and also places harbouring disease, 'bad air', dirty water and so on (Uchiyamada 1998, 2000). If garden land (*paṟampu*) stands for fruit trees, the possibility of building a good permanent house, proximity to temples, bus-stops and shops, then the paddy field lands stand for temporary huts and relative isolation from services. We will begin this paper by setting out some ways in which houses and people are grafted onto domesticated and auspicious garden land—positive spaces and moments in the lives of the respectable bourgeois and higher status families—before moving on to a greater appreciation of the significance of flows of influence and qualities by way of thinking about some spaces and moments considered by those mainstream families as disruptive and dangerous: death and funerals, and the flooding of the paddy lands during monsoon.

Land and landscape in Kerala are alive and, like the humans and animals seen on them, subject to continual flux. There is a lively market in land, as since the 1960s many of the village's wealthier and more educated professionals (notably Nāyars and Christians) sell up and move out to the cities while upwardly-mobile families (especially Īḻavars and lower-status Christians) buy up the vacant plots and sometimes also houses, shifting into more prestigious areas of the village. Daniel records the importance for rural Tamils of ensuring compatibility between land and people, often expressed in terms of caste, such that the soil in certain areas is said to be 'sweet' and hence suitable for members of a certain community. In Kerala's crowded and highly mixed coastal belt settlements, the various zones of the main village do not have such strong associations with particular social groups; here it is an individual plot that is assessed in close detail, and whose characteristics may turn out to be completely different from those of the plot next door.

When land is bought or transferred, a horoscope is drawn up for the plot, using the date of purchase or access as birth date: 'When we buy or get a plot of land, it is like giving birth to it' explained one Āśāri (building artisan). The horoscope can be drawn by anyone with knowledge of astrology, but clients prefer to consult a member of the Āśāri caste, a group which in rural areas continues in the caste occupation of building and carpentry work. The *nakṣatram* or 'ruling star'/asterism of the house is calculated according to the name of the plot. For example, the initial of a plot to be known as 'Vellayil Tekketu' is the Malayāḷam letter 'Va', and the *nakṣatram* which corresponds to this letter is *rōhiṇi*. Such information will be needed by the diagnosing astrologer if there are later disturbances or problems with the house or land.

According to Āśāri informants, during a fight between the Dēvanmār (gods) and Asuranmār (demons), Mahāviṣṇu fell to earth and became Vāstupuruṣan (land man—see Madan 1987: 139). Each and every marked plot of land contains one Vāstupuruṣan, plus the 81 gods who live on his body.[3] When humans wish to settle on a plot of land, the Vāstupuruṣan dwelling there must be made comfortable and his body respected, as we will outline below. Melinda Moore (1990), writing about the ideal Kerala house, has suggested that there is only one Vāstupuruṣan covering the house, but our informants were clear that there are always at least two to be considered: the one whose body maps or fixes a plot of land, and the one(s) whose body/ies form(s) the house. Against Moore's understanding that Vāstupuruṣan actually is the land, we shall work with an assumption that is both in agreement with what has generally been written about land in India (e.g. Fuller 1992: 43, 193), which certainly seems to make more sense of our data and which is also suggested in Caldwell's recent notes on land in northern Kerala (1999: 104ff). This is that land which is a female divine being (Bhūmi-Dēvi) who, like other female beings, must be pacified by a male being if her transformative and protective powers are to be safely used in the human world (cf. Östör 1980: 199). Menon and Rajan (1989: 1) state that when Kerala was formed: 'The newly reclaimed land presented many problems—floods, landslides, earthquakes. [. . .] Parasurama is believed to have stabilized the land and made it habitable through the installation of 108 Sivalingas and 108 Shakthipeedhas (fixed seats for male and female generative powers) and consecrating them with tantric rituals.' Vāstupuruṣan is not, then, the land itself but the consort of the land who, by binding and containing her, domesticates her: if Bhūmi-Dēvi is life, Vāstupuruṣan is form.

Where we depart sharply from Caldwell is in then refusing to consider this human body/land body homology as a totalizing metaphor. We therefore avoid assuming a consistency or durability across discourses and realms, so that, for example, we do not wish to suggest or assume that Vāstupuruṣan necessarily for all Malayāḷis at all times is focused on stabilizing Bhūmi-Dēvi by means of sexual intercourse. We will suggest a far more cautious interpretation, which is that at sometimes, certain parts of natural phenomena are held to resemble each other. Some features of the human body or particular aspects of human reproductive processes are pilfered to make metonyms with which to explain animal and paddy reproduction and vice versa, but these metonymic relationships of resemblance, contrast or homology are not drawn into neat metaphors by means of which any phenomenon can then be understood in terms of another.

We also differ considerably from Melinda Moore in our positioning and orientation of Vāstupuruṣan on the land and in house. When we worked with village practitioners in the field of Āyurvēda we found a close correspondence, with only minimal variation, between the 'authorized version' as presented in pan-Indian texts and actual local practice, but in the realm of architecture/geomancy (*taccuśāstra*) we claim the existence of a semi-autonomous local tradition. But this does not mean that Kerala Āśāris are less scrupulous about respecting *śāstra* or more informal in their knowledge-practices; the Āśāris we interviewed did not rely on memory or oral transmission, but had their own hand-written manuals, passed down from father to son and consulted carefully.

While Moore expresses ambiguity and doubt on the subject of Vāstupuruṣan's orientation (1990: 182), our informants were very clear that land man fell to earth face down, his arms and legs outstretched, and that he touches the earth at four cardinal points, i.e. at his spread hands and feet. His buttocks are raised, his back is straight, and his head is raised to look south-west, towards the Ocean. His position as described (and acted out) to us is similar to a four point prostration, like that adopted when greeting a deity in performing the *sūryanamaskāram* (see Fig. 5.1). It therefore differs considerably from the orientation given by Beck (1976) and picked up by Moore (1990), in which land man lies, arms and legs folded inwards, flat on his back or stomach, and always facing north-east.[4] The places where his hands and feet touch earth according to our informants' positioning (Fig. 5.1), named by Āśāris as the four *kōṭi* (knots or bound points), turn out to correspond exactly to the four cardinal points. This makes sense in view of the understanding that space is something to be held down and bound, and land something to be stabilized: with his extremities firmly flat on the ground, land man not only maps but also ties and fixes physical space. When building a house, Vāstupuruṣan of the land plot must not be disturbed, so the Āśāri's first job is to locate him and map him out.

The directionality given here reproduces exactly what Āśāris told us. Thus, while Europeans are accustomed to a geography and a

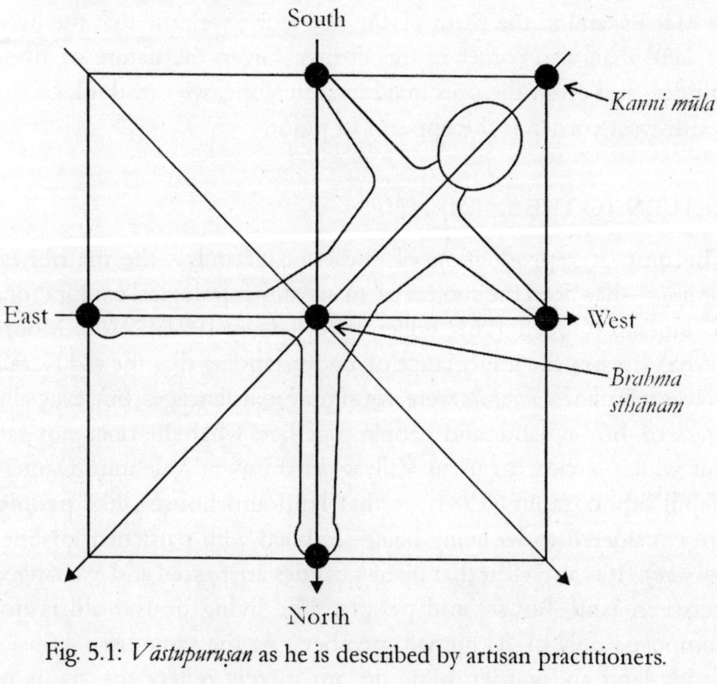

Fig. 5.1: *Vāstupuruṣan* as he is described by artisan practitioners.

cartography in which north is the top and in which north-south is the direction of the primary axis, the Āśāris we met spoke of a south to north axis, while in diagrams they draw 'upside down' from the orientation usually given in western conventional maps. In this ethno-geography, south is 'up', while north is 'down'.[5] Another particularity is that the land—in this coastal region, apparently totally flat—is actually said to have an unseen slope, running from south-west to north-east—in the direction also taken by monsoon winds, a fact also confirmed by Moore (1990; see her discussion pp. 187ff on 'the presumed underlying and universal cline' and 'an underlying flow of good influence from the south-west towards the north-east', p. 189). Water runs from south-west to north-east, which is why, for example, a house well is placed at the north-east corner, to take advantage of the ease with which water will flow at this corner. While Moore, following building manuals, places the goddess Nirṛti in the south-west corner, our informants placed Dēvi there—both as Bhūmi-Dēvi embodying or protecting the land and as Mahālakṣmi in the form of the rice-store; we note that the head of land man also comes in this corner. Given the nature of these entities, and given the presumed unseen slope, we can think of the south-west corner as the uppermost point.

RETURN TO THE *TAṞAVĀṬU*

The unit of reproduction of the Nāyar family—the matrilineal *taṟavāṭu*—has been the subject of many anthropological explorations of kinship (Gough 1961; Fuller 1976; Jeffrey 1994 [1976]). Moore (1985) stresses the importance of understanding that the old Kerala Nāyar matrilineal *taṟavāṭu* were not simply matrilineages, but, crucially, units of house, land, and people together: what she does not say, but which is clear to us in Valiyagramam as in Valentine Daniel's Tamil ethnography (1984), is that land and houses, like people, are considered to be living beings imbued with particular qualities (*guṇam*). It is also clear that many qualities are passed and exchanged between land, house, and people. The living household is not composed only of its human members. At the same time, houses, paddy-land and garden plots do not merely reflect the status of their owners: they constitute, like individual persons, objectifications of the wider family group, of the latter's name and reputation, and, like people, act both as a source and as a target of quality. Moore also neglects to mention the house-land-people units of other communities: many families among Kerala's Tīyyar and Īḻavar communities were also matrilineal and ran large *taṟavāṭu*, while patrilineal Christian families built large homes modelled either on *taṟavāṭu* or on colonial styles. Brāhmans meanwhile had their *illam* and Kṣatriyas their *koṭṭāram* (palaces). All such buildings of 'big families' are better thought of not simply as 'houses' but as large structures supporting many dependants and servants. Dilip Menon has explored the historical significance and working practices of the nineteenth-century *taṟavāṭu* and demonstrated the politico-economic indivisibility of its component parts: land, house, people, animals, and crops (1994).

While the number and extent of a house's dependants and attached properties have generally declined and while the *taṟavāṭu* as such no longer exists since the legal abolition of matriliny (in a range of legislation between 1912 and 1976), an idealized *taṟavāṭu* model still prevails. Whether named as *taṟavāṭu*, *illam*, *koṭṭāram* or simply house (*vīṭu*), the house is the long-lasting and concrete embodiment of a family's success or failure, its relative worth and reputation, indicated in the identity between family and house-names. In Taussig's terms, it is a monument to the family (1997). It is particularly understood as the objectification of the worth of the family's senior male, the householder, who provides the cash to buy land and build the house.[6] A man's first duty, after marrying and fathering children—taking on Hindu householder status—is to build or improve the family home, leaving behind (usually to his youngest son) something of value and which speaks of a certain status. Buying, renovating or building a house is a priority, as brick and tile houses replace thatched or wooden huts, and concrete or costly granite and teak replace brick. As considerable capital is required to build a new house, this is usually a long-term goal (an average of between Rs 1,50,000 to 2,50,000 in 1990, Rs 4,50,000 to 7,50,000 in the early 2000s for a prestigious concrete three bedroom house, excluding the cost of the land).

Since concrete houses have become relatively common, wealthy villagers have begun to maintain distinction by having their new houses built either brickwork style, or according to traditional *nālukeṭṭu* design (traditional Kerala four-sided house built around a central courtyard, discussed below). Houses are constructed over a period of years: the ritual placing of a foundation stone is like a vow (*nērcca*), in which the Hindu carpenter (Āśāri) acts as priest, and is a public commitment to build, years before the cash to continue work is raised. Side extensions, verandas, extra storeys, may all be added long after the original house has been built. A house is a never-finished project: as a family's wealth, reputation, prestige and membership grows, the house will also grow. But this growth is far more than a matter of symbolic capital or embodiment of householder's *mānam* (prestige, standing). Growth is an attribute of living things, and successful growth testifies to the auspiciousness of the house and the land on which it is built, a positive quality which will act favourably upon residents (cf. Carsten and Hugh-Jones 1995).

BUILDING A HOUSE

Melinda Moore (1990; see also 1985) has already described the layout of a traditional Kerala high-caste four-sided house, or *nālukeṭṭu*, and has discussed the *taccuśāstra* (manuals about the science of house building). Although most new houses now are built using non-traditional materials, and often to new designs, Hindus and Christians alike continue to consult and employ the Hindu Āśāris,[7] since the choice of suitable site and layout depends upon factors which only these specialists understand. Migrants may buy plans from a Gulf-based architect, but take the Āśāri's advice on alterations necessary to bring the house structure into line with *śastrik* principles. Āśāris allow leeway in interpretation to permit desires for a filmi-style house rather than a *nālukeṭṭu*. For example, strings of small holes which should be placed in house walls to allow the passage of *vāyu* (wind) (Moore 1990: 175) can be improvised: 'We can count a door or window as a hole, and put more windows and doors into the house in the necessary places', Vasudevan Āśāri explained. A recent counter-trend to the extravagances of the 1970s is to turn to the restoration of existing properties or to build anew, but in traditional style.[8] Often the existing *aṟa* (paddy-store) of an old house, referred to as the heart of the house or as Mahālakṣmi, is preserved, renovated, and used as the core of the new building. The *aṟa*, as much as the kitchen fire, is a core living part of a building which itself lives, having a life-span, a horoscope, and being subject to the same laws and forces as those which affect other organic bodies.

In house-building, first the plot must be squared-off and measured out, and the lines of force mapped, so that Vāstupuruṣan is correctly aligned. Thankappan Āśāri told us that there are 10 or 12 types of house, classified according to size and directionality, and that a *nālukeṭṭu*, four-sided single atrium house, actually holds not one but four land men. The *nālukeṭṭu*, a four-sided building around an open central courtyard, is the basic model or prototype for all houses; an *eṭṭukeṭṭu* (double atrium house) is just two *nālukeṭṭu* side by side. The majority of houses in Valiyagramam are what the Āśāri call *adharma gṛhaṅṅaḷ* (adharmic houses), being half (the commonest house) or one quarter of a *nālukeṭṭu* (cf. Moore 1990: 171).[9]

Nālukeṭṭu means 'four knots' or 'tied down in four places'. Lines are drawn in on the squared-off land plot as a whole before placing the first *kōṭi* or knots which will tie and stabilise the plot and enable building (see Fig. 5.2):

1. East to west = *Brahma sūtram*, the line of Brahma, supreme god.
2. South to north = *Yama sūtram*, the line of Yama, death or darkness. The centre cross of the south to north and east to west axes is marked as Brahma *sthānam* (Brahma's place, at the centre of the plot, considered by Moore (1990) and Beck (1976) to be the location of the navel of the land man, but according to our informants and diagrams, it is at the *naṭu*, the lower back (see Fig. 5.1). In a house, the point where the axes cross corresponds to the open courtyard, a square of earth left open to the sky, where a sacred basil may be planted.

3 South-east to north-west = *Mṛtyu sūtram* (the line of death); if the house touches this line, death will come.

4 South-west to north-east = (given by informants in Malayāḷam as) *Kaḻunan sūtram*, and translated by a research assistant as the

line of the neck or jugular vein. Moore (1990: 175) gives the name of this axis as *karṇan*, and translates it as ear, diagonal or corner line, from Sanskrit.

In deciding where on the plot to build the house, some rules are followed: the house must be situated in one of the eight spaces produced by drawing the above four axes, in such a way that it does not intersect any of the lines (see Fig. 5.2). Permissible locations for the house are the following triangular spaces within the original plot: south-south-west, west-south-west, north-north-east and east-north-east. The house then sits either in the upper portion of land man's body, or in the space between his legs. In other words, it cannot be placed externally to his body, but must be encompassed by it; the house must be tied or held in place by the land. Vāstupuruṣan therefore acts as an unseen bridge holding together and merging into

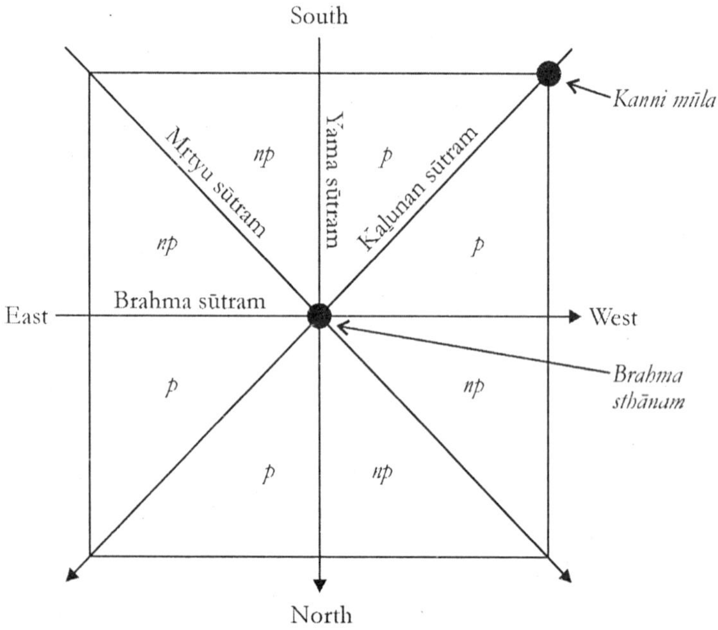

p = -permissible location for building a house
np = not permissible

Fig. 5.2: Lines of influence as they are drawn in on a land plot, and permissible locations for building a house.

one object two physical entities, earth and the house. The rules about axes not intersecting make clear that the earth is subject to cosmic influences which travel across the land and which have effects on the built structures upon it. It is perhaps the body of Vāstupuruṣan, connected to both, which acts as transmitting medium for these influences to pass from earth to house. The 'rules' are of course normative expressions of ideals, such that while we have never seen a Brāhman *illam* which contravenes any of the Āśāris' ideals, there are houses in Valiyagramam which flout one or more of them. At the same time, problems in the families of those living in such homes are quickly attributed to the *adharmic* nature of the buildings.[10]

The house itself is also built by human bodies, in the same all-fours, head raised, buttocks-raised attitude described above for the land man on the plot, but with the arms and legs less widely spread to allow for the fact that the spaces to be fixed here are not squares, but rectangles (see Fig. 5.4). The *nālukeṭṭu* is considered by Āśāris the basic and best model, consisting of four full men.

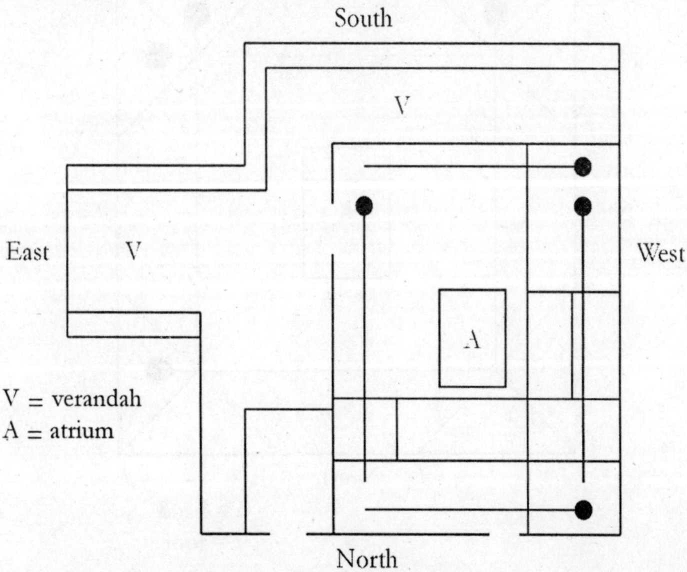

Fig. 5.3: How more than one *Vaśtupuṛusan* are put together in a *nālukeṭṭu*.

'All other houses are just portions of a *nālukeṭṭu*', and this is then what makes them *adharma gṛhaṅṅaḷ* (demonic/amoral buildings): our diagrams clearly show the way in which they would then be incomplete, holding dissected portions of what should ideally be whole bodies of Vāstupuruṣanmār or land men (Figs. 5.3 and 5.4). This is, after all, appropriate, since they are traditionally the houses of Christians or *avarṇa jāti*, who by orthodox reckoning are incomplete persons: Nampūtiri *illam*, Kṣatriya *koṭṭāram* and high-status Nāyar *taṟavāṭu* alone are alleged to be complete *nālukeṭṭu*.[11]

In the arrangement of space-fixing male bodies around a house, the positions of the hands and feet show that the general principle of arrangement is that the men are oriented towards the south-west corner. Of the four men who form the four sides of the house around the central atrium, one is considered pre-eminent, the *tekku pēru* (south-side person). The south side of the house is the most important side, referred to by Āśāris as *sthāyi* (fixed); it is the side

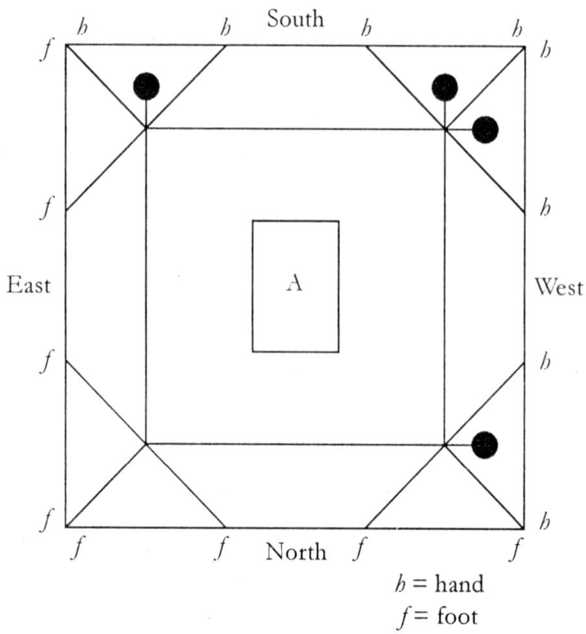

Fig. 5.4: *Nālukeṭṭu* and the four *Vāstupuruṣans*.

along which the main veranda runs and is, we note, firmly held down by four hands.[12]

When a house is to be built, the Āśāri and householder together first plant a splint of jack-fruit, a white latex-bearing tree, at the compound's south-west point. Here, post-cremation, family members' bones will be buried, to be later transformed into fertile substance (discussed below). This south-west corner is the most significant angle: it is where the initial foundation-stone is laid, often years before any further building work takes place, where the first splint of jackfruit wood is planted, and where all initial *pūjās* are done. After this will come the doorframe and then the east-west roof frame, house-man's spine. *Tekku pēru* is the man on the principal (south) side of the house, he whose head lies in the south-west corner of the building, whose spine forms the east-west axis which 'holds everything together'[13] and whose ribs mark out important south-north axes (Fig. 5.4). In the best and commonest sort of *nālukeṭṭu*, the *paṭiññāṟu* (west) house, whose front porch and main entrance are to the east, the beams of wood—whose 'heads' (tops of the beams) must always face west—run in exact concordance with south-man's spine, the top of which is also in the west. The three lesser men whose spines form the other roof-beams are arranged as shown in Figs. 5.3 and 5.4, the rule being that no head should lie in the north-east corner, which must be left clear.

The central atrium, which Moore perspicaciously links to the empty centre and to the Hindu cosmos (1990: 199), is in our understanding empty not, as she claims, because it corresponds to the navel of a single house-man, but because it is the central point where the axes cross and the *Brahmasthānam* of the house. Here the earth is left empty and unbound, free to connect with the universal source of power and energy (*paṟaśakti*), while all lines of cosmic influence come together in a 'hot spot' of power (Fig. 5.2).

The doorframe of the main entrance to the house, which is the first structural part to be placed after the foundation stone and jackfruit wood splint at the south-west corner, is, according to Āśāris, the anus of the main house-man (see Figs. 5.3 and 5.4). We have double-checked this assertion, even if it is clear from the diagrams that the entrance does correspond indeed to an anus. Perhaps any problem we have in assimilating this information lies in thinking of this door as an entrance: for family members, whose proper place after all is not outside the house but within it, this door is more appropriately an exit. Family members and friendly visitors rarely use this main 'entrance', preferring to skip around the side (males) or via the kitchen (females).[14] Often the door is placed there simply for *taccuśāstric* requirement, and is actually left closed up and never used. Knowing that this 'official main door' is land man's anus also throws extra significance on the fact that corpses and departing new brides are ceremoniously exited by this door, excreted, as it were, from the house.

All these initial steps—foundation stone, jack-split, doorframe, east-west roof frame—before building proper commences are accompanied by *pūjās* performed by householder and chief Āśāri together. A small piece of gold, a little paddy, some red flowers, and some milk—items clearly related to the material world, to prosperity and fruitfulness—are buried under the foundation stone. Thankappan Āśāri told us: 'I do all these *pūjā* myself, I get *dakṣiṇā* for it: money, betel-nut, a new cloth. Brāhmans know nothing about all this, they cannot do it.' What the Āśāri is stressing here is that he has knowledge and a power for action which the Brāhman does not, remunerated and respected exactly like Brahmanical knowledge, with *dakṣiṇā*. This knowledge and technical skill relates to the material world and to the life-processes of organic beings. Even a Brāhman must call an Āśāri to plan his house and do the necessary *pūjā*; his knowledge is not powerful enough to allow him to act here for benefit in the realms of material prosperity and fertility.

After the ceremonial inauguration of construction-work, the Āśāris are left to finish the house. In house-plans, twelve boxes representing the months of the Malayāḷam year are drawn surrounding the house, in exactly the same way as is done when preparing a person's birth-chart; Āśāris referred to this as drawing up the house's horoscope (Fig. 5.5). The scheme for placing rooms and facilities is done by reference to the horoscope and not to the cardinal points (cf. Moore 1990: 172ff), since houses need not always be built facing east; an east-facing house is the best but not the only possible *dharmic* building (also Moore 1990: 174). We can, however, draw

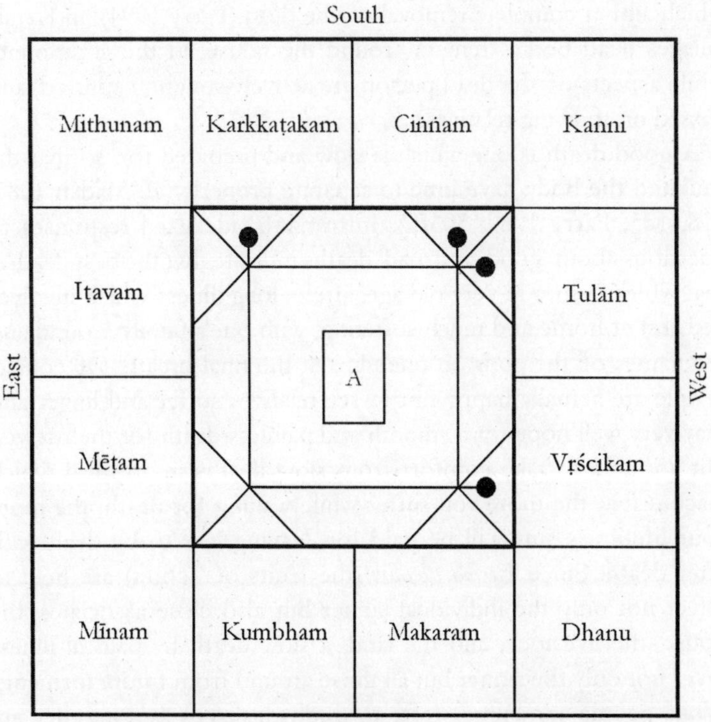

Fig. 5.5: The house and the months of the calendar.

out a general implication that life-sustaining powers of fertility and increase are highly concentrated around the rice store (*aṟa*) and the foundation-stone, while physiological processes bringing pollution (childbirth, excretion) are kept in the next corner (moving clockwise). In an ideal home, these would be the south-west and north-west corners.

RECYCLING THE DEAD

An aspect of Kerala life which never fails to provoke unease or even horror among north Indians is the practice of keeping the family dead very close by. Unlike north Indian funerals, in which a polluting dead body is removed to a cremation ground outside the village or the urban residential area, and subjected to rites which aim at complete removal of the dead (Parry 1994), in Kerala villages dead bodies remain around the house, in the compound, while aspects of the dead person are actively sought, captured, and passed on to living relatives.

A good death is one which is slow and prepared for, so that the soul and the body have time to separate properly (cf. Madan 1987: 118, 125; Parry 1989: 503ff.). Informants' idealized responses to questions about 'good' and 'bad' deaths indicate that the best death is that which comes in very old age, after a long illness which involves bed rest at home and much suffering, with one's family around and the names of the gods on one's lips at the final breath. Of course, people are actually happy not to see relatives suffer and linger and may very well hope for a smooth and painless death for themselves, but are able to take comfort from slow deaths in an ideal which teaches that the more you suffer while waiting for death, the more your lifetime's sins will be paid for, leaving less to be dealt with after death. Since *karma phalam* (the fruits of action) are held to affect not only the individual sinner but also close associates, the house, the livestock, and the land, a slow death by painful illness saves not only the sinner but all those around from future torments. While people sometimes refer to (individualized) *karmam* they are more likely to express these ideas in terms of (more generalized) *dōṣam*. As we will explain in more detail below, the negative fruits of the actions of a sinner affect not simply their individual soul but the entire family group, and are transmitted largely through the land and house.

Death, then, should be slow, at home, and at an appropriate time with regard both to one's own age and place in the family (e.g. a son should not die before his father), when it will be accepted gratefully as a liberation from the body and from this world. A painful death is often spoken of as the sinner paying for their sins before dying, thereby, as we will see, leaving less *dōṣam* to be dealt with by descendants. The souls of young people (who still hold desires or attachments to the world), of those who die suddenly without preparation, or of those weighed down by unpaid for sins, are unlikely to be able to leave the world Their spirits are expected to hover around, trying to re-embody themselves via possession, in order to experience the earthly life which they still crave, to take revenge on those who caused their untimely death, to pay for or pass on to others their sins, or to stay near their loved ones from whom they cannot yet bear separation.[15]

We interviewed informants from all the Hindu communities, plus funeral specialists like barbers and woodcutters, about the funeral procedures; there was substantial disagreement over fine details. Nowadays in Valiyagramam washermen and the drummers refuse to come to funerals, so all the *karmam* and preparations—apart from the woodcutting, which is still done by the Tanṭāns (woodcutters)—are conducted for Nāyars and Īḻavars by the community's own barber; Pulayars do everything themselves, while Brāhmans have their own funeral priests. Partly because of the difficulty of finding barbers, washermen and so on to participate in the rites, the NSS and SNDP community associations (Nāyar and Īḻavar respectively) have published booklets explaining how to conduct a 'do-it-yourself' cremation.[16]

There are five rites, cremation, exhumation and purification, food sacrifice/*piṇḍam* balls, feasting, taking to the ocean. Death day is day one, and even if the cremation is not performed on this day, it is always treated as though it had been; from that day, a family may decide to keep pollution (*pula*) and do the first four rites spaced over seventeen, eleven or—as is usual—five days, depending upon convenience.[17] The usual practice now is to keep five days' pollution and then end the *sañjayanam* (purification and burial under jack-tree of cremains[18]), *bali* (sacrifice) and *valiya kāpi* (pollution-breaking feast) all together on the fifth. One year after day one, the purified cremains are dug up and taken to the sea. Brāhman funerals are even more complex, while for pragmatic reasons Scheduled Caste and poor Īḻavar funerals are often stripped down to a simple and inexpensive burial on the compound land.

Persons in Kerala do not suddenly disappear at death. At death and in the ensuing rituals, they must be subjected to extreme fragmentation and many transformations. Cremation and the ensuing rites appear, like birth, as similar to the original creative sacrifice (Beck 1976; Parry 1989: 503ff.). This is not surprising, because birth and death are often associated: a death in one arena is a birth into another (Beck 1969; Kapferer 1991: 298). This does not mean that the one is an exact metaphor for the other; and again, we reiterate our unwillingness to force the data into the sort of interpretation which would make the one (and already one would need to ask: which one, death or birth?) into a template for the other. We are instead dealing with an association of two semantic domains by virtue of drawing metonymically on looser and mutually resembling principles, in this case more general processes of union and separation (Östör 1980: 180-1). In such processes, what is held together is broken apart and spilled, yielding both the regenerative seeds of new life (cf. Shulman 1980) and also some unwanted negative residues. This type of process is, as we shall outline below, also observable in paddy agriculture.

Over the course of funeral rites, through a great many successive transformations which take place at increasing distances from the death-place, various parts of the person become less and less personalized and more anonymous or undifferentiated; these parts, good and bad, are refined and separated out by the actions of persons, trees and land. The component parts of the person which are broken down are many. First, there is elemental matter in combination which is first broken back down into its constituent *pañcabhūta* and returned to the immediate physical environment of the house compound (on the *pañcabhūta* or five elements, see Subbarayappa 1966). This breakdown is achieved by prayer (Īḻavars) or by ritual actions (Nāyars) done before the pyre is lit. The pyre itself effects a second transformation. After it burns for two or three hours, people watch to see the body break in half and collapse inwards. When the burning body breaks at the lower back, *pāpam* or *dōṣam* (sin or faults, evils including and bringing with them bad luck, illness and so on) are said to be liberated into the air along with the soul, as the stomach bursts and the lower back breaks (note, not the skull as in north India, but the *naṭu*—the part corresponding to the empty bare earthen courtyard in the house and the crossing-point of lines of force in the body of Vāstupuruṣan). At this point further transformations are effected, when the barber performs rituals using a pot of milk to try to 'catch' and neutralize the released *dōṣam.* What is not caught will settle on the land and contribute to its characteristics. Some substances, however, remain in the ashes and bones in the pyre pit (the cremains). After cremation, some of these cremains are ritually washed (purified with holy water, cow's urine, and so on) and taken away to the compound's south-westerly jackfruit tree by the chief mourner. The remainder is left in the pyre pit, which will then be dug over.

These early-day transformations of the dead body which begin to break the person down and settle different components in different places around the compound, transformations which are begun by living persons, are then continued over the next years by the actions of trees and the land. Because household members do not disappear to cremation grounds but remain around the compound, actually becoming part of the compound and its vegetation, a plot can become 'ancestral' land very quickly and easily—as soon as one person has died there—facilitating Kerala's fast-moving land market. When new people move into a plot, they generally take over and adopt the ancestral spirits already existing around there; the possibility of incorporating high-status ancestors and high-quality influences and substances from the land into one's own household is actually a strong motivating factor for families seeking to buy land from city-bound high-status families, such as the many Īḻavars who have moved into former Nāyar plots or the few Nāyars who have managed to buy old Brāhman plots and houses. The wealthy ex-untouchable Paṇṭāram (*pappaṭam*-making) family with a son in the USA who have managed to buy an old Kṣatriya *koṭṭāram* are an extreme example of this 'capturing' of auspicious and high-status qualities. At the same time, a plot with undesirable ancestral spirits or influences can easily be diagnosed and 'cleaned' by the actions of an astrologer and appropriate rituals.

After *sañjayanam* (cremain purification), the pyre pit is planted with three important fruit and root bearing plants; banana at the south (head) side, coconut in the stomach (central) side, and a tuber at the north (feet) side. The dug-over pit, with its cremains, is then left on the land to feed (to become the food of, i.e. to be transformed by) trees, which will then feed the house dwellers. Before the pit is filled in and planted, some fragments of the bones have been taken and washed in *sañjayanam*; after this purificatory ritual washing, these cremains—which must include skull fragments—are then buried for a year underneath the jackfruit tree at the extreme south-west corner of the compound, left to be transformed by the tree. Any residual *dōṣam* left in the cremains will go into the newly-planted pyre pit plants and the jackfruit tree. The jackfruit, which yields a cold white fluid and large fruits made up of hundreds of smaller seeds, objectifies household fertility, prosperity, and increase; the fruit is a good icon for all members together on the ancestral plot, for the '*janiccuvāl, mariccuvāl*' (all *taṟavāṭu* members, including those yet to be born and those already dead) invoked as such during funeral rites. The tree will during the year transform the purified cremains; something from them will remain in the cremains and something will enter the tree. This jackfruit tree must never be cut down, and gives continuity of cool refined ancestral substance, distilled by the tree from cold white bones.[19]

The final remnants of transformed matter are dug up from under the jackfruit tree after one year, presumably completely transformed by now, and are taken by the chief mourner to the Ocean.[20] If the soul is now ready to detach itself from the land and family, it will go with (in) the purified and transformed cremains to be released into the ocean. The scattering into fast-flowing water of the soul can be understood as enacting *mokṣa*, the final obliteration of the self, merger with godhead. The highly refined remains (the exhumed cremains) going into the water also contribute to the continuance of a larger and less differentiated circular flow of life. We can, following the funeral's sacrificial logic (see e.g. Beck 1976; Parry 1989: 503ff. Hiltebeitel 1989: 357), think of them as the sacrificial remnants which contribute to new life (the cooled-down 'fiery seed'—Shulman 1980: 90-3). If the *jīvātmāvu* (individualized soul) successfully de-differentiates itself during its post-cremation year of wandering, it will settle in the bone fragments and go willingly to the ocean, where it might go to heaven or into total dissolution. If it remains attached (to the land, to the people living there), it might stay in the compound[21] as a domesticated and now deified ancestor, tied and fixed into a *kuryāla* (ancestor shrine), or as a disembodied and unsatisfied ghost (*piśācu*), who will eventually find its way to the paddy fields, where many disembodied spirits wander.

We see, then, that the qualities of the person are also fragmented. Some sin is burnt off by the bodily suffering immediately prior to death, which is why a long debilitating illness is preferred. Some is burnt in the pyre; the more it smokes, the more *dōṣam* and sin are burnt off. 'To make more smoke' is given as a reason why green wood is used on the pyre and why men must smoke cigarettes at funerals. Some more *dōṣam* and sin comes out of the corpse's stomach when it bursts and the lower backbone breaks. Some of this goes into a pot of water carried by the chief mourner, from where it may be neutralized by the barber through the addition of cows' milk. Any residual *dōṣam* which remains firmly 'stuck' to the bones and ashes after all the rites are concluded will go into the three trees planted in the pyre pit, and from there, into the bodies of the descendants who eat the fruit of the tree. The fate of the soul meanwhile is uncertain. People simultaneously claim that it remains on the compound land, wandering; wanders around the village until it is reincarnated; goes into the *kuryāla* (ancestor shrine); stays under the jackfruit tree; goes to heaven; merges with 'Viṣṇu's leg'; and goes to the sea and dissolves there into universal spirit.

Most often, a soul is too differentiated and too attached to the earth to be able to go off to the sea in purified bone remnants, and it stays wandering around its old neighbourhood. It may be weighed down by *dōṣam* which is said to be so 'sticky' and 'heavy' that it will not pass from it. Or it may simply be attached because of unfulfilled desires: to see a grandson born, to stay around a much adored wife, to continue living in the house it loved. If the funeral rites were not carried out properly, or if the death was a bad one, the soul will certainly be unable to detach from the death place. In all the above cases, it will initially be unhappy. and probably cause disturbance to the family, so that they will realize that it is there, and help it. *Bhūmi dōṣam* and *bhavana dōṣam* (problems with the land and with the building respectively) are common causes of family troubles such as illness, unemployment, and family squabbles. If *dōṣam* needs to be put right, the astrologer can diagnose it and advise treatment, after which the spirit can be comfortably settled in the ancestor shrine.

If a spirit has no *dōṣam*, but is simply attached, wanting to carry on being part of the family, then it can; but only on condition that it accepts its new status and stays in the place now appropriate for it, the *kuryāla* (ancestor shrine). It may travel the slow road to *mokṣa* (release) like this. After a while, it will merge with the other familial spirits in the *kuryāla*, until it becomes only part of de-differentiated Appuppan (granddad) the group spirit of all dead family members. From here, it is a short step to total dissolution.

Not only the soul and the *dōṣam* but other qualities and parts of the person also remain in the earth of the family compound. There they will be transformed by the land to give substance to trees whose fruits will be eaten by family members. Any sticky (extremely bad, severe) residual *dōṣam* or sins which resisted transformation by the pyre and have also resisted transformation by the land and by the tree, will then be passed on to the descendants. When they eat the jackfruit, banana, coconut and tubers, they will be eating transformed ancestral substance: in Kerala, *karma phalam*, the fruit of the actions of the ancestors, is not an empty figure of speech but is literally ingested and assimilated by the living descendents.

FLOODS AND PADDY LANDS

The monsoon, breaking shortly after harvest, brings chaos to the village: canals and rivers overflow their banks, wipe out many of the roads, travel is difficult everywhere and in places impossible, the rain destroys houses, sometimes crops and animals, and finally departs. It leaves the paddy fields flooded to a depth of 2 m with a sea of water in which float rotting plants, dead small animals, human excreta, the wreckage of houses, and scores of tiny fish swimming in the silt rich water. Fish is valued only second to rice as a food by non-Brāhmans, is served daily in those homes which can afford it, and its relative absence in the diets of the poorest is sorely lamented. Monsoon is a time of abundance of this food, as boys from all the non-vegetarian castes go to fish in the canals and paddy fields.

This water then, contains life, in the form of food and a multiplicity of living creatures; and death, in the form of chaos, destruction, and excreta, all abundantly mixed. It is also out of control, overflowing, threatening to invade the ordered centre of the village, where the temples are, and where the higher castes live. Higher castes guiltily picture the Harijan colonies as even more dirty and miserable than usual during the monsoon, and arrange alternative emergency accommodation in the village primary school for the season. But many refuse to go, moving in with family who live nearer the edges of the *puñja*, or, if they are lucky enough to have brick houses, staying put, ignoring the water which laps around and even in through the front door, travelling to market and receiving visitors by boat. When the monsoon arrives, many Pulayar young people told us, 'You must come out in the boat with us to see the flooding'. We assumed that they wanted us to see the extent of the damage suffered by their community; many had their entire houses destroyed. But there was another, equally strong, reason, that we should see and share their enthusiasm for the beauty of the flooded paddy-fields.

The beauty of the *puñja* was a recurrent theme of our conversations year round. Pulayars spoke about the *puñja* (our *puñja*, they always called it) with more attachment and sentimental regard than even the most traditional high-caste landlord. High-caste informants told us, 'We are attached to the land, that's why we don't like to migrate, that's why we shouldn't sell it', but in truth they are mostly attached to their garden land. As regards the paddy-fields, they are attached only to their refined end product and to the concept of land-owning, of being rooted within the village (Miller 1954; cf. Strathern 1990 [1988]: 81ff.).

The Pulayars, who often jokingly reminded us that they were the 'true sons of the soil', living and working on the paddy land, had a qualitatively different relationship with it from any other group: they continually praised its beauty and power, and their attachment to it. When we asked whether they felt it was unfair that they were stuck in colonies at the edges of the village, and asked whether they would like to move nearer the centre, they were emphatic that they would not. Even during the monsoon, they pointed out, only those most desperate and with nowhere else to stay went to the village school; everyone who could, stayed on the *puñja*. What they wanted, they told us, was to stay living in that place, but in solid brick houses instead of huts. When we talked about land reforms, they acknowledged that they had done badly, compared to the middle communities who, having been tenants, got the right to buy at fixed prices. The Pulayars had never legally controlled land, and so had no right to buy. However, they continued to regard the *puñja* as their own land; on paper, they pointed out, it had been unrightfully usurped years ago by outsiders, but in spirit it still belonged to them. They lived there, their dead were buried there, their ancestors, and other spirits which only they knew how to deal with, walked there (Uchiyamada 1998, 1999, 2000).[22] The upper castes have usurped the products of the land, but they have not really managed to take control of it; they do not go there that often, some only once a year, to supervise the harvest, and all of them, including the Christians and the ex-untouchable Īḻavars, are terrified to go near the *puñja* at night. Only people from the lowest castes—Pulayars and Paṟayars—are completely unafraid and happy to be on the *puñja*.

As monsoon water levels recede, 'bundhs' (dykes) and irrigation channels (sealing, bounding, channelling flow) are built by Pulayar men, while cleaning and weeding (refining, transforming) is done by Pulayar women, to clear out the dirty or unwanted life-forms and to prepare the ground for the cultured crop of rice. From the point of view of high-caste villagers, the water is now channelled, under control, its rotting and unwanted elements disposed of by ex-untouchable caste members and its fertility put to the social purpose of agriculture. Just as low-caste ritual specialists deal with a polluting corpse, trying to neutralize sin and *dōṣam* in milk while liberating a person's soul to become a benevolent resident ancestor, the Pulayar labour in filth to turn the chaotic rot of the paddy fields into a bounty of rice. As might be expected, among Pulayars another viewpoint exists. This accepts the abundances (fish and rice; progeny) brought about by floods and accepts that the forces and powers which energize and move the material world into productivity must, of necessity, scrabble in the dirt. Unlike the Nāyar bank-clerk, the Brāhman schoolteacher, and the Īḻavar shop-owner, all of whom have a horror of manual labour and a general ambivalence about the mess and disorder involved in productive and generative processes, the Pulayars, who still have no option other than manual work and residence on the site, are more accepting of the ambivalence inherent in material life (Kapferer 1991: 298; Kapadia 1996). The Āśāri, making his point about the laying of the foundation stone as being a *pūjā*, also reminds us of the complexity of life-processes such that, as another Āśāri remarked, when talking about menstruation and childbirth, 'even these things have their own sort of purity'.

FLOWS AND CONNECTIONS

Bringing together what we can understand about the land plot, house building, and funeral rituals, we can see that what is being stressed in all cases (as also in Āyurvēda) is connection and flow, with a need for the non-obstruction of channels. These channels exist within the bodies of Bhūmi-Dēvi, Vāstupuruṣan—land man and house-men—and persons, living and dead. Bodies—seen and unseen—should be bounded externally and fixed while still permitting flux within and permeability to the outside, so that forces and substances are able to circulate healthily. This can be done by marking out a plot, building walls and a roof, and always respecting lines along which influences move and substances flow. Spaces must always be left within the boundaries, to allow circulation and the exchange of qualities and substances between bodies: human and non-human. Particular emphasis is placed upon enhancing and fixing the re-generative qualities of paddy, cattle, and humans within the land; lines of flow of substance circulation sustain this process (transmission of ancestral qualities to the living via cremains transformed into food; of the lines of flow, the most important is that which originates in the south-west (Moore's 'underlying flow of good influence from the south-west towards the north-east', 1990: 189). Tracing its course inwards, it moves past (not across, since none of the diagonals must be intersected) the jackfruit tree in the compound under which cremated family members' bones are buried, the foundation-stone of the house, the newly-weds' bedroom, the paddy-store and/or *pūjā* room, the head of the major house-man, the atrium, the kitchen and the well.

Flows, although they may appear to be linear because our knowledge permits only part of their course to be tracked out with relation to the house,[23] actually appear to be like flows within the human body—continuous, re-cycling and transforming the matter that passes through their spheres of influence and touching various stopping-off points along the way. If we plot the movement of paddy—the substance of life—it can be seen to flow anti-clockwise. It is brought upwards from the paddy fields on the village's west side to the *aṟa* (paddy-store), where it becomes an embodiment of Mahālakṣmi in the house's south-west corner; thence it moves downwards to the kitchen, where it is again transformed by the cooking fire in the north-east corner; it is further processed in eating and digestion by the humans of the house; finally its residues are excreted in the latrine, usually placed towards the north-west corner of the compound, at a convenient distance from the north-easterly well. Eventually, this human excreta will be broken down by the land, and more crops will be produced.

Human beings meanwhile appear to follow a complementary clockwise trajectory. If we plot their movements, they are born in the north-west quarter, moving upwards to live and eat in the north-east corner. They die and are laid to rest in the south-east quarter and are transformed into spirits and fragmented subtle substance in the topmost south-west corner. The soul (*jīvātmāvu*) may well stay on the land, fixed into a *kuryāla* (ancestor shrine) at the south-west. Part of their subtle matter and possibly also their spirits (if they have not been fixed, but are still wandering) will continue to be re-cycled, moving towards the *puñja* to the west, helping to fill it and contribute to its nature as a place full of spirits, ghosts, influences and untied substances.

We also notice that architectural principles place the jackfruit tree (containing white fluid, pure refined substance of the ancestors) directly opposite the latrine. This splitting of the final end-products of human beings into two parts, a refined and pure precious white fluid associated with ancestors and a dirty and polluting unwanted part, underlines by metonymic resemblance similar processes taking place within the paddy land. In the case of humans, the agent of transformation is the garden land and its trees; for paddy plants, it is ex-untouchable humans who refine and separate out the harvestable rice from the initial chaos of the flooded field. Human persons clearly stand in opposition to the growing paddy: they mature and grow inside the house, and on the east side of the atrium, while paddy matures and grows outside of the house/compound, and on the west side. Flows of humans and of paddy run parallel to each other, crossing and connecting, and being transformed and re-cycled by the land, the house and the persons within.

Cecilia Busby (2000) and Rich Freeman have both recently proposed that we can best understand the complex and shifting nature of persons in Kerala and the ways in which Malayāḷis act to alter the environment and the people around them by means of ethnosociologically-derived concepts: permeability, flux, and so on. Freeman notes, 'in a culture where personhood can be bestowed on inanimate objects, invested in architectural sites and projected onto entire polities, and where even mundanely human bodies throng inwardly with multiple individuated beings, and extend outwardly into invisible zones of pollution, everyday western models of the person and its powers are hardly a helpful guide' (1999: 173).

Noting that the temple is considered the deity's physical body, Freeman is picking up on a fact which could lead us towards the sort of analysis given in 1976 by Beck, in which the perfect (male) human body is given as a sort of template for the temple and indeed the cosmos (Freeman 1999: 167; Beck 1976). Like Beck, Das (1985) too is preoccupied with the ways in which human and cosmic bodies mimic each other, and takes the human body as a sort of root metaphor or primary motivator. But Freeman's complex understanding of what Kerala personhood represents, and hence what a Malayāḷi human body actually is, means that his analysis does not suffer from the literalism of the 'master metaphor' as explored by Beck and Das. Freeman's insistence on holding on to the fluid and partial nature of the embodied person also echoes Busby's exploration of how Malayāḷi persons come to be gendered (2000). As Busby notes, '(T)he incorporation of substances through eating, intimacy and exchanges is an important part of understanding bodily identities and relationships, and thus what men and women *do* is very much understood as part of what they *are*' (2000: 219). What Freeman and Busby reiterate in the case of personhood and the human body goes then also for other entities, which themselves often draw upon principles embedded in the realm of the human.

Another recent writer on Kerala, Sarah Caldwell, has unfortunately gone against the fresh and nuanced current proposed by Busby and Freeman and instead slipped back into a literalist and heavily formalist style of analysis, rooted in conventional understandings of normatively stable and unitary personhood, in which the body is taken as an a priori fact and in which the realm of the body and especially sexuality is taken to provide the principal motivator (both in terms of psychic, personal and symbolic motivation) of cultural life (1999). In our own (1993) theses we traced out in some detail many parallels between human and paddy reproduction, but still refused to consider these as constitutive of an all-encompassing correspondence between realms. Caldwell has been less restrained and has enthusiastically argued for human sexual reproduction as a sort of master-metaphor (1999).[24]

The data which we have presented on land and territory, which has necessarily broadened out to consider houses, persons, and spirits, suggest that human reproduction and the life-cycle are not modelled on or mimicking paddy production, but stand in a relation to it which is similar in some aspects but also in opposition. Humans are not crops but are complementary to crops, while humans and crops feed each other and contribute to each other's processes of growth and change. Correspondences between domains are based on metonymic principles, and not on an all encompassing root metaphor which can then be used to understand every cultural domain from gardening through cooking to social organization. That no 'model', which entails predictability, coherence, consistency and so on actually exists, becomes apparent when it is measured against actual processes. The notion of resemblances and correspondences based upon immediately observable (externally motivated) internal metonymic principles, at first appears to be far less powerful than that of a consistent cultural (internally motivated) metaphor (see Barley 1983). However, this type of bricolage may in the long run turn out to be far more generative and suggestive of connections, since it does not straitjacket data or force certain interpretations.

Indeed, thinking about Kerala itself—densely populated, with no clear boundaries between villages which themselves also have no central nucleus, shows us the way forward for thinking about

Malayāḷi persons, houses and land plots (Miller 1954). *Nālukeṭṭu*, after all, means 'tied down in four places': the corollary may then be that the rest of an entity is not tied down, but remains fluid. While land needs to be stabilized and tied down at the cardinal points, the rest of a plot is carefully left open to the outside: house-builders purposely leave extra holes in houses to permit the flow of influences and qualities; the entire centre of the home is left as bare earth and described as a major crossing-point where cosmic influences flow. Meanwhile, Vāstupuruṣan's (form) attempts to stabilize and hold down Bhūmi-Dēvi (life) are best thought of as a continual process, not an accomplished fact. The annual transformation of the west side *puñja* offers another clear reminder of life's flux and of the inability of humans to control their lived environment as monsoon rains flood roads and houses but new life forms suddenly proliferate, and the visible environment is completely transformed. Kerala's landscape is constantly in flux, while land in the rice-growing villages of Kuttanadu, lying at and below sea-level, has a close relationship to the sea. Coastal backwater villages, where dense habitation nestles between lagoons, also mark the closeness of Kerala's relationship with the sea and the ease with which land can be transformed into water. Popular geography, meanwhile, remind us that when Kerala was formed, 'the newly reclaimed land presented many problems—floods, landslides, earthquakes' (Menon and Rajan 1989: 1). Zimmerman has explored the classical opposition between the north Indian dry lands, the jungle (*jāṅgala*) and the marshy lands (*ānūpa*) where buffalo roam (1987). Perhaps we need a different south Indian ecology and geography in which the ocean—surrounding the subcontinental tip and offering us the breathtaking spectacle of the place where three oceans meet—is given its due importance, and where the importance of the fluid in the life of the land is not lost.

Acknowledgements: We have received support for various periods of fieldwork in Kerala and writing-up from June 1989 to the present from: the Economic and Social Research Council of Great Britain; the London School of Economics; the Leverhulme Trust; the Nuffield Foundation; the Wenner-Gren Foundation; and the Society for South Asian Studies. We have been affiliated to the Centre for Development Studies, Thiruvananthapuram, Kerala; Madras Institute for Development Studies, Chennai; the Centre d'Études de l'Inde et de l'Asie du Sud, Paris. For generous and thoughtful comments on earlier versions of the paper, we thank Gilles Tarabout, Daniela Berti, Chris Fuller. Andrew Kingston made the diagrams.

NOTES

1. Paddy land also forms part of this complex, but for reasons of space we have opted not to discuss or include it here.
2. See Osella & Osella 2000 for a full-length ethnographic monograph.
3. The art or science of knowing how to deal with land and houses and Vāstupuruṣan(s) is generally known in north India as *vāstu*, but in Kerala was referred to as *taccuśāstram*—'carpenter's knowledge'.
4. Beck (1976) and Kramrisch (cited by Moore 1990) writing about space, were actually working from temple building manuals. House-building is not analogous to temple-building: see Klostermaier 1989: 300ff.
5. This disposition is indeed peculiar in that it does not follow either the one in use in India, or in Kerala by other specialists in architecture and astrology, where it is the east which is always placed at the top of diagrams (Editors' note).
6. Generally, young couples stay for some years with the husband's parents, until they have enough capital to construct a separate house. Nuclear families are the norm, with youngest sons remaining at home to look after the ageing parents. In patrilineal (Christian) families, youngest son inherits, but among ex-matrilineal (Nāyar and Īḻavar) families even now the family home may be given to a daughter as dowry, leaving the youngest son to construct his own new home where he will take his parents to live with him.
7. Also used as a generic for the wider community of artisans/craftsmen, divided into carpenters (Taccāśāri), stonemasons (Kalāśāri), blacksmiths (Kollan), goldsmiths (Taṭṭān) and so on.
8. Laurie Baker, an architect of English origin settled for over 40 years in India and recently awarded citizenship, has long worked with the Kerala government and HUDCO (Housing and Urban Development Corporation) to encourage low-cost housing built using as far as possible traditional materials (including mud) and house-building principles. The demand for his houses among the fashionable of Tiruvananthapuram city is helping the movement away from the expensive and uncomfortable concrete Gulf/filmi-style mansions (see Bhatia 1991).

9. We are here synthesizing and cutting a large body of information collected on *taccuśāstra* in order to present only what seems pertinent to this paper.
10. An interesting development in Delhi is a shift away from *vāstu* (as it is there known) and towards the use of Chinese *feng shui*. This is perceived as a cheaper and easier alternative means of making one's living space auspicious (personal communication, Radhika Chopra).
11. Even today, there is only one four-sided house in Valiyagramam owned by an *avarṇa* family; the rest all belong to the higher *jāti*.
12. Moore (1990: 183) quotes Kramrisch as claiming that in the temple, the north side is considered most fixed, but goes on to admit that she found no such idea among her own Kerala informants relating to houses.
13. The *mōntayuttaram*, compound of *mōnta*, face and *uttaram*, roof beam.
14. We are not suggesting that people know that the main door is an anus; apart from specialists who have access to house-plan knowledge, they certainly do not. However, this door is normally kept locked in many houses, and people clearly do have some sense—perhaps because they see that Brāhmans do not use the 'front' door—that it is not an everyday entrance, but a formal exit.
15. The worst death is in childbirth, after which the thwarted and jealous mother will surely return as a *yakṣi* (female spirit) to harass more fortunate women. Other bad deaths include suicide, violent accidents, murder, and the deaths of people who have not yet satisfied their earthly desires for marriage and children. Young unmarried women who die are especially prone to return and, out of jealousy and a desire to experience married life, take possession of the bodies of brides. In an attempt to avoid this, they are sometimes buried dressed in bridal finery, but the numbers of such spirits around indicates that this subterfuge often fails.
16. This may have contributed both to the standardization of the rite among those members of the non-twice-born castes who have seen and used such booklets, and to the confusion about 'correct' practice among those who have not, but who are relying solely on the barber to have what knowledge was once shared between himself, the drummers, and the washermen.
17. Different communities used to keep different lengths of *pula*, as would be expected from the literature (see e.g. Orenstein 1968, 1970; Panikkar 1918; Gough 1959). Nowadays, *pula* is something not related by most people to caste status, and families choose for how long to observe it. Nāyar and Īḻavar barbers told us that 'in the old days' Brāhmans and

Nāyars kept 10/11 days, Īḻavars and Pulayars 16, but 'now we're all the same, so we all do the same. For convenience everybody can do the rice balls, *sañjayanam*, and tea-party on the fifth day if they want'. This is the 'reformed' funeral as promulgated by the NSS and SNDP caste associations. Brāhmans still keep 11 days *pula*, because they reason that it takes 10 days to build a new body for the spirit (cf. Parry 1985); most other people do not know that this is what is supposed to happen. This novel situation reverses two of the usual features of death-pollution lengths: the highest caste keeps the longest period of *pula* (cf. Orenstein 1968; Marglin 1977); in line with this fact, observance of *pula* is thought to be an index of orthodoxy, so that longer *pula* means higher status. For non-Brāhmans, it is normal to collapse all the ceremonies into five days, and break the *pula* on the fifth; it is ostentatious to do more unless you are a Brāhman. Nobody keeps 17 days: it is a theoretical possibility entertained only by barbers. It should be noted that the reformed practice of keeping five days, and of ending the ceremonies into one day, is more economical: this fact was often pointed out by informants.

18. A now widespread term in English to designate the remains after a cremation.
19. The jackfruit tree yields a very 'cold' fruit, and a white latex. The white latex, as cool and highly refined substance, is then like semen or breast milk. When a new house is built on the compound, some of this substance is placed in the foundation-stone. The fruit is a many-held-together in the one, having many tiny seeded fruits held within one skin. Jackfruit is both an extremely cold food, and is renowned for causing wind, i.e. to be indigestible. Pregnant women often immediately go off jackfruit; its taste and even smell makes them sick. It is then apparently a powerfully symbolic plant. While Caldwell notes several aspects of the jack, especially the fruit's likeness to breasts (1999: 111), and associates it with Bhadrakāḷi, we prefer to think of it as a multi-valenced and ambiguous, over-productive symbol which cannot be fixed as male or female, the fluid neither breast-milk nor semen, nor even characterized as being about death or regeneration, but as offering possibilities of associations with all these things.
20. Preferably Kanyakumari, the place where three oceans meet.
21. Never in the house. Persons are kept on the Inside, but spirits belong to the Outside.
22. Of course, some of this 'tough talk' is part of a self-conscious and politicized 'sons of the soil' rhetoric. One imagines that if a Pulayar

family were to make enough money to be able to move into the centre they too, like the Paṇṭāram family mentioned here, would relish the chance to buy up an old high-caste *taṟavāṭu*.

23. An illusion compounded by our diagrams' use of straight lines.
24. See Malamoud 1975 for a similar exercise, in which cooking rather than sex becomes the master-metaphor for all. We plan to argue elsewhere in more empirical detail against Caldwell's highly partial view of Kerala society, which appears to us to be influenced by mechanisms of projection and orientalist sexualizing fantasy and to make rather sweeping claims, considering that it is somewhat lightly rooted in anthropological participant-observation fieldwork (two weeks continuous residence in a village plus longer-term fieldwork of trips out from a large town to view performances and conduct interviews, Caldwell 1999: 51, 201).

REFERENCES

Barley, N., 1983. *Symbolic Structures: An Exploration of the Culture of the Dowayos*, Cambridge: Cambridge University Press.

Beck, B., 1969. 'Colour and Heat in South Indian Ritual', *Man*, n.s., 4: 553-72.

———, 1976. 'The Symbolic Merger of Body, Space and Cosmos in South Indian Ritual', *Contributions to Indian Sociology*, n.s., 10, 2: 213-43.

Bhatia, G., 1991. *Laurie Baker: Life, Work, Writings*, Delhi: Viking/Penguin.

Busby, C., 1997. 'Permeable and Partible Persons: A Comparative Analysis of Gender and Body in South India and Melanesia', *JRAI*, n.s., 3: 261-78.

———, 2000. *The Performance of Gender: An Anthropology of Everyday Life in a South Indian Fishing Village*, London: Athlone.

Caldwell, S., 1999. *Oh Terrifying Mother: Sexuality, Violence and Worship of the Goddess Kali*, Oxford: Oxford University Press.

Carsten J. and S. Hugh-Jones, 1995. *About the House: Levi-Strauss and Beyond*, Cambridge: Cambridge University Press.

Daniel, E.Valentine, 1984. *Fluid Signs: Being a Person the Tamil Way*, Berkeley: University of California Press.

Das, Veena, 1977. *Structure and Cognition: Aspects of Hindu Caste and Ritual*, Delhi: Oxford University Press.

———, 1985. 'Paradigms of Body Symbolism', in *Indian Religion*, ed. R. Burghart and A. Cantlie, London: Curzon Press, pp. 180-207.

Freeman, J.R., 1999. 'Dynamics of the Person in the Worship and Sorcery of Malabar', in *La Possession en Asie du Sud: parole, corps, territoire*, ed. J. Assayag and G. Tarabout, Paris: EHESS, pp. 149-81.

Fuller, C.J., 1976. *The Nāyars Today*, Cambridge: Cambridge University Press.

———, 1992. *The Camphor Flame*, Princeton: Princeton University Press.

Gough, K., 1959. 'Cults of the Dead among the Nāyars', *Journal of American Folklore*, 71, 281 ('Traditional India: Structure and Change'): 446-78.

———, 1961. 'Nāyar: Central Kerala; Nāyar: North Kerala; Tiyyar: North Kerala; Mappilla: North Kerala', in *Matrilineal Kinship*, ed. D. Schneider and K. Gough, Berkeley: University of California Press, pp. 298-442.

Hiltebeitel, A., 1989. 'Draupadi's Two Guardians. The Buffalo King and the Muslim Devotee', in *Criminal Gods and Demon Devotees: Essays on the Guardians of Popular Hinduism*, ed. A. Hiltebeitel, Albany: State University of New York Press, pp. 339-71.

Jeffrey, R., 1994 (1976). *The Decline of Nāyar Dominance*, Delhi: Manohar (2nd edn.).

Kapadia, K., 1996. *Śiva and Her Sisters: Gender, Caste and Class in Rural South India*, Boulder: Westview Press.

Kapferer, B., 1991 (1983). *A Celebration of Demons: Exorcism and the Aesthetics of Healing in Sri Lanka*, Oxford: Berg/Washington: Smithsonian Institution.

Klostermaier, K., 1989. *A Survey of Hinduism,* Albany: SUNY.

Madan, T.N., 1987. *Non-Renunciation: Themes and Interpretations of Hindu Culture*, Delhi: Oxford University Press.

Malamoud, C., 1975. 'Cuire le Monde', *Purusartha*, 1: 91-135.

Marglin, F. Appfel, 1977. 'Power, Purity and Pollution: Aspects of the Caste System Reconsidered', *Contributions to Indian Sociology*, n.s., 11, 2: 245-70.

Menon, D.M., 1994. *Caste, Nationalism and Communism in South India: Malabar 1900-1948*, Cambridge: Cambridge University Press.

Menon, P.A. and C.K. Rajan, 1989. *Climate of Kerala*, Cochin: Classic Publishing House.

Miller, E.J., 1954. 'Caste and Territory in Malabar', *American Anthropologist*, 56: 410-20.

Moore, M., 1985. 'A New Look at the Nāyar Taravad', *Man*, n.s., 20: 523-41.

———, 1990. 'The Kerala House and the Hindu Cosmos', in *India through Hindu Categories*, ed. McKim Marriott, Delhi: Sage, pp. 169-202.

Orenstein, H., 1968. 'Towards a Grammar of Defilement in Hindu Sacred

Law', in *Structure and Change in Indian Society*, eds. M. Singer and B. Cohn, Chicago: Aldine.

———, H., 1970. 'Logical Congruence, in Hindu Sacred Law. Another Interpretation', *Contributions to Indian Sociology*, 4, pp. 22-35.

Osella, C., 1993. 'Making Hierarchy Natural: the Cultural Construction of Gender and Maturity in Kerala, India', London: London School of Economics (Ph.D. thesis).

Osella, F., 1993. 'Caste, Class, Power and Social Mobility in Kerala, India', London: London School of Economics (Ph.D. thesis).

Osella, F. and C. Osella, 2000. *Social Mobility in Kerala: Modernity and Identity in Conflict*, London: Pluto Press.

———, 2002. 'Quelques points de vue sur l'inné et l'acquis au Kerala, Inde du Sud', in *Images du corps dans le monde hindou*, ed. V. Bouillier and G. Tarabout, Paris: CNRS Editions, pp. 467-95.

Östör, A., 1980. *The Play of the Gods: Locality, Ideology, Structure and Time in the Festivals of a Bengali Town*, Chicago: University of Chicago Press.

Panikkar, K.N., 1918. 'Some Aspects of Nāyar Life', *JRAI*, 48: 254-93.

Parry, J., 1985. 'Death and Digestion: the Symbolism of Food and Eating in North Indian Mortuary Rites', *Man*, n.s., 20, 4: 612-31.

———, 1989. 'On the Moral Perils of Exchange', in *Money and the Morality of Exchange*, ed. J. Parry and M. Bloch, Cambridge, Cambridge University Press, pp. 64-93.

———, 1994. *Death in Banaras*, Cambridge: Cambridge University Press.

Subbarayappa, B.V., 1966. 'The Indian Doctrine of Five Elements', *Indian Journal of the History of Science*, 1, 1: 61-7.

Shulman, D., 1980. *Tamil Temple Myths*, Princeton: Princeton University Press.

Strathern, M., 1990 (1988). *The Gender of the Gift: Problems with Women and Problems with Society in Melanesia*, Berkeley: University of California Press.

Taussig, M., 1997. *The Magic of the State*, London: Routledge.

Uchiyamada, Y., 1998. '"The Grove is Our Temple": Contested Representations of *kāvu* in South India', *The Social Life of Trees: Anthropological Perspectives on Tree Symbolism*, ed. L. Rival, Oxford: Berg, pp. 177-96.

———, 1999. 'Soil, Self, Resistance: Late-Modernity and Locative Spirit Possession in Kerala', *La possession en Asie du Sud: parole, corps, territoire*, ed. J. Assayag and G. Tarabout, Paris: EHESS, pp. 289-311.

———, 2000. 'Passions in the Landscape: Ancestor Spirit and Land Reforms in Kerala, India', *South Asia Research*, 20, 1: 63-84.

Zimmermann, F., 1987. *The Jungle and the Aroma of Meats: An Ecological Theme in Hindu Medicine*, Berkeley: University of California Press.

PART III

RELIGIOUS AND POLITICAL TERRITORIES

6

Territory, Death and Local Deities in Newar Villages of the Kathmandu Valley

GÉRARD TOFFIN

Grouping by kinship and grouping by contiguity have long been recognized in anthropological theory as the two main ways of forming a local political community. The classic distinction was put forward by Henry Maine in the mid-nineteenth century (*Ancient Law*, 1912 [1861]) and can be paraphrased as that between the two principles of 'Blood' and 'Territory'. Though Maine saw kinship or 'blood' as the earlier institution, he also referred to the historical process by which the basis of a community that originally might have been formed through territorial association could come to be recast or reinterpreted in terms of blood relations. As a matter of fact, the general salience of these two principles of land and blood continues to have some application in modern industrial societies. Since the French Revolution of 1789, which brought with it the concept of a liberal and democratic nationalism, France, for instance, is strongly attached to land rights, *jus loci*, as far as national identity and citizenship are concerned, in contrast to Germany, where blood rights, *jus sanguinis*, are still prevalent. Conversely, tradition-based societies of low economic development sometimes give precedence to locality over kinship.

In a recent article, the late anthropologist Graham Clarke (1995) has shown the relevance of these two principles of association for the formation of modern ethnic and national identities in the Himalaya. He stressed in particular the importance of the topography, of bounded local territories, and of parallel valley systems for the understanding of the recent political history of

Himalayan countries. Clearly, the topographical fragmentation of that region has acted as a baffle against modern ideas of nationalism and political integration based on a 'same blood' idiom. Mountains hinder communication, and promote enclaves with their local identities that cut across the wider 'tribal' or 'caste' divisions of kin that appear to fuel fundamentalist conflict in the plains. Within its own highland territory, the Himalayan chain still continues to act as a barrier to the integration that may be sought by any such overall nationalist movements as have been seen in the northern Gangetic plain. The larger national identities that exist today in Nepal do not appear to be homogeneous or exclusive in the manner we may associate with a developed nationalism in the West.

Unfortunately, Clarke did not make any reference to the local cultures of the Himalaya. No mention is made, for instance, of the pervading influence of the concept of territory and residence in Tibet even though ethnographic studies on this country show without ambiguity that kinship bonds are frequently depreciated or overdetermined by ties based on territory. In *Lieux de neige et de genévriers* (1989), Pascale Dollfus has demonstrated that the main social units of Ladakhi Tibetan villages were territorial units, and that local society could be called, after Claude Lévi-Strauss (1991), a 'société à maisons', quite different from societies organized primarily by patrilineal kinship groups. In the village she studied, residence clearly overshadows lineality. Similar data have been reported from Central Tibet (D'ing-ri) by Barbara Aziz (1978, chapter 4). Besides, recent researches inspired by the pioneering study of the Tibetologist René de Nebesky-Wojkowitz (1956) have revealed the importance of the cult of sacred mountains (associated with a sacred lake) in determining local groupings and in structuring Tibetan village societies as distinctive units. As a matter of fact, territorial units were traditionally self-contained all over Tibet, with a great deal of local autonomy *vis-à-vis* the central state.

As far South Asia is concerned, it was until recently accounted scientifically incorrect, especially in France, to stress the importance of territory in village organization. Louis Dumont's theory, set out in *Homo hierarchicus* and other works, emphasizes caste links and hierarchy. It was difficult for this influential author to recognize communal relationships based on village ties. He straightforwardly asserted that 'the conception of "village solidarity" in India seems all too often to be a presupposition imposed upon the facts' (Dumont and Pocock 1957: 27). The main 'social referent' was supposed to be the dominant caste and hierarchy. The concept of territory was thus evicted from anthropological debate. It was Indian scholars such as M.N. Srinivas, and anthropologists from the UK and the USA. Dissatisfied with Dumont's views on caste, who devoted their time to show the relevance of 'horizontal links' as against 'vertical links' in India's villages.[1]

Recent historical and anthropological studies, such as Nicholas Dirks' (1987) ethno-history of a little kingdom of south India, and Dennis Hudson's (1993) study of Madurai, have shown that territorial links across the lines of caste are an important element in the sociology of India, and cannot be excluded from the discussion. William Sax, a specialist on Garhwal, has argued that 'throughout India, persons and places are believed to mutually (though of course not exclusively) determine each other' (1991: 74). They are engaged in 'a continuing set of exchanges' (ibid.: 72). According to this anthropologist, many South Asians think of their places of residence as biophysical entities. They believe themselves to be substantially affected by the place where they reside. W. Sax quoted the study of E.V. Daniel on south India, which reports that upon migrating to a new village, people often immediately look up their castemates, not so much to make their acquaintance as to establish whether or not the local soil is compatible with persons of their nature (1984: 67).

In this paper, I am concerned with the roles of blood and territoriality among the Newars of Nepal, especially among the Jyāpu (agriculturist) caste of this ethnic group. Newars form a very complex Himalayan community, having inhabited the Kathmandu Valley for more that two millennia and speaking a Tibeto-Burmese language. They are deeply indianized and are divided into more than 30 castes, from the Brāhmans at the top of the hierarchy to the former 'untouchables' at the bottom. Hinduism and Mahayana Buddhism coexist in their religious life. The Jyāpu are the largest among these castes. They live in rural areas as well as in old urban centres.[2]

As most of the studies have shown, territory is of utmost importance in Newar society and culture. The Kathmandu Valley was divided during the late medieval period into three autonomous kingdoms, Bhaktapur, Lalitpur and Kathmandu, which fought each other for centuries and were extremely jealous of their individuality. Political fragmentation and conflict have left traces in the religious and social structures. The Newars are traditionally organized in small territorial units, villages or city quarters. People remain strongly attached to their original settlements, even if they have migrated to other places. They usually come back to visit their relatives and friends at the time of the main local festival. Settlements are protected from the dangers outside by a ring of deities, often supplemented in the past by defensive walls. Although they are divided into castes, the inhabitants collectively worship common deities linked to a particular territory, their own individual *kṣetra.* Interdependence among the castes, and the complementarities of ritual duties during festivals and in the cult of local deities obliterate at least in part the religious hierarchy of the pure and the impure. Obviously, village solidarity within the Kathmandu Valley is not 'a simple architectural and geographical fact' as is claimed by Pocock and Dumont (1957: 26) of the Indian subcontinent. The importance of locality is so great in villages as well as in the cities that, as in Tibet, it is territorial ties rather than kinship that determine social relationships. As will be shown later, kinship units tend to be absorbed by residence groups and by the local ritual associations called *guthi* (from Skt. *goṣṭhī* : association) which play a central role in Newar society (Toffin 2005).

The Newar case is of special interest for this volume because it explicitly links territory with death. Here, the social links woven around the soil are in close relation with the celebration of mortuary rites. To be more exact, the affiliation of a person to a given territorial unit depends explicitly on his membership in a specific funeral group attached to this territory. It is an original situation compared to the Indian world of castes, where cults of the dead do not create well-delimited social groups and where, with some exceptions, ancestors do not contribute to affirm the cohesion of a kinship group. Only persons who died accidentally or in an unusual way, as well as ascetics or charismatic religious figures, are durably remembered (Blackburn 1983; Tarabout 2001).[3] On the other hand, the Newar case is to be compared with the Indian tribal religions, at least partially. As will be recalled, some Indian tribes give to the spirits of the departed a crucial role in social life and establish clear connections between ancestors and territory.

I shall focus my presentation on the rural areas of the Kathmandu Valley, which are less known and which admittedly have better preserved old traditions than have the cities. My data derive primarily from Newar peasants, more specifically from Jyāpu villages. They have been mainly collected in two localities (Pyangaon and Theco) where I did intensive fieldwork during the 1970s and 1980s. I also used material I collected between 1995 and 1999 during a survey of eight of these units. This recent research sheds new light on the social and religious organization of these communities.

VILLAGE SPACE AND KINSHIP UNITS

Newar villages of the Kathmandu Valley are predominantly inhabited by farmers from the Jyāpu (Maharjan) caste. Some of them, like Pyangaon and Sunaguthi, are entirely single-caste villages. Others, like Thecva or Khokana, consist of a majority of Jyāpu, along with other castes such as Gathu gardeners, Śreṣṭha traders and peasants, non-agricultural castes of low status (Nāy butchers, Nau barbers) carrying out ritual services for the Newar farmers, and low castes such as the Kau blacksmiths, indispensible for the manufacture and repair of agricultural implements. In a few cases, such as Satungal, the population is divided almost equally between Jyāpu and Śreṣṭha. Generally, the multi-caste structure of the population is marked spatially: nearly every minority caste-group is settled within a concentrated spot or compound. 'Untouchables' for their part have their quarters towards the edges of the settlement, beyond the pale of 'civilized' society. Their position outside the locality demonstrates that such villages constitute a hierarchically ordered society. Interestingly, these villages are not mixed: no other ethnic groups such as Indo-Nepali Parbatiya or Tamang, live in them. They are purely Newar. Such homogeneity plays an important role in the cohesion of the locality. Size, too, is a crucial matter in this connection: the populations of these rural localities range from 600 inhabitants up to 5,000.

Let us say a few words about the physical setting and rural economy. The Newar villages of the Kathmandu Valley are mostly constructed on high ground and on flat terraces hanging 50 to 100 m over the valleys. The area around the village is cultivated with dry crops, such as maize, non-irrigated rice, mustard, and various kind of pulses. Irrigated rice is grown in the lowlands during the rainy season, in rotation with wheat in winter. These Newar settlements are quite rich. Their inhabitants are able to sell an important part of their agricultural products, vegetables as well as rice, to the urban market. The land is very fertile, and yields are traditionally high compared to those of other areas of Nepal or elsewhere in Asia. Recently, the introduction of improved varieties of rice and wheat has markedly increased yields. Although agriculture forms the foundation of the local economy, an increasing proportion of the population have a paid employment outside the village.

The Newar village units of the Kathmandu Valley are characterized by a very concentrated pattern of settlement, very different from the dispersed structure characteristic of the Indo-Nepalese (Parbatiya) castes that speak Nepali as their maternal language. The long rows of attached houses of three to four storeys with their tile-covered roofs along well-designed streets give a compactness to the overall layout. Fields and gardens start from the back of the houses and lie all around. With the exception of the broader streets, which are nowadays sometimes covered with asphalt and used by cars and trucks, the lanes are narrow, less than 5 m wide. The buildings, with their decorated façades oriented towards them, are constructed either along these axes or perpendicular to them, behind the streets. As in urban settlements, back extensions towards inner blocks often constitute inner courtyards, to which small covered passages provide public access. Occasionally, streets widen to form small squares that act as the centres of neighbourhoods.

Most of the localities are divided into quarters, *tvāḥ*, known by particular names. These smaller units earlier had organizational and administrative functions, such as collection of taxes and minor cases of justice. They have lost their importance since 1950, but remain an important element of the village structure, especially in ritual affairs. Their boundaries are nearly always clearly defined in the memories and consciousness of the inhabitants. In addition, Newar villages are divided into moieties: an upper part, *cue*, and a lower part, *kve*.. Their respective positions are fixed by the orientation (upstream/downstream) of the nearest river. As I have shown (Toffin 1996), this dual division is an important aspect of spatial structure and the mapping of the locality in the inhabitants' eyes. It has no social content, but in most cases entails some ritual implications. Theco's two moieties, for instance, are under the protection of two different tutelary goddesses: Bālkumārī in the upper part and Brahmāyāṇī in the lower part.

This compact structure is associated with a clear symbolic image of the settlement. As in the former (thirteenth to eighteenth century) Malla capitals of the Kathmandu Valley, such as Patan, Bhaktapur, and Kathmandu, there is a need to establish a religious centre. This central point is marked off either by a temple dedicated to either a Hindu or a Buddhist deity, or by a small Buddhist *caitya* (the Newar farmers are in principle Buddhist), or by an uncarved stone embodying Kṣetrapāl, protector of the land. Kṣetrapāl is identified by the villagers with Bhairava. He is worshipped during all communal events, and the blood of animals is occasionally offered to him. The villagers also have a very strong idea of the religious boundaries of their settlement. In contrast with what happens in cities, the ritual boundaries are not made up of a circle of temples dedicated to Aṣṭa Mātṛkā goddesses and located in the eight directions of space. The village is, however, demarcated from the outside by one or two *pīṭh* sanctuaries (from the Sanskrit *pīṭha*), which play a religious role during festivals. Furthermore, the boundaries are more often than not characterized by numbers of ritual rubbish dumps, where polluting materials, impure substances and remains of religious feasts are thrown away. These sites, inhabited by supernatural beings of an ambiguous nature, protect the villagers against various evils coming from the outside, especially epidemics. Various rituals related to possession by bad spirits take place here.

The cohesion and unity of the village are reinforced by the worship of common gods. Generally, each village has its own Gaṇeś and a Nāsadyaḥ (local god of music) temple. Gaṇeś is worshipped daily by each household, especially by the women, with incense, an oil-lamp, uncooked rice and vermilion paste. He is also revered at time of festivals and during life-cycle rituals, such as the rice-feeding ceremony, boys' initiations, and marriage. He drinks local beer and alcohol. Only in the larger rural localities is there more than one Gaṇeś temple. Nāsadyaḥ for his part is worshipped by all the musicians of the community, drummers, flautists and cymbal-players, as well as by masked dancers where they exist. He is identified by most of the population with Nritināth, the dancing Śiva (Naṭarāja), and is represented by one or three triangular openings in the wall of the dedicated altar. In some cases, as in Khokana, two temples of Nāsadyaḥ are found in the village, one associated with each side of the village.

Additionally, these villages focus on one (or two) temples of a tutelary deity who ensures their protection and about whom more will be said later. Often associated with the origin of the locality, this deity can be either male or female. In the south of the Valley (in the district of Lalitpur), one can mention: Bālkumārī, Brahmāyāṇī, Rudrāyāṇī, Harasiddhi, Bhailadyaḥ Bhṛṇgāreśvar Mahādev, and Kāleśvar Mahādev. These deities are worshipped at fixed times by the whole village in public festivals, as well as during the life-cycle rites of various families. The priests of the local temples are mainly chosen from the Jyāpu caste. As will be shown, the whole religious life of the settlement revolves around this deity. Similarly, in the case of multicaste villages, the whole locality pays homage to the tutelary god.

It should be noted that most of these rural settlements are ritually enclosed several times a year to mark them off from what lies outside. At the Gaṭhā Mugaḥ festival, which falls during the rainy season, for instance, evil spirits are driven out from the locality at night and offerings are made at the cult sites on the boundaries. Afterwards, each house is barricaded and cut-off from all contact with the outside world. Similarly, in several communities, the space of the village is ritually isolated for a certain period of time. Theco village is completely cut-off from the outside during one month every twelve years, at the time of the great festival of the masked dance of the local Nava Durgā. Such ritual enactments, which are widely distributed in other parts of Nepal, in Assam and in South-East Asia (Macdonald 1975), are of paramount importance for the representation of the local space as a clustered unit.

Jyāpu village society, the main topic of this paper, is divided into small patrilineages four to six generations deep called *khalak*, *bhu*, or *kavāḥ*. These units, which are not named, are rather weakly structured. They fall apart as soon as the memory of a common agnatic ancestor has faded, usually after five generations or so. No written genealogies are recorded. Kin-groups are pre-eminently defined in religious terms, and manifest themselves most clearly at the time of funerals. On the demise of a close agnate (*phuki*) a mourning period of thirteen days is observed. During this time, *phuki* are held to be in a state of pollution. For the death of more distant agnates (*ba phuki* or *jhina phuki*) or married daughters, by contrast, the mourning period is only four days. As a rule, no marriage may take place within these patrilineages. Cross-cousin marriage is forbidden.

As with all Newar castes, the other religious attribute of the Jyāpu's lineage is the cult of a common tutelary god called *digu dyaḥ*. Each *kavāḥ* or *khalak* collectively worships this divinity once a year, either in the month of Māgh (January–February), or in Baiśākh (April–May). Members of the kin group gather on that day on open sites located at the edge of the locality and make offerings to the god, represented by a series of uncarved stones. An ornament called *kikaṃpā*, which is kept in normal times inside the sacred room of the house of the eldest man of the lineage, is placed on the top of the non-iconic divinity. It has the form of a diadem or of the carved halo on Hindu and Buddhist statues, and serves as a symbol of the god. A collective feast for the men, women, and children, is held on the spot. In some villages, such events still attract a great number of relatives. In other cases, only a small group of people is present. When a split occurs inside the group, the new lineage orders another ornament from the goldsmith. After transferring the divine spirit from one *kikaṃpā* to the other, the newly-made ornament is worshipped as the lineage deity. From that moment onward, two different feasts will be held successively in the same sanctuary.

Village endogamy is another important social feature of these Jyāpu localities. In Pyangaon, until recently there was a ban on marrying a girl from outside, on pain of expulsion from the community. In other villages, such restrictions are not in force. Yet, statistically, the rate of endogamous marriages is, or was until quite recently, over 80 per cent in nearly all major Jyāpu settlements. For some scholars, this tendency applies to most of the Newars. Declan Quigley writes, for instance: 'In theory, and still very much in practice, Newars marry Newars not only of their caste but of the local sub-caste. By "local" I mean usually within half an hour's walk and often much less' (Quigley 1984: 160). The strength of affinal kinship is in part responsible for this village endogamy. There are a number of obligations between the in-laws. The marriage ceremonies, for instance, are followed by a series of formal visits between the two sides of the family. Exchanges of gifts and food between the two households are also made during nearly all ceremonies. Moreover, married daughters are under an obligation to conduct numerous ceremonies in their natal house during funerals. It is thus appropriate for them to marry into a house in close proximity to that of their parents. The introversion of Jyāpu social units also militates in favour of such matrimonial ties. A preference for marriage inside the settlement of course tends to multiply the bonds one has within the village community and to strengthen the unity of the Jyāpu locality.

It is clear that these villages are a strong sociological reality and constitute well-defined structural entities. However, they are not totally autonomous or isolated. Administratively, they are attached to wider units of which they form only a part. Economically, they are dependent on nearby markets and on one of the three former Malla capitals (Kathmandu, Lalitpur, and Bhaktapur). It is in these centres that villagers sell their foodstuffs and buy what they are not producing themselves. The very land that is cultivated by the farmers is sometimes owned by Śreṣṭha or high Buddhist Newar castes from outside. In the ritual sphere, too, an attribution of self-sufficiency does not correspond with the facts. Most of the villages call upon the services of external high status priests, Buddhist or Hindu, to celebrate certain ceremonies: funeral rites, the consecration of a *stūpa*, the pacification of a house, the initiation of local Tantric officiants, etc. Most of them use the services of castes living outside their own locality. Besides, the inhabitants of these Jyāpu villages also participate in the main festival of the nearby town and worship its main divinities. The inhabitants of Theco, Pyangaon, Bulu, and Harsiddishi, all located in Lalitpur district, thus pay regular homage to Rāto Matsyendranāth (Bugadyaḥ in Newari). This god holds the same position in relation to his district as village divinities do in relation to their villages. In recent years, the opening up of these peasant communities has been greatly accelerated in all fields, including that of matrimonial alliances with Newar outsiders.

DEATH IN THE LOCALITY

Kin groups, however, are encapsulated in multifunction groups of the *guthi* type. In this concern, the key social grouping is the funerary association called *sī guthi*, *sanāḥ guthi*, or *murdā guthi*[4] in Newari. Such organizations are essential for full integration into the community. To be excluded from one's *sī guthi* is to be excluded from one's lineage and one's caste. Moreover, a Jyāpu peasant who moves to another village or to the nearest urban centre will remain affiliated to his natal funerary association, at least so long as he keeps regular relations with his natal locality. Socially, this group is characterized by three main features. First, it is a compulsory association: all the Jyāpu members of the village must belong to one such *guthi*. Second, it is based on a fixed and inherited membership: one is affiliated to the *guthi* of one's father and one is not supposed to change *guthi* during his lifetime. To move from one *guthi* to another is traditionally rare, and must be approved by the heads of the two associations. Third, such groupings are mainly residential groups: membership of a *sī guthi* belonging to a village different from the one where one is born or actually lives is unthinkable. In all these respects, the *sī guthi* of village peasants differs from Newar *guthis* of the other castes (with few exceptions), formed for various special purposes and operating either in villages or in an urban context. These alternative associations are purely voluntary, and can be changed over the years.

Several traits of these Jyāpu funeral groups merit emphasis. Membership of *sī guthi* is restricted to males, although women can benefit from the ritual services of the funerary association of their husbands at the time of their funerals. Another important point is to be noted: only the heads of households may be members (*guthiyār*) of a *guthi*, so that one becomes a member of the association only when a separation happens in the household. A son will thus be considered a real member only after he separates from his father. In Sonaguthi village, where the number of members of the *sī guthi* is extremely large, the affiliation is formalized only after the death of the father.

Although these groupings are not clans or lineages, they are often made up of kinship units closely related to each other. But, as was stated earlier, genealogical memory is not deep, and members of the group cannot trace their descent to a common ancestor. Furthermore, accidents and conflicts in the history of the families mean that some members are not agnatically related. The frequent adoption of children from the sister's family in the absence of male children has also changed the agnatic composition of the kin-groups. This is why marriage alliances within the death society are not prohibited so long as they fall outside a *phuki* relationship.

The peasant community of each village is divided into two, three, four, or more *sī guthi*. In several cases, a single association is said to have split over the years into separate groups. In general, these funerary associations are not strictly localized. In some exceptional cases, the whole Jyāpu population of the locality is affiliated to a single association. In Sonaguthi village, for instance, the single *sī guthi* of the village gathers together a population of over 600 households. Each *guthi* has its own common house in the village, called either *guthi ché*, lit. 'the house of the *guthi*', or *capāḥ*, which designates in principle a ceremonial rest-house. As we shall see, this common house is used for the annual feast and various meetings.

Each funeral *guthi* has a common deity who presides over the activities of the group and is worshipped by all the members at least once a year. This supernatural being, called Sī dyaḥ in Newari (from New. *sī* death), is in normal times kept in the house of the eldest person of the group, *thakāli*, or in the house of the member in charge of the association for the year. This person worships the Sī dyaḥ once a week, in the evening. The Sī dyaḥ is represented by a statue, mask, or earthenware vessel vested with strong magical power. It is kept in a concealed place in the attic, and is greatly feared by the members of the group. It is associated with cremation, and is frequently identified with Bhairava (Āju). The patron deity plays an important role in the self-identification of the group. Women are not allowed to touch him. The same is true of children whose first teeth have not yet been shed: these children are considered to be immature, *kaci*.

The principal function of the *sī guthi* is to organize the funerals of its members. It oversees the transfer of the corpse to the funeral pyre and takes care of the cremation. It is also charged with the dispersal of the final remains of the body to the four corners of the Kathmandu Valley.

Normally, all the members of the *sī guthi* have to participate in the funeral procession from the house to the cremation ground on the riverside, generally to the west of the settlement. Women are included in the procession. One of them, a married daughter of the bereaved family, throws rice and paddy along the route. But as soon as the womenfolk reach the boundaries of the locality, they return to their respective houses. Once at the cremation site, the *guthiyār* as well as the near agnates sprinkle the corpse with water. The pyre is constructed by the members of the association from wood kept in a small store in the village belonging to the *sī guthi*. Finally, in the days following the cremation, both the men and the women of the funerary association come to present their condolences to the family of the deceased. This ceremony is called *bicāḥ vanegu* in Newari.

Moreover, the members of the organization gather together every year, on a fixed date, for various religious ceremonies and a large feast. In Theco, this event takes place during the main village festival, on the occasion of Thilā punhī, the full moon of the month of Maṇsir (November–December). During the four days of the festival, the various *sī guthi* of the locality focus on their respective *guthi*-house. The Sī dyaḥ god of the funeral association is brought out into the common house and is worshipped with sacred water, vermilion paste, oil lamps, and incense. In Theco as in some other villages, the tutelary god is housed in a special hut made of bamboo strips and straw temporarily constructed inside the *guthi*-house. The feast takes place in a religious atmosphere, marked by gravity and reserve.[5]

Outsiders cannot attend these meals and are not permitted to watch the proceedings. *Sī guthi* meetings and ritual procedures are the business only of those who are members; others are physically debarred from attending, kept away by a screen or guards at the entrance. The funerary association is hence much more than a way of earning religious merit or an association formed simply for a charitable purpose. It is a secret society, impregnated with sacramental values, which contributes to defining a sense of mystical community. It should be noted that the food taken at these ceremonial meals is first offered to the Sī dyaḥ god of the group. The dishes are thus sacred in many ways. Eating together binds the assembly into a spiritual group. Especially significant in these ceremonies is the *sī kāḥ bhvay* ritual, during which the head of a sacrificed buffalo or goat is divided up and consumed, the various parts going in a prescribed order to the eight most senior members. Given the spiritual values attached to the head of the body (honour, spirit, sacredness) in Newar and Nepalese society, such a sharing has a crucial significance beyond mundane issues. The affinity felt by those who periodically join in the performance of these rites and feasts is extremely strong. At the same time, the line between the elders and the juniors is strongly demarcated.

Jyāpu funerary *guthi* play an essential role in social control. The elders of the association, *thakāli*, are the key figures of the village (the same is true in towns) and the custodians of traditional usage. They have ceremonial privileges such as to be served first at feasts and they wear white turbans on ritual occasions. They are periodically invited by influential members of the community to feasts called *deś bhvay*. These *thakāli* are in fact the headmen of the village. They are in a position to expel from the community any person who has had sexual relations with women from impure castes or has married a non-Jyāpu girl. Bad behaviour, breaking caste rules, theft within the village, especially of religious objects, and violence against other members can also be sanctioned after a proper meeting by exclusion from the group. The social and religious status of the concerned person will be deeply affected, no other associations in the village willing to accept him. Nobody will help him to perform funeral rites and to take away the corpse at death. Such excommunication is in fact synonymous with exclusion from one's caste and from one's lineage cult group. Besides, in several villages, the importance of the death societies for the proper integration of individuals into the community is even greater. In Pyangaon, for instance, marriage alliances have to be approved in all cases by the heads of one's funeral group. This is done in the following way. Some weeks after the marriage (minimal) ceremony, a feast is held in the groom's house, to which the *thakāli* of the various *guthi* of the village are invited. If they refuse to come, the marriage is not formally approved. As a rule, funerary associations indicate who are acceptable marriage partners and who are not. They provide an unambiguous marker of caste status.

THE CULT OF THE TUTELARY DEITY OF THE LOCALITY

As has been indicated earlier, every Newar village has its own patron deity, belonging either to the Hindu or to the Buddhist pantheon. Such a god carries important values and representations attached to the territory. He is strongly attached to the community, even if he can be worshipped by neighbouring villagers at certain times of the year. It is often said that if an unscrupulous person should try to steal its statue or its ornament, the representation of the god will become abnormally heavy, so that the robber cannot move it. This patron deity is sometimes believed to be the sovereign and is taken to be responsible for the general prosperity of the locality. He can also take the life of persons living under his jurisdiction. Moreover, regular offerings to his altar are a tribute to him. At all events, this type of deity is a living symbol of the settlement and he expresses the identity of its inhabitants. In many ways, he is playing the part of a god of the land, and can be compared to other Bhūme deities all over Nepal, combining two aspects, one benevolent, the other violent and dreadful.

This tutelary god is housed in a specific temple, often of the Nepali style, with one, two, or three storeys. In Jyāpu single-caste villages or villages dominated by Jyāpu, priests are chosen from the locality and belong to the Jyāpu caste. They receive a Tantric initiation, *dekhā* (from Skt. *dīkṣā*), to perform their sacerdotal functions. Generally, the offices are hereditary from father to son.

The social and religious life of the community focuses upon this temple.[6] The deity is worshipped daily by a woman from each household early in the morning according to a fixed religious route that makes the circuit of all the notable gods and sacred sites of the locality. In most cases, women do not enter the temple, but throw the offerings from the outside toward the altar, ringing the outside ceremonial bell, if there is one. The deity also has its annual festival, fixed by the lunar calendar, and this constitutes the 'village festival', *deś jātrā,* or the 'main festival', *mū jātrā*, of the religious calendar. On that occasion, the god is carried by young boys through the streets of the village in a palanquin. He is considered so powerful that he is supposed to cause the death of one villager during each celebration of the festival.

Most of these divinities receive regular animal sacrifice. Blood is shed on the statue or on the stone representing the god as well as on the soil of the locality and on the villagers watching all around the sacrifice. Such practices are supposed to be auspicious and guarantee prosperity. As a rule, it seems that blood, violence, and even in some villages (Theco, Harasiddhi) human sacrifice are periodically required to regenerate the locality, ensure its well-being, and establish a new link between the tutelary god and its inhabitants. Such offerings transform the village space into a sacrificial ground and legitimize the primacy of the god in the local hierarchy.

Interestingly enough, funeral societies of the Jyāpu villages investigated are also dedicated to the worship of these local deities. As such, they are not only concerned with death and social control, but also with life and the general welfare of the locality. Such a close association between bad sacredness and good sacredness within the same institution is peculiar to Newar socio-religious organization. Guthi death societies clearly combine these two opposing fields. This is how funerary associations have a crucial role in the definition of territoriality and in the religious life of the whole village.

Let us take Theco village. In the upper part of the locality, each of the four funerary associations has separate duties towards the goddess Bālkumārī, who presides over the destinies of this part of the community. The first one offers cooked rice to the goddess every month on the eve of the new moon. The second offers rice-beer on every full moon day. The third presents rice, vermilion paste, incense, and flowers on the first day of the lunar month. And the last one takes responsibility for the cult of the Bhairava located in the upper part of the village.[7] The tasks of watching over the temple, guarding the statues, and cleaning the roofs rotate among the membership according to an age-set division called *pui* in Newari. It is estimated that within each moiety of Theco every inhabitant will have to undertake such work at least once in his life.

But this is not the whole story. The funerary associations of the locality ensure also the performances of the various rituals of the land god. In Theco village for instance, the funeral societies of the lower part form the Brahmāyāṇī *guthi*, and the funeral societies of the upper part, the Bālkumārī *guthi*. These two expanded associations are funded by rice-fields, held as *rāj* (state) *guthi* and registered in the national corporation in charge of these religious holdings (Guṭhi Sāṃsthān). In 1975, these lands were cultivated by tenants from Theco and neighbouring villages. In addition, each *guthi* owns a common house near the temple of its goddess. To run such estates, the two associations concerned have generated a complex hierarchical structure. The Brahmāyāṇī *guthi* for instance is headed by a body of 21 notables called *thakāli*, who include the five most senior members of the association, six cooks, six accountants, and six watchmen. Some of these functions rotate among the membership; others are permanent. These 21 persons are fed more than 12 times a year with great abundance of food and beer. These meals place the elders of the group in conscious opposition to the younger generation. Furthermore, like all other *guthi* feasts, these gatherings transform the village community into a collective body, separate and distinct from outsiders.

The festivals of the local deities are also organized by funeral groups. In Khokana, for instance, the festival of the main divinity of the village, Śikālī, which is celebrated from the third until the seventh day of the bright fortnight of Āśvin (September–October), includes the preparation of nine earthenware jars of rice beer. The three death societies of this Jyāpu village prepare three of these each a few days before the celebration. These pots are sacred (some of them are decorated with a head of Bhairava). The beer, prepared from fermented 'black rice', is said to contain special power, *śakti*. Everybody inside the association has to drink a little of it.

In Theco village the festivals of Bālkumārī and Brahmāyāṇī are held at the same time as the feast of the funerary associations: between the end of the lunar month of Maṇsir and the beginning of Pus. This is the main event in the year's calendar. On the first day of the festival, the statues of the two goddesses are carried to their common *pīṭha* (New.: *pigã*), a sacred place outside the village proper, towards the south. A Hindu Tantric priest comes at night from the small neighbouring town of Chapagaon to perform a fire-sacrifice in front of the two deities. Next morning, Bālkumārī and Brahmāyāṇī are taken back to the village and carried in separate palanquins through the streets of their respective moieties.

In summary, *Sī guthi* groups are much more than death associations. They have multifarious functions embracing many fields of the socio-religious life. They are in fact the keystone of the village structure. More particularly, they establish a connection between the dead and the cult of local divinities. Each male villager is simultaneously bound to a funeral group and to a territorial god. In my opinion, this organic link is a marked characteristic of Newar social structure. Consequently, funerals appear in the traditional Kathmandu Valley as events that create social bonds. Among Jyāpu peasants, as among most of low or medium Newar castes, death is more important than marriage. From the religious point of view, marriage is not a marked ceremony, especially among Jyāpu, and does not entail complex rituals. By contrast, funerals are linked with extremely complex and long ceremonies that mobilize the bereaved family for months. In this connection, Newars are much more like the other Tibeto-Burman hill groups of Nepal[8] than the Indo-Nepalese and north Indians, where marriage is the great event of the family group, especially among high castes.

CONCLUSION

Some important conclusions can be drawn from this ethnographic analysis. First, cult units are a crucial element of Newar social structure. Without a patron god, a group has no legal existence, no legitimacy. A kingdom's capital becomes a political entity through the collective cult of the tutelary deity of the former Malla king, Taleju/Kumārī. A village is transformed into a distinct and cohesive entity through the worship of a tutelary and protective deity. Funeral groups become legitimized through their god of death, Sī dyaḥ. Furthermore, kin groups are defined preferably by reference to a common god, the Digu dyaḥ, worshipped at regular intervals by patrilineal kin. Everywhere in the Newar setting, space is identified and validated by the divinities who reside in it: in all cases, territoriality is thought of as a religious space. At every level, sacralization is a compulsory process by which a group becomes a distinct structural entity. Even Malla royal cities have up to the present been conceptually imagined as religious diagrams (*maṇḍala*) enclosing a series of Tantric divinities. Identity and separateness derive primarily from common reference to a tutelary deity or to a group of gods attached to a specific spatial unit. Such divinities are a sign of the individuality and independence of the local group.

On the other hand, attention has to be drawn to the low structuring power of kinship. Admittedly, the exchange of ritual duties between wife-givers and wife-takers, agnates and affines, is very important in the life-cycle ceremonies. Yet, on the whole, as has been demonstrated in this paper, Newar descent units do not form corporate groups. They do not constitute the organizing framework of the society. To become influential, they have to be transformed into a religious unit. It is widely known to anthropologists the world over that in such cases other types of groupings, such as age classes, secret societies or various voluntary associations tend to become prominent.

Newar death and cremation associations have to be seen in this light. They are the main locus of the society, and are at the foundation of the social system as a whole. At the same time, they clearly have a hybrid character: they are not defined exclusively by either kinship or residence, but by a mixture of the two. For instance, the language of kinship remains important in the *guthi* pattern. Funerary associations are often thought of in terms of consanguinity: they generally form exogamic groups, they each have a common tutelary god, and most of all, their strong patrilineal inflexion (as the cult units linked with the main local divinity) is akin in spirit to the patrilineality of the kin groups. As a matter of fact, women are barred from all the sacred ceremonials important for the community. Such a prohibition helps incidentally to reproduce social relations of male domination and female subordination. Obviously, peasant funeral associations are conceptually recast into kinship idioms.

What about the link between death and territory, so decisive in the cultural repertoire of the Newars, especially of the Jyāpu agriculturist caste? The importance of death in connection with territory is often explained by the presence of ancestors in the earth. The burial of dead persons incorporates a mystical element in the soil. Local units and landscape thus store memory: they are memorials to departed relatives and founders. As is widely known, death is a means of cementing of territorial bonds. In French villages, the fact of having dead relatives buried in the local cemetery is an important step toward better integration into the local community. The same can be said of many other European countries. On the other hand, the cult of the deceased is an important element in the construction of a nation's identity. Erecting a memorial to the memory of these dead is an essential part of the representation one village makes of its past. In this perspective, death is a crucial medium through which a grouping establishes links with the territory it occupies. Accordingly, territory gives permanence to the ancestors and legitimizes the position of the living beings in their present life.

Paradoxically, ancestrality is secondary in the Newar idiom. The dead are cremated and not buried in the Kathmandu Valley (with some rare exceptions). Their ashes are dispersed in rivers. Suggestively enough, the cult of ancestors is not very developed among the Newars. Ancestors are propitiated only occasionally during *śrāddha* rituals and very rarely further back than the grandfather. They are not granted great importance. The main preoccupation of the relatives is to make the dead disappear or to shuffle them as rapidly as possible into a collective category (Vergati 1995: 19). Even the lineage deity of the Newars, of whom I gave a brief description above, is transformed in a way into a god of the land: he has no name (to the uninitiated) and he establishes primarily a link between the blood relatives paying homage to him and the territory on which they live.[9]

The real ancestors of the Newars are the living elders, the *thakāli*, of the various *guthi* groupings. These elders, the most senior persons in the group, preside over all religious affairs and are consulted at every critical moment of the life of the group. Everybody pays respect to them and bows down in front of them in token of submission. To reach this position, they have more often than not to undergo a special ritual, *thakāli luiyegu*, which is a kind of consecration. Furthermore, they often wear rings in one ear, a sign that they have undergone another ceremony, the *burā jāko*, celebrated by persons of both genders who have reached the age of 77 years. After this old-age ritual, Newars are considered as quasi-divine and progressively relinquish active control over daily-life subsistence activities. But, once vanished, these respected old persons are rapidly forgotten. They lose their social identity.

Newar culture contrasts sharply in this regard with that of other Nepalese populations, such as the kinship-dominated Tamang or Gurung hill tribes, where kin groups get their cohesion through the memory of a well-established list of ancestors, and where marriage with a cross-cousin is prescribed. As a matter of fact, it seems that the strength of ancestrality in Nepal (as in other countries) is proportional to the strength of the unilineal kin groups. Speaking of Nepalese hill tribes, Nick Allen for instance has suggested that: 'As caste society infiltrates the clan-based village of the once territorially segregated tribe, as temporary contractual relationships tend to replace hereditary ones, and as national language displaces the tribal, the cult of the tribal ancestors become more and more peripheral' (1976: 526).

I would argue that the patron gods of the Newars, and more particularly their land gods, are assuming the role played by ancestors in other custom-based societies. Some explicit links exist. Several local divinities are considered, for instance, to be former ancestors. The clearest case is Bhairava, called currently Bhailodyaḥ in Newari, but also Āju, 'grandfather'. A former king of Kathmandu Valley, Yalambara, is said to have been transformed into a god. Similarly, Mātṛkā goddesses are called 'Ajimā' in Newari, a title in which the word *aji*, 'grandmother', can be discerned. It seems that ancestors turn rapidly into deities, and that a link between the two is often present. Such merging is sometimes reported in studies of Nepalese tribal groups, such as the Gurungs and the Tamangs (Strickland 1982; Toffin 1990). Evident parallels can also be drawn with cognatic societies of Tibet and Ladakh, where a similar situation has been described (Dollfus 1989). Such various forms of 'territorial kinship' are important to document. It is to be hoped that further comparative research will be carried out on this topic in order to arrive at a better understanding of Himalayan symbolic representation.

Finally, I want to draw attention to some parallels with tribal groups in India. Among the Santals of north-east India for instance, the idiom of ancestrality is strongly attached to the figure of the local headman, *nāike* (Carrin-Bouez 1986), representative of the founder of the locality. In most cases, these chiefs are the officiants of the various cults celebrated in the sacred grove of the village —a grove linked with the creation and the mythical history of the territory. As such, they establish a link between the first ancestors of the locality and the present-day situation. Among the Raj Gonds of central India, the deceased members of the clan dwelling in the company of the clan deities form part of a community that remains a unit, even though divided by the line between life and death. As reported by C. Fürer-Haimendorf (1974, 1979), the rite by which the spirit of the dead (*sanal*) is formally introduced to the departed members of his clan is a crucial element of funeral and memorial ceremonies. Not surprisingly, Raj Gond ancestral shrines often evolve into cult centres for the clan gods.

Among the Sora of Orissa and Andhra Pradesh on the other hand, the dead are difficult to forget and continue to interfere in the daily life of the villagers long time after their death. As vividly established by Piers Vitebsky (1993), they continue to revert and to transmit their original condition to others. Both horizontally and vertically, ancestors themselves live in different places of the inhabited house and village. These sites play a prominent role in the making up of the memory of the group, in lineage segmentation and sharing-out inheritance. Other similar cases could be pointed out from amidst the Muria of Andhra Pradesh. These examples attest to the strength of the link between ancestors and territories in the tribal world, even if this link is materialized through different means. It would be interesting to determine if this observation concerns only the tribal world or the Hindu low castes as well.

Acknowledgements: A first version of this paper has been presented at the University of Oxford, on the occasion of the 2000 Radhakrishnan Memorial Lecture (All Souls College). I thank Daniela Berti and Gilles Tarabout for their useful comments.

NOTES

1. See *India's Villages*, ed. M.N. Srinivas (1955), with contributions, among others, of F.G. Bailey, McKim Marriott, Kathleen Gough and D.G. Mandelbaum.
2. For a general presentation of the Jyāpu agriculturist caste of the Newars, cf. Toffin (1984), as well as Gellner and Quigley (1995). On Newar religion, see also Toffin (2000).
3. For an overview on classical conceptions about ancestorship and the cult of the dead in India, see Dumont (1980) and Malamoud (1982). For an overview on classical conceptions about ancestorship and the cult of the dead in India, see Dumont (1980) and Malamoud (1982).
4. These terms are often abbreviated by rural Jyāpu and transformed into *gu*.
5. For parallels in Newar cities, van den Hoek and Shrestha (1992: 665).
6. The preponderant role of these village temples reminds one of the village

monastery (*gompa*) of the Sherpa communities of Helambu in Nepal. In his thesis (1980), G. Clarke has demonstrated that such *gompa* play a determining part in the social life of the villages concerned.

7. In Theco village, this Bhairava is associated with the cult of Bālkumārī.
8. See also Toffin (1997) for the importance of death and death funerary associations among the Pahari (Pahi) located to the south of the Kathmandu Valley.
9. As a rule, the resemblance between the *pīth* sanctuaries of the tutelary gods of the village (Mātṛkā goddesses for instance) and the sanctuaries of the lineage deities *digu dyaḥ* is striking. Cf. G. Toffin (1984) and A. Vergati (1995: 40). Both are established outside the locality and are built with stones of the same shape and with the same decoration.

REFERENCES

Allen, Nick, 1976. 'Approaches to Illness in the Nepalese Hills', in *Social Anthropology and Medicine*, ed. J.B. Loudon, London: Academic Press, pp. 500-52.

Aziz, Barbara, 1978. *Tibetan Frontier Families (Reflections of Three Generations from D'ing-ri)*, Delhi: Vikas.

Blackburn, Stuart H., 1983. 'Death and Deification: Folks Cults in Hinduism', *History of Religions*, 24, 3: 255-74.

Carrin-Bouez, Marine, 1986. *La Fleur et l'os. Symbolisme et rituel chez les Santal*, Paris: EHESS.

Clarke, G., 1980. 'The Temple and Kinship among Buddhist People of the Himalaya', Oxford: Lincoln College (Ph.D. dissertation).

———, 1995. 'Blood and Territory as Idioms of National Identity in Himalayan States', *Kailash*, 17, 3-4: 89-131.

Daniel, E.Valentine, 1984. *Fluid Signs: Being a Person the Tamil Way*, Berkeley: University of California Press.

Dirks, Nicholas B., 1987. *The Hollow Crown: Ethnohistory of an Indian Kingdom*, Cambridge: Cambridge University Press.

Dollfus, Pascale, 1989. *Lieux de neige et de genévriers. Organisation sociale et religieuse des communautés bouddhistes du Ladakh*, Paris: CNRS.

Dumont, Louis, 1970 [1966]. *Homo hierarchicus. Essai sur le système des castes.* Paris: Gallimard (rpt.).

———, 1980. 'La dette *vis-à-vis* des créanciers et la catégorie de *sapiṇḍa*', in *La dette*, ed. C. Malamoud, Paris: EHESS, pp. 15-37.

Dumont, Louis and David F. Pocock, 1957. 'Village Studies', *Contributions to Indian Sociology*, I: 23-41.

Fürer-Haimendorf, C. von, 1974. 'A Central Indian Tribal People: The Raj Gonds', in *South Asia: Seven Community Profiles*, ed. C. Maloney, New York: Holt, Rinehart and Winston, pp. 202-57.

———, 1979. *The Gonds of Andhra Pradesh: Tradition and Change*, London: G. Allen and Unwin, pp. 363-93.

Gellner, David N. and Declan Quigley, 1995. *Contested Hierarchies: A Collaborative Ethnography of Caste among the Newars of the Kathmandu Valley, Nepal*, Oxford: Oxford University Press.

Hoek, A.W. van den and B.G. Shrestha, 1992. 'The Sacrifice of Serpents: Exchange and non-Exchange in the Sarpabali of Indrayani', *Bulletin de l'Ecole Française d'Extrême-Orient*, 71: 57-75.

Hudson, Dennis D., 1993. 'Madurai: The City as Goddess', in *Urban Form and Meaning in South Asia: The Shaping of Cities from Prehistoric to Precolonial Times*, ed. H. Spodek and D.M. Srinivasan, Washington: National Gallery of Art, pp. 125-42.

Lévi-Strauss, Claude, 1991. 'Maison', in *Dictionnaire de l'ethnologie et de l'anthropologie*, ed. P. Bonte and M. Izard, Paris: PUF, p. 436.

Macdonald, A.W., 1975. *Essays on the Ethnology of Nepal and South Asia*, Kathmandu: Ratna Pustak Bhandar.

Maine, H., 1912 (10th edn) [1861]. *Ancient Law*, London: John Murray.

Malamoud, Charles, 1982. 'Les morts sans visage. Remarques sur l'idéologie funéraire dans le brâhmanisme', in *La mort, les morts dans les sociétés anciennes*, Paris: Cambridge University Press/FMSH, pp. 441-53.

Nebesky-Wojkowitz, René de, 1956. *Oracles and Demons of Tibet (the Cult and Iconography of the Tibetan Protective Deities*), Den Haag: Mouton.

Quigley, Declan, 1984. 'The Social Structure of a Newar Trading Community, East-Central Nepal', London: London University (Ph.D. dissertation).

Sax, William, 1991. *Mountain Goddess: Gender and Politics in a Himalayan Pilgrimage*, New York-Oxford: Oxford University Press.

Srinivas, M.N. (ed.), 1955. *India's Villages*, Bombay: Asia Publishing House.

Strickland, S.S., 1982. 'Beliefs, Practices and Legends: A Study in the Narrative Poetry of the Gurung of Nepal', University of Cambridge (Ph.D. dissertation).

Tarabout, Gilles, 2001. 'Ancêtres et revenants. La construction sociale de la malemort en Inde', in *De la Malemort en quelques pays d'Asie*, ed. B. Baptandier, Paris: Karthala, pp. 165-99.

Toffin, Gérard, 1984. *Société et religion chez les Néwar du Népal*, Paris: CNRS.

———, 1990. 'Ancêtres claniques et esprits féminins dans l'Himalaya népalais', *Revue de l'Histoire des Religions*, CCVII-2: 159-88.

———, 1996. 'The Moiety System of the Newars', *Contributions to Nepalese Studies*, 23, 1: 65-88.

———, 1997. 'Le dieu Bhyaldyaḥ et la fête des confréries funéraires chez les Pahari du Népal central', in *Les habitants du toit du monde*, ed. S. Karmay and P. Sagant, Nanterre: Société d'ethnologie, pp. 565-82.

———, 2000. *Entre hindouisme et bouddhisme: La religion néwar, Népal*, Louvain-La-Neuve: Peeters.

———, 2005. *From Caste to Kin: The Role of Guthis in Newar Society and Culture*, Lalitpur: Social Science Baha.

Vergati Anne, 1995. *Gods, Men and Territory: Society and Culture in Kathmandu Valley*, Delhi: Manohar/CSH.

Vitebsky, Piers, 1993. *Dialogues with the Dead: The Discussion of Mortality among the Sora of Eastern India*, Cambridge: Cambridge University Press.

7

The Annamanada Case: A Hundred Years of Conflict over Rights and Territories in Kerala

GILLES TARABOUT

Foreigners coming to the south-western coast of India have produced seemingly contrasting statements in the past regarding the existence of territories there. Two examples may serve as illustrations. Ibn Battûta, who travelled throughout this coast in the 1340s, states:

> There are in Malabar twelve idolatrous sultans. . . . Between the States of each of them, there is a wooden gate on which is engraved the name of the one whose domain starts from this point. It is called the safety gate of 'N'. When after some offence a Muslim or an idolatrous has fled the State of one of these princes, and has reached the safety gate of another prince, he is in security, and the one he flees cannot seize him even though he be powerful and heading numerous armies. (Ibn Battûta 1982: III-197—my translation from the French version)

In contrast, Van Reede, the first Dutch Governor in Cochin, writes in 1677:

> The extent of each realm is expressed in terms of the number of soldiers the Chief could command—the territorial extent not being taken into consideration. Of course there are traditional boundaries for each Nad [principality] over which the individual chieftains held sway. (Van Reede, quoted by Raman Menon 1936: 12)

Thus, on the one hand sacrosanct boundaries marked by gates are mentioned, while, on the other hand, soldiers are said to be more relevant for the definition of a realm than the land effectively controlled (though limits are acknowledged). Such a basic opposition is illustrative of a more general debate about the existence or importance of conceptions of territory in India. Contrary to the many scholars who have argued that territory was altogether absent, or of secondary importance, this paper aims to show its crucial role in the social organization and dynamics, and at understanding why there could have been any doubt on the matter. The discussion will bear on the region corresponding nowadays to south and central Kerala. The point, however, is of relevance to India as a whole.

PRELIMINARY DISCUSSION

Van Reede's statement may at first sight be interpreted as corresponding more to the strategic interests of the Dutch—an evaluation of the armed forces of the respective rulers in a context of colonial expansion—than to an actual portrayal of local conceptions. As a matter of fact, however, it borrows from a past effective usage in the region, where small regions, *nāṭu*, and sometimes 'villages', *dēśam* (with the nuance that settlements are dispersed), were referred to by numbers. This has been sometimes interpreted by historians as corresponding either to the number of families of the martial peasant caste of Nāyars, or to the number of notables who were members of local assemblies.[1] Thus, according to one historian,

> The *Nadu* and *Desam* in Kerala differed from similar territorial divisions elsewhere in so far as they consisted not of so many towns and villages but of so many Nair [Nāyar] families such as the '*Five Hundred*' of Kodakaranadu, the '*Four Hundred*' of Annamanada, and the '*Three Hundred*' of Chengazhinad (Sreedhara Menon 1962 : 146—reproducing a study published in 1911 by C. Achyutha Menon)

Though the figures used by Van Reede were of a different order (armed men being counted by the thousands), a similar logic seems at work, which defines 'territorial divisions' through groups of people rather than through boundaries. Since, *contra* Sreedhara Menon, considering a chiefdom with reference to its inhabitants appears to have been a widespread practice in South Asia, some scholars have been led to contest the very validity of the term 'territory' when applied to former political units. For instance, according to André Wink, 'the concept of territory becomes fallacious' in the context of eighteenth-century Maratha rule in the Deccan (Wink 1986: 47); this is because 'territory cannot be seen as a primary constituent of the Indian state. Instead we find a people-cum-territory or *janapada*, shot through with vested rights' (ibid.: 161). The same argument is forwarded by political scientist Christophe Jaffrelot when he considers that territory gets only 'a subordinate and ambiguous place' in ancient Indian political tradition (Jaffrelot 1996: 75). Jaffrelot here relies on the work of anthropologist Louis Dumont. For Dumont, the socio-political sphere, and therefore kingship and territory, belong to a secondary, empirical level which is not recognized as such at the 'ideological' one (the latter being reduced to an opposition between purity and impurity characterizing caste hierarchy—Dumont 1966: 196).

All these authors, however, seem to base their arguments on an implicit comparison with a model of territory typical of the modern nation state—itself often an ideal construct as Ronald Inden has pointed out (1990: 265). Taken to its logical extreme, this model would imply that no 'real' territory ever existed before the apparition of nation states. This restrictive understanding of territory tends to shape the discussion in Manichean terms about its existence or non-existence, as if only a 'yes' or 'no' answer was to be expected—and more often than not, the answer is negative as a direct consequence of the very definition. I prefer to follow here the dictionary definition. A territory, as understood here, is any extent of land (or water) under a jurisdiction. The question then becomes one of studying modes of land appropriation and political control.

The denial of the importance of territory in India has sometimes taken advantage of an anachronistic use of studies on Vedic texts. According to these texts, territorial rooting was either dismissed as undesirable (see Angot in this volume), or altogether ignored. For instance, Sanskritist Charles Malamoud explained that the 'word *grāma*, ordinarily translated as "village", designates a human concentration, a network of institutions, rather than a fixed territory; differing from Latin *pagus* which evokes territorial rooting, the Vedic *grāma* is essentially a troop if we are to believe its etymology. . . . The stability of the *grāma* depends more on the cohesion of its constituent group than on the space it occupies' (Malamoud 1976: 4-5). However, to conclude from this that territory in India was of secondary importance from Vedic times to comparatively recent periods would be a big leap. Malamoud is always cautious to restrict his statements to the ancient period and literature he studies; but the general feeling about the secondary character of territory in India was so prevalent among scholars at a time that, in this case, it led him to extrapolate to contemporary society, adding that 'the weakness of the Indian village's "territoriality" can also be seen in the fact that in India, ancestors have no terrestrial abode' (ibid.: n. 7). This was a reference to funerary practices mainly among Brāhmans and other high-ranking castes, but not necessarily among mid or low-status groups, at least in south India. Strikingly, however, the same argument has been put forward about today's Kerala by Yasuchi Uchiyamada, a social anthropologist whose general stance may be seen as post-modernist and 'subalternist'. Contrasting Brāhmans with non-Brāhmans and especially Dalits, he argued that the latter had stronger bonds with land because they bury their dead and install their ancestors in shrines (Uchiyamada 2000). As this example suggests, there is thus more in this than mere so-called 'Orientalism', as the question could be too easily dismissed.

Thus, be it at the level of kingdom, village, or high-castes' landed property, territory in India has often been said to be of little relevance.[3] Considering this was a society practising settled agriculture for more than two thousand years, one cannot be but surprised by such assertions. Could scores of successive kings and chiefs be uninterested in political boundaries? Could villagers be uninterested in village limits? Could high-caste landlords be uninterested in the lands they controlled because their ancestors were (hopefully) in heaven? There is here a major problem in interpretation, which seems to come from confusion between practice and discourse, assigning to some discourse an overarching import. For instance, Kesavan Veluthat (1993) has pointed out a confusion often made between what he calls the 'self image of royalty' and the forms taken by power and authority. Ronald Inden (1990: 268), for his part, rightly underlined that though 'the makers of India's polities were anti-utopian', it does not follow that Indians devalued the political. 'On the contrary they have treated the political aspects of life as integral.'

My paper explores how social and political life was territorially organized in Kerala. How were territories thought of and discussed?[4] How did notions and practices related to them evolve as part of the general changes in society?

The use of the past tense needs a word of explanation. The Indian Union, and as part of it, the state of Kerala, is conceived in terms of a modern nation state with its associated notions of territory, heirs to a complex heritage of Indian and Western political thought and practice (Goswami 1998; 2004). A study of present-day conceptions would be interesting in its own right, but would not therefore directly address the issues previously summarized.

True, a lot of ethnographic evidence on today's society points to a deep rooted, ancient sense of territory in Kerala.[5] Names of persons refer most of the time to the specific place of origin of the family, thus rooting genealogies in the soil. A large number of temple cults are still closely linked to the families of notables who hold sway over a remembered, well-delimited past territory. Deities themselves have often very precise jurisdictions,[6] whose limits are ceremonially marked by processions. Temple festivals are organized on a territorial basis, in which territory-based factions compete (Tarabout 1986; 1993; 1999). But while such evidence gives one a strong feeling that territory is central to current social life, and is not a new phenomenon, it has not by itself the capacity to address the debate about the importance and nature of territorial conceptions before the advent of colonial political formations. Hence my attempt to introduce a discussion about past conceptions of territory in the region, and about their evolution.

The paper will proceed in the following manner. After a presentation of some characteristics of the landed elite prior to the twentieth century, the discussion will focus on a particular dispute which opposed the two former kingdoms of Cochin and Travancore for more than a century, and which concerned the rights each of them claimed over the Annamanada temple and its lands. A remarkable number of claims, arguments, and counter-arguments were put forward in the course of the dispute, shedding light on the conceptual elaborations relevant at that time and in these circumstances.

A LANDED ARISTOCRACY

Throughout the period to be considered, from the early eighteenth to late nineteenth centuries, the society on the south-western coast (as in other parts of India) underwent important changes in relation to which the Annamanada dispute has to be understood. A few characteristics of the landed elite, applying to this period, may be summarized.[7]

Land control and political power was mainly in the hands of two castes, deemed superior in terms of purity: the patrilineal Naṃpūtiri Brāhmans and, ritually below them, the matrilineal Nāyar peasant-warriors (considered by Brāhmans to belong to the broad category of 'servants', Śūdras, but locally of high status in relation to other castes). Of intermediate status between these two castes, a few princely lineages were also part of this landed aristocracy, at the core of the political power. There was a flourishing commerce in spices (especially pepper) in the hands of the appreciable Muslim and Christian minorities, but this did not lead to political dominance, except in a few instances.[8]

The Naṃpūtiris, Nāyars (at least the most affluent and powerful among them) and princely lineages had in common a few characteristics. They were organized in extended lineages possessing undivided rights over land. Usually Naṃpūtiris had superior rights, and Nāyars held subordinate but more or less permanent ones; cultivation was in the hands of Nāyars of less affluence or of lower-status castes. A lineage or branch-line (sometimes consisting of more than a hundred persons) would live together in the same house or manor-house. The name of this lineage was the name of the house and its surrounding compound.[9] It was thus the name of a plot of land, unique in the whole of Kerala, which localized and identified at the same time each lineage, testifying to the crucial importance until very recently of locality in the definition of the social units within these castes.

The preservation through time of the continuity of these localized lineages, together with their economic and political rights and the positions of honour (*sthānam*) they could detain, was of vital concern for this aristocracy. Whenever their perpetuity was at risk they resorted to adoption (including of adults), a fact already noticed and underlined in the sixteenth century by the Arab traveller, Sheikh Zeen-ud-deen (Rowlandson 1833: 66), and well-supported by evidence throughout the later period. In order to account for all these characteristics, I have suggested in previous papers to apply the notion of 'House' or 'Manor-house' to these lineages constituting the local 'nobility'. This notion gained a new anthropological relevance following the work of C. Lévi-Strauss (1979; 1984), who introduced this concept to characterize social units where the preservation of economic and political interests strongly interferes with the ordinary logic of blood relationships in the definition and perpetuation of lineages.[10]

In most parts of Kerala, settlements are of a dispersed pattern. They are typically spread over comparatively elevated, dry land bordering the inundated lowlands where paddy is grown. Some Nampūtiris may live in separate houses, without constituting a Brāhman settlement; but some other Nampūtiri Houses may form together a dispersed Brāhman settlement, called specifically a *grāmam*, that formerly controlled comparatively large areas of agricultural land. Nāyar Houses, as a rule, are part of a dispersed Nāyar settlement or neighbourhood, usually of much smaller size than Brāhman ones, and commonly called *tar̲a* (elevated ground, platform) or *kara* (bank, ridge). Members of other castes may also live there (with the exception of castes of much lower status who used to live in separate hamlets), or may have their own settlement. A Nāyar residential unit could well overlap with a Brāhman unit (or with others from other castes), but all had limits, and a name that their members are eager, to now, to defend on ceremonial occasions.

We shall return later to Brāhman settlement organization. Regarding the Nāyars and other castes, a group of neighbourhoods constituted a *dēśam*, usually (though inappropriately) translated as 'village'. A *dēśam* was under the authority of a 'village chief', a *dēśavaḻi*, who was the leader of the local militia and claimed economic, political and ritual privileges (this is a thing of the past, except sometimes for a few ritual privileges). The 'village chief' for his part owed allegiance to a regional ruler, *nāṭuvaḻi*, subordinate in his turn to a raja. In the early eighteenth century, however, political fragmentation in the southern half of Kerala made such a pyramidal model a rather ideal one, with many *nāṭuvaḻis* largely asserting their autonomy. A *dēśavaḻi* was usually the largest landowner in his *dēśam*, and derived most of his income from his land, with the exception of a few fees and ceremonial gifts. By contrast, *nāṭuvaḻis* and rajas had, in addition to their domains, much wider sources of income: capitation fees, succession fees, adoption fees, fines, ceremonial gifts, taxes on specific trees, taxes on wild game and, most importantly, tolls on various trades (Padmanabha Menon 1929: 324ff.). Depending on the regions, however, there was in the early eighteenth century generally either no land taxation, or taxation on only a small fraction of the lands—those that were not owned by Brāhmans, temples, or other princes. The major part of the income of *nāṭuvaḻis* or of rajas thus derived from trade tolls or demesne lands. This was the result of an accumulation process made possible by a general expansion of the spice trade (particularly in pepper) with Asia, and a corresponding development of the cash economy, of new cultivated areas, and of a new, non-Brāhman, military landowning class (to which most of the *nāṭuvaḻis* and *dēśavaḻis* belonged).[11] Superior rights on land (*janmam*) were sold, sometimes with the correlated power to administer justice (Logan 1951: cxxiv). Lands became regularly mortgaged, providing for a growing dissociation between landownership and land-control (Ganesh 1999). Even *dēśavaḻi* rights could be mortgaged and sold (for instance Logan 1951: cxxxv, cxxxviii, cxlvi, for deeds between 1622 and 1731). These transactions were precise in evoking the limits of the land or of the *dēśam* which was sold or bought; they were also detailed and extensive in enumerating its 'components' (including, where land was concerned, the sky above and the *pātāḷam* or underworld beneath). All this points to a strongly expressed notion of ownership of precisely delimited lands, often linked to politico-religious jurisdictional rights.

As far as political structure was concerned, it was made particularly complex due to the fact that there was a 'multi-dimensional' quality to the rights that could be held by a single House. A House could, for instance, assume a *nāṭuvaḻi* title on a region in which other Houses could have *dēśavaḻi* rights on some of its 'villages', while itself possessing at the same time *dēśavaḻi* titles on 'villages' outside its own region; in addition, it could as well have landed 'property' (under a variety of landowning or land-controlling rights) in various places.[12] This was a situation of intense competition between Houses for accumulating more titles, more rights, and more power. In this contest, many big temples held by Nampūtiri Houses became crucial stakes, not only (as has often been said for south India) because they were important economic redistribution centres, or because they provided a public stage where to demonstrate prestige through donations,[13] but also—quite simply—as a source of divine power and legitimacy couched in terms of devotion or *bhakti* (Narayanan 1994; Namboodiri 1999). The Annamanada case, to which we shall now turn, has to be understood in such a light.

THE ANNAMANADA CASE: OUTLINE

Annamanada is the name of a temple situated a few kilometres from the small and busy town of Chalakudy in central Kerala.[14] Since 1761, and for more than a century, this temple and a few villages connected to it (representing approximately 10 sq miles) were at the core of a dispute between the Raja of Cochin, in the territories of which Annamanada was situated, and the Raja of Travancore. The latter had emerged in the course of the few preceding decades as the main local power, covering the southern half of today's Kerala. The former had been weakened by successive invasions from the north by the Sāmūtiri (Zamorin) of Calicut, and by the Mysore rulers (Hyder Ali and Tipu Sultan) against whom he had had to ask his powerful neighbour, the Raja of Travancore, for military help. His territories were both reduced and discontinuous, dispersed in the central part of Kerala. By a first exchange of agreements in 1761, slightly modified in a second exchange in 1765, both rajas recognized the respective boundaries of their territories, with the proviso that the Raja of Travancore would continue to exercise the ceremonial rights that he had obtained in a few important temples situated in

Cochin's territories. Annamanada was one of them. This in itself was no exceptional feature. It was not uncommon to have two, even three, chiefs or rajas exercising ceremonial and executive rights in important temples, sometimes quite far from their territories.[15] But in this case, difficulties emerged and conflict between the local representatives of the two rajas steadily worsened.

By the end of the eighteenth century, the British were the main power in south India. They annexed the northern part of today's Kerala, which then became the Malabar district, first of the Bombay Presidency, and later of the Madras Presidency. Cochin and Travancore were maintained as Princely States, under indirect rule. A Resident was installed in both courts, to shape the (officially independent) policies of the rajas. As far as the Annamanada case is concerned, conflicts between the two rajas continued unabated, so that successive residents had regularly to intervene. By the end of the nineteenth century, both rajas asked for a final arbitration on Annamanada and four other similar longstanding disputes (out of which three concerned rights over temples).[16] In October 1880, J.C. Hannyngton, then District and Sessions Judge of Salem, was appointed by the Madras government as arbitrator. He heard both sides, and in 1882 gave a judgement in favour of Cochin as far as Annamanada was concerned. This arbitration process provides the main source of the present study. A compilation of papers related to it was published by the Travancore government in 1900 under the title *Important Papers Connected with the Dispute between Travancore and Cochin Regarding the Annamanaday Devaswom and the Desoms thereof, Including Adoor Gramom*—referred to in the following pages as *IP*.[17]

The limitations imposed by such a source should be clear. The frame is a judicial contest, in which officials and lawyers on both sides come forward with tactical arguments orienting all presentation of 'facts'. Besides, only a few original documents pertaining to the early stages of the dispute were submitted (some of them deemed to be downright forgeries by the opposite side). Thus, the present discussion largely relies on historical reconstructions and claims that were made in the 1880s by people living already in a very different intellectual, political, and administrative context. But we can cross-check these reconstructions with the ones provided by recent historical studies,[18] so that a plausible picture regarding past territorial logic may emerge. I would argue that the differences between the situation in the eighteenth century and the discourses recorded in the late nineteenth century, and the very conflicting nature of arguments regarding the interpretation of earlier rights (as expressed in the 1880s), may prove illuminating about the changes that occurred between the early stages of the dispute and the arbitration procedure.

As a first step the paper will propose a reconstruction of the situation at the time of the agreements between Cochin and Travancore in 1761 and 1765. This will be followed by an evocation of the conflicts between Travancore and Cochin. I will then proceed to present a discussion of a few important vernacular terms, as they were considered at the time of arbitration. Through these three stages, I hope to illustrate the changes in the conception of territory in the course of a century and a half, until about 1910.

THE ORIGINS OF THE DISPUTE

In 1881, at the beginning of the arbitration, Cochin proposed her own reconstruction of what the situation was supposed to have been prior to the treaty of 1761. This went unchallenged by Travancore in its counter-statement. It does not follow, of course, that this was an accurate picture, but merely that it seemed acceptable to both parties. We can compare and cross-check with other sources taken from epigraphy, from legal deeds, or from European descriptions of the seventeenth and eighteenth centuries.

Let us first see how the place is described in the document drawn up by Cochin,[19] under the subheading 'The foundation and endowment of Annamanada Devasom and how Travancore came to acquire a footing therein': 'The Devasom or Pagoda is situated in the Adoor Gramam' (*IP:* 4).

'Devasom', *dēvasvam*, is properly speaking 'God's belongings'. This is usually not only the temple (here called 'Pagoda'), but also the lands put in the name of the god. The statement situates the temple geographically by including it in another territorial unit, a *grāmam*—a

Naṃpūtiri dispersed residential unit. Adur (or Atavur) *grāmam* was one of the 32 *grāmam* said to have been at the origin of Naṃpūtiri implantation in Kerala.[20]

> The Devasom [*dēvasvam*] was founded and endowed by ten Nampoories [Naṃpūtiris], namely [name of the ten Houses[21]], though the exact date of its foundation and endowment is involved in obscurity, and the Sankethom [*saṃketam*] of the Devasom comprises 12½ villages, i.e. [names of 13 villages[22]]. Of these, [two[23]] lie outside while the other villages lie within the limits of the Gramom. (*IP:* 4)

As in many other cases in Kerala, the temple is presented as a Naṃpūtiri foundation and endowment. In this case, the temple's original and supreme rights are said to be collectively owned by the ten Naṃpūtiri Houses of the Adur *grāmam*. The endowment consists of lands in 12½ villages ('½' is an often used formula in ancient Kerala for enumerations),[24] with the enumeration of 13 names. The lands as such, which may not necessarily form a continuous stretch, constitute the Annamanada *dēvasvam* lands. We learn from another statement in the arbitration files that there were two other, smaller *dēvasvam* situated in the same *grāmam*. We have therefore to understand the word *saṃketam* as designating an overall territory under the Annamanada's temple jurisdiction and constituted by the 13 'villages' (*dēśams*) in which were situated the temple lands, though not all these lands may have belonged to the god (there was land of other temples, as well as Brāhman domains and possibly some chieftains' personal domains). It nevertheless was considered as constituting a territorial jurisdiction with important powers attributed to the temple committee of Brāhmans. Quite clearly, the description suggests (and this is historically attested in other cases) that *saṃketam* (temple 'territory' as distinguished from God's land ownership) and *grāmam* (Brāhman settlement's 'territory' as distinguished from Brāhman personal landownership) did not necessarily coincide.

> Through the Gramom runs the river or stream called Annamanadapoya. On the eastern side of the stream is situate [*sic*] the village of Ariancoodi, while on its western banks lie [name of the 10 other villages of the

grāmam]. Thus the Adoor Gramom proper consists of only 10½ desoms or villages. (*IP:* 4)

After having thus geographically located the temple and its territory in relation to a Naṃpūtiri *grāmam*, the text proceeds to evoke a different set of territories intersecting with the previously mentioned ones. First it mentions rights over 'villages', *dēśaṃs*, detained by village chiefs (*dēśavaḻis*) and rights over regions, *nāṭu*, held by *nāṭuvaḻis*. Such rights entailed a control over various sources of revenue and over the residing population (especially armed men), and were linked to various ceremonial privileges and obligations towards higher rulers. They were known under the generic appellation of *sthānam*, positions. Positions were attributed by higher rulers, and could be inherited, conquered, begotten through alliances, or, at times, bought. The head of a House could hold several positions, and in rare cases a single one was shared by different Houses. In the case of Annamanada, the picture evoked by Cochin's document is the following:

To one Kodur Malayan originally belonged the Nadoovai Stanom [*nāṭuvaḻi sthānam*] of the 9½ villages lying to the west of the Annamanada river; while the Nadoovai Stanom of the single village lying to the eastern side of the river as well as the two villages situated beyond the limits of the Gramom was owned by Koratti Kymal. The Kymal at the same time possessed the Deshavai Stanom [*dēśavaḻi sthānam*] of the villages of Annamanada and Palashari, while the Deshvai Stanom of the village of Kalloor belonged to Villiarvattom Swaroopam [a local small dynasty]. (*IP:* 4)

Let us sum up. The temple is situated in a Brāhman settlement (*grāmam*), the extent of which is smaller by two villages than the temple's overall territory (*saṃketam*). The 13 villages that are said to form this *saṃketam* are divided between two regional chiefs. One has *nāṭuvaḻi* rights over ten villages, while the other has *nāṭuvaḻi* rights over three villages as well as *dēśavaḻi* rights in two villages situated in the other chief's territory (likewise, a third village in this chief's jurisdiction is headed by a third regional chief from the outside). We do not know who had *dēśavaḻi* rights in the other villages, but we can imagine it could have been either the *nāṭuvaḻi* himself (of the region in which the villages were situated), or the head of a local House. This multiplicity of territories, their imbrications and overlaps might give an impression of 'fuzziness' to an outside observer. But, if anything, far from having no territory, we have too many of them!

The picture is rendered still more complex by the existence of various kinds of rights (*sthānam*, position) related to the supervision of the temple's affairs, which included collection of revenue, ceremonial privileges, and authority on the lands attached to the temple.

> Koratti Kymal on the foundation of the Devasom, further more, became Aka-koima [*kōyimma*] or director of affairs within the Pagoda. On the occasion of the Oolsavem or festival, accompanied by an armed suite, he used to proceed from Koratti to the Devasom, have the festival flag hoisted and the necessary ceremonies performed. On the . . . last day of the festival, he was required to proceed to the . . . portico of the Pagoda, receive the customary rod and stick from the Tandri [chief priest], accompany the Daven [*dēvan*, god] or idol in state [to the bank of the river] and after the Daven had gone through the usual ablutions return to the Pagoda. (*IP:* 4)

The term *kōyimma* was the object of a specific controversy during the dispute, and will be discussed below. Let us translate it as 'authority'. *Akakōyimma*, literally 'internal authority', is deliberately presented by Cochin as a mere 'director of affairs'. But the holder of such a *kōyimma* had also clearly a decisive, and much valued ceremonial role. In other Kerala accounts, this authority is regularly presented as a kind of delegation of power from the Naṃpūtiri supreme authorities: finding themselves unable to take proper care of the temple, they ask Nāyars or members of a princely lineage to exercise the armed authority required for the proper functioning of the cults. Whatever be the case, it is important to note here (and there is general agreement on this point) that such a role is explicitly distinguished from the prerogatives of regional rulers or village chiefs as such. Of course, it was a ruler or a chief who would hold it, but it may not necessarily be the one in whose territorial jurisdiction the temple was located. As a consequence, conflict was quite frequent.

The 'Koratti Kymal' is frequently mentioned in the document. *Kaimal* is a title frequently applied in the Cochin area to the head of a chieftain Nāyar House. For instance, the Koratti Kaimal is evoked by the Dutch in 1716 as being at the head of 3,000 Nāyar soldiers (Galletti et al., 1911: 20). In 1743, J.V. Stein van Gollenesse, then Dutch Commander of Cochin, in a memorandum makes explicit his disagreement with the economic policy of the Koratti Kaimal —who was at the time, so it appears, the senior lady of the Koratti House: 'The territory of the female Caimal of Coretty . . . is of no great importance, still it exports 120 candies of pepper; which this worthless woman causes to be carried elsewhere' (ibid.: 62). In the first decade of the twentieth century, this House was 'still in existence and in fairly good circumstances' according to Achyuta Menon (cited in Galletti et al., 1911: 62, n. 3).[25]

Let us sum up what were the rights and jurisdictions concerned with the Annamanada temple in the early eighteenth century, according to the document forwarded by Cochin at the time of the arbitration. There were four levels or kinds of territories: *grāmam*, *saṃketam*, *dēśam* and *nāṭu*. Various rights are also distinguished in the document. The Nampūtiri Houses exercised a collective control over the temple (and over the *grāmam* and *saṃketam*), and this right was termed *ūrāyma*. The heads of Nāyar and princely Houses exercised their authority at the level of *nāṭu* and *dēśam* (and occasionally, when called for by the Nampūtiris, at the level of *saṃketam*). Such Houses could, in addition, hold special rights in the temple, such as *akakōyimma*.

Political fortunes varied greatly during the first half of eighteenth century with incessant wars between rulers occasionally backed by Dutch and English forces. In the case of Annamanada, this led to a proliferation of *sthānam* (which suggests that the corresponding authority may have been somewhat ineffective in reality). The events told by Cochin being rather complex (*IP:* 5-6), I will summarize them very cursorily.

First, Kodur Malayan (the name suggests a chief belonging to a low-status caste), exercising *nāṭuvaḻi* rights over most of the *grāmam*, fell out with the Nampūtiri Houses. Since the latter detained superior *ūrāyma* rights, they asked the help of a Nāyar chieftain in order to get rid of the Malayan. The Nāyar killed the Malayan and took his place, assuming all his properties and positions. Later, this Nāyar

House became heirless. The Cochin Raja, as overlord, proclaimed the adoption of another chief, the Kodasseri Kaimal,[26] into the house of the Nāyar, declaring him the Nāyar's heir. This conferred on the Kodasseri Kaimal all the Nāyar's privileges (in addition to the ones he already enjoyed as Kaimal), including the rights which had been originally exercised by the Kodur Malayan. Similarly, the rights of Villiarvattam (one *dēśam* within the Adur *grāmam* as far as Annamanada was concerned) were conferred by the Raja of Cochin to another noble of his court.

Around 1715, there was an invasion of the territories of Cochin by the Sāmūtiri of Calicut, helped by rebel chiefs of Cochin and by rebel factions within chieftains' houses (for instance Kodasseri). The Sāmūtiri appointed one of his own noblemen as authority over the temple. The latter, together with the Naṃpūtiri Houses, delegated effective control to nine local 'lords', *prabhū*. These *prabhū* were from different principalities: four of them (including the Kodasseri Kaimal) came from the principality of Kodasseri, two from Parur, and three from Alangad.

In 1755-8, there was a second war between Cochin and the Sāmūtiri. In 1761, the Raja of Cochin entered into an agreement with Travancore as a result of which the Sāmūtiri forces were eventually repelled. The Raja of Cochin made then a new and different nomination for 'conducting the affairs' of the temple.

But the Naṃpūtiris of the *grāmam* were dissatisfied and in 1762 solicited the direct protection of the Raja of Travancore, who then sent his own nominee. Besides, the agreement of 1761 stipulated that Travancore would annex the principalities of Parur and Alangad, which had obtained rights over Annamanada through their *prabhū* (five *prabhū* out of nine came from these two principalities). While these moves created the conditions for Travancore's intervention in the temple's affairs, the Cochin Raja, who had already acquired 'by surrender and otherwise' all the rights formerly detained by the Koratti Kaimal, benefited by the transfer of *ūrāyma* rights by two Naṃpūtiri Houses shortly after 1765.

My purpose here is not to check in details the reality of the facts mentioned, though I accept their overall plausibility. Travancore did not specifically contest them during the arbitration, either, and the dispute between the two states mainly bore on the meaning to be given to such facts: what meant, for instance, to be invited to be a 'protector' by the Nampūtiris? But as the preceding summary of events might have shown in an impressionistic way, a few characteristics emerge from the very complexity of the story, which have more or less general relevance in the region as a whole:

– *dēśam* and *nāṭu* formed the general political structure of the society, in terms of effective control over territories and armed men. Their chiefs were seldom removed, even during times of conquest, but eventually they submitted. What was at stake was therefore not so much to alter the boundaries of principalities or *nāṭus*, but who was to be overlord and what would be the rights the latter would exercise. While transfers of *nāṭuvaḻi* or *dēśvaḻi* rights (when houses became extinct) led to a concentration of prestigious titles in a few Houses (like the Kodasseri Kaimal), there was conversely a proliferation of new rights and of newcomers as far as the 'supervision' of temples was concerned. Such a proliferation of notables is well in line with the general increase in new landowners that may already be noticed in the preceding centuries, and suggests an erosion of the former chieftains' effective power, together with an increase in the ascendancy of the Rajas.

– as territories, *grāmams* and *saṃketams* appear to have been different from *nāṭus* and *dēśams*. As they were respectively the territories of Brāhmans and deities, they were thought of as being 'divine', but could not exist without 'protectors' from ruling Houses. These were territories with a legal and sanctified existence, but devoid, in themselves, of the (military) power to enforce their maintenance and regulations. Correlatively, in the shifting balance of power between Rajas and chieftains, the capacity to have representatives attached to temples outside one's own territory was a major stake.

– such outside protectors could have different sources of legitimacy. For instance they could inherit a position from another House, or gain it through conquest, or be 'elected' by the Brāhmans. Thus, the Nampūtiri Houses remained a major legitimating force throughout the period, when temple and *grāmam* offices were proliferating.

It should be stressed that, whatever the fragmentation of rights, their possible superposition and the fluidity of their circulation, what remained undisputed were the territorial limits to which they applied. True, rights were contested, but the dispute developed precisely because these rights applied to territories with defined boundaries. This point will be made clear by examining the succession of administrative and political skirmishes which took place between Cochin and Travancore from about 1800 to the arbitration in the 1880s.

Before coming to this, it should be noted that in 1765 an agreement between Cochin and Travancore simplified considerably the presentation of the situation: both Rajas agreed to sum up the rights held by Travancore as being 'the Samudaya Stanom of the Annamanada Devasom and the Koima Stanom of the Adoor Gramom' (*IP*: 4). According to the arguments presented by Cochin during the arbitration, these were mere offices for conducting and supervising the affairs of the temple and the *grāmam*. According to Travancore, the two terms meant 'sovereignty'. We shall return to this discussion later. Whatever the meaning advocated by the two parties, this agreement reduced drastically the multiplicity of rights evoked in the preceding pages. This has to be understood in relation to the development of centralization processes throughout the eighteenth century, in Travancore since the 1730s, in Cochin after 1762: at the time of the agreement, the two emergent centralized states could overrule the rights of local chiefs.[27] We will hear no more of *dēśavaḻis* or *nāṭuvaḻis*, then, as the effective power of such houses became progressively reduced to a few ceremonial privileges.[28] The local actors, in the later part of eighteenth century and during the nineteenth century, will be more and more government officers, nominated agents of the two states, part of a gradual process in which old obligations and customary authority were first incorporated in an administrative framework, before becoming fully dissociated from any political relevance.[29] Sanjay Subrahmanyam has described this process in Travancore as 'a form of centralizing royal power in the eighteenth century that uses a "traditionalist" vocabulary precisely to subvert earlier arrangements' (Subrahmanyam 2001: 13).

This corresponds also to a reduction in the types of territories: *nāṭus* and *dēśams* would not have any political reality any more. However, the two states and their growing bureaucracy would still have to tackle territories that did not fit into the centralization process: those of the *grāmam* and the *saṃketam*. It may be argued, in fact, that it was the very dispute under scrutiny that helped to keep these units somewhat alive, though in a constantly modified form, even though elsewhere, by the end of eighteenth century, they were losing all social and political relevance.

OVER A CENTURY OF TUSSLE

As Cochin stated, after the agreement of 1765 'the Devasom affairs continued to be managed by the Ooraimakars [holders of *ūrāyma*] and others, but constant disputes arose between the managers themselves' (*IP:* 6). As we have seen, there were quite a number of these managers, some of them taking their orders from Cochin, others from Travancore. In order to see on which points, precisely, conflicts erupted, I will briefly enumerate a few instances.

Around 1773-4, there is a contestation about which lands in the *grāmam* may be submitted to the few taxes levied by Cochin.

In 1792, there is a conflict between the two states concerning agents of Travancore in the *grāmam* collecting a land tax, which had been initiated at the time of the Sāmūtiri. In addition, according to Cochin, Travancore unduly wanted to impose her pepper monopoly in the area and had sent troops in order to enforce her claims.[30]

In 1798-9, the collection of pepper by Cochin in some parts of the *grāmam* that did not belong to the temple or to the Nampūtiris, is opposed by Travancore. This starts what Cochin calls in the document 'a series of aggressions and usurpations, which but for the fact of its [Travancore] being the more powerful of the two, would have left to open war between it and Cochin' (*IP:* 7).

We may note that this takes place when the British have already established their overall supremacy in the region, and installed a British Resident in the two royal courts. As incidents multiply, a new agreement mediated by the British is made in 1805.

In 1812, Travancore, as part of a general policy initiated by the then British Resident, Col. John Munro, declares that all temples under her supervision are 'state temples', their revenue being affected to the Finance department.[31] This applies also to Annamada, despite Cochin's protests.

In 1813-14, Travancore attempts to conduct a survey of the *grāmam* garden lands for tax settlement, but Cochin opposes the move—each state having the support of its own respective British Resident. The same year,

Travancore objects to the sale of salt (a State monopoly) by Cochin agents in the *grāmam*, and opens a local office for levying duties on goods against the remonstrations of Cochin.

In 1814-15, it is Cochin's turn to try to survey the lands, a move opposed by Travancore.

In 1816-17, Travancore manages to survey *grāmam* lands.

In 1823, after many other skirmishes concerning monopolies (salt, pepper, tobacco), a new agreement is concluded between the two states, following British arbitration. It is also decided that the *grāmam* is a *saṃketam,* equating thus what previously seemed to have been territories of a different nature. The Resident, Major E. Cadogan, tries to set up a committee of Naṃpūtiris in charge of elaborating a definition of what is a *saṃketam.* The very working of this committee becomes a subject of dispute.

In 1828, Cochin opens up different offices, especially for controlling duties on goods, despite protests by Travancore.

In 1830, Cochin objects to Travancore's endeavour to fully control pepper trade and accuses her of forcing people to buy her salt.

In 1834, Travancore attempts to oppose the rebuilding of Cochin's local customs-house, destroyed by fire for the second time in a few years.

In 1837, Travancore conducts a new survey, despite the renewed protests of Cochin.

And so on.

What emerges from these examples is a climate of constant rivalry, of claims and counterclaims, moves and countermoves. The causes for contention are remarkably the same throughout the period. They concern the imposition of land taxes and the corresponding survey operations, the right to impose taxes on various goods, and the monopoly over pepper, salt and tobacco (plus the licensing of alcohol production and commercialization). Even when these monopolies were abolished during the second part of the nineteenth century as part of liberal economic policy, and were replaced by licenses, trade conflicts remained at the core of the dispute between the two states. This is important, because we are brought back to the statement of Ibn Battûta quoted in the opening of this paper: the very necessity of imposing tolls on traders meant that along routes of trade there were posts signalling boundaries. In the Annamanada case, the right to levy trade taxes was a crucial stake disputed by

Cochin and Travancore. What was not contested was the existence of territorial limits allowing for such a taxation.

Earlier taxes, such as personal taxes akin to capitation fees, came to be discontinued, as were various other small taxes on numerous activities. By the time of the arbitration, in the late nineteenth century, the conflict focused mostly on land relationships, the building of customs-houses, and the overall question of 'sovereignty'. The way the question was put, however, seems to have been quite different from what could be understood to have been the case in earlier times. As arbitrator Hannyngton wrote in his decision,

> this arbitration has merely to determine whether at *any time* [original emphasis] Travancore acquired a Sovereign right or a proprietary right over the tract.
>
> By a proprietary right I understand to be meant such a right as is exercised by a Jenmum [*janmam*] proprietor of lands in Travancore—a complete right of ownership subject to the laws of the State within which his possessions lie. (*IP:* 81)

The *janmam* right was the superior right detained by (mostly) high-caste Houses on lands over which there were many other rights. As part of the land settlement process initiated in India from about 1800 by the British in the provinces they directly controlled, or in the kingdoms in which they imposed their influence, 'proprietary rights' in an absolute, exclusive sense had to be established by law so as to identify who would be responsible for the collection of land revenue. Depending on the regions in India, 'owners' were identified at various levels of the hierarchy of land rights. In Travancore, successive legislations were passed between 1865 and 1896 that conferred ownership rights on the tenants of government lands. In this part of Kerala in the 1850s, this corresponded to some 80 per cent of the cultivated land in the state, as a result of the annexation of the domains of chieftains and temples during the preceding decades. At the time of the arbitration, Travancore was thus a state that directly owned most of the land, and that could confer private property in the modern sense of the word (Cochin did not reach this point until well into the twentieth century).[32] It is significant that the Arbitrator could consider the Annamanada dispute as a question bearing on 'sovereignty' or 'proprietorship' in an absolute, exclusive perspective, much akin to the one developed during the debates on land tenure some fifteen years earlier.

In trying to define sovereignty, both Cochin and Travancore States agreed on enumerating a multiplicity of rights. We may take the list established by Travancore in the arbitration files, in her refutation of Cochin's claims (*IP*: 52):

> It is further alleged in . . . the Cochin statement that (1) Cochin has from the earliest times exercised civil and criminal jurisdiction, (2) She established and maintained within the Gramom [mention of three offices], (3) She has levied taxes on property within the Gramom and is still levying them, (4) She compelled every Nair family in the Gramom to send a man when there was a conscription in her territories in [1762-63], (5) She holds the salt, tobacco, and pepper monopolies as well as the Abkari farm [right of distributing licences for making and selling alcohol],. (6) permission for the celebrity [*sic*] of marriages and other ceremonies by the inhabitants is obtained from the Rajah of Cochin on payment of fees, (7) sanction to adopt is granted by His Highness.
>
> A complete statement, no doubt, of rights of sovereignty. Whether such statement is well sustained by evidence is the question.

Each state claimed to have held such rights in exclusivity in the past. However, as the first part of Cochin's statement illustrates (and as is brought out by external available evidence), such rights were in fact often held by different persons. *Dēśavaḻis*, we may recall, were entitled to services, revenues and 'gifts' and exercised judicial and executive powers, as were *nāṭuvaḻis* at a higher level and with wider power. In terms of territory, each right was applicable only within certain limits, so that a multiplicity of rights held by different houses meant a multiplicity of territories. In the arbitration files, the claim by both rajas to have held all the rights from early times is in line with the affirmation of the existence of only one kind of political territory, the territory of the state. This, of course, seems to have been the projection on past times of a nineteenth-century situation. The conflict between Cochin and Travancore bearing on taxes, surveys, customs and monopolies, is therefore a conflict bearing all along on crucial aspects of sovereignty, which are still expressed through fragmented rights inherited from the past, but which are also understood in a new centralized economical and political perspective, with a new, unified territorial frame of reference in mind.

Such a new perspective visibly affected the relationship between political power and temples. Temples and Brāhmans were lords in their own right for a long period until the eighteenth century. In the Annamanada dispute, they seem to maintain a certain political identity thereafter, with territories such as *saṃketam* and *grāmam*. But this must have increasingly become a survival, an anachronism, and a thorn in the process of political centralization. In a way, the Annamnada dispute and its arguments about the 'true nature' of *grāmam* and *saṃketam*, does not so much aim at preserving these territories than at legitimating their eventual absorption in state administration. This is obvious in the arbitration files, in the discussion fostered by Travancore on the semantics of a few terms, and especially on the supposed meaning, in older days, of *saṃketam* and *kōyimma*.

THE SEMANTIC DISPUTE

These two terms, among a few others of lesser importance, are discussed in a statement placed before the Arbitrator in July 1881 by the Travancore Commissioner, S. Shungrasoobyer, in the name of the Travancore government. Shungrasoobyer begins his arguments by discussing the notion of *saṃketam* in order to establish that it was formerly a distinct and autonomous political body (underlining that by their agreement of 1823, Cochin and Travancore had recognized Adur *grāmam* to be a *saṃketam*). This departed from the description provided by Cochin about the past situation, where *grāmam* and *saṃketam* were distinct territories, differing in the case of Annamanada by two villages (*dēśam*). If we accept the plausibility of this statement, it is possible that by about 1800 *dēśams* were no more the locus of a distinct, though subordinate political power, and that the difference between the limits of the *grāmam* and those of the *saṃketam* did not have the same relevance. Moreover, there could have been changes in the settlements themselves. Whatever be the case, the fact is that when the Travancore representative enumerates the villages constituting the 'Gramom commonly known as the Adoor Gramom Sankethom', he mentions some seventeen villages (*IP:* 37). This list includes the '10½' villages constituting the Adur *grāmam*, the two additional villages making for the *saṃketam* according to Cochin, plus four villages not mentioned as part of the 'original' concerned territories.

We do not know the exact reasons of these discrepancies, though they suggest an already well-engaged process of administrative centralization at the time of the 1823 agreement. Territorial simplification equating *grāmam* and *saṃketam* forms the basis of Travancore's subsequent argumentation.

What is supposed to be a *saṃketam* in this new understanding? In order to define it, Travancore exhibits a document whose genuineness is contested by Cochin, and which is said to be the advice given in the 1830s by a committee of two Naṃpūtiri experts nominated by Travancore (*IP:* 57-8). Whether deriving or not from their advice, the definition proposed by Travancore in 1881 is the following:

> The substance of their answers is that the term Sankethom applies to a village over which no Sovereign has any right or jurisdiction; . . . that the Sovereign whose territories surround a Sankethom has, as such, no authority of any kind over it, but all powers are vested in the Sankethom authorities conjointly with the Sovereign elected by them; that the civil and criminal jurisdiction over Sankethoms vest in the constituent members elected or in the Sovereign protector of their choice; that the terms Koima, Aka Koima, Samudayom are applicable to the managing members who are generally Sovereigns elected for the purpose. In short, then, a Sankethom means an independent constitution governed by its own members and presided over by a Sovereign elected by them. (*IP:* 39)

After an enumeration of arguments tending to show that the 'Adoor Gramom Sankethom' is precisely such a *saṃketam* (*IP:* 39-40, countered by Cochin in *IP:* 59-60), the Travancore Commissioner thus concludes:

> In fact, we find all the elements that go to constitute a body politic, which though of a primitive structure was self-working and independent owning no Sovereign except one of its own choice. I may venture to submit that the

Adoor Gramom Sankethom was as independent of its neighbour, Cochin, as Cochin was of the Sankethom. (*IP:* 40)

This stand was of course strongly opposed by Cochin, who in the counter-statement signed by Commissioner Geo H. Gunther and Counsel William S. Gantz, proposed the following definition:

Sankethom is a tract of territory, belonging to a Pagoda, the limits of which are defined. Within those limits no act calculated to pollute the Pagoda, to which the tract belongs, can be committed. Such lands as are exclusively set apart for the performance of ceremonies etc. at the pagoda are said to be lands comprised in the Sankethom; and the Sovereign, within whose dominions the tract is situated, has as much Sovereign supremacy over it as he has over other portions of his territories. (*IP:* 60)

It is now quite clear why Cochin was putting so much emphasis on a reconstruction of the past in terms of multiple rights, all subordinated to Cochin as paramount sovereign, while conversely Travancore's interest was to portray a *saṃketam* as a separate political entity.

The exact nature and extent of the privileges that a *saṃketam* did enjoy are not easy to determine with precision from the available sources. Some certainly had a considerable degree of autonomy—there are cases of people seeking refuge from a raja's wrath, much as in churches in Western countries. However, it does not appear to have been considered a separate 'body politic', and the offices detained in it by rulers seem to have been more considered in terms of supervision than in those of sovereignty.[33] Whatever be the case, it has to be noted that both parties do not discuss a minute the fact that a *saṃketam* is a territory, though Cochin suggests a subtle definition: only lands dedicated for the service of the temple are deemed to constitute the *saṃketam* (a definition which helps to maintain Cochin's initial distinction between *saṃketam* and *grāmam*).

Let us return to Travancore's contentions. Having defined a *saṃketam* as an autonomous 'body politic', the Commissioner proceeds to define the nature of the authority (*kōyimma*) that Travancore is entitled to exercise on it.

The meaning of the term Koima in this document is the most important as bearing directly and materially on the controversy in hand. It is a term peculiar to this part of the coast and signifies, as has been already stated, sovereign. (*IP:* 41)

He enumerates various examples illustrating this use, while acknowledging a change of meaning in present times, where the term is 'sometimes used to designate, more by way of analogy, the superintending employe [*sic*] of a pagoda' (*IP:* 42). He goes on then to criticise the position of Cochin for translating the term as 'pagoda dignity'. Taking as example *dēśakōyimma* (and noting that at the time he is writing it did not exist anymore, which shows the extent of political transformations since early eighteenth century), he affirms that 'in former times, it meant the sovereign or the highest authority in the Desom or tract of country' (ibid.). This, of course, deliberately ignores that *dēśams* were subordinated to higher political units (*nāṭus* and kingdoms), but it is in line with Travancore's arguments that the *sthānam* this kingdom obtained in the past should be considered as implying its sovereignty in the modern sense.

As a consequence, the Travancore Commissioner is lead to assert (quite oddly) that all *kōyimmas* are the same. Whether 'inside *kōyimma*' (*akakōyimma*) or 'superior *kōyimma*' (*mēlkōyimma*), 'the prefix is not of so much significance as the substantive term. Whether "Mel" or "Aka" is used, it is agreed that the meaning conveyed by the term Koima is sovereign' (*IP:* 43). This, in fact, goes against all available evidence, as in some temples different, hierarchized *kōyimmas* are historically attested.[34] Nonetheless, the interpretation of Travancore is that the treaty of 1761 was stipulating the right of both states 'to exercise, as before, the Koima rights enjoyed by each within the limits of the territories of the other', which rights are to be understood as sovereign rights since 'the two States came to possess sovereign jurisdiction over small tracts within the limits of each other' (ibid.).

Quite understandably, this is not Cochin's point of view. While pointing to the fact that an interpretation in terms of sovereignty would be absurd in the case of multiple *kōyimmas* for a same temple or a same tract of land, Cochin explains:

Every person exercising control over, or entrusted with duties relating to, any particular dignity connected with a temple has a Koima Sthanom in respect of that dignity. The person holding such a dignity need not necessarily have the entire management of the temple with which he is associated. His superintendence may be confined to one of the several departments of the same institution. (*IP:* 66)

Besides, in her reply, Cochin distinguished sovereign rights from positions such as *kōyimma sthānam*, which in the present case, 'were only the citizen or private rights of appointing persons attached to pagodas situated within other parts of Cochin' (*IP:* 61). Thus, the interpretation of the treaty of 1761 proposed by Cochin is that

Travancore acquired certain Sovereign rights as well as certain private rights, Sovereign rights in and over [the two ceded principalities of] Parur and Alangad; and private rights of appointing persons to pagoda Sthanoms (office or dignities) appertaining to Parur and Alangad, but held in Cochin territory. Cochin had possessed a similar private right of making appointments to pagodas in territories belonging to Travancore. Inasmuch as the exercise by the one power of such private rights within the dominions of the other led to constant disputes between the subordinate servants of the two powers, a change in the mode of making appointments to the pagodas became necessary. Hence the treaty of . . . 1765. This treaty . . . , therefore, dealt exclusively with the private right of making appointments to temple offices or dignities'. (*IP:* 61-2)

The language used is extremely significant. *Kōyimma* is defined in terms of both administrative logic (it becomes a kind of superintendence) and private rights as opposed to the sovereignty of the state. This is an anachronism. The hierarchy of rights evoked for earlier periods should not be restricted to a purely bureaucratic hierarchy, as it involved various rights including religious ones, nor to an opposition between private and public. In this sense, Cochin and Travancore have the very same understanding of sovereignty, as being the exclusive possession of a territory. But the cause that Cochin has to defend leads her to take the opposite stand of Travancore in the semantic dispute, and argue that a *saṃketam* is not a body politic but a name for temple lands; a *kōyimma* is not sovereignty but the private right to nominate administrative agents. In this very confrontation, we get a glimpse of both the complexity of former territorial rights, and the difficulty to give an account of them in terms of nineteenth-century notions of private property *versus* state territory.

THE ARBITRATION AND ITS AFTERMATH

On 9 January 1882 the case was eventually decided in favour of Cochin. The Arbitrator, J.C. Hannyngton, who was to later become British Resident in Cochin and Travancore, asserted that 'the whole idea of the existence of a Sankethom corporation is as baseless a stretch of imagination as can be conceived and has as little real existence as the kingdom of Liliput' (*IP:* 82). Thus it could not have the power to elect a sovereign. Furthermore, according to the Arbitrator, the treaty of 1765 was to be understood as relating 'not to dominion or sovereignty, but to the management of pagodas' (ibid.). The judgement was thus:

> I decide, therefore, that Travancore has no Sovereign right to the Adoor Gramom or the Annamanada Devasom, and I direct that she do on or before the first July 1882, withdraw from all interference within the disputed tract. (*IP:* 82)

Travancore preferred an appeal. By an order of 30 October 1882, the Governor of Madras upheld the Arbitrator's decision, as long as the 'withdrawal from interference' was not understood as affecting 'the spiritual rights which rest in Travancore', that is, her rights to conduct ceremonies within the temple (*IP:* 91). This decision, inspired by a newly affirmed dichotomy between spiritual and temporal, was perhaps diplomatically well-advised, but led in fact to new complications. Soon, Travancore complained of having to bear all the temple expenses while at the same time being unable to recover any rent from the temple's tenants, as she had been declared by Cochin's civil courts 'incompetent to sue for rent or to give leases to tenants' (*Withdrawal of Management, etc.*, p. 2). Travancore decided then to withdraw totally from the management of the temple. The transfer to Cochin was completed by the end of 1909. By 1910, the process of territorial centralization was achieved in both kingdoms as far as such cases were concerned.

CONCLUSION

This case study should not be taken as an isolated instance of territorial complexity and change. As far as the whole of Kerala is concerned, at least, there is overwhelming evidence that superior rights on land could be exercised on very dispersed lands, sometimes far apart (this was especially true of temples); that rulers' territories could be discontinuous (but their limits well known); that different rulers could have diverse complementary rights over lands and over temples sometimes situated in other rulers' territories. In other words, the story of Annamada is exceptional only in the richness of the documentation that has reached us.

Thus, not only did territories exist in Kerala before colonial supremacy but, indeed, they were of many different kinds. The fact that territories could and did often overlap, does not preclude their being clearly delimitated. Boundaries (for divine jurisdiction, for trade, for land ownership, for control of agricultural production, for the exercise of military force) could be, and were contested, but they were so because boundaries existed! Territories were at the heart of social life, the object of long-standing disputes, and can in no way be considered of secondary importance. Objects of transactions, they were a legal reality and not just an expression of military control over men.[35] They cannot therefore be restricted to a mere 'empirical' level, to use one of Dumont's expressions. True, caste organization was interwoven with the structure of power (and therefore with territorial units), but it cannot be equated with it; the fact that caste repartition intersected with territorial units does not disqualify the reality and the ideological relevance of the latter.

This paper illustrated the changes that occurred during the eighteenth and nineteenth centuries regarding notions of territory. If we do not restrict ourselves to a definition of territory applying only to the modern nation state, we must study various modalities of spatial rights and jurisdictions. In this perspective, it was argued in the course of this paper that the multiplicity of territories of the early eighteenth century was linked to the fragmentary nature of power. This in turn gave rise to contests, such as the one concerning the Annamanada temple. Conversely, the progressive concentration of power during the later period, leading to the two modern nation states of Cochin and Travancore, induced an exclusive conception of sovereignty applied to an unified political territory. The prolongation of the controversy about Annamanada until the 1900s was in some ways a consequence of the will from both states to appropriate this small tract of land and treat it as a mere administrative division.

Such observations should not be dismissed as only referring to some kind of 'Kerala exception' in this matter. On the contrary, they find widespread echoes throughout India. The details may vary, as no two regions will be identical, but the overall characteristics and the general evolution are of a similar pattern. Just one example will suffice. Speaking about Bihar in the eighteenth and nineteenth centuries, Jacques Pouchepadass (1991: 27) suggests that the imposition and development of colonial rule was a process of confrontation between an earlier state of society 'where the political and the social were intricately interwoven' (the accompanying details show a situation akin to that described for Kerala), with a colonial conception of a 'liberal State as an institutional organ distinct of society, the source of cohesion for the collectivity of individual citizens, exercising the monopole of force and taxation, linked to society through a set of impersonal rules applying universally —that is, law' (we recognize the very process of state centralization described in our case study). According to Pouchepadass, this meant building up a 'public space', instituting a separation between public and private—a colonial project not completely realized along these lines at the local level in Bihar (Pouchepadass 1991: 46). As far as Kerala is concerned (as well as other parts of south India), we should add that such an evolution, though definitely shaped in its later stage by colonial rule, had already started before and independently of it. Already by 1750 a form of separation between political power and civil society had already begun to take place in Travancore (Ganesh 1990: 30)—in the case of Annamanada we have followed its consequences as the process gained impetus in the following decades. In nearby Tamil Nadu, the Nayakas in Tanjavur were able in the sixteenth and seventeenth centuries to exploit 'the ambiguous social space between trade and landed power' for opening new public spaces and new sources of legitimacy (Subrahmanyam 1998:

82f.). Moreover, as Subrahmanyam reminds us, the distinction between private and public has very ancient cultural roots in South Indian literature, and we should not be 'excessively naïve about the specifically European, and modern, trajectory of the public/private distinction' (ibid.: 80).

Last, to recognize that territory is politically unified in the modern nation state should not lead us to imagine that we are not living also, in the contemporary, so-called globalized world with a multiplicity of territories. Be it for commercial purposes or for a variety of administrative ones, the state's territory is subdivided into an extremely complex set of overlapping concessions, jurisdictions, sectors, circumscriptions, etc., where the opposition private *versus* public is sometimes less marked than we like to imagine. The transformation which led from a variety of political territories to the present 'unified' one should therefore not be understood so much as a reduction and as a simplification process, than as a change in the nature and organization of power relationships. As Jacques Pouchepadass summarized the development of the bourgeois state in Western countries, this was 'a multi-secular social process marked by the objectification of power relationships (progressively dissociated from the persons involved in these relationships) and by the emancipation of the economic as distinct from the political' (Pouchepadass 1991: 26).

This certainly was not the case in 1758 when a deed was granted to the 'linguist' of the British East India Company in one of the kingdoms immediately north of Cochin, for when this man acquired land, he indivisibly acquired 'the power of administering justice, both civil and criminal, even to the cutting off the hands of a thief'.[36] If possible, territory was even more a determining factor in the definition of social rights than now.

Acknowledgements: I thank D. Berti, K. Veluthat and M.R. Raghava Varier for their keen reading of a first draft of this paper, and for the help extended to me in preparing this study. The remaining mistakes are mine. I am also grateful to Professor Pier Giorgio Solinas for having given me the opportunity to make the initial presentation of this material in 1999 at his seminar in Sienna University, and for the stimulating discussion that ensued.

NOTES

1. These interpretations are criticized in Narayanan 1977: 107ff.
2. A conclusion explicitly made by A.T. Embree, when the author equates the notion of boundary with 'a fixed line, marked on the ground, accurately represented on a map, and described in a treaty by two impinging sovereignties recognizing each other's territory . . . a feature associated with the rise of the modern nation-state' (1977: 258).
3. The present writer, in a former work (Tarabout 1991: 97ff.), is no exception.
4. According to M.R. Raghava Varier (personal communication), the *Līlātilakam*, a fourteenth-century treatise on poetics, 'seems to recognize both a cultural-geographical and a socio-political territory; some verses seek to imagine a geographical entity while some others talk of political territories'.
5. See for instance Miller (1954).
6. 'Their jurisdictions [of gods and goddesses] are even geographically and territorially delimited. It is in the jurisdiction of the goddess at "Thirumaandhaankunnu" that our family house is situated. . . . If we just reach across the river that flows adjacent to the house, we are in the territory of a different god' (Namboodiripad 1976: 5).
7. While this historical reconstruction relies solely on the work of other authors, mostly Kerala historians, its perspective (and the corresponding simplifications) is adapted to the kind of study I have been engaged in (see Tarabout 1986; 1991; 1993; 1997).
8. Susan Bayly (1984; 1989) argues in favour of a much more important military and political role of Christians in the southern half of Kerala, an inference from available and well-known documents she is alone among modern historians to draw.
9. The compound surrounding the house and giving its name to the lineage is both a garden and a place where important rituals are performed, including cremation of the dead and (at least in former times) burial of the charred remains—in contradistinction to regular funeral practices among high status castes elsewhere in India (and at variance with Uchiyamada's affirmation that this is characteristic of only Dalits in Kerala). As M.A. Moore (1985) has pointed out in the case of the Nāyars (but it has wider relevance in Kerala), the house-compound unit is symbolically self-contained, like a small realm.
10. This contrasts with one of Dumont's conclusions regarding the relationships between territory and kinship (Dumont 1957: 165).

11. For the expansion of pepper trade and cultivation, see Kieniewicz (1969; 1986). For the development of a cash economy and its socio-political implications, see Ganesh (1991; 1999; 2002); also Raghava Varier (2002). For the development of subordinate tenures, see Shea (1959).
12. A remarkable illustration is to be found in the papers collected and published by K.K.N. Kurup (1984). See also Miller (1954).
13. The importance of the economic and political functions of the major temples in Kerala has been underlined by many authors. For a recent study, see Veluthat (2002); on the Brāhman oligarchy and its relation to the early medieval State, see Narayanan (2002).
14. There are only brief references to the temple in the literature—see Namboodiri (1999: 317), Shungoonny Menon (1878: 142), Sreedhara Menon (1962: 161, 170, 607).
15. Sreedhara Menon 1962: 147; Tarabout 1991.
16. The arbitration was required for 'the dispute regarding the Devasom of Elancoonnapolay and the Desoms thereof', 'the dispute regarding the Annamada Devasom and the Desoms thereof including Adoor Gramam' [this is the one that provides for the present case study], 'the dispute regarding the villages of Pallipooram, Poorathoor, and Perincherry of the Perumanur Devasom', the dispute regarding the Tachudaiya Kaimal [a position-holder in the Kudalmanikkam temple], and a dispute regarding the Idyaramad hills.
17. A few years later, a new dispute erupted on questions of management, leading Travancore to abandon all claims on Annamanada in 1910. A selection of papers concerning this new dispute was published in 1929: *Elangunnapuzha and Annamanada Devaswoms: Withdrawal of Management (1901-1910)*, Trivandrum: Government Press, 1929.
18. The historiography for the period immediately preceding the one under consideration is abundant. Among recent works, the reader may refer to Cherian (1999), Ganesh (1990; 1991), Kooiman (1990), Narayanan (1977; 2002), Rajan Gurukkal (1992), Veluthat (1993). See also the remarkable collections of deeds published in Kurup (1984) and Narayanan (1987).
19. 'Written Statement of the Dewan of Cochin on the dispute between Travancore and Cochin regarding the Annamanada Devasom and the villages belonging thereto' (*IP*: 4ff.).
20. Veluthat 1978: p. 28 the author notes that this *grāmam* is nowadays no more in existence.

21. 'Poorakatpully Nampoory, Aravatha Nampoory, Muyivattatha Nampoory, Kachankodatha Nampoory, Kudakvattatha Nampoory, Chatheri Nampoory, Madona Nampoory, Maprampilly Nampoory, Mangalapilly Nampoory, and Thekkanadatha Nampoory' (*IP:* 4).
22. The names are given thus: 'Annamanada, Kallur, Allatoor, Vennoor, Vayantala, Meladoor, Keyadoor, Vyanatkara or Arasheri, Kumbidi, Palasheri, Aiancodi, Valloor and Kayikodom' (*IP:* 4).
23. Valloor and Kayikodom.
24. Compare Galletti (1911: 129, including the note by C. Achyutha Menon): we hear about 18½ villages, 8½ families, etc.
25. Both Koratti Kaimal and Kodasseri Kaimal, mentioned in the documents discussed here, are well-known historical houses of central Kerala. Besides Galletti (1911), see for instance Shungoonny Menon (1878: 116ff.), Sreedhara Menon (1962: 157ff.), Poonen (1978: 81).
26. The Dutch seem to have had uneven relations with the Kodasseri Kaimal's principality. In 1743 for instance, Stein van Gollenesse writes in his memorandum: 'It exports 125 candies of pepper and the best cardamom', but not to the Dutch Company as the Kaimal is reported to complain 'I have become a laughing-stock because I have sold this product to the Hon'ble Company for 13 ducats while the other chiefs have received 24 ducats.' To make things worse, the Dutch Company was also in conflict with the Jesuits, allies of the Kaimal and controlling 'the cardamom and the wax' despite the vain efforts of the Company 'to rout out this mischievous rabble'. The Kaimal himself, as described by Van Gollenesse at the time of the memorandum, 'is about 50 years old, a shrewd and crafty gentleman but very much addicted to drink; his successor is a bad lot, who has filled the country with counterfeit fanams [money]' (Galletti et al., 1911: 61-2).
27. Sreedhara Menon (1962: 162 ff.), Ibrahim Kunju (1976), Ganesh (1990; 1991; 1999). On the new 'court culture' and 'new rituals of state' associated with such processes—conferring a different but still crucial importance to control on temples—see Bayly (1984: 189 ff.).
28. The evolution was already heralded in the mid-eighteenth century by the multiplication of 'lords' as is evident from the case of Annamanada, suggesting that *nāṭuvaḻis* had already lost effective power. Still, for some time, the corresponding titles were kept in use. For an example, see Kurup (1984: 11-16) where acts dated 1817 enumerate 'prominent persons', i.e. *nāṭuvaḻis* and *dēśavaḻis*, along with landlords possessing temples and other ones, 'those who are without anything herein

mentioned but who are rich and capable' or 'who are rich and unemployed' (!)—in these two latter cases, mostly Nāyars.

29. Velu Pillai (1940, II: 507-11); Ganesh (1999: 172); for highlighting (and valorizing) the specific role of Col. Munro in these transformations in early nineteenth-century Travancore, see Yesudas 1977.
30. Travancore first proceeded to a revenue settlement in her territories in 1751-4, followed by a second one in 1773, marking the end of 'earlier autonomous authority of the Brahmanas and temples' (Ganesh 1999: 169, 171). In Cochin, the first survey was made later, in 1777-81 (ibid.: 172). Trade monopolies were also enforced as part of the same process of state centralization—in Travancore as early as 1743—so that 'the king came forward not only as the state's military leader and temple manager but also as its overall pepper merchant' (Kooiman 1990: 17; also Shungoonny Menon 1878: 123ff.; Sobhanan 1981). This was marked by the rise of 'state brokers', notably a few affluent Christian families (Bayly 1984: 188), as well as by a multiplication of smaller traders (Jeffrey 1994: 31).
31. According to Velu Pillai (1940, I: 558), this concerned some 1567 temples, whose lands thus came to be owned by the state.
32. Varghese (1970: 30ff., 64ff.).
33. M.G.S. Narayanan and K. Veluthat (1983: 269) define *saṃketam* as 'temple corporation', with forces for self-protection, under the supervisory authority of a prince selected for the purpose. Such a territory was supposed to be kept away from outside military activities (Ganesh 1999: 161), and might even have provided refuge (Velu Pillai 1940, II: 203). Commenting on an important collection of deeds, M.G.S. Narayanan (1987) defines *saṃketam* as 'a quasi-autonomous territory with feudal ecclesiastical tenure' (p. xvi) or 'a quasi-autonomous territory consisting of several villages organized around a Brahmanical temple' (p. xvii) but he specifically makes the point in the same page that 'the *Sanketam* depended very much on the neighbouring chieftains for everything including . . . the maintenance of law and order in their territory'.
34. Achyuta Menon (1911: 393), Sreedhara Menon (1962: 147).
35. Compare with Dharma Kumar (1998: 127), writing about the notion of landownership in pre-colonial south India: 'Legal rights are not simply a reflection of the distribution of power'.
36. Logan 1951: cxxiv, n. 1.

REFERENCES

Achyuta Menon, C., 1911. *The Cochin State Manual*, Ernakulam: Cochin Government Press.

Bayly, Susan, 1984. 'Hindu Kingship and the Origin of Community: Religion, State and Society in Kerala, 1750-1850', *Modern Asian Studies*, 18-2 : 177-213.

———, 1989. *Saints, Goddesses and Kings: Muslims and Christians in South Indian Society, 1700-1900*, Cambridge: Cambridge University Press.

Cherian, P.J., ed., 1999. *Perspectives on Kerala History: The Second Millennium*, Thiruvanthapuram: Government of Kerala (*Kerala State Gazetteer*, vol. II, part II).

Dumont, Louis, 1957. *Une sous-caste de l'Inde du Sud: Organisation sociale et religion des Pramalai Kallar*, Paris-La Haye: Mouton.

———, 1966. *Homo hierarchicus: Le système des castes et ses implications*, Paris: Gallimard.

Elangunnapuzha and Annamanada Devaswoms: Withdrawal of Management (1901-1910), Trivandrum: Government Press, 1929.

Embree, Ainslie T., 1977. 'Frontiers into Boundaries: From the Traditional to the Modern State', in *Realm and Region in Traditional India*, ed. Richard G. Fox, Delhi: Vikas, pp. 255-80.

Galletti, A., the Rev. A.J. van der Burg and the Rev. P. Groot, 1911. *The Dutch in Malabar, Being a Translation of Selections nos. 1 and 2 from the Records of the Madras Government*, Madras: Government Press.

Ganesh, K.N., 1990. 'The Process of State Formation in Travancore', *Studies in History*, 6-1: 15-33.

———, 1991. 'Ownership and Control of Land in Medieval Kerala: *Janmam-Kanam* Relations during the 16th-18th Centuries', *The Indian Economic and Social History Review*, 28-3: 299-323.

———, 1999. 'Agrarian Society in Kerala (1500-1800)', in *Perspectives on Kerala History: The Second Millennium*, ed. P.J. Cherian, Thiruvanthapuram: Government of Kerala (Kerala State Gazetteer, vol. II, part II), pp. 123-79.

———, 2002. 'Land Rights and Political Structure in Medieval Vēṇāṭu', in *State and Society in Pre-Modern South India*, ed. R. Champakalakshmi, Kesavan Veluthat and T.R.Venugopalan, Thrissur: Cosmo Books, pp. 144-71.

Goswami, Manu, 1998. 'From *Swadeshi* to *Swaraj*: Nation, Economy, Territory in Colonial South Asia, 1870 to 1907', *Comparative Studies in Society and History*, 40-4: 609-36.

———, 2004. *Producing India: From Colonial Economy to National Space*, Chicago: Chicago University Press.

Ibn Battûta, 1982. *Voyages* (tr. from the Arabic by C. Defremery and B.R. Sanguinetti, 1858; introduction and notes by S. Yerasimos), 3 vols., Paris: Maspéro/La Découverte.

Ibrahim Kunju, A.P., 1976. *Rise of Travancore: A Study of the Life and Times of Martanda Varma*, Trivandrum: Kerala Historical Society.

Important Papers Connected with the Dispute between Travancore and Cochin Regarding the Annamanaday Devaswom and the Desoms thereof, Including Adoor Gramom, Trivandrum: Government Press, 1900.

Inden, Ronald, 1990. *Imagining India*, Oxford: Basil Blackwell.

Jaffrelot, Christophe, 1996. 'La question du territoire en Inde: de l'universalisme aux particularismes ?', *Cultures et conflits*, 21-2: 75-102.

Jeffrey, Robin, 1994 (1976). *The Decline of Nair Dominance*, Delhi: Manohar (2nd edn.).

Kieniewicz, Jan, 1969. 'The Portuguese Factory and Trade in Pepper in Malabar during the 16th Century', *The Indian Economic and Social History Review*, 6-1: 61-84.

———, 1986. 'Pepper Gardens and Market in Precolonial Malabar', *Moyen Orient et Océan Indien*, 3: 1-36.

Kooiman, Dick, 1990. 'State Formation in Travancore. Problems of Revenue, Trade, Armaments', paper delivered at the 11th European Conference on Modern South Asian Studies.

Kumar, Dharma, 1998. *Colonialism, Property and the State*, Delhi: Oxford University Press.

Kurup, K.K.N., ed., 1984. *Kavalappara Papers*, Calicut: Calicut University.

Lévi-Strauss, Claude, 1979. *La Voie des masques*, Paris: Plon.

———, 1984. *Paroles données*, Paris: Plon.

Logan, William, 1951 [*c.* 1887]. *Malabar*, vol. 2, Madras: Government Press (rpt.).

Malamoud, Charles, 1976. 'Village et forêt dans l'idéologie de l'Inde brâhmanique', *Archives Européennes de Sociologie*, XVII: 3-20.

Miller, Eric J., 1954. 'Caste and Territory in Malabar', *American Anthropologist*, 56-3: 410-20.

Moore, Melinda A., 1985. 'A New Look at the Nayar Taravad', *Man*, n.s., 20-3: 523-41.

Namboodiri, N.M., 1999. 'Cultural Tradition in Medieval Kerala', in *Perspectives on Kerala History: The Second Millennium*, ed. P.J. Cherian, Thiruvanthapuram: Government of Kerala (Kerala State Gazetteer, vol. II, part II), pp. 265-325.

Namboodiripad, E.M.S., 1976. *How I Became a Communist* (tr. from Malayalam by P.K. Nair), Trivandrum: Chinta Publishers.

Narayanan, M.G.S., 1977. *Re-Interpretations in South Indian History*, Trivandrum: College Book House.

———, ed., 1987. *Vanjeri Grandhavari* (*vaññēri granthavari*), Calicut: University of Calicut.

———, 1994. *Foundations of South Indian Society and Culture*, Delhi: Bharatiya Book Corporation.

———, 2002. 'The State in the Era of the Cēramān Perumāḷs of Kerala', in *State and Society in Pre-Modern South India*, ed. R. Champakalakshmi, K. Veluthat and T.R. Venugopalan, Thrissur: Cosmo Books, pp. 111-19.

Narayanan, M.G.S., and K. Veluthat, 1983. 'A History of the Nambudiri Community in Kerala', in *Agni, The Vedic Ritual of the Fire Altar*, 2 vols., ed. F. Staal, Berkeley: Asian Humanities Press, pp. 256-78.

Padmanabha Menon, K.P., 1929. *A History of Kerala*, vol. 2, Ernakulam: Cochin Government Press.

Poonen, T.I., 1978. *Dutch Hegemony in Malabar and its Collapse (A.D. 1663-1795)*, Trivandrum: University of Kerala.

Pouchepadass, Jacques, 1991. 'L'Etat et la structuration de l'espace politique dans l'Inde coloniale', in *De la royauté à l'Etat. Anthropologie et histoire du politique dans le monde indien*, ed. J. Pouchepadass and H. Stern, Paris: EHESS, pp. 25-54.

Raghava Varier, M.R., 2002. 'State as *Svarūpam*: An Introductory Essay', in *State and Society in Pre-Modern South India*, ed. R. Champakalakshmi, Kesavan Veluthat and T.R.Venugopalan, Thrissur: Cosmo Books, pp. 120-30.

Rajan Gurukkal, 1992. *The Kerala Temple and the Early Medieval Agrarian System*, Sukapuram: Vallathol Vidyapeetham.

Raman Menon, V.K., 1936. 'The Old Chiefs of Malabar', *Bulletin of the Sri Rama Varma Research Institute*, 4: 11-19.

Rowlandson, M.J. (tr.), 1833. *Sheikh Zeen-ud-Deen: Tohfut-ul-Mujahideen*, London: Oriental Translation Fund of Great Britain and Ireland.

Shea, T.W. (Jr.), 1959. 'The Land Tenure Structure of Malabar and its Influence upon Capital Formation in Agriculture', University of Pensylvania (unpublished Ph.D. dissertation).

Shungoonny Menon, P., 1878 (1983). *A History of Travancore from the Earliest Times*, Trivandrum: Government Press (rpt.).

Sobhanan, B., 1981. 'Trade Monopoly of Travancore', *Journal of Kerala Studies*, 8-1/4: 29-38.

Sreedhara Menon, A., 1962. *Kerala District Gazetters: Trichur*, Trivandrum: Government Press.

Subrahmanyam, Sanjay, 1998. 'Hearing Voices: Vignettes of Early Modernity in South Asia, 1400-1750', *Daedalus* (special number on 'Early Modernities'), 127-3: 75-104.

———, 2001. *Penumbral Visions: Making Polities in Early Modern South India*, Ann Arbor: University of Michigan Press.

Tarabout, Gilles, 1986. *Sacrifier et donner ā voir en pays Malabar. Les fêtes de temple au Kérala (Inde du Sud) : étude anthropologique*, Paris: EFEO.

———, 1991. 'Au "royaume" des brahmanes, les guerriers sont rois. Souveraineté, pouvoir et statut au Kérala', in *De la royauté ā l'Etat. Anthropologie et histoire du politique dans le monde indien*, eds. J. Pouchepadass and H. Stern, Paris: EHESS, pp. 75-122.

———, 1993. 'Ritual Rivalry in Kerala', in *Flags of Fame: Studies in South Asian Folk Culture*, ed. H. Brückner, L. Lutze and A. Malik, Delhi: Manohar, pp. 81-108.

———, 1997. 'Une configuration sociale régionale: le Kérala', *Historiens et Géographes*, 356: 243-56.

———, 1999. 'Corps possédés et signatures territoriales au Kérala', in *La possession en Asie du Sud. Parole, corps, territoire*, ed. J. Assayag and G. Tarabout, Paris, EHESS, pp. 313-55.

Uchiyamada, Yasushi, 2000. 'Passions in the Landscape: Ancestor Spirits and Land Reforms in Kerala, India', *South Asia Research*, 20-1: 63-84.

Varghese, T.C., 1970. *Agrarian Change and Economic Consequences: Land Tenures in Kerala, 1850-1960*, Bombay: Allied Publishers.

Velu Pillai, T.K., 1940. *The Travancore State Manual*, 4 vols., Trivandrum: Government of Travancore.

Veluthat, Kesavan, 1978. *Brahman Settlements in Kerala: Historical Studies*, Calicut: Sandhya Publications.

———, 1993. *The Political Structure of Early Medieval South India*, Delhi: Orient Longman.

———, 2002. 'The Temple and the State: Religion and Politics in Early Medieval South India', in *State and Society in Pre-Modern South India*, ed. R. Champakalakshmi, Kesavan Veluthat and T.R.Venugopalan, Thrissur: Cosmo Books, pp. 96-110.

Veluthat, Kesavan and M.G.S. Narayanan, 1983. 'A History of the Nambudiri Community in Kerala', in *Agni, The Vedic Ritual of the Fire Altar*, 2 vols., ed. F. Staal, Berkeley: Asian Humanities Press, pp. 256-78.

Wink, André, 1986. *Land and Sovereignty in India: Agrarian Society and Politics under the Eighteenth-century Maratha Svarâjya*, Cambridge: Cambridge University Press.

Yesudas, R.N., 1977. *Colonel John Munro in Travancore*, Trivandrum: Kerala Historical Society.

8

Divine Jurisdictions and Forms of Government in Himachal Pradesh

DANIELA BERTI

> Like the flowers of a garland, the inhabitants of a *hār* (territory of a God) are bound together.
>
> Vidyachand Thakur, Kullu, 2001

Travelling on the roads in the Kullu Valley in Himachal Pradesh, one may notice a visible sign that suggests a territorial division according to divine jurisdictions. The more you enter into such a jurisdiction, the more you will come across vehicles with the name of the specific god of the area written in self-adhesive letters on their windscreen.

That village gods live in delimited territories is a common feature attested throughout the subcontinent. Studies on regional pantheons, particularly in the Himalaya, have shown the political, administrative, and economic dimensions involved in such local cults. In Tehri Garhwal, for instance, Sax (1991) notes that the public processions of the deities' palanquins carried by villagers in the territories of earlier kingdoms, cancelled out 'in practice the academic distinctions among politics, economics and ritual' (Sax 1991: 203). In a similar perspective, Toffin (1993) considers the structure of the Indo-Buddhist Newar pantheon in the Kathmandu Valley as 'a total social phenomenon . . . at once religious, territorial and politico-administrative' (Toffin 1993: 120).

Such interrelations between various dimensions of social life are not without theoretical consequences in the field of Indian studies. There has been a strong and lasting influence (particularly in France) of Dumont's general theory on Indian society, according to which political and economic power, as well as territory, are separate from the ideological sphere of religion, since they are encompassed by it and subordinated to it.[1] According to Dumont and Pocock, 'the territorial factor, the relation to the soil is not, in India as a whole, one of the primary factors in social organization. It is a secondary factor in relation to the two fundamental factors of kinship and caste' (Dumont and Pocock 1957: 18). Territory, being not included in what Dumont calls the 'ideology' or system of ideas, beliefs, and values (Dumont 1966: 15), is thus devoid of cognitive significance.

The present paper concerns a Himalayan region that corresponds to the former Kullu kingdom. I analyse how territory has been taught, organized, and transformed in various ways and in different periods, according to a plurality of interrelated logics: ritual, political, fiscal, administrative, and electoral. My aim is to show that territory is not only the basis of ritual and political organization or individual identity; it is also a central topic of reflection and of explicit discourse.

The analysis will focus on the notion of *hār*, used in the region to designate the area considered to be the jurisdiction of a specific god. A lawyer from Kullu, V.C. Thakur, suggested the following definition:

> *Hār* indicates the area in which devotees of a particular deity reside. It refers, essentially, to a territory inside which the inhabitants use to honour a specific deity. In a wider sense, *hār* can designate the people who live in a particular territory (*kṣetra*) belonging to a deity, which are called also its *hārye* (inhabitants of the *hār*) and which are considered as the political subjects (*prajā*) of the deity. The inhabitants of a *hār* are territorially linked one another by the ties they have with the deity.

This definition points towards different aspects of the notion of *hār*: it is a clearly delimited divine territory; it points to the sovereignty of the deity over the inhabitants of this territory, defined as its 'political subjects'; it entails territorial ties between the inhabitants at a same *hār*. These various aspects will be analysed in the following pages by taking into account successive forms of government in the region: first, a kingdom progressively came to be established in the seventeenth century; then the British colonial administration took over by the end of the nineteenth century; last, the region became part of the democratic Indian state, following Independence. The scale of observations will also vary, taking into account either a village, or a group of villages, or the territory (once corresponding to the kingdom of Kullu) which nowadays forms an electoral constituency. The first part of the paper considers the *hār* from a historical perspective, by using oral accounts as well as colonial reports. In the latter case I will mostly refer to the manuscript of W.H. Emerson, a British administrator of early twentieth century. This document is full of details about the territorial jurisdictions of the local deities, and shows how British administrators were occasionally called upon to interfere in the management of the cults of village deities. The second part of the paper will focus on the contemporary period, for which I will use ethnographical material collected during different spells of fieldwork between 1995 and 2001.

First, I will briefly describe the main characteristics of the deities concerned.

VILLAGE GODS AS 'SOCIAL ACTORS'

The expression *devī-devtā* (literally 'goddess-god') is used in the Kullu Valley to speak of the deities of the village temples. The worship of these village deities involves the intervention of various temple functionaries—priest, medium, administrator, musicians. Each deity is considered to exercise his/her power within a delimited area, the *hār*, and the inhabitants of this area turn to him/her to ask for rain or sunshine, or to cure a villager's disease or solve a problem, or to arbitrate village conflicts.

Each village deity has a medium, the *gur*, who undergoes public initiation. When consulted, the medium shows (culturally expected) signs of divine possession, and begins to speak on behalf of the deity. A village deity can also express itself through the movements of its palanquin, the *rath*, carried on the shoulders of the villagers at festivals. These movements are supposed to be provoked by the deity and not the bearers. Villagers decode such movements as expressing the deity's feelings, intentions and desires in response to a specific situation. For the devotees, the medium's words and the palanquin's movements allow village gods to communicate, to participate in village life, and to take decisions.

The worship of these deities is in the hands of an administrator (*kārdār*) and a group of villagers who form the temple committee; they usually belong to high castes. Low-caste villagers participate in the worship, too, as musicians, medium, and devotees.[2] Most of the village gods were previously the lineage deity of some dominant families in the region. Even today the worship of a deity may be the responsibility of one or several families. The god Balu Nāg, for instance, in the Banjar area, has ties with the Bhatta family, whose members still take the most important decisions concerning his worship. If we consider the god's story, however, priority is clearly given to territorial links over those of lineage. According to one story, Balu Nāg settled in the region of Banjar on arrival from the nearby district of Mandi, and the Bhatta family happened to be the first to worship him. Even when a village deity is linked to a particular family in the region, he differs from the category of 'lineage deity' by holding sovereignty over all those who live in his territory. These people form the *hār*, or *hārye*,[3] independently of kinship ties or caste status. The way for the deity to expresses his/her sovereignty is to bring benefits and punishments upon those living within his/her jurisdiction.

AUTHORITY OVER LAND AND TERRITORY

The influence that village gods still exercise on the inhabitants of their territories through their mediums is often presented by local scholars as one of the reasons that forced past kings of the region to establish political relations with them, by means of alliance or subjugation. It is at least in these terms that M.R. Thakur interprets the decision of King Jagat Singh (seventeenth century) to introduce the worship of an outsider, Raghunāth (a form of Rāma), into the kingdom. The king declared this god to be the real 'king of Kullu', to whom all local deities had therefore to bow in reverence and obedience.[4] In addition to this act of politico-religious centralization, Jagat Singh also assigned land to different village gods, who then became *muāfīdār devtā* (landholding deities). Following this, and as a sign of political subordination, the village gods were obliged to pay an annual tribute (*nazarānā*) to Raghunāth. They also, for fear of being fined, had to visit the capital once a year during the annual festival in order to pay homage to the royal god and to his human delegate, the Raja of Kullu.

The king exercised control over the management of worship in the villages by influencing, for example, the choice of a medium, the nomination of the temple administrator, or even by imposing the specific style in which a god's palanquin had to be built. He could also exercise some 'pressure' on village gods in connection with the power (*śakti*) they were supposed to have over atmospheric conditions within their territorial jurisdiction. In times of drought, for instance, the king used to organize in the palace a 'universal consultation' (*jagtī pūch*) of all the deities of the kingdom (through their mediums) in order to ask them to give rain. Local narratives add that, when the demand was not satisfied, the king would consider the mediums answerable for the gods' failure and would threaten to have their heads cut-off if the rain did not come at once.

Villagers could also call upon the king's mediation to solve cases of more limited 'territorial droughts'. The measures to be taken in such circumstances were normally decided by the king or, in his absence, by one of his representatives. When the region fell under British control, the Administrator occasionally had to assume a royal role. One of them, Emerson, reports such an instance. When he was governing the region of Shimla, one day he received the visit of some villagers. They had come to ask him to punish the mediums of a very famous god in the region, Kamru Nāg, considered to be responsible for the rain shortage.

> It was clearly up to me to do something, and as all arguments failed to convince the people, I finally gave orders to the Wazir to call the erring diviners, and without ill-treating them in any way to attempt to bring them to a sense of their duties. The peasants were more or less content with this show of activity, but the results were not satisfactory, and when a few weeks later, the diviners themselves appeared before me, I took the opportunity of

reminding them of their duties, and the punishments prescribed for their neglect. They were refreshingly candid. Kamru Nag's job, they admitted, was to send sunshine and rain in their proper season. If he failed to do so, they (the diviners) were called to the police station and kept confined. If the rain did not then come within a reasonable time, they were made to stand naked in the sun; or in fine weather was needed and rain fell, they were made to stand up to their waists in the river until the sun shone. They knew of no reason why the same measures should not now be taken, but they would like four days of grace, and if no rain came within that time, they would bow to whatever punishment was ordered. So they were given their four days, and as rain fell before they ended, no further action was necessary. (Emerson, *Manuscript*, 62)

If the king—as reported by Emerson—had the right to punish inefficient gods through their mediums, he rewarded with land gifts or privileges those deities who satisfied his requests. Many stories of royal donations tell how a deity received a certain amount of land from the king as a reward for having brought rain in times of need.[5]

The relations between the central authority, exerted by the king on behalf of god Raghunāth, and the local authority, exerted by villagers on behalf of village deities, seem to have always been complex and ambiguous. In his study of the economic and political importance of village gods in Kinnaur, Singh (1989: 89) notes that the kings 'used the devtas as their representatives for manifesting royal presence in remote areas. . . . Since the Raja did not frequently visit Kinnaur, the devta's frequent tours on his behalf manifested divine sanction for the Raja's rule.'

The territorial implications of local cults thus appear to have been a crucial element in royal politics. On the one hand, the assignation of land (*muāfī*) to village deities can be interpreted as a political and religious form of centralization, for the prerogatives that local deities already enjoyed in their own territories now had to be sanctioned by the palace. Consequently, the king could also delegate to a local god his royal presence in distant regions.[6] On the other hand, the control exercised by the king over the management of the cults had politico-territorial implications, for instance, the protection of the boundaries of the kingdom. As a rule villagers were not allowed to change the style of their god's palanquin unless so authorized by the king (Emerson 1920: 64); this was due to the fact that, since the style of a palanquin is associated with a specific kingdom, it would have meant that the god's supporters had established alliances with neighbouring kingdoms (Vidal 1998: 64). Thus, the need to control boundaries appears to be very present in the Kullu kings' political preoccupations. True, this way of constructing politico-territorial boundaries did not necessarily involve map-making or physical delimitation, but was established through other symbolic means. It suggests in any case the need to reconsider the idea that that territory in India was defined by taking into account its centre, not its boundaries.

Another stereotype likely to be refuted by the present data is the assertion that the king ruled over territory not conceptually differentiated from a population, as suggested by the term *janapada*, which Dumont translated as 'population-cum-territory' and which he relied on to discriminate between what he claimed to be the ancient Hindu conception of kingship and the modern Western idea of nation, where territorial sovereignty implies the property of the land (Dumont 1966: 393).[7] A different interpretation of the territorial conceptions linked to ancient Indian kingship is, however, given by R. Lingat (1967), which better fits the data for the kingdom of Kullu. In studying the Dharmaśāstra, the author identifies two main notions associated with kingship: the notion of *rājādharma*, the duties and obligations of the king to which he is submitted independently of the extension or localization of his territory, and the notion of *kṣatra* which is, by contrast, 'a power which is territorial in character, not only because it is applied within a territory and ends at the frontiers of the kingdom, but because it is conceived . . . as a regal right over territory, akin to a proprietary right that gives direct power over land and soil' (Lingat 1967: 237, my translation).

In any case, the overall property of the land itself was far from being an unknown component of sovereignty in the Himalayan kingdoms (at least), a fact already fully emphasized by the British administrators as shown by this passage from Lyall's Gazetteer: 'Under the Rájahs, the theory of property in land was that each

Rájah was the landlord of the whole of his "Ráj" or principality. . . . The Rájah was not, like a feudal king, lord paramount over inferior lords of manors, but rather, as it were, manorial lord of his whole country' (Lyall 1874: 24).

The donation of land to village gods as well as the donation of the kingdom to Raghunāth emphasizes the importance given to landed property in the exercise of political sovereignty, which is directly legitimated here by deities.

DIVINE PROPERTIES AND AREAS OF INFLUENCE: THE BRITISH PERIOD

With the beginning of the colonial period we have more information about divine territories and how they were managed by the British. When the latter settled in the region in the second half of the nineteenth century and undertook a revenue settlement, the first thing they noticed was the importance of land which came under the name of village gods. In his field notes, Coldstream[8] wrote that in the subdivision of Prini:

> [The god] Jamlu has a muafi [property exempted from taxes] of 94 [acres] in Prini and [the goddess] Sawari one of 42 [acres]. Two other deota [gods] have pretty assignments . . . [In the sub-division of Vashisht] seven gods have muafi in Vashist and four have temples as well. [The god] Thakur Ram Chandra owns 65 acres of land and has an assignment of 64 rupees.

The divine properties (*muāfī*) were usually confirmed by the British administrators. To adapt these assignations to the norms of British legislation, the administrators introduced a 'legal artifice' (Vidal 1988: 76): a decree equated deities with 'moral persons' with the legal status of children, and granted them the right to basic amenities needed for maintaining their cult (ibid.). These properties were managed by a temple administrator (*kārdār*) who was considered to be the god's 'tutor'.[9]

The British administrators reported the difficulties they had in registering these assignations for which often no kind of documents was available:

In taking a general view of the temple maafis in Tahsil Kullu, the first thing that strikes one is the great amount of land they possess. . . . I have thought that the amount of land belonging to temples in Kullu was most excessive, and should somehow or other be reduced, but after taking up and investigating a number of cases I came to the conclusion that it must be treated in a free, not technical manner. In the absence of sanads [written assignations] or ancient list of maafis [holdings], and for lack of maps or field books, which were not produced at the original settlement, it was not possible with all the untrustworthy evidence to say what the area originally granted by the Rajas was. . . . There was no doubt that temple lands had often been held without sanads, and that many sanads had been lost in the disturbances before annexation.

Even if British colonial policy, as a rule, was to avoid interfering with local practices, it is quite possible that the survey they conducted favoured this or that local deity. A traveller in that period, Enriquez, informs us that a deity in the area was extremely angry because the revenue settlement did not properly ascertain the extent of his lands. The author also reports an episode showing how frequent it was at the time for a villager to transfer part of his land to a deity:[10]

the priests [of the temple] insisted on the sanction of Government being obtained for such a gift, because they said, the transfer under the Land Alienation Act, could not legally take place without such sanction, except to an agriculturist, and the deota, as they pointed out, was a god and not an agriculturist. The case was sent up to Government, and sanctioned.

(Enriquez 1915: 44)

The Gazetteers show that at the time of the arrival of the British in the region, the extension of a deity's areas of influence (*hār*) never coincided with land cultivated in its name (*muāfi*). Emerson reports many cases in which a 'deity' tried to assert its own influence over the territories belonging to other neighbouring deities, also asking the inhabitants of these territories to pay tribute as a sign of their submission. The case of god Mahāsū, whose worship spread all over the region of Shimla, is a good example:

For twelve years on end he is continuously on tour, visiting the various tracts where his worship has been adopted, accompanied by a retinue that grows fat on the offerings of the people. He [the god] chooses the richest and most pleasant villages to halt in, which have to bear the burden of his exactions. But the neighbouring villages do not escape scot free. Every family of his subjects in this districts through which he passes has to contribute one rupee and eight annas towards his expenses, the rupee being kept by his priest and the annas paid into his treasury. . . . Many other contributions were also exacted such as ghi, goats and supplies of various sorts. . . . To check these exactions, summary orders were passed in the presence of the assembled elders, banishing the god and his attendants from one district, and commanding his Wazir to abstain from accepting any invitation on the part of Mahasu without the sanction of Government. (Emerson, *Manuscript*, pp. 11-14)

Emerson's observations do not allow us to grasp the social implications of such conquering actions. They show, however, how the British administration could disapprove of what the text describes as 'exactions' and could intervene therefore, through official actions, in order to put a stop to the expansionistic plans of a deity.[11]

What also emerges from a story like this is how the extension of a deity's *hār* and the importance a deity assumes in the regional pantheon are subject to historical transformations. The worship of certain important deities may disappear, while that of new deities may be adopted by an increasing number of people.

Such expansion does not imply, however, that the territory within which a deity receives tribute is its 'property'. Land assignations, in fact, could be carried out in the form of *muāfī* only by the king, and subsequently by the British administration. A deity's area of influence therefore does not correspond to its landed property, even if a deity endowed with a large amount of land is considered powerful and influential throughout the region.

Following Independence, an event provoked a radical transformation in the regional pantheon's equilibrium and in relations between village deities and their land. In 1972, Indira Gandhi's government promulgated the 'Pass Tenant Act', giving the opportunity to cultivators, including those who cultivated the gods' lands, to become owners. As a consequence, village deities, also called *paisevāle devtā*, 'deities with money', lost a large part of their holdings. All the deities that had given their land for cultivation at the time of the reform were deprived of their means of subsistence; the others have been able to preserve considerable holdings up to the present today. Some deities, whose land was formerly not cultivable, found themselves suddenly rich as a consequence of the introduction of apple orchards on land unsuitable for rice or other grain (Vidal 1988). Since this reform, those who cultivated gods' land in exchange for services rendered to the temple (priests, mediums, and musicians) have become owners; they were no longer obliged by law to continue providing services to the temple.[12]

It is difficult to ascertain the impact of this reform on local cults. The registers dating back to colonial time show that at the beginning of the twentieth century some deities whose cult is today abandoned or is extremely reduced, possessed an important amount of land. However, we cannot be sure that a lapse in worship was caused only by the impoverishment of the divinity. Long before land reforms, Emerson, reports, many stories showing how abandonment of cults were frequent and could result from a decision by villagers to react to the 'inefficiency' of the deity.

> [The god of rain, Goli Nāg] originally dwelt in Kulu, where for many generations he never failed to send the rain and sunshine at their proper season. Suddenly, however, ... he began to send nothing but rain, forgetting all about the need of sunshine. His followers tolerated this for some time [until when] they thought it time to give him some experience of the element he loved so much. So one wet day they took his idol, images and litter in procession to the river Sutlej and threw them into the torrent, an act of justice which, no doubt, gave them some satisfaction for their ruined crops. (Emerson, *Manuscript*, pp. 9-10)

The story goes on. After Goli Nāg's palanquin was thrown into the river, one of his metal masks was found on the riverbank by a passer-by who, happy to find such a treasure, took it home. In his village the god then started to manifest his presence by sending impressive floods, which destroyed the whole harvest and spread terror among the people. Local mediums were consulted. They revealed that the one responsible for these disasters was Goli Nāg, whose mask was somewhere in the village. Through the mediums the god asked to be set up in place of a local goddess, and to receive daily worship.

So Goli Nag passed through the waters of tribulation to a lofty temple, where he has dwelt in ease and honour ever since. Only occasionally, bored by the unfailing alternation of the season, he turns summer into winter, or sends the rains at harvest time.

This story illustrates the kind of transformation to which divine territories have been submitted: a village god abandoned by his own people in his own jurisdiction, and whose palanquin is thrown into the river, can be adopted by the inhabitants of a neighbouring village as the main god, with a new jurisdiction. The following pages will detail the ties established between a village deity and the inhabitants of its jurisdiction, and will also show how the rituals followed within the *hār* are related to the system of land taxation applied in the region during the colonial government.

RITUAL TERRITORIES AND FISCAL UNITS

In order to define a god's territory, Kullu people make reference to ancient administrative units that existed before the colonial period, and which were adopted by them in order to organize the collection of land taxes: the *phāṭī*, which includes a group of villages, and the *koṭhi*, which includes a number of *phāṭī*.

An administrator, Lyall, reports that at the time of the Rājā's rule, *koṭhi* meant a granary in which the grain that the peasants gave to the king as land tax was collected. The term was also applied to indicate the boundary of villages whose tax was put into the same granary. The *phāṭī* was a sub-division of the *koṭhi*, a term referring not so much to a territory as to a population sharing the services or the forced labour due to the king (Lyall 1874: 119).

The two terms were later adopted by colonial administrators in order not only to organize their revenue settlement and the collection of land taxes, but also as a criterion to distinguish various *devī-devtā* by referring to the extension of their area of influence. Thus, Lyall writes in his official gazette:

> Most of these deotas [deities] are merely objects of worship of a single hamlet, or of one or two neighbouring hamlets; many, however, are known as the deo or devi of the whole of a *phati*, or of a whole *koṭhi*. A few of the larger and more noted shrines are generally respected, and their

festivals attended by men from all the surrounding *koṭhis*, or by men of one or more waziris.

According to Lyall, the divisions in *phāṭī* and *koṭhi* reflected the dominions of the ancient chiefs who had controlled the region before the centralization of the kingdom. In his view, the borders of a deity's *hār* were once political, being associated with the power that a lineage or a local chief exercised on one or more villages.

The divisions in *phāṭī* and *koṭhi* are today used in administrative language, and still define a deity's *hār*.[13] In some regions, this *hār* covers a certain number of *phāṭi* included in different *koṭhi*; in this case, people will speak of a 'five *phāṭī* deity' or of a 'seven *phāṭī* deity'. A clear indication of the limits of a divine jurisdiction is the contribution to the expenses for annual or occasional ritual activities celebrated in honour of the deities. The frequency of the contribution varies according to the territorial level of the divinity: the inhabitants of a village regularly participate in all the rituals celebrated in their village deity's temple, whereas they contribute on an irregular basis to those organized for the deity of the *phāṭī* or of the *koṭhi*.

Moreover, the multiple and relative territorial limits concern the influence that every divinity exercises on the territory and on its inhabitants. Such influence is also expressed during séances. For instance, Takṣak Nāg, the deity of a *koṭhi* of eight villages, used to say during consultations made at his temple: 'blue sky here, blue sky in eight places; rain here, rain in eight places'. Or else: 'rain from Nagar to Kullu [one *koṭhi*], blue sky from Nagar to Vasist [another *koṭhi*]; blue sky from Nagar to Kullu, rain from Nagar to Vasist'. Sometimes it is also a greater unit of the region which is evoked: a deity can say for instance 'good things in a place; good things in seven *wazīrīs* [groups of *koṭhi*]'.

Mediums often explain an excess of rain or a drought as a result of the frequent conflicts amongst villagers, and which demand ritual reparation. In the northern part of the valley (Parol), the logic of such reparation is the same in all the different *koṭhi*: if the conflict occurs inside a village, all the villagers should be involved in the ritual reparation.

The territorial influence of a *devī-devtā* is not limited to an area of worship—village, *phāṭī*, or *koṭhi*—but is a sort of logic determining a network of ties encompassing territories controlled by different deities. For instance, the deity of a particular village may be said to exercise influence over the entire territory of the *koṭhi*, even if inside his territory other village deities control one *phāṭī* or simply one or several villages. In the case of individual or village problems, only the village deity will be consulted. If the dispute affects several villages, the deity of the whole *phāṭī* or *koṭhi* will be asked to arbitrate the debates.[14] In the northern part of the valley, the logic of this interpretation is the same in all the different *koṭhi*: if a mistake has been made within a village, all its inhabitants are summoned to participate in the ritual reparation; if it involves two villages of a same *phāṭī*, all the villages of this *phāṭī* will be considered responsible; if it involves two villages of a same *koṭhi*, the whole *koṭhi* will be asked to participate. Such a rule has the effect of mobilizing all the villagers included in one *phāṭī* or one *koṭhi*, who will try to encourage a compromise between the parties in conflict. If they succeed, they perform a collective ritual to pacify the deity.[15] All the villages have to participate physically and economically in the ritual—not only those who are in conflict but also those that are included in the same ritual subdivision, without even having any direct part in the conflict.

Let us see how this interdependence between ritual-territorial logic and the colonial fiscal-administrative system has left its imprint on the current situation.

TERRITORIAL PUNISHMENT AND FISCAL RESPONSIBILITY

In 1995 there was no rain in the Jagatsukh *koṭhi* for several months. There was a risk that the harvest would be completely destroyed. The inhabitants of the eight villages that formed the two *phāṭī* of this *koṭhi* were desperate. They constantly consulted the mediums of the village deities in order to find out the reasons for such a drought, and to ask for rain. The deities' answer was always the same: there was no rain and there would not be any till the two villages of Prini and Banara, fighting each other within the same *koṭhi*, put an end to their dispute. The god of Prini, Phāl Nāg, exercised his influence on a whole *phātī* which included three other villages. His brother, the god Takṣak Nāg of Banara, dominated the other *phātī* of the *koṭhi*. One of the consequences of the dispute was that the two villages refused to bring their deities' palanquins to common village festivals, in order to avoid each other.

The dispute lasted for more than a year.[16] All efforts to find a solution had been in vain, until Śravaṇī's medium, the goddess of one village in the *koṭhi*, promised to bring rain as soon as the villagers reached a compromise. The negotiations began, facilitated by the fact that the rain started to fall in neighbouring territories. Let us look at a passage in one séance, during which Śravaṇī, speaking through her medium, linked the lack of rain to punishment inflicted by her.

Goddess Śravaṇī's medium: Put your dispute on your head! You fight each other and you separated us! You play with swords and sticks but we . . . we have Indra-Samundra [we control the rain[17]]. These two brothers [the gods of the two villages in conflict] put the pillow in the opposite directions.[18] It was in this way that they brought rain. When Śandal Ṛṣi [the god of a nearby village] came here, it started raining in other places. But it is in these eight villages that the rain doesn't come!

People of the village: Yes! In other places plenty of rain has come, but here nothing! Why doesn't the rain come here? You must tell us!

The goddess thus reveals the territorial extent of her divine wrath. Simultaneously, by stressing these limits, she reinforces the conviction that the shortage of rain was because of her disappointment at the fight between the two villages. But villagers belonging to other villages in the *koṭhi* protested about being associated with the two guilty ones, and considered it unjustified to suffer the consequences of their misdeeds.

Villager to the goddess Śravaṇī: O Mahārāja! [term of address for any deity] You should punish the two villages of Prini and Banara but you should do nothing to the others. If someone makes a mistake, you don't have to punish the entire world! Tell us who is guilty and then you punish him. Otherwise, if you do this, all of us will suffer! The administrators of god Phāl Nāg and of god Takṣak Nāg must find a compromise. [*addressing the two administrators*:] You both, you take the decision, here, now!

Those who found themselves involved in the dispute without being responsible for the fight tried to convince the temple administrators to reach a compromise. An agreement was eventually found. On the goddess's demand, the eight villages were required to participate financially in a reparation ritual. The decision was facilitated by the fact that during the séance, some drops of rain began to fall. On the day of the compromise, the rain arrived in abundance and all the villagers pointed out that it fell just within the limits of the *koṭhi*!

This case confirms that as far as the god is concerned, the inhabitants of a *hār* are jointly responsible. In this case, since the dispute arose between two villages whose deities dominated two *phāṭī* included in the same *koṭhi*, all the inhabitants of the *koṭhi* suffered the consequences of the divine disappointment and had to contribute to the reparation.

Now, these rules of 'divine justice' find a curious parallel in the system of land taxation introduced by Barnes, a British administrator who introduced the revenue settlement in the region in 1851. According to this system, all the cultivators of the lands included in a *phāṭī* or in a *koṭhi* were *jointly responsible* for the payment of the land tax (*Punjab District Gazetteers* 1917: 145). We may wonder if the existence of a 'joint ritual responsibility' may have influenced the British decision to adopt a similar logic for land tax collection.[19] However, according to Lyall, before the arrival of the British, there was no system of joint fiscal responsibility (ibid.: 144 ff.).[20] In 1851, when Barnes introduced the new system, a headman was named for every *koṭhi* (or, if the *koṭhi* was too large, for every *phāṭī*) and all the tenants were made collectively responsibly for tax collection (ibid.: 145). In Kinnaur, a region near Kullu, such a procedure was not well received and there were widespread protests:

> [The ministers] did not remain passive spectators in the face of this development but reacted strongly and got this Settlement cancelled within two years . . . [They] justified it by saying that the 'principal god of the country had expressed an opinion that the cholera which was then raging was solely attributable to the money assessment. (Singh 1989: 106)

Some administrators too criticised this system, finding it inappropriate for the socio-geographical conditions of the region. Barnes himself observed that in Kullu, contrary to villages in the north Indian plains, the land:

> instead of being a coparcenary estate, reclaimed, divided, and enjoyed by an united brotherhood, is an aggregation of isolated freeholds, quite distinct from each other, and possessing nothing in common, except that for fiscal convenience they have been massed together under one jurisdiction. (Barnes 1885: 56)

We cannot say what motivated Barnes to introduce joint fiscal responsibility, and it is not possible to deduce from his reports whether he had any knowledge of the existence of a similar procedure in ritual contexts. Whatever the case, the consequence of this new system was that at the level of fiscal territorial units as well as of divine jurisdictions, the same logic was now adopted. In fact, in the northern part of the region (Parol), the villages named by British administrators in their official lists of *phāṭī* and *koṭhi* are the same as the ones jointly responsible at ritual level.

The correspondence between the ritual and fiscal system appears even more meaningful if we compare the northern part of the region with the southern territory that was assigned as *jāgīr* to the Rājā of Kullu. Whereas since 1846 a great part of the region was submitted to direct British rule, the region of Rupi in the southern part of the valley was assigned as rent-free *jāgīr* to the then Rājā of Kullu, Thakur Singh. Until Independence, the fiscal system in the two parts differed, and such a diversity seems to have had some effects at ritual level.

Colonial administrators inform us that at the time the revenue settlement was revised in 1868, the ex-Rājā (*jāgīrdār*) and Rupi people:

> applied to the Settlement Officers to revise their record of right so as to bring it into accordance with the existing custom. The effect of the change *was to do away with joint responsibility* within the *koṭhi*, the *jāgīrdār* having to look to each individual landholder for payment of his quota. (*Punjab District Gazetteers* 1917: 159, my emphasis).

Contrary to Parol, the joint ritual responsibility in Rupi never concerns a whole *phāṭī* in one *koṭhi*. It only affects some of their villages, sometimes even separate villages belonging to different *koṭhi*. Wherever joint fiscal responsibility has not been applied or, as in Rupi, has been rapidly abolished, it would seem that the most important ritual unit is not the *koṭhi* but the *phāṭī*, i.e. the group of people who share the services or the forced labour due to the king. The fact that in the north the *koṭhi* is also involved in joint ritual responsibility may have been a result of the application of joint fiscal responsibility introduced during the British period.

In any case, what is certain is that in the whole region of Kullu and in nearby regions, the lists of fiscal *phāṭī* and *koṭhi* reported in the British gazetteers correspond to the multiple *hār* of *phāṭī* and *koṭhi* deities. This should be taken as a trend, since the limits of the ritual territories as well as of the fiscal ones have been subjected in the course of time to slight variations. For instance I could observe in *koṭhi* Jagatsukh (in the north of the region) that one of the three *phāṭī* of the ancient fiscal *koṭhi* has been recently been dropped from the joint ritual responsibility as a consequence of unresolved conflicts.

Thus, the overall correspondence between fiscal-administrative territories and ritual territories does not exclude changes in their respective limits as a consequence of the social and political transformations that have taken place in the region. Even today the administrative system and the ritual system are not rigidly fixed. In fact, village panchayats overlap with ancient fiscal units of the *phāṭī*, still in use. Moreover, at ritual level, transformations are obvious if one takes into account the cults of the so-called 'new deities' (*naī devtā*). At the origin of these new cults, there is usually the 'discovery' in the earth of a statue or of a metallic face, and the consequent manifestation of the deity possessing someone—usually its future medium; it reveals its name and asks to be set up in a temple and adopted by the entire village, whose territory will come under its influence.

We have seen that transformations in the pantheon also took place in the past, before and during the colonial period: some deities might lose their dominion while others might conquer more territories. If, for the past, we are not able to document in detail such transformations in their historical and sociological context, ethnographic data show how such transformations can be linked to political interests or motivations at various levels.

This last section will try to bring to light how in contemporary democratic India, divine territories continue to have politico-ritual relevance and, in some cases, can even influence the delimitation of electoral constituencies.

DIVINE JURISDICTIONS AND ELECTORAL CONSTITUENCIES

Within their own territories, *devī-devtā* express their will on all private or public issues, including the choice of a candidate to regional elections. J. Singh (1989) shows that in nearby Kinnaur, the success of a political leader depends both upon his personal charisma and on the approval he receives from the local deity:

> No discussion of politics in Kinnaur can ever be complete without a mention of ubiquitous devi/devtas. No politician can dare to publicly cross swords with a village deity. Candidates for elections begin their campaigns by presenting offerings to the local deity and by seeking his blessing. Should the devta express his wrath towards a particular candidate, the latter would have an uphill fight on his hands (Singh 1989: 37).

Most political leaders who stand for local elections belong to the region and have strong personal and devotional ties with village deities. A candidate who receives the approval of a local god will be more readily supported by the people living in the god's jurisdiction. In this sense, the *hār* can become an important factor in polls: the larger the *hār*, the more the deity's support can influence the results.

Some episodes that took place after Independence show how political leaders took into account these divine territories when reorganizing the electoral constituencies for the elections for the Himachal Pradesh Assembly in 1967. One example concerns the region of Banjar, 40 km south of Kullu. There the god Śṛṃgā Ṛṣi dominates a *koṭhi* (Banjar) next to the jurisdiction of the Balu Nāg deity, which covers a territory of about three *koṭhi* (Sikari, Tiloknath, and Fatehpur). The worship of Balu Nāg is in the hands of an influential family. One of its members, Beli Ram, an influential political leader, wanted to be elected from a constituency that included the *koṭhi* of Śṛṃgā Ṛṣi. According to Beli Ram's son, the Congress party, in power at the time, refused to give him the ticket and supported another local leader, nearer to this god. Beli Ram then decided to contest the election as an independent candidate. Since his influence in the subdivision controlled by Balu Nāg would have discredited the Congress candidate, the Congress party—he said—managed to prevent the constituency from being cut in two, incorporating the territory of Balu Nāg within a reserved constituency (Ani) and thus eliminating any chance of Beli Ram winning the elections.

The importance of Śṛṃgā Ṛṣi's *hār* in the electoral results is still taken into account by contemporary political leaders. The elected representative of the corresponding constituency to the Legislative Assembly was up until recently Karan Singh, a brother of the Rājā of Kullu, both leaders of the Hindu right-wing party, the BJP.[21] According to a widespread opinion among Balu Nāg's supporters, the Rājā, Mahesvar Singh, is today Śṛṃgā Ṛṣi's ally because he wants the inhabitants of the corresponding constituency to go on supporting his brother. According to them a manifestation of such an alliance takes place at the annual festival of Dussehra, when all the *devī-devtā's* palanquins are brought by their villagers to the capital to pay homage to Raghunāth and to his human representative, the Rājā. Since the latter was up until recently also a member of the New Delhi Parliament, and president of the festival committee,[22] Balu Nāg's people accuse him of using his power to place Śṛṃgā Ṛṣi's palanquin in the highest place during the two main Dussehra processions: immediately to the right of Raghunāth's ceremonial chariot. While they consider instead that their own god should have been given this honorific position by tradition, they accuse the king of interfering in the ritual rules with his electoral politics.

Śṛṃgā Ṛṣi and Balu Nāg are both 'landholding' deities (*muāfidār devtā*), whose *hār* is sufficiently large to assume political weight, at least in regional elections. But even the so-called 'new' deities, devoid of property, and whose worship is recent, can assume an important role in this political-ritual system of alliances. This is the case, for instance, of goddess Pañcālī who is regularly gaining in importance since her current medium, a rather charismatic person, has been active now for about ten years. It is said that the goddess manifests herself with all her power and many people come from far to consult her and ask for her protection. Mahesvar Singh shows a special predilection for this goddess as he thinks she has decisively supported his political career. One of the last episodes taken as proof was when the king was elected to Parliament, in 1998. An inhabitant of the village of Pañcālī recounted the episode to me:

> The party of Raja [the BJP] was not in power at that time and the goddess [consulted by the raja through her medium] said 'if you come here with your heart, I will change the kingdom of Delhi'. Six months later, in 1998, the Government of Delhi changed [the Hindu right came to power], and the Raja became a member of the Indian Parliament!

In order to thank the goddess, the king is said to have contributed to the building of a new temple for her. The consecration ceremony as described by the priest of Pañcālī shows how this goddess, lacking a traditional *hār*, has tried to extend her area of influence by taking advantage of the king's support:

> On the day of the ceremony, the goddess, through her medium, gave an order to a messenger to go to the palace and to tell the king to come to the temple. During the celebrations, the raja started trembling [manifesting divine possession]. When they were setting up the statue of the goddess in the new temple, tears came to the Raja's eyes. There were thousands of people here and they all were scared of what the goddess might do. During the consecration ceremony, the goddess covered [in procession, with her palanquin] more than twenty villages. She was in a violent mood and asked for many sacrifices. [Her palanquin] went to all the nearby localities, to Balu Nāg's *hār*, Markhanda Ṛṣi's *hār*, and also to the village of Alva. There she set up her boundary. Nobody could stop her. Five kilometres away there is the village of Manglore and behind that, Tipri. Her procession made its way there. Thanks to the king and to the participation of all these villages, we offered a great sacrifice [with a lot of animals].

The procession thus enabled the goddess to declare the ambit of her influence in order to recruit new 'supporters'—as people in Kullu often say. Processions are frequent in this part of India for marking a deity's influence within a territory. In the nearby region of Tehri Garhwal, for instance, pilgrimages carried out with the deity's palanquin through several administrative units 'represent and unite the territories in which they occur by circumambulating them' (Sax 1991: 204).[23]

The example of Pañcālī, as well as those described by Sax or by Emerson (reported previously) and concerning the colonial period, show that if the regional pantheon of these Himalayan regions appears 'almost always [to reproduce] some political-ceremonial areas . . . referring to a more or less distant royal past' (Toffin 1993: 100), they are nevertheless still likely to be re-defined and re-shaped on the basis of power relationships between villages or according to the vicissitudes of electoral politics.

Like the kings of the past, the political leaders of Kullu (and not only those belonging to royal families) create ties with the local territorial deities and establish alliances with them, thus provoking some transformations in the structure of the regional pantheon. What is significant is that Mahesvar Singh announced a proposal to assign all the sterile lands of Kullu to temple deities. Had it been accepted, such a gesture would have increased, albeit with sterile lands, the gods' holdings, offering 'new' deities the opportunity to become 'landowning' deities, and reinforcing the identification of Mahesvar Singh in his ritual role as a king, donor of land to deities for whom he demands respect and obedience.

CONCLUSION

In his study on 'small kingdoms' in Orissa, Schnaepel (1994: 153) distinguishes two levels of political-territorial authority corresponding to two categories of deities, having different links with territories: one which is associated with local territories and with deities considered to be autochthonous; and the other covering the whole kingdom and with which deities introduced from the outside are associated.

We have seen that the contrast between these two levels of authorities is also present in Kullu. The god-king Raghunāth, whose worship was introduced from the plains by the king, does not have the same kind of relation with territory that local deities have within their jurisdiction. Raghunāth does not have a specific *hār*, and having neither medium nor palanquin he cannot be consulted directly by the inhabitants of his kingdom. The relationships that villagers maintain with him are limited to royal festivals, when *devī-devtā's* palanquins are brought to the capital to pay him homage. If he is the sovereign authority in the kingdom, over the people and the *devī-devtā*, he does not directly intervene in its prosperity or in the inhabitants' well-being.

By contrast, the *devī-devtā's* relationship with their respective territory does not rely on the sole exercise of a sovereignty in their jurisdiction, but also involves the demonstration of the power (*śakti*) they have over land, the weather, and disease. We have seen god Goli Nāg lose his territory because he let rain pour down uncontrollably, and conversely goddess Pañcālī gained some territory thanks to the power she manifested in satisfying the demands of those who consult her.

Both the models show, however, how the territorial factor is a referent around which the social, political and religious life of the region is organized. Moreover, territory is not solely associated with political power, but is situated, according to Dumont, outside so-called 'ideology'. If 'ideology' is for Dumont 'a system of ideas and values' and includes 'the conscious aspects' of the social system (Dumont 1966), the material presented here shows that territory, far from being reducible to an 'empirical' dimension of the social organization, plays an important role in local discourse and is used as a theoretical and 'ideological' dimension framing social behaviour and religious and ritual activity.

Territory is not only linked to the political sovereignty of Raghunāth or of local gods, but is also taken as a referent for social identity and for the ritual solidarity of the inhabitants of the different *hār*. During village festivals, in which *hārye* of different deities participate, each villager identifies himself with his own 'god-palanquin', who thus becomes a referent not for defining his lineage or his caste, but for defining the place from where he comes or, more exactly, where he lives. As opposed to what Malamoud suggested in relation to the Vedic notion of *grāma*, 'village', here the referent for defining the *hār* is not 'the cohesion of the group which forms it', but rather the very area that constitutes it.

The importance of divine territoriality also explains the sustained political importance of village gods in the different systems of government that have historically succeeded one another in the region. Thanks to their mediums, their palanquins and the inhabitants of their jurisdictions, local gods not only participate in local, political and religious life but, in the past as much as in the present, they establish close alliances with the central form of authority—the Rājā, the British administrators, and now political leaders. In this sense, the cults of *devī-devtā* show that territorial dimensions are not exclusively associated with the political domain of society but are at the very focus of the religious and ritual activities and discourses.

NOTES

1. For a discussion of these theories, cf. (among others) Galey (1989), Dirks (1996), Burghart (1987).
2. The main caste of the region is the Kanet, who now call themselves Rājpūt or Thākur. The Dāgī, of low status, are also numerically important. Brāhmans are present but few in number, or concentrated over a few villages.
3. A change of residence does not necessarily sever the links of a deity with the original *hār*. For instance, village women used to marry outside their natal village and to go to live in the in-laws' village, because of the virilocal system of residence. During periods of hardship, a married woman tends to become closer to her natal village deity again. This deity, consulted through his/her medium, may say that he/she wants to be set up in the in-laws' house and be worshipped there. If this demand is accepted, the deity will settle in the in-laws' house not as a village deity, but as a family or house deity. This does not prevent the woman, once married, from being under the authority of her husband's lineage deity or of her husband's village deity (compare Sax 2000).
4. From that moment on, the official acts of the kingdom were issued in Raghunāth's name. The statue of this god, which according to local stories comes from Ayodhya, is still worshipped by the descendants of the royal family. Four or five priests are in charge of daily worship. They wake the god and his consort, wash them, apply their make up, dress them in royal robes, worship them and seat them on a throne so that visitors to the temple may receive their *darśan* (vision).

5. Vidal (1988: 56) reports how the ruler of Bashar assigned five villages to a deity of the Rohru district to thank him for having brought rain.
6. In Orissa, Kulke (1986: 154) notes that by giving land to gods the Oriya kings wanted to have 'a nominal leadership among the Hindu rajas of east and south India'. According to him 'In order to justify this claim and to strengthen his power, both inside and outside of Orissa, he declared the Lord of Puri the Supreme King of his empire.' Reference to this kind of gift is also found in the dynastic stories of Himalayan kingdoms near Kullu: for the district of Kinnaur, for example, Singh (1989: 88) writes that no act of the state 'was performed without the approval of Bhima Kami, who was regarded as the ruler of the land'. Land gifts to gods are also attested in southern India (Waghorne 1989: 405).
7. This idea of Dumont has been adopted by some historians (cf. Wink 1986) and taken for granted by other scholars (for example: 'in the Indian political tradition, such as it appears for instance in the Arthashastra, territory has an ambiguous and subordinate place', Jaffrelot 1996: 75).
8. Coldstream was responsible for revising the system of land taxation in 1910. The manuscript can be found in the Land Office in Kullu.
9. In various parts of India, village temple deities have land registered in their name. Sontheimer (1964) shows that god as landowner has been the topic of a longstanding discussion, not only among jurists but also among philosophers and theologians who linked this to the debate on the nature of the idol—whether or not it could be considered as the deity's body, endowed with intelligence and sensory organs. Sontheimer shows the difference between positions defended by jurists and by materialistic philosophers, for whom the land was given to a god only in a figurative and metaphoric sense (thus implying that the priest was the real beneficiary), and the popular belief also shared by theistic philosophers, for whom the god was the real owner. This idea, according to the author, was somewhat reified when British administrators in the nineteenth century surveyed the lands of village gods—even if the notion of god was then reduced to an abstract juridical, purely ideal entity. Also Annoussamy (1979), Derrett (1968), and Colas in this volume.
10. In this kind of situation British administrators often considered the god as the subject, thus adopting the local point of view. In some cases I will respect this usage.
11. Vidal analyses some stories collected by Emerson, which illustrate how

a deity could try to impose himself on another deity's territory, and the hostility that this could provoke between the two gods' respective supporters (Vidal 1988: 64ff.). In some cases, the territories for which the gods were competing seem to correspond to those of rival political groups (quoted in Vidal 1988: 55).

12. Nevertheless, temple functionaries, even after officially becoming owners of the temple lands they cultivated, usually continue to offer their services to the temple for fear of provoking the deity's anger. Cf. Vidal (1988) and Berti (2001).
13. They coexist with the panchayat divisions which roughly coincide with the *phāṭī*. While *phāṭī* and *koṭhi* are still referred to by the land administration, it is the panchayat that are otherwise referred to for most other administrative and political purposes.
14. A parallel to these subdivisions can be found in Kinnaur where, instead of *koṭhi* or *phāṭī*, the terms used are *khund* and *ghori* (Raha 1978: 95).
15. The ritual is decided by the deity and may consist in the sacrifice of an animal or in a Brahmanic ritual of vegetable oblations in a sacred fire.
16. For a detailed analysis of this conflict, see Berti (2001: chap. X).
17. It is the god Indra, one of the gods of the classical Indian pantheon. In local myths this god gives rain to the god Takṣak Nāg, implicated in the conflict. The association with Samundra, the primordial ocean, emphasises the capacity to give rain.
18. It means that the brothers Phāl Nāg and Takṣak Nāg sleep in the same bed side by side—i.e. they are very close.
19. The opposite hypothesis seems improbable, since the joint ritual responsibility is applied at all levels of worship units (village, *phāṭī*, *koṭhi*) and for a number of different situations—not only in times of conflict but also for all kinds of ritual work (work to build or repair the temple or the god's images, etc.).
20. We know that the system, at least in theory, has also been used elsewhere in India since medieval times, as well as in some regions of Nepal (Regmi 1978: 142).
21. Even if British administrators have withdrawn the title of rājā from the kings of Kullu, this decision did not have any effect from a ritual point of view: they keep intact their role *vis-à-vis* the local deities as Raghunāth's first devotee and representative. They continue to live in the Kullu palace and to finance worship of Raghunāth. Thus, though

Mahesvar Singh, the actual rājā, has neither power as rājā nor any official title, he still continues to be called 'rājā' by the local people. It is in this sense that the term rājā is used here when referring to him.

22. Since the 1970s, the annual festival in honour of Raghunāth has become a 'National Festival' and is partly financed by the state of Himachal Pradesh. Consequently a Festival Committee has been created, whose President changes according to the party in power. When the rājā was a Member of Parliament, he assumed two roles during the celebrations: a ritual one as delegate of Raghunāth, and a political one as MP and President of the Festival Committee. He alone takes decisions concerning the relative positions to be attributed to the deities' palanquins. The distribution of these positions is crucial in defining the hierarchical relations between villages, and plays an essential role in the alliances between political leaders and groups of villagers (Berti 2005).

23. On palanquin processions in the Katmandu Valley see Toffin (1982)

REFERENCES

Annoussamy, David, 1979. 'La personnalité juridique de l'idole hindoue', *Revue Historique de droit français et étranger*, 4: 611-21.

Barnes, G.C., 1855, *Report on the Settlement in the District of Kangra in the Trans-Sutlej States*, Lahore.

Berti, Daniela, 2001. *La parole des dieux. Rituels de possession en Himalaya indien*, Paris: CNRS Editions.

———, 2005. ' "Now It Is all Politics". Quelques discours sur les transformations de la fete du Daśahrā ā Kullu (Inde du nord)', in *Rites hindous. transferts et transformations*, ed. G. Colas and G. Tarabout, Paris: EHESS, pp. 305-42.

Burghart, Richard, 1987. 'Gifts to the Gods: Power, Property and Ceremonial in Nepal', in *Rituals of Royalty*, ed. D. Cannadine and S. Price, Cambridge: Cambridge University Press, pp. 237-70.

Derrett, J.D.M., 1968. *Religion, Law and the State in India*, Delhi: Oxford University Press.

Diack, A.H., 1897. *Gazetteer of the Kangra District, Parts II to IV (Kulu, Lahul and Spiti)*, Delhi: Indus Publishing Company.

Dirks, Nicholas B., 1996. *The Hollow Crown: Ethnohistory of an Indian Kingdom*, Ann Arbor: The University of Michigan Press.

Dumont, Louis and David Pocock, 1957. 'For a Sociology of India', *Contributions to Indian Sociology*, 1: 7-22.

Dumont, Louis, 1966. *Homo Hierarchicus. Le système des castes et ses implications*, Paris: Gallimard.

Emerson, W.H., 1920. *Mandi State Gazetteer*, Lahore: Government Printing.

———, *Manuscript*, London: Indian Office Library (MSS. EUR. E.321).

Enriquez, C.M.D., 1915. *The Realm of Gods: A Tale of Travel in Kangra, Mandi, Kullu, Chamba, Kishwar, Kashmir, Ladak and Baltistan*, Calcutta/ Simla: Thacker, Spink & Co.

Galey, Jean-Claude, 1989. 'Reconsidering Kingship in India: An Ethnological Perspective', *History and Anthropology*, 4: 123-87.

Jaffrelot, Christophe, 1996. 'La question du territoire en Inde: de l'universalisme aux particularismes?', *Cultures et Conflits*, 21-2: 75-102.

Kapur, Anuradha, 1993. 'Deity to Crusader: The Changing Iconography of Ram', in *Hindus and Others: The Question of Identity in India Today*, ed. G. Pandey, Delhi: Penguin Books India, pp. 74-107.

Kulke, Hermann, 1986 [1978]. 'Early Royal Patronage of the Jagannath Cult', in *The Cult of Jagannath and the Regional Tradition of Orissa*, ed. A. Eschman, H. Kulke and G.C. Tripathi, Delhi: Manohar, pp. 139-55.

Lambert, Helen, 1996. 'Caste, Gender and Locality in Rural Rajasthan', in *Caste Today*, ed. C.J. Fuller, Delhi: Oxford University Press, pp. 93-123.

Lingat, Robert, 1967. *Les sources du droit dans le système traditionnel de l'Inde*, Paris: Mouton.

Lyall, J.B., 1869. *Religious Institutions in Kullu of the Kangra District*, The Punjab Record, vol. IV, 2.

———, 1874. *Report of the Land Revenue Settlement of the Kangra District, Panjab, 1865-72*, Lahore: Central Jail Press.

Malamoud, Charles, 1976. 'Village et forêt dans l'idéologie de l'Inde brâhmanique', *Archives Européennes de Sociologie*, XVII: 3-20.

Punjab District Gazetteers, 1917. Vol. XXX A, *Kangra District*, parts II, III, IV, Lahore: Punjab Government Printing.

Racine, Jean-Luc, 1993. 'Rama et les joueurs de dés. Questions sur la nation indienne', *Hérodote*, 71 (L'Inde et la question nationale): 5-42.

Raha, M.K., 1978. 'Stratification and Religion in a Himalayan Society', in *The Indo-Tibetan Interface*, ed. J.F. Fisher, Paris: Mouton, pp. 83-102.

Regmi, M.C., 1978. *Land Tenure and Taxation in Nepal*, Kathmandu: Ratna Pustak Bhandar.

Sax, William S., 1991. *Mountain Goddess: Gender and Politics in a Himalayan Pilgrimage*, Oxford: Oxford University Press.

———, 2000. 'Residence and Ritual in the Garhwal Himalaya', *Himalaya Past and Present*, IV (1993-1994): 79-114.

Schnaepel, B., 1994. 'Durga and the King: Ethnohistorical Aspects of Politico-Ritual Life in a South Orissan Jungle Kingdom', *Journal of Royal Anthropological Institute (n.s)*, 1: 145-66.

Singh, Jogishwar, 1989. *Bank, Gods and Government: Institutional and Informal Credit Structure in a Remote and Ṭribal Indian District (Kinnaur, Himachal Pradesh 1960-1985)*, Wiesbaden: Franz Steiner Verlag.

Sontheimer, Gunther-Dietz, 1964. 'Religious Endowments in India: The Juristic Personality of Hindu Deities', *Zeitschrift für Verglichende Rechts Wissenschaft*, 87: 44-100.

Toffin, Gérard, 1982. 'Analyse structurale d'une fête communale néwar: le *deś jātrā* de Panauti', *L'Homme*, XXII: 57-89.

———, 1993. 'Le territoire des dieux. Essai sur la géographie politique du panthéon de la Vallée du Népal', in *Classer les dieux? Des panthéons en Asie du Sud*, ed. V. Bouillier and G. Toffin, Paris: EHESS, pp. 99-129.

Vidal, Denis, 1988. *Le culte des divinités locales dans une région de l'Himachal Pradesh*. Paris: Editions de l'ORSTOM.

Waghorne, Joan P., 1989. 'From Robber Baron to Royal Servant of God? Gaining a Divine Body in South India', in *Criminal Gods and Demon Devotees: Essays on the Guardians of Popular Hinduism*, ed. A. Hiltebeitel, Albany: State University of New York Press, pp. 405-26.

Wink, André, 1986. *Land and Sovereignty in India: Agrarian Society and Politics under the Eighteenth-Century Maratha Svarâjya*, Cambridge: Cambridge University Press.

9

Mapping the Nation's Body: Territorial Processions in Propaganda Videos of the Hindu Right

CHRISTIANE BROSIUS

This paper discusses the creation of Indianness as it was generated and put on display by means of employing specific notions of territory and society in the video media of the Hindu Right in India during the early days of economic liberalization.[1] My focus will be on how and why particular visuals, metaphors and narratives came to be combined through the performative practice of 'patriotic pilgrimage' (*deshbhakti ki teerth yatra*) or procession in the late 1980s and 1990s. Through the yatras, the Hindu nationalist agents intended to communicate and heighten an idea of national identity by linking it to spatial, somatic, and familial metaphors. In this chain of associations and cross-references, the nation became identified with territory, territory became personified as a human being with a biography (Mother India, *Bharat Mata*) nurturing society and providing national identity, harmony, and welfare.

In the discussion of two major territorial processions conducted by the BJP with the support of different Hindu Right organizations and at various stages between 1990 and 1992, a variety of concepts is explored which make up the complex rhetoric of territorial identity. The two videos presented here, *From the Sea to the River Saryu* and *Unity Pilgrimage*, document nationalist processions led by the BJP, organized by a range of representatives within the Sangh Parivar.[2] Before the individual processions and the videos made on them are introduced, some general issues on the context shall be examined.

The processions and videos reflect the Sangh Parivar agents' attempt to shape common denominators for a notion of Hindu superiority and mainstream culture. In this process, the Hindu nationalist organizations, making up a diverse and heterogeneous fabric, presented themselves as a united brotherhood and as speakers of the so-called 'people's will for revolutionary national reawakening'. For the BJP, these patriotic pilgrimages were ideal and spectacular means of mass-education and contact. Says Narendra Modi, the All-India Secretary of the party at the time of the interview and key organizer of several BJP processions in the 1990s:[3] 'Through yatra you can have mass contact! It is a . . . mass communication system. It's not simply a cultural, religious, traditional activity . . . it was there in my country since the last thousands years. . . . But even today we are feeling that *direct* communication, . . . *heart to heart talking*, is the best way' (personal interview, June 1997).

The rhetoric of patriotic pilgrimage demonstrates that, in order to project itself as a 'party of the people', the BJP engaged in a large project of fusing Hindutva ideology and politics, drawing heavily on the wide sphere of popular culture, particularly religious imagery, narratives and practices. The conscious blurring is reflected in this extract from an interview conducted with L.K. Advani.[4]

> I hold that in India the religious appeal is very intense, *extremely* intense. It cuts across all caste and linguistic divisions. So, when we undertook—I undertook—this *rath yatra* (chariot procession) to affirm that is a temple, this should be a temple, and that the whole country should contribute towards the construction of the (Ram) temple (in Ayodhya) . . . we tried to interpret it as a political campaign against pseudo-secularism. But there were *masses* who viewed it as a religious issue. And so there was a *massive* appeal. (personal interview, February 1997)

The standard argument of the Hindu Right was that a Ram temple once stood at the site of the Babri mosque, a building that was constructed under the Mughal invader Babur's rule in 1528. Not only had it been a temple to worship Ram but allegedly it had been no less than his birthplace. Turned into a symbol of century-long suppression and humiliation of the 'Hindu psyche', the reconstruction of the 'lost' Ram temple at the same site came to be identified with the resurrection of Hindu pride, Hindu history, and Hindu territory. The procession of 1989 served to spread and dramatize this message by performative means. As Advani put it elsewhere, pilgrimage became a means to draw the 'map of nationalism'.[5] In an issue of the BJP magazine *BJP Today* (vol. 6, no. 11, June 1997: 6), the leader states that 'Yatra has a unique significance in Indian tradition and national life. It is not only a spiritual exertion in the form of a journey, undertaken with reverence and a measure of toil, but also an exercise in the experience and assertion of India's millennia-old cultural civilisational unity.' These comments give a clear indication that territorial procession was desired as a vital mode of political mobilization and 'national unification' because, as the political leader proclaims, 'it cuts across all caste and linguistic divisions'.

It requires mentioning at this point that political parties (as well as social reformists) in India have struggled with the riddle of 'unity in diversity' since the nineteenth century. For the Hindu nationalists to find common denominators that would bridge and bond the Hindu people despite their regional, linguistic and/or religious or sectarian loyalties has so far been an almost impossible task. Organizers of the Ram Rath Yatra claimed that it challenged the government in power and other parties with what Advani coined as 'pseudo-secularism'. With this, he sought to shape a notion of opportunist governance that only pretended to be truly secular in that in the distribution of power and access to it, it did not discriminate on the basis of either religion or caste. However, so the argument runs, religion and caste proved to play a major role in politics and increased fragmentation. The BJP's critique was that the Hindu people had to bear the cost of such politics by being sidelined in the favour of widespread 'pampering' of minorities such as the Muslims, or of the Dalits on the levels of employment and education and that, likewise, those minority groups abused such privileges and instrumentalized them to put pressure on the government. The projection of Ram as a 'national leader' and divine king who accepts food even from Shabri, an 'untouchable' woman or the appropriation of pilgrimage as a religious custom practised by all Hindus (and members of other religions), were part of an effort to create a virtual storehouse of 'shared' heroes and histories, ideals and practices. India's diversity becomes particularly evident and loaded with tension during election times, when, despite the rhetoric of unity, the BJP addresses its electorate according to caste and religious categories, hoping to gain the support of whole 'vote-banks' (see Shah 1998). In fact, the political action of the BJP diverges from the official ideology of unity and harmony that is presented in the procession videos. Running below the surface of the rhetoric of harmony is a rhetoric of conflict and threat that leads towards a heightening of tensions between members of various castes and religions. As a consequence, such electoral politics are based on the creation of social tensions.

The aim of the processions in the early 1990s was to transform the political and public sphere in order to pave the ground for the BJP,—then still in the opposition, to take power at the centre. Often processions preceded or paralleled State Assembly or General elections. The Ram Rath Yatra, for instance, documented in the video *From the Sea* was conducted by then BJP president Lal Krishna Advani in autumn 1990, a few months before the General Elections in 1991, where, for the first time, the BJP saw 54 of its members in Parliament.[6] The territorial processions explored here show clearly that a key rhetoric of challenging the government was enacted through reference to the notion of territory on geographical, metaphorical, and performative levels, all interconnected. Through territorial processions, territory was made 'real', visible and tactile. Furthermore, it became a catalyst for the creation of social and political conflict through which the BJP could claim and assert legitimacy and authority. With the videos the party attempted to further propagate its agenda and display itself as a legitimate representative of the 'people's will'. The videos examined here did not solely address ordinary voters. They were intended to mobilize Sangh Parivar activists and grassroots networks. A tension-filled field of discourse was shaped, by which the Sangh Parivar could rhetorically attack secular government and Muslim groups, stereotyping them as manipulating, aggressive, or destructive anti-national forces. In doing so, 'counter'-aggression could be legitimized and even sanctified. Processions and procession videos are thus also connected with a chain of violent clashes between Hindus and Muslims as well as the demolition of the disputed Babri mosque in Ayodhya on 6 December 1992 by thousands of male Hindutva supporters, that in return sparked off nation-wide rioting in which approximately 2000 people died and many more made homeless and traumatized.[7]

If we explore procession videos, we also need to ask how the 'message' was brought to the audiences. And who, for instance, made the video? Around 1990, the video production house Jain Studios in New Delhi was one of the few studios that had specialized in political marketing and offered political agents the technological facilities and professional staff to make videos in a few weeks, sometimes even days. At that time, there were hardly any alternatives of media production to the official state broadcaster, Doordarshan (DD; see Ohm 1999, Butcher 2003), a part of the Ministry of Information and Broadcasting that was clearly biased towards the respective party in power. Video technology had only just arrived in the mid-1980s and Jain Studios quickly became a welcome alternative and way to circumvent the monopolization of DD through the government. The videos made by Jain Studios were not restricted in time and subject, but tailored to the agenda and expectations of the clients. To improve the impact of political propaganda for election purposes, Jain Studios set up a fleet of mobile vans, known as *Videos on Wheels*, or VOW. These vans could be hired by individual politicians and parties for political campaigns. VOW did not only facilitate the circumvention of government monopolies and restrictions, it enabled a dissemination that went beyond the existing infrastructure of privately owned television-sets. Even in the late 1980s, television sets were luxury items, particularly in rural areas. VOW offered to present the client's message as a 'packaged event', along with a chain of film clips from famous Hindi movies, with popular devotional or pop songs or political speeches. Last but not least, videos were easy to copy and not exorbitantly expensive and could be easily distributed among party and cadre workers. Besides BJP leaders even politicians such as Rajiv Gandhi and film star-turned-chief minister N.T. Rama Rao turned to Jain Studios to get additional support for their local election campaigns.[8] This way, opposition parties could also circumvent censorship and address their audiences 'directly'. In the case of propaganda videos made for the BJP or the Sangh Parivar as a whole, the sidelining of the government monopoly on media distribution also succeeded through the systematic use of the elaborate networks of grassroots networks of the RSS and BJP offices. With respect to propaganda videos such as *From the Sea to the River*, the studio's facilities ensured that enough video copies were provided to party members and leaders. These made further copies of the videos, thus producing a snowball-system through which thousands of video films could then be distributed. In BJP shops, these sold at Rs 100 each. They were shown at private and semi-private meetings, on roof-tops, in courtyards, at public squares, folk and religious festivals and political meetings, to name only a few occasions. It is difficult to distinguish how many copies of a video circulated, where and how they were received by audiences. But they are to be seen as an important complement to political face-to-face communication and emotional mobilization. And their rhetoric certainly enables us to gain a deeper understanding of Hindutva ideology and practices.

Let us now take a closer look at the audio-visual material. Two issues based on crisis and confrontation gained momentum in the early 1990s and find reflection in the procession videos. They are the support of the BJP for the Ayodhya campaign and the Kashmir issue, another highly emotive issue used to mobilize against regional separatism and militancy in the northern province bordering Pakistan. The first video, *Sagar se Saryu tak* (*From the Sea to the [River] Saryu*, 1990, Hindi, produced by Jain Studios,[9] documents and accompanies then party president L.K. Advani on his Ram Rath Yatra from Somnath, a sacred town by the sea in Gujarat, and site of a Jyotirlinga temple that was reconstructed in the 1950s, towards Ayodhya, another sacred city by the banks of the Saryu in Uttar Pradesh, a city said to have been the capital of Ram's kingdom. Time and again Advani is shown taking a bath in the jubilant crowds following and receiving him along the route of 10,000 kilometres. One aim of the procession was to increase pressure both on the government and Muslim groups to 'hand over' the Babri mosque so that the requested Ram temple could be built.

How were the religious symbols selected and transferred into the political domain? Ram is not only one of the main gods in the Hindu pantheon, the Sangh Parivar defines him as a symbol of national unity and identity. With such a definition, the Sangh could present the destruction of an imagined Ram temple for the purpose of building the Babri mosque as a sign of brutal invasion and ongoing humiliation. The claim, as mentioned above, was that with the reconstruction of the temple at the same spot, the alleged primordial hurt 'Hindu sentiment' and lost home of the Hindu people could be recreated and revitalized. The Ram Rath Yatra was executed to further dramatize this claim by actually performing the return of Ram from exile as it was narrated in the *Ramayana*, thus restoring the former glory of the 'lost' Hindu kingdom. At the same time, allegorical reference is made to the *Mahabharata* also: Krishna who authorizes Arjuna to fight a holy war against his cousins in order to reinstall order on earth, and in the video film a bazaar print of Krishna and Arjuna placed on the chariot in the battle is repeatedly shown. In demanding the substitution of 'the symbol of slavery' with a 'symbol of national pride and self-confidence', the video's voice-over commentary relates this act to the Hindu people's liberation.

Ekta Yatra Vande Mataram (Unity Procession, Hail to Mother India, 1992, Hindi; also *Unity Pilgrimage*), a video produced by Matthew S., a former employee of Jain Studios in 1992, is presented as a 'living map of India' related to another patriotic pilgrimage that was undertaken by then party president Murli Manohar Joshi, a VHP hardliner (Jaffrelot 1996: 450 ff.), from Kanyakumari, at the southernmost tip of the Indian Peninsula, to Srinagar in the contested state of Kashmir between 11 December 1991 and 26 January 1992 (Republic Day), covering a distance of several thousand kilometres. The proclaimed aim of the patriotic pilgrimage was to hoist the national flag over the main bazaar of Kashmir's provincial capital, Srinagar, in order to promote India's unity in the light of growing feelings of separatism and alienation among the Muslim majority in Kashmir from the politics conducted in India's capital Delhi. Instead of placing Ram at centre-stage, this procession promoted Mother India as the key figure of mobilization. Her identification with the national territory and welfare enabled the BJP to perform narratives of crisis and threat. The voice-over commentary in *Unity Pilgrimage* announces that the procession was to 'preach patriotism, to challenge the politics of the bomb and the gun with the intense power of *Vande Mataram*.[10] From the sea to the mountains . . . the Ekta Yatra was formulated to manifest patriotism as national unity' (Fig. 9.1). Through this political iconography, the reference to the

Fig. 9.1. Mother India, panel mounted on the back of a procession chariot. Photograph taken at the Swarna Jayanti Rath Yatra, 1997 (photograph: C.B.).

unofficial anthem, 'Vande Mataram' and the symbolic act of flag hoisting, the clear message was communicated that Kashmir will always remain part of Indian territory and that no alien force should dare to further threaten this 'sacred' organism and homeland of the 'real' Indian people.

Both videos' strategies of persuading their viewers by promising them better access to, or security of, societal and political resources were part of calculated politics of electioneering and winning votes of particular groups, especially of the urbanized high-caste middle classes. A key narrative of mobilization was that of the Hindu people's search for 'their home territory', or soil.

MAPPING THE NATION-HOME

The mapping of identity aligns maps, somatic metaphors, and nationalist politics to the Hindutva effort to invoke in the viewers a realist feeling of *Heimat* (homeland) by means of paying devotion to the nation (*deshbhakti bhav*). With this notion declared to be a common denominator of Indianness, the Indian people could simultaneously be imagined, represented, and positioned as an entity. Likewise, the audiences could be shaped into an ideal disciplined, moral, and sacred communion of brothers and sons of Mother India. *Heimat* referred this familial unit to a territory in which it was said to be rooted, and where it could safely dwell.

Both videos propose that this primordial desire for *Heimat* was not only endangered but destroyed in the process of history as well as current politics. The fundamental basis of national identity was threatened by territorial (separatist) claims made by all sorts of particularistic groups. For example, *Unity Pilgrimage* carries an animated scene showing a map of India as it virtually disintegrates, 'losing' its most problematic states Punjab, Assam, and Kashmir to separatist forces. As a consequence, so the argument went, the Hindu people became 'refugees in their own country'. In *From the Sea to the River* this homelessness can be assured by claiming back 'lost' territory and rebuilding the Ram temple; in *Unity Pilgrimage,* home can be reinstalled if the 'displaced' Hindu people can be granted that Kashmir will always remain a part of India. The necessity of 'coming home' is heightened through the association of the Hindu people with the territorial body of the nation as well as the creation of a familial relationship between the citizenry as children of Mother India. People, mother, and nation form a natural organism connected through mutual interdependence. Territorial processions and devotion, according to Hindutva ideologue Barthwal in a book on Bharat Mata, are linked to the task to 'wake us up to the urgent and paramount need for putting our Hindu house in order for ensuring the eradication of all such blots of foreign domination' (Barthwal 1997: 4).

To put the 'Hindutva house in order', the two key mythic figures of Ram and Bharat Mata give a face and a body, a history and a family-tree, but most of all, a 'virtual human touch', to the rather abstract idea of the nation and national identity. Quite like the geographic and symbolic sites of Ayodhya and Kashmir, Ram and Mother India are meant to serve as 'emblems' and catalysts for the creation of models of human agency (we have to defend ourselves and our home) as well as the elaboration of invisible borders and strategies of inclusion and exclusion on this map of imagined Indianness (intruders need to kept out/shown their place). Furthermore, because they offer scope for the identification and projection of fears, desires, and hopes, Bharat Mata and Ram can be employed to increase drama and conflict, feelings of pleasure and discomfort in the viewer. The then government in power and the Muslims are presented as essentially anti-national because they do not recognize the importance of Ram and Mother India for the formation of national identity and thus not the relevance of territorial devotion.

The procession videos enabled Hindutva spokespeople to successively construct layer upon layer of a complex net of cartographic practices and spatial metaphors, so dense that the display of connections seemed credible and real. This comes close to what Walter Benjamin in his groundbreaking essay 'The Work of Art in the Age of Mechanical Reproduction' (1973, written in 1935) meant when he referred the power of 'surgery' of the camera eye to the invisible signature of the technology by which an apparatus-free patterning of experience could be created that goes 'under the viewer's skin' as a 'seamless reality'[11] or second nature. Special effects, editing, the use of mixed media such as comics and footage from other films, or a voice-over commentary, devotional songs, and quotes from scriptures were the means used to heighten this virtual reality. Compared to the actual procession, in particular the technique of editing diverse footage heightened the idea of Hindutva as a legitimate authority and the procession as 'successful' event (even though, for example, the *Unity Pilgrimage*, to some extent, failed to be successful). The images and narratives employed in this performative flow were consciously appropriated from the familiar spheres of popular culture, be it from mythological texts or religious practice, but also from official state rhetoric and political iconography. Once integrated into Hindutva's diverse pantheon of deities and heroic martyrs, they could then be reinterpreted and moulded into an authoritarian and linear narrative.

THE FUSION OF MAPS AND TERRITORIAL PRACTICES

Both *From the Sea to the River* and *Unity Pilgrimage* create notions of Indianness by identifying sacred with national territory and the sacred family of Hindus with the Indian citizenry by drawing upon the popular practice of pilgrimage. The videos indicate that Hindutva's re-mapping strategies are a result of, reaction to, and partly fusion of, various spatial concepts and practices. First, there is the notion of a sacred land as it evolved with the ritual of religious pilgrimage and cosmological maps. Second, there was a range of cartographic maps and picturesque landscapes deriving from colonial activities in India. Third, we find maps that shaped with the rise of the secular state in post-colonial India. The videos document that Hindutva maps are based upon, or against, those various territorial notions and practices. Using processions, the BJP attempted to develop an alternative 'counter-map' as a stage on which narratives of home and exile, conflict and resolution could be displayed and attributed with the idea of the national identity and devotion to the country.

PILGRIMAGE AND SACRED TERRITORY

From the Sea carries a lot of footage of pilgrims bathing in a river or singing devotional songs while circumambulating a sacred shrine. The 'sacredness' of the journey undertaken by Advani as well as Joshi is repeatedly mentioned. This reference to both the sacredness of soil and pilgrimage is not coincidental. Pilgrimage maps and practices are deeply intertwined with everyday or special ritual practices in India and have been crucial factors of community constitution. As an expression of religious duty and loyalty, pilgrimage is an activity to be performed by every devout Hindu, irrespective of his or her caste or sect. It leads the pilgrim a step closer to salvation (*moksha*). And it temporarily detaches him or her from everyday bindings, giving utmost priority to the collective experience and performance of belief and suggesting an intimate closeness to the divine. The meaning of *yatra* is 'journey', but the term is generally associated with the journey of a *yatri* (traveller, pilgrim) to a holy place or *tirtha,* that is a crossing place and site where the borders between the sacred and mundane, micro- and macro-cosm, oscillate where the devotee can be close to the divine. Often, these sacred zones are located on the banks of particular rivers or lakes, for water, often coming from springs high up in the mountains, is perceived as sacred as well as liminal. In fact, the physical movement practised in the yatra, it is implied, is sacred and fulfils a purifying function. The first Hindutva procession to draw upon the idea of sacred territory and purifying water was the Ektamata Yatra, conducted by the Vishva Hindu Parishad (VHP) in 1983 to kick off the Ayodhya controversy by organizing hundreds of large and smaller processions starting from different sites in India and Nepal and assembling in Nagpur where the RSS was founded and has its headquarters (see McKean 1996; Jaffrelot 1996).

The notion of pilgrimage enabled the BJP to project the ideal Indian citizen as a devotee (Fig. 9.2) and the vision of a sacred brotherhood unified through ancient devotional practices and rituals, themselves intrinsically linked to territory (Fig. 9.3). Transposed from the religious to the political level, the cult and devotion of the god or goddess, the site, shrine and pilgrim activities were tied up with the cult of the nation state, with devotion to the nation being defined as salvation from allegedly bad governance. The citizens-as-pilgrims could be fused into an imaginary entity of equals. With these associations, as mentioned above, the BJP attempted to tackle and gloss over the diversity of Hindu society. Ram and Mother India were consciously displayed as 'casteless' deities. In turning them into national icons rather than holding on to a particular religious

Fig. 9.2. Devotee immersed in prayer by a river.
Sangh Parivar new year card, 1990s. Artist: Balraj, New Delhi

Fig. 9.3: 'The Real Existence of the Race of the Aryas'.
Saints seated on the map of India, performing a fire ritual.
Sangh Parivar book cover, 1990s.

code and practice, the BJP could increase its self-presentation as a revolutionary and secular party that was concerned with the elimination of difference. This way, the party attempted to challenge the others by accusing them of privileging ('pampering', or 'vote-banking') particular castes for electoral purposes. It further tried to circumvent a fragmentation of the electorate through reservation politics that had been enforced in the late 1980s and that granted religious minorities and particular castes access to government jobs and to education in the context of the Mandal Report (Shah 1998).

The country is imagined as a sacred body covered by a complex network of pilgrimage routes and sites, each linked and referring to the other. This creation of direct references also corresponds with the pilgrimage practice of ritual circumambulation (*pradakshina*). One of the most well-known nets of sacred sites and pilgrimage routes in India is made up of the four main pilgrimage sites, Badrinath, Puri, Rameswaram, and Dwarka. The Sangh Parivar makes use of the sacred cartography (Fig. 9.4). As Diana Eck has elaborated, India in Hindu sacred geography is covered by polycentric and plural nets of pilgrimage sites, rivers, temples, the sea, and snow-clad mountains where sacred stories are enacted, where the gods and goddesses descend, dwell, and mingle with human beings, and where every site has been sanctified and has a story to tell. The organizers of the political processions drew upon this topography, trusting that most Hindus were familiar with the idea of sacred landscape. When L.K. Advani crossed the country in his chariot, from the sacred site of Somnath to that of Ayodhya, he conjured up the idea of the Hindu gods' epiphany on earth, to a journey through 'their' kingdoms in which the earth is sanctified, very much as in the illustration of Bharat Mata leading 'her' people through a sacred landscape, here followed by Hindutva icons such as M.S. Golwalkar, K.B. Hedgewar or Swami Vivekananda (Fig. 9.5).[12]

The idea of the sacred national territory is common to most national movements claiming sovereignty. In India, it was linked to the struggle for independence from colonial rule. The most militant vision of territorial passion was developed in the pamphlet *Hindutva: Who is a Hindu?* (1989 [1923]) by Veer D. Savarkar. This ideologue

Fig. 9.4: 'The Universal Guru Shri Shankaracharya'. First Adi Shankaracharya seated on map of India, with four sacred sites. Sangh Parivar book cover.

Fig. 9.5: Bharat Mata leading her sons through a sacred landscape. Sangh Parivar book cover, *Our Festivals*, by H.V. Seshadri, published by the Hindu Council in Bangalore, 1983.

considered territorial devotion as a tool of resistance against an external threat, colonial oppression and Islamic infiltration, as well as a cure to the internal threat of diversity within Hindu society. Savarkar's concept was that in their love for the national territory, the Hindu people would finally transgress the social and religious boundaries dividing them, and become 'one caste' of Hindus, a sacred brotherhood (Savarkar 1989: 129-36). Savarkar drew upon the idea that territory is loaded with sacred and national history, that the land of the Hindus is both a playground of the gods, and a 'sacred' graveyard for heroic martyrs:

> Ah! Every hill and dell is instinct with memories. . . . Here the divine Cowherd (Krishna) played on his flute. . . . Here the son of Bandabahadur was hacked to pieces before the eyes of his father. . . . Every stone here has a story of martyrdom to tell! Every inch of thy soil, O Mother! has been a sacrificial ground! (Savarkar 1989: 112)

Religious and national devotion are tied together by means of the highest ideal of selflessness through martyrdom for the nation. But Savarkar's comment is also reminiscent of the myth of the dismemberment of goddess Sati's dead corpse. Here, the places where Sati's limbs fell are said to have become *pithas*.[13] The play on this Hindu myth not only involves a gendering of landscape and divine action, but a certain degree of eroticism. Savarkar's citation further relates to the importance of collective remembrance through worship of the earth.

The BJP profited from such a complexity of the sacred landscape: For the Unity Pilgrimage, for example, Narendra Modi had the soil of martyrs from all over the country collected in urns (*kalash)* and incorporated in a martyr's cult. National memorials were revered as if they were sites inhabited by the divine (*pitha*). Above, I mentioned that the BJP processions attempt to re-map India as *Heimat,* and it is in the performance of such imagined landscapes, I argue, that the notion of homeland is most strongly dramatized and instrumentalized as a tool for the intimate loyalty of the citizen to the nation.

Both videos carry a lot of footage of the chariot (*rath*) on which the leaders traverse the country from west to east, and from south to north. The chariot is another 'link-image'. Advani's *rath* in 1990 was a van with attached hoardings of religious symbols such as the lotus flower, 'drawn' by two cut-out lions mounted on each side of the van. In 1991, Joshi's mode of transport for the Unity Pilgrimage was also a converted Toyota van, 'dressed up' as a Hindu temple. On the one hand, the chariot enables association with religious festivals and pilgrim processions during which deities are said to visit the earth and make themselves and their laws manifest. Catching a glimpse of the gods while they are on such a journey through the countryside is meant to be an event of particular religious significance for every worshipper. The participation in such a festive act is itself defined as a sacred and blessing experience (*darshan lena*). On the other hand, the chariot is also a reference to the *Mahabharata*, in which the noble warrior Arjun rides into battle against his enemy-cousins, accompanied and authorized by the god Krishna.[14] These references clearly play upon the potential of the procession to create charismatic leadership and enhance violence.

Pilgrimage videos such as *From the Sea to the River* utilize their Hindu audience's assumed familiarity with the fact that, in pilgrimage, sacred and profane maps overlap, and are tied to each other in manifold meaningful ways, thus leaving scope for the attribution of historical events and sites. However, with those processions, the Hindutva representatives have turned the concept of pilgrimage upside down. Instead of asking the Indian citizenry to go on a pilgrimage, they did it themselves by inventing 'new' pilgrimage routes, sites, and reasons for pilgrimage, merging these with already established routes and sites. Such a strategy reminds us of what sociologist Veena Das calls a reference to ideas of the 'traditional community as a resource for building an alternative vision of . . . modernity' (Das 1995: 53). The idea of alternative visions of modernity is important in that the BJP must not be seen as a party that attempts to return to the past, but that employs visions of the past in order to place and interpret the present in a new light.

MAPS OF INVASION AND COLONIZATION

References to pilgrimage maps and practices are but one frame of reference in the procession videos. To a great extent, they serve the purpose of shaping ideas of a 'Golden Hindu Age'. Juxtaposed with another frame of territorial references, this imaginary 'Arcadia' is further heightened. How is this performed? The sacredness of India, and the city of Ayodhya in particular, is evoked in a montage scene in *From the Sea to the River*. The commentary claims that the task is to rebuild the 'lost Hindu sentiment' and homeland by means of reconstructing Ram's alleged birth-temple at the site of the Babri mosque. In an animated scene, a revolving globe of the world emerges out of the dark, referring to the cosmic creation of the world. The globe moves towards the camera, which then takes a close-up shot of 'Greater India' (*Akhand Bharat*). This is in association to a claim within the Sangh Parivar based on the assumption that the national territory should be identical with the 'cultural' space of Hindu spread from Afghanistan to Singapore. Ayodhya is marked by a star (Fig. 9.6). The commentary furthermore mentions that by Ram's grace Bharat, pre-Mughal India, was en-

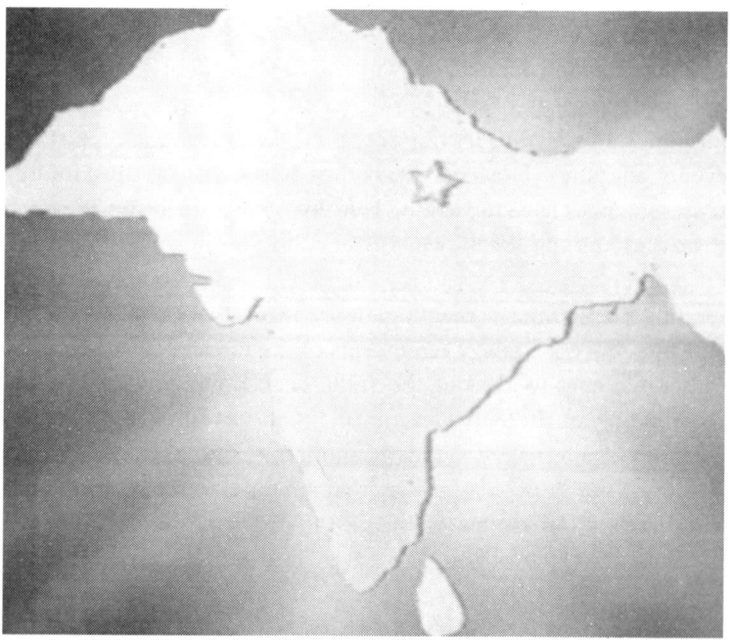

Fig. 9.6: Map of Greater India with the sacred town of Ayodhya highlighted as star. Video still from *From the Sea to the River*.

lightened by sacred knowledge. Therewith follows the footage of a video film allegedly depicting Mughals invading India in 1528 very much like a news-report (Fig. 9.7). We learn that under Mir Baqi, Babur's general, the Ram temple was destroyed and replaced by the mosque. The commentary claims that Ram was, is, and will always remain, a major pillar of Indianness:

Why did the Muslims do this? They didn't want to build a place of worship, they wanted to break the symbol of India's pride. The mosque is the symbol of their military victory. And a symbol of India's defeat and slavery. We have to remove this symbol of slavery . . . and build a temple on that place, a symbol of national pride and self-confidence. This is our national *dharma*.

Shots of pilgrims are added to enhance the idea of a mass movement, identifying the citizenry with pilgrims. The voice-over continues: 'It is our fortune to sacrifice ourselves for this task. For centuries Hindus have been struggling for this and the clarion call of this revolution never ceased.' Over the cartoon images of Hindus fighting Muslim forces on the battlefield, a devotional song now

Fig. 9.7: *Invading Mughals* Video still from *From the Sea to the River.*

begins to talk about the lovers and devotees of freedom who went out to a battle in the name of Ram. Throughout the video, landscape, religious sites and history are thus re-invested with meaning and transposed into sites of alleged primordial nationality.

The employment of sites is a strategy to create a mental map and history of oppression and humiliation of Hindus *versus* the passionate courage of Hindus to challenge those threats. This polarization, by means of drawing upon iconographies of war and peace, is evident in both procession-videos, carried in countless shots of the sun rising over the sacred townscape, *ghats* leading down to a bathing site and bathing devotees of Ayodhya, or snow-clad mountains, wild rivers, and the lakes of Kashmir. Against these pleasure-promising shots of seemingly untouched landscapes, the footage of territorial invasions is crudely inserted. They are to enhance in the viewers feelings of discomfort and anxiety through the voice-over's reference to ongoing geographic threat and national fragmentation. The reference to Mughal invasion projects the Hindus as the original inhabitants and inheritors of the land, a people made homeless, and united in their previous incapacity to assemble in solidarity under a stern (Hindu) leadership. In the montage of sights of sacred rivers versus footage of invaders galloping across Indian soil, the videos create a mental map of 'shields of protection and security . . . against the foreign aggressors' and 'bulwarks for preserving the nation's psyche' (Barthwal 1997: 4).

What we find in this re-interpretation of history is a fragmentation of two pasts. Indianness is trapped between a pre-Mughal utopia of cosmological maps and paradisiacal landscapes and a cartography of foreign infiltration and alienation that stretches from the Mughal Empire to the Nehruvian model of the secular state. It is interesting that this iconography was appropriated and put on display through the lens of what had already been elaborated as 'typically' Indian (and Muslim) by colonial and orientalist agents. Reflected in this is a fascination with (1) the potential of European picturesque landscape paintings and early photography to translate notions of, and a desire for the poetry of idyllic Arcadian settings; (2) the disciplining power of modern mapping practices (see Archer 1980: 7; Edney 1997: 54-62) through which land and people could be measured and classified; and (3) the stereotype of an essentially aggressive Islam.

The British rulers had introduced the notion of cartography as an ideological as well as pragmatic instrument of colonial power and expansion. The first map of 'Hindoostan' was published in 1782 (Kalpagam 1995: PE87). According to Matthew Edney, this 'provided the definitive image of India for the British and European public' (Edney 1997: 9), but also for Indian nationalists of various kinds. For the first time, India could be gazed upon and conceptualized as a single, self-referential geographical unit. In response to this, Veer Savarkar outlined classifications and a history of Hinduness, personifying territorial identity as a primordial given and sacred land (*punyabhoomi*) to the Hindu 'race' (*jati*).[15]

'COUNTER-MAPS' FOR INDIA'S SONS

The processions and spatial concepts documented in the edited scenes described above are the foundation-stone on which the BJP attempted to establish 'counter-maps'. The interpretation of territory through these maps was to challenge previous maps and notions of nationality that, so the argument runs, led to a weakening of Hinduness. The alternative maps are rhetorical strategies to stage the erasure of sites of foreign rule from the topography of collective memory by their replacement with 'authentic' Indian sites. As mentioned above, an important factor through which the Sangh Parivar attempted to bring national devotion to a diverse and disseminated audience was the personification of the nation in the figure of Bharat Mata and of governance in the figure of the semi-divine warrior, Ram. Mother India's 'career' evolved from a colonial and orientalist context that refined a gendered language of nationalism, for example in identifying India as a beautiful and chaste woman, and as the keeper of tradition and familial values and stability (Chatterjee 1995). In order to project narratives of national self-empowerment and devotion against those of colonial humiliation, anti-colonial agents in the late nineteenth century created a nationalist 'counter-figure', Bharat Mata.

This impacts on the 'counter-maps' produced in the BJP processions. In *Unity Pilgrimage*, the voice-over commentary recapitulates the

Mughal and colonial period. Here, heroic agency and self-sacrifice against foreign oppression became intertwined with the idea of 'natural' devotion for the Motherland. In the commentary, Mother India's traditional dress personifies not only a Hindu woman's chastity but calls attention to the identification of territory with a woman's body (Fig. 9.8):

> History is a witness that Indian heroes have never left the sari of Mother India empty with their sacrifices. Guru Gobind Singh, Shivaji, Rani Lakshmibai, Chandrashekar Azad, Bhagat Singh, heroes like these, gave their sacrifices willingly, along with Savarkar and Hedgewar, Shyama Prasad Mookerjee and Deendayal Upadhyaya. They gave the coming generation the eternal message of patriotism.

Fig. 9.8: Mother India's body as Greater India.
Sangh Parivar new year card, 1990s.

The people's fate could be identified with and tied both to the life and body of the personified nation and the generations of martyrs who allegedly all died to protect Bharat Mata's integrity and honour. Allegedly, those figures gave their life for the territorial sovereignty and independence of their mother, thus becoming protecting and selfless martyr-sons. Yet the history of this rhetoric can be traced back to the beginnings of anti-colonial agitation (Ramaswamy 2001). A powerful document is the picture of socialist and revolutionary Bhagat Singh and his two comrades (who sought India's independence from colonial rule by militant means, and were hanged by the British in 1930) offering their heads to Bharat Mata whose body has merged with the map of India[16] (Fig. 9.9).

The idea of the nation and citizenry as one moral, physical, and spiritual entity is essential to mobilize in the audiences not just desires, but fears and anxieties. Most prevalent are suggestions of this familial body's dismemberment and mutilation. Partition is particularly important in this connection. The reference to the bloody borderlines then drawn enabled Hindutva spokespersons

Fig. 9.9: Three Martyrs devoting their heads to Mother India.
Nehru Memorial Museum & Library. Photographic Collection (no. 36508).

today to invoke Partition, and relate it to the current nationality crisis and separatism in states such as Punjab, Assam, and Kashmir, aligning them consensually to political weakness. This is done by means of using metaphors (rather than visuals) of pain: devastation, torture, and the fragmentation of Mother India's body (Fig. 9.10), as well as suggesting the economic marginalization and paralysis of her sons.

But the Hindutva maps of the early 1990s are also a response to Jawaharlal Nehru's privileging of a new, secular topography that was to be covered by canals, dams, and steel plants instead of religious sites. The leaders of the young nation state found that socialism, secularism, planned industrialization, and mass education of the citizens required new forms of mapping. To engender identification with the young nation state, territorial boundaries and sites had to be both defined and filled with prospects of development. The nation space projected by Nehru was not based on sacred cosmologies or colonial geographies, but on maps that related India to economic and technological development, to altogether different concepts of time and space. For instance, India was no longer depicted as 'timeless' and 'passive', but as a force actively shaping time and space, by 'making history'. Religious identity and sites were to a great extent sidelined because of the tragic events following Partition and the assumption that religion should never again be turned into an instrument for the heightening of tensions between Hindus and Muslims. The Indian nation was now imagined as a 'neutral' community of producers dedicated fully to the task of secular nation-building, with no other personal attachment than that to the welfare of the state and its people.

In response, the 'secularized maps' and practices of re-mapping Indianness through sites of economic and technological development are treated by the BJP as a step towards further alienation of the Hindu people from their homeland. The commentary in *From the Sea to the River* describes Somnath and Ayodhya as utopian sites:

L.K. Advani has to fulfil his pledge which he gave in the election manifesto, the promise to build the Ram *mandir*. That is why the BJP undertook that devotion to Saryu. Just as Vallabhbhai Patel, the former Home Minister, restored [*sic*] the ancient Somnath temple to its former glory to protect and

Fig. 9.10: 'Call of the Mother', Mother India calling for help. Sangh Parivar booklet.

consolidate the country's freedom, so will L.K. Advani, by constructing the temple at Ramjanmabhoomi, restore India's lost pride. In this holy land of Shiva, Ram's traditions will be fulfilled again. *Bharat Mata ki Jai* (Victory to Mother India)!

Against Jawaharlal Nehru's visions of the Indian development into an industrialized country and secular state, his Home Minister Patel sought to secure his own visions of an 'ancient' and 'eternal' India and highlighted the interests of the so-called 'Hindu majority'. He was a reluctant bystander as the ruined Somnath temple was brought down and a new temple was built.[17] In the eyes of many Sangh Parivar ideologues today, Nehru's giving in to Patel's conservatism set the example of a 'positive' secularism that had finally come to recognize the relevance of Hindu culture to the reconstruction of its religious sites and territory.[18]

The video presents Advani as a leader following the footsteps of Patel. The metaphor of Ram's revolutionary exile mentioned above combines various associations of 'coming home' and aligns Advani's leadership to a mass movement with a direction, purpose and legitimacy. Where Somnath came to represent the possible 'beginning in the cultural reassertion of the nation' (BJP 1993: 18), Ayodhya was thus turned into the memory site of an unfulfilled dream of an 'authentic' homeland, to be installed in the near future; the liberation of the Hindu people from the alleged humiliations of the past as well as the secular state-as-prison.

I conclude this analysis by taking the temples of Ayodhya and Somnath, and the way they are presented in *From the Sea to the River*, as what Michel Foucault, lecturing on 'Other Spaces' in 1967, called a 'heterotopia'. According to Foucault, we live in an epoch of spatial simultaneity and juxtaposition, where sacred and profane sites, closed and open spaces, fuse and overlap, creating relations of friendly neighbourhood and hostile Otherness (Foucault 1991: 34; see also Deshpande 1998). The Hindutva maps as they appear in the videos are such hyper-real heterotopias as they accumulate and generate histories, memories, and experiences, layer upon layer. They are normative, condensed, and dynamic spaces that offer panoramic views of the imaginary Self and the Other, the past and the future.

For political agents like the BJP, they serve as normative tools to establish control over the citizen-devotees by means of positioning, the creation of chains of associations through particular images and narratives and in the drawing of boundaries. The Hindutva processions ultimately aimed to mobilize support through a discourse of fear. This brings us to the last section of the paper.

SHAPING CARTOGRAPHIC ANXIETY

I mentioned the nation's personification as a woman, the national territory as her body, and the citizens as her devout sons, all making up a seemingly natural organism. In such an imaginary space, Mother India could be a passive victim, humiliated and threatened by external and/or alien forces. Her sons, there are hardly any references to daughters in this highly gendered rhetoric, have the lifelong duty to protect her, and are thus actively involved in the process of making history and re-mapping identity.

From this organic and familial analogy derived concrete strategies of identity constitution that lead to the stereotypical fixation of the 'Hindu sentiment' as essentially tolerant, and Muslims as dangerous, aggressive, and anti-national others. The body metaphor enabled Hindutva ideologues to create a discourse of fear, or what Sankaran Krishna calls 'cartographic anxiety', that is the creation of fear of infiltration and fragmentation both of the 'geobody' and the social organism.[19]

As in *From the Sea* scenes from *Unity Pilgrimage* clash images of paradise with evocations of a present state of chaos and misrepresentation. A song refers to different aspects of the motherland and the fact that people still keep marching together under the national flag. Against this backdrop of social unity, other scenes are inserted, carrying the footage of bombs exploding and staged scenes of militants seemingly preparing for a guerrilla war by smuggling weapons into India and attacking invisible goals. These shots are edited against footage of the picturesque, beautiful Valley of Kashmir and Srinagar's Dal Lake, itself the incarnation of romantic love manifest in poetry and Hindu films. The commentary identifies senior BJP leaders as Mother India's sons as it claims that:

. . . poisonous separatism is seeking to divide the country. And Kashmir, heaven on earth, is humiliated by the Kashmiris [read 'Muslim separatists']. Our national flag too, is humiliated. Now the goal of these brave sons of Mother India is to unfold again the national flag of India at Srinagar and to challenge the treacherous forces. They have pledged to restore the pride and dignity of Mother India. This journey is a warning, it is a warning to divisive forces, it is a warning to the government which has submitted itself to separatism and terrorism.

Unity Pilgrimage starts with the 'guardians' of Hindutva's perspective on India's integrity and territorial wholeness—Ram and Mother India, each superimposed on a map of Greater India (Fig. 9.11). Then, an animated poster of Pakistan and India is presented, with images shaped like missiles moving from Pakistan across the border and entering India (Fig. 9.12). The blurred, staged 'documentary' footage of men carrying machine-guns, emerging from behind bushes and pointing their weapons towards goals outside the camera frame add to the heightening notion that the Hindu people's 'home

Fig. 9.11: Ram superimposed on map of Greater India.
Video still from *Unity Pilgrimage*.

Fig. 9.12: Missiles from Pakistan entering into India.
Video still from *Unity Pilgrimage*.

territory' is about to be invaded and threatened once more by 'anti-national' forces. With the authority of a news reader, the commentator reports that Pakistan encourages terrorism and seeks further fragmentation of India by supporting militants along the disputed line of control between India and Pakistan. Reference is made to the sacred and anthropomorphic nature of the Indian territory and to *deshbhakti* as a national ideal. The voice-over then takes the viewer back on a journey in time to show India's history as the drama of territorial invasions and the endless struggles of brave Indians to defend India's territorial integrity, and concludes by stating that the aims of the so-called terrorists are:

> . . . to cut Bharat Mata into pieces. But they don't know that the unity of India rests on its cultural heritage which is based on the idea of equal respect for all religions and that Mother and Motherland are higher even than heaven. This gives us the power to prevent attacks and that is why India is still able to withstand all different invasions.

The mention of the tie of nationalist devotion to Bharat Mata that bonds the brotherhood and nation together against external threats is important: it represents the nation as a joint family. With it, Hindutva ideologues can tie in further narratives such as the life-long obligation and duties of Mother India's children to respect and protect their Mother's honour and integrity. This, in return, grants them the right to call India their home and to hoist the Indian flag as a demonstrative symbol of possession-taking. Yet, both *From the Sea* and *Unity Pilgrimage* issue indirect 'warnings' to those unwilling to succumb to the 'joint Hindu family' rules. In the case of the Ayodhya controversy, those Muslim groups refusing to hand over the Babri mosque to the Hindus prove that their loyalties are towards the Mughal invaders. In the case of the Kashmir issue, we encounter associations with Muslims as anti-nationals because they are willing to see Mother India being mutilated.

The videos indicate that the Hindutva rhetoric of *deshbhakti* consciously involves the use of religious and ethnic stereotypes for the purpose of self-constitution.[20] The video sequences enhance the uncanny thrill and spectacle of dealing with Sameness and Otherness through editing and commentary. Imbued in this is the cynical suggestion by the Sangh Parivar that over the centuries of Islamic presence in India, the Muslims *could* have assimilated to the Hindu mainstream and become part of the Hindu family. But they still pay primary loyalties to foreign 'ancestors' such as Babur and to holy places and territories outside India, such as Mecca. Furthermore, they say, many of today's Muslims were previously Hindus who converted to Islam (by force or because they wanted to transcend caste discrimination). Thus, *they* decided to 'drift away' equally betraying the 'essences' of the Hindu homeland and of the fraternity of nation-devotees. Identifying familial loyalty and territorial loyalty, the BJP can now engage in the rhetoric of legitimate anger, and even violence, against the 'traitors'. As the following proclamation of senior BJP-leader Rajmata Vijaya Raje Scindia in the *Unity Pilgrimage* video shows:

> I want to tell the terrorists *and* those Muslim friends who want to be separated from us that we are one family, we will not be happy if you try to divide our family. *We will live as one family, India is our mother and*

we are her children. This is the tradition in the BJP that we uphold. We don't consider you to be separate. The success of this yatra has troubled the terrorists. They have written slogans that 'if you have drunk your mother's milk, come to Srinagar and unfurl the flag'. I want to tell them that this is exactly what we will do. It will then be decided who has drunk their mother's milk.

Here, Muslim 'friends' or 'brothers' are associated with anti-national militants, traitors, and lost sons. The message is clear: Hindutva nationality is *per se* tolerant and peaceful. But once provoked, the son of the nation transforms into a heroic warrior prepared to even give his life for the country's/family's integrity.

For the BJP, the whole procession and in a condensed way, the flag hoisting ceremony are a symbolic exercise of taking possession of land. The performance of such a 'ritual of (territorial) possession',[21] made visible and creating an audience through the video media—is the public declaration of superiority on the behalf of the BJP and its potential supporters.

Furthermore, in the context of the riots that accompanied Advani's Ram Rath Yatra in 1990, leading to the demolition of the Babri mosque in December 1992, it became evident that the rhetoric of brotherhood and traitors gained momentum in its performative enactment. The religious-political processions carved out a space that could be loaded with intense emotions and ruptures, where borders into very sensible physical and symbolical territories of 'the Other' were consciously crossed in order to provoke conflict, and claim authority, or possession. This could range from the provocative act of a procession passing through Muslim neighbourhoods (*mohallas*), often involving the violent clash of local Hindu and Muslim groups, or the flag hoisting ceremony, further dramatized in the video media by situating the act among staged 'terrorist' attacks.

CONCLUSION

Analysis of the videos has enabled us to trace how a complex 'counter-map', very much like an archaeological excavation site, evolved with the Hindutva project of re-mapping the nation by means of re-investing religious traditions and practices with nationalist meaning, and by inventing a set of shared memories and experiences of pre-colonial and colonial history, all of which were related to Indianness as territorial devotion. A whole range of maps, images and practices were employed in the Hindutva processions. They provided metaphoric, visual, and narrative material for an identity construction that appealed to territory through a dramatization of seemingly existential crisis and loss: lost homeland, lost history and lost or rather, dispersed joint family. After having evoked feelings of loss and cartographic anxiety, the BJP could now promise to challenge and provide solutions for both. On this basis, hierarchical categories and strategies of inclusion and exclusion were elaborated and performed that enabled Sangh Parivar spokespeople to demarcate a mental map of 'authentic Hinduness' *versus* one of 'threatening and alien Others', in particular the Muslims. The territorial processions of the early 1990s were thus a highly performative strategy of provoking violence through conflict creation.

In the aftermath of 11 September 2001, the stereotype of 'the Muslim' as essentially aggressive and anti-national has come to enjoy new popularity among Hindutva spokespeople, this time in line with the so-called 'international alliance against terrorism'. This has heightened a rhetoric of infiltration and growing instability of the national geobody, among radical representatives within the BJP but in particular in the context of non-parliamentary representatives of the Sangh Parivar. Yet, by and large, the metaphors of cartographic anxiety seem to have weakened in the public discourse on nationality. The relationship between Pakistan and India has improved of late, due to government initiatives that were started under then Prime Minister Atal Behari Vajpayee and followed up by the current Prime Minister, Manmohan Singh (e.g., regular bus transport facilities between the two countries). Whether the slogans of territorial danger can be restored and turned into signs of new fields of conflict, remains to be seen and largely depends on the ways in which nationality is defined and enacted.

Acknowledgements: I thank Daniela Berti and Gilles Tarabout for their invaluable comments on the paper.

NOTES

1. 'Hindu Right' is a term used to refer to a very heterogeneous alliance of groups and organizations whose agenda, broadly spoken, is the proliferation/spread of Hinduness as a superior 'Indian way of life' (Hindutva). The key political organization referred to here is the Bharatiya Janata Party (hereafter BJP, founded in 1981). It is usually referred to as a sub-branch of the 'Mother-organization', the Rashtriya Swayamsevak Sangh (hereafter RSS, founded in 1925), as well as another sub-branch, the non-parliamentary Vishwa Hindu Parishad (World Hindu Council, hereafter VHP, founded in 1964). See Brosius (2005), Gopal (1993), Jaffrelot (1996), Ludden (1996) and Pandey (1993).
2. Parivar is a term employed by Hindu Right organizations in order to refer to the whole body of organizations aligning themselves to Hindutva ideology (see Nandy et al., 1995).
3. At the time of writing, Modi was Chief Minister of the state of Gujarat. He played a highly controversial role in the context of the Gujarat riots in 2002, where more than 2,000 people, mostly Muslims, died in pogroms organized by supporters of the extreme Hindu Right with only a little resistance from within the BJP. His 'Gaurav Yatra' (Procession of Pride) was conducted during and after the communal turmoil of 2002 and in the approach to the parliamentary state elections of that year.
4. At the time of the interview, Advani was party president; between 1998 and 2004, he was Home Minister and Deputy Prime Minister. He resigned from the post of party president in September 2005 due to tensions within the Sangh.
5. L.K. Advani, in *BJP Today*, vol. 6(12), 15-30 June 1997: 4-5.
6. Roy (1996: 35), Jaffrelot (1996), Malik and Singh (1995).
7. Along the route of the Ram Rath Yatra, riots were reported in 26 places, 99 people were reportedly killed between 1 September and 20 November 1990. See Shah (1998: 248); also Brass (1998), Deshpande (1998: 269-77), Gopal (1993), Nandy et al., (1995); van der Veer (1994: 123 ff.).
8. In 1989, Rajiv Gandhi had commissioned an election video with Jain Studios and hired VOW vans for his campaign in the southern state of Tamil Nadu.
9. Until the mid-1990s, the studios produced several dozen propaganda videos for the Sangh Parivar (and other parties too), many directly related to the Ayodhya controversy. See Brosius 2005.

10. *Vande Mataram* is a poem/song derived from Bankim Chandra Chattopadhyaya's novel *Anandamath* (1882), translated by Aurobindo Ghose between 1894 and 1909.
11. Benjamin writes that film offers this intimacy because it does not reveal the technical apparatus producing the scenes (Benjamin 1973: 226-30).
12. See Eck (1999: 137, 167).
13. *Devibhagavata Purana* 7.30.44-50, *Mahabhagavata* 11.32-118. See O'Flaherty (1975: 249ff.). I am grateful to David Smith (Dept. of Religious Studies, Lancaster University) and Sophie Hawkins for their advice on this matter.
14. Krishna's presence at the side of Arjun consecrated the killings and guaranteed victory as everything was said to be executed according to *dharma*. See Biardeau (1997: 114-16).
15. On national devotion as territorial passion, see Hindutva ideologues Golwalkar (1996: 81-150) and Savarkar (1989: 111-18, 129-36). On Savarkar, see McKean (1996: 71-96).
16. The three men fought for a socialist republic. Their ideas on militant activism did not aim at a nationalist movement based on a particular ethno-religious agenda. Rather, they envisaged India's sovereignty as carried by a community of workers engaged in socialist revolutionary activities. See Grover (1987), Noorani (1996).
17. This temple was built around 1000 AC. It had been repeatedly demolished and rebuilt since then, and was turned into mosque in the early eighteenth century. It was K.M. Munshi, another member of the Cabinet, who devised the whole project. See Khilnani (1997: 33-4), van der Veer (1992: 90ff., 94), Thapar (2005).
18. The mouthpiece *Organiser* commented on the Jyotirlinga temple in Somnath as 'more than a temple. It is the sovereign symbol of our living nationalism. It is a national institution, a national memory' (*Organiser*, 12.3.1951: 3).
19. The idea of Islam as the anti-national, threatening Other is an essential part of Veer Savarkar's pamphlet *Hindutva*. 'Geobody' is a term used by Thongchai Winichahul (1994, in Ramaswamy 2001) in his analysis of the relationship between nation, gender, and territory. The 'geobody of the nation' seeks contextualization as a cultural-specific discourse of power. See also Najmabadi (1997: 442-3). Sankaran Krishna explores cartographic anxiety in his analysis of Congress(I) election campaigns in 1989 and references to separatism as 'balkanization' (1996).

20. See Bhabha 1994, especially chapter 3.
21. Stephen Greenblatt, describing Columbus's strategies of power in the Americas, argues that 'rituals of possession stand in for negotiated contracts', thereby fixing 'a set of public linguistic acts, giv(ing) them official standing, mak(ing) them "historical" events' (1992: 58).

REFERENCES

Archer, Mildred, 1980. *Early Views of India: The Picturesque Journeys of Thomas and William Daniell 1786-1794*. London: Thames and Hudson.

Barthwal, Harishchandra, 1997. *The Integral Spirit of Bharat: An Eulogy. Bharata Ekatmata Stotra.* Delhi: Suruchi Prakashan.

Benjamin, Walter, 1973. 'The Work of Art in the Age of Mechanical Reproduction', in *Illuminations* (Introduction by Hannah Arendt, tr. by Harry Zohn). London: Fontana Press, pp. 197-210.

Bhabha, Homi, 1994. *The Location of Culture*, London and New York: Routledge.

Biardeau, Madeleine, 1997 [1981]. *Hinduism: The Anthropology of a Civilisation.* Delhi: Oxford University Press.

BJP, 1993. *BJP's White Paper on Ayodhya and the Rama Temple Movement.* Delhi: BJP.

Brass, Paul R., 1998 [1997]. *Theft of an Idol: Text and Context in the Representation of Collective Violence.* Calcutta: Seagull.

Brosius, Christiane, 2005. *Empowering Visions: The Politics of Representation in Hindu Nationalism.* London: Anthem Press.

Butcher, Melissa, 2003. *Transnational Television, Cultural Identity and Change: When STAR came to India.* Delhi: Sage.

Chatterjee, Partha, 1995 [1993]. *The Nation and its Fragments: Colonial and Postcolonial Histories.* Delhi: Oxford University Press.

Das, Veena, 1995. *Critical Events: An Anthropological Perspective on Contemporary India.* Delhi: Oxford University Press.

Deshpande, Satish, 1998. 'Hegemonic Spatial Strategies: The Nation-Space and Hindu Communalism in Twentieth-Century India', *Popular Culture*, 10(2): 249-83.

Eck, Diana L., 1999. 'The Imagined landscape: Patterns in the Construction of Hindu Sacred Geography', in *Tradition, Pluralism and Identity: In Honour of T.N. Madan.* Special Issue of Contributions to Indian Sociology. 32(2), ed. Veena Das, Dipankar Gupta and Patricia Uberoi. Delhi: Sage, pp. 165-88.

Edney, Matthew H., 1997 [1990]. *Mapping an Empire: The Geographical*

Construction of British India, 1765-1943. Chicago and London: University of Chicago Press.

Foucault, Michel, 1991. 'Andere Räume', in *Aisthesis. Wahnehmung heute oder Perspektiven einer anderen Ästhetik*, ed. Barck, Karlheinz, Peter Gente, Heidi Paris and Stefan Richter. Leipzig: Reclam Verlag, pp. 34-46.

Golwalkar, M.S., 1996 [1966]. *Bunch of Thoughts*. Delhi: Sahitya Sindhu Prakashana (revised and enlarged 3rd edn.).

Gopal, Sarvepalli (ed.), 1993 [1991]. *Anatomy of a Confrontation: The Babri Masjid-Ram Janmabhoomi Issue*. Delhi: Penguin Books.

Greenblatt, Stephen, 1992 [1991]. *Marvelous Possessions: The Wonder of the New World*. Chicago: University of Chicago Press.

Grover, D.R., 1987. *Civil Disobedience Movement in the Punjab 1930-1934*. Delhi: B.R. Publishing.

Jaffrelot, Christophe, 1996. *The Hindu Nationalist Movement and Indian Politics, 1925 to the 1990s: Strategies of Identity-Building, Implantation and Mobilisation (with Special Reference to Central India)*, Delhi: Penguin/ Viking (French original, 1993).

Kalpagam, U., 1995. 'Cartography in Colonial India', *Economic and Political Weekly*, 30(30), 29 July: PE-87-98.

Khilnani, Sunil, 1997. *The Idea of India*. Delhi: Oxford University Press.

Krishna, Sankaran, 1996. 'Cartographic Anxiety: Mapping the Body Politic in India', in *Challenging Boundaries: Global Flows, Territorial Identities*, ed. Michael J. Shapiro and Hayward R. Alker. Minneapolis and London: University of Minnesota Press, pp. 193-214.

Ludden, David (ed.), 1996. *Making India Hindu: Religion, Community, and the Politics of Democracy in India*. Delhi: Oxford University Press.

Malik, Yogendra K. and V.B. Singh, 1995 [1994]. *Hindu Nationalists in India: The Rise of the Bharatiya Janata Party*. Delhi: Vistaar.

McKean, Lise, 1996. *Divine Enterprise: Gurus and the Hindu Nationalist Movement*. Chicago and London: University of Chicago Press.

Najmabadi, Afsaneh, 1997. 'The Erotic *Vatan* [Homeland] as Beloved and Mother: To Love, To Possess, and To Protect', *Comparative Studies in Society and History*, 39(3): 442-67.

Nandy, Ashis, Shikha Trivedy, Shail Mayaram and Achyut Yagnik, 1995. *Creating a Nationality: The Ramjanmabhumi Movement and Fear of the Self*. Delhi: Oxford University Press.

Noorani, A.G., 1996. *The Trial of Bhagat Singh: Politics of Justice*. Delhi: Konark Publishers.

O'Flaherty, Wendy Doniger, 1975. *Hindu Myths*. London: Viking/Penguin.

Ohm, Britta, 1999. 'Doordarshan: Representing the Nation's State', in *Image*

Journeys: Audio-visual Media and Cultural Change in India, ed. Christiane Brosius and Melissa Butcher. Delhi: Sage, pp. 69-98.

Pandey, Gyanendra (ed.), 1993. *Hindus and Others: The Question of Identity in India Today*. Delhi: Viking.

Ramaswamy, Sumathi, 2001. 'Maps and Mother Goddesses in Modern India', *Imago Mundi: The International Journal for the History of Cartography*, 53: 97-114.

Roy, Meenu, 1996. *India Votes: Elections 1996-7: A Critical Analysis*. Delhi: Deep and Deep.

Savarkar, V.D., 1989 [1923]. *Hindutva—Who is a Hindu?*. Delhi: Bharti Sahitya Sadan.

Shah, Gyanshyam, 1998. 'The BJP's Riddle in Gujarat: Caste, Factionalism and Hindutva', in *The BJP and the Compulsions of Politics in India*, ed. Thomas B. Hansen and Christophe Jaffrelot. Delhi: Oxford University Press, pp. 243-66.

Thapar, Romila, 2005. *Somanatha: The Many Voices of History*, Delhi: Verso.

Van der Veer, Peter, 1992. 'Ayodhya and Sonmnath: Eternal Shrines, Contested Histories', *Social Research*, 59(1): 85-109.

———, 1994. *Religious Nationalism: Hindus and Muslims in India.* Berkeley, London: California University Press.